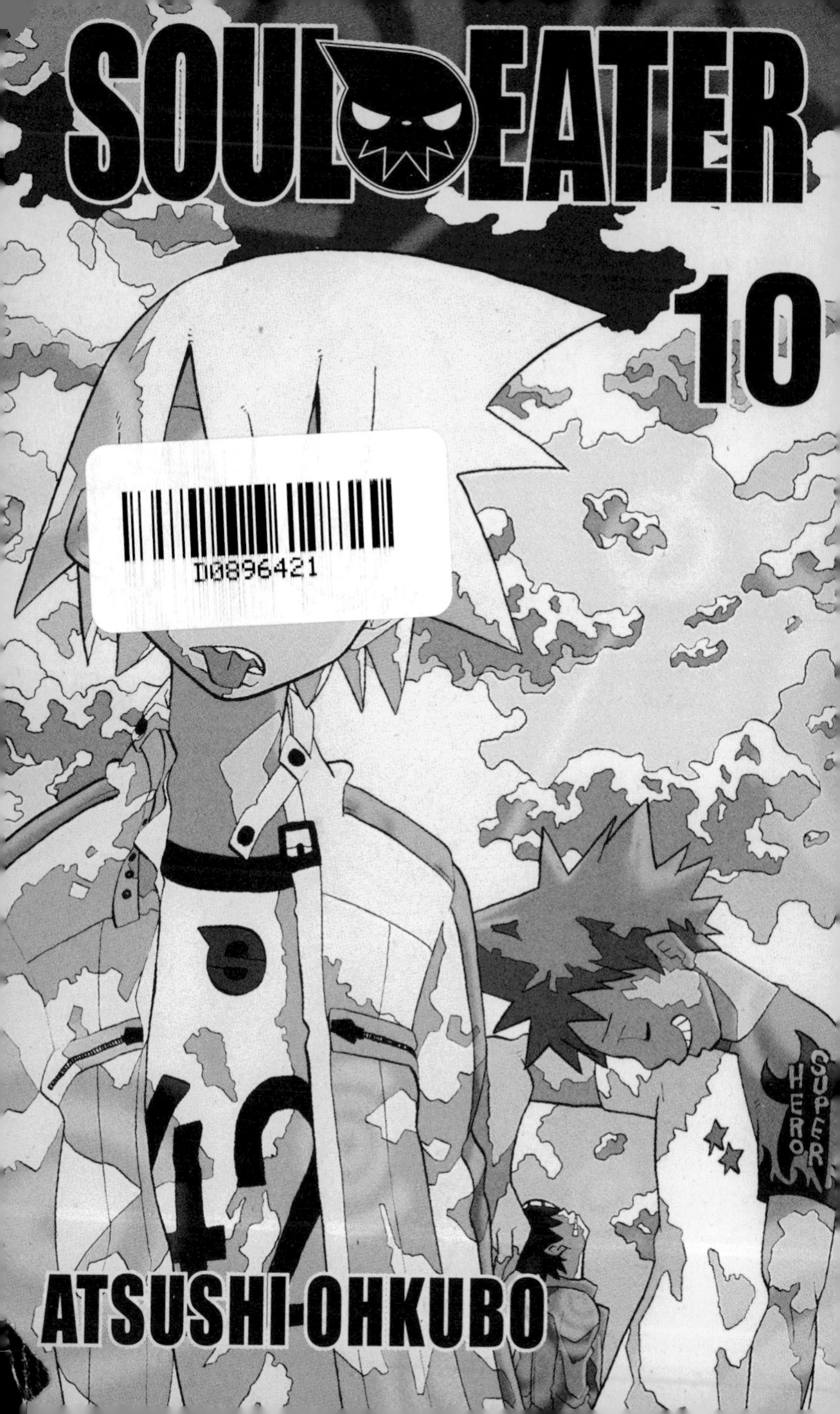
SOUL EATER
10
SUPER HERO
ATSUSHI·OHKUBO

SOUL EATER

vol. 10
by ATSUSHI OHKUBO

MIND SHUT, EYES SHUT, SOUL SHUT IN

SOUL EATER 10

BUTTATAKI

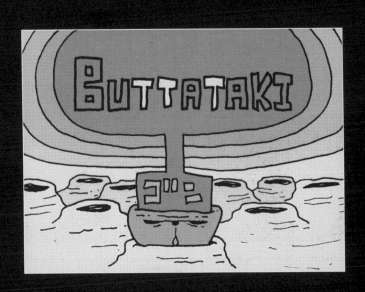

CONTENTS

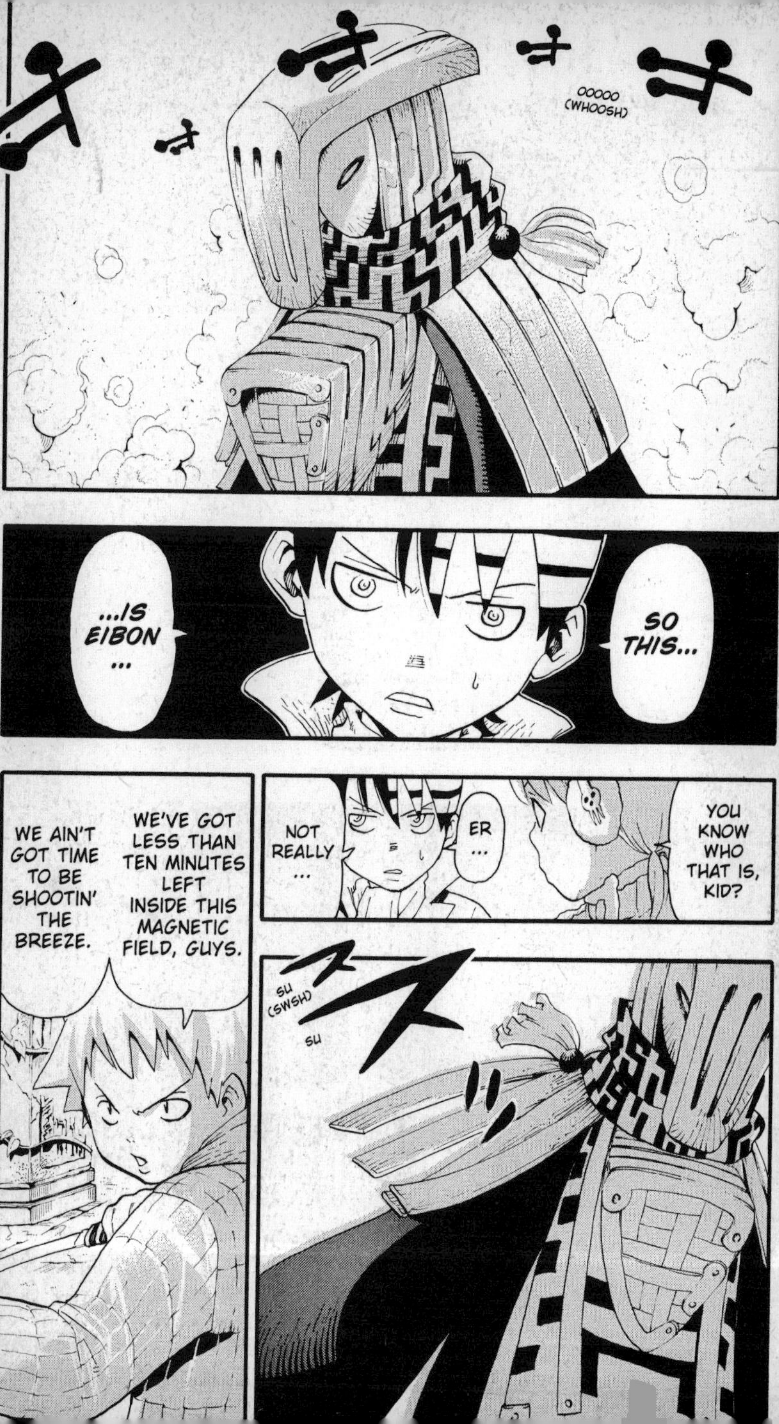
OOOOO (WHOOSH)
SO THIS...
...IS EIBON ...
YOU KNOW WHO THAT IS, KID?
ER ...
NOT REALLY ...
SU (SWSH)
SU
WE'VE GOT LESS THAN TEN MINUTES LEFT INSIDE THIS MAGNETIC FIELD, GUYS.
WE AIN'T GOT TIME TO BE SHOOTIN' THE BREEZE.

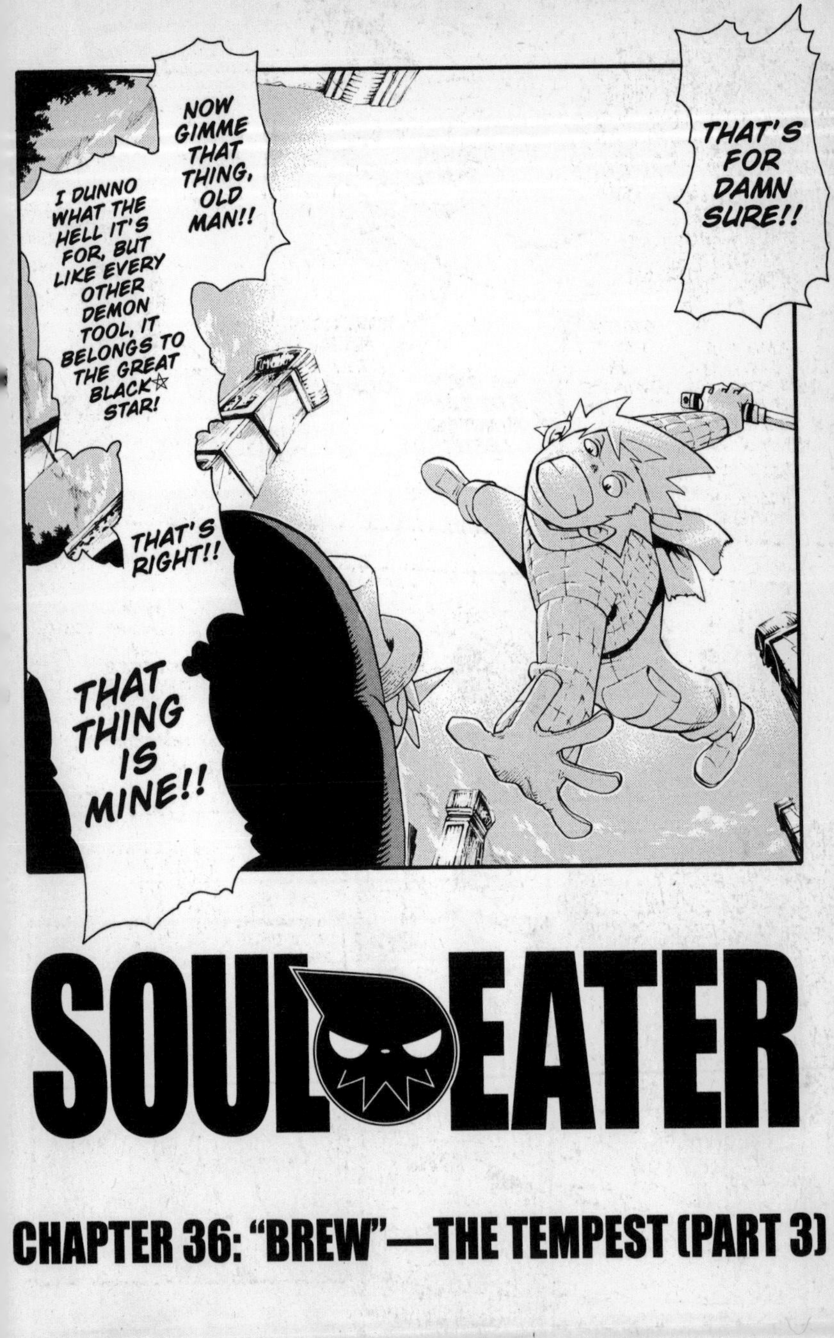
THAT'S FOR DAMN SURE!!
NOW GIMME THAT THING, OLD MAN!!
I DUNNO WHAT THE HELL IT'S FOR, BUT LIKE EVERY OTHER DEMON TOOL, IT BELONGS TO THE GREAT BLACK☆STAR!
THAT'S RIGHT!!
THAT THING IS MINE!!

SOUL EATER

CHAPTER 36: "BREW"—THE TEMPEST (PART 3)

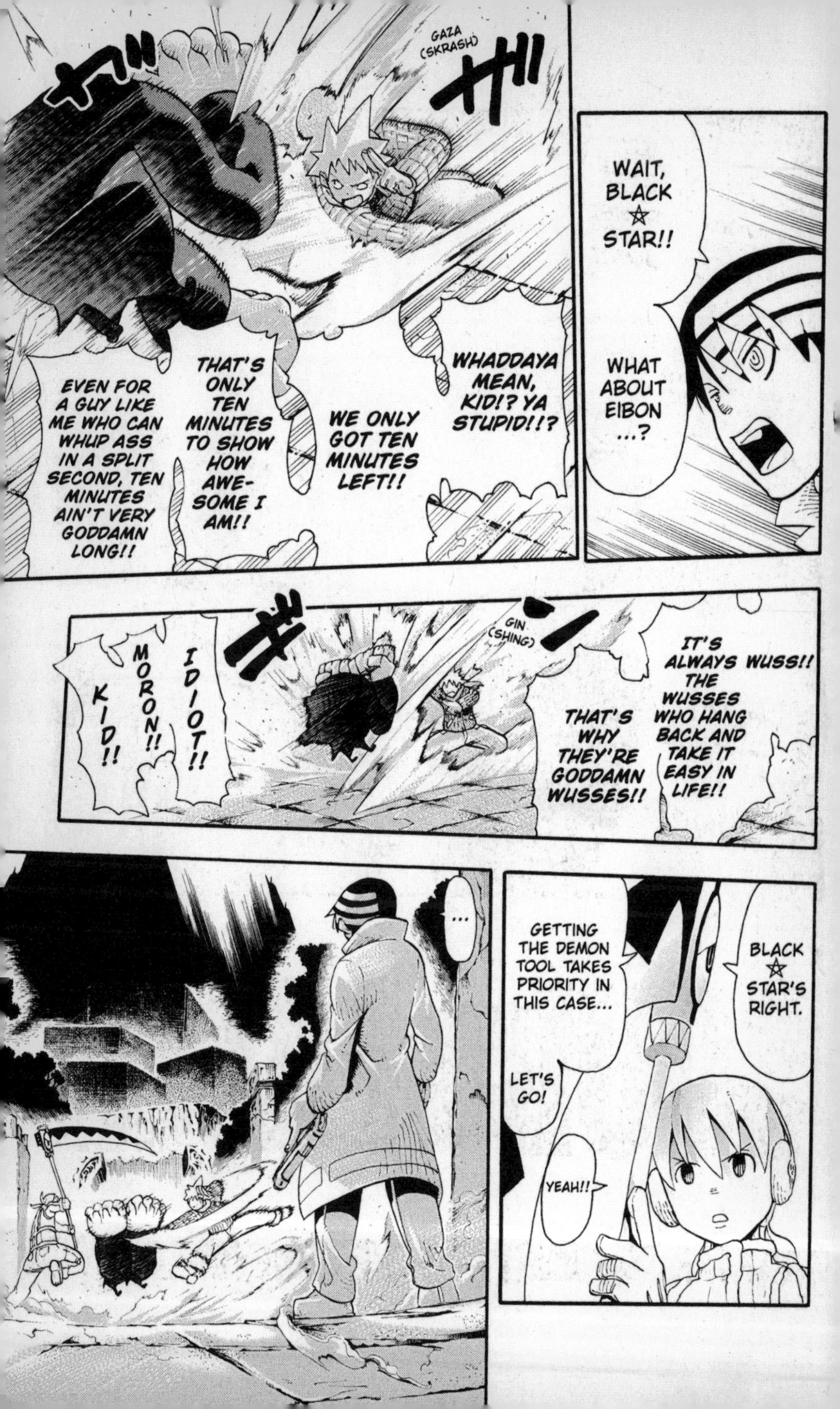
WAIT, BLACK ☆ STAR!!
WHAT ABOUT EIBON ...?
GAZA (SKRASH)
WHADDAYA MEAN, KID!? YA STUPID!!?
WE ONLY GOT TEN MINUTES LEFT!!
THAT'S ONLY TEN MINUTES TO SHOW HOW AWE-SOME I AM!!
EVEN FOR A GUY LIKE ME WHO CAN WHUP ASS IN A SPLIT SECOND, TEN MINUTES AIN'T VERY GODDAMN LONG!!
GIN (SHING)
IT'S ALWAYS WUSS!! THE WUSSES WHO HANG BACK AND TAKE IT EASY IN LIFE!!
THAT'S WHY THEY'RE GODDAMN WUSSES!!
IDIOT!!
MORON!!
KID!!
BLACK ☆ STAR'S RIGHT.
GETTING THE DEMON TOOL TAKES PRIORITY IN THIS CASE...
LET'S GO!
YEAH!!
...

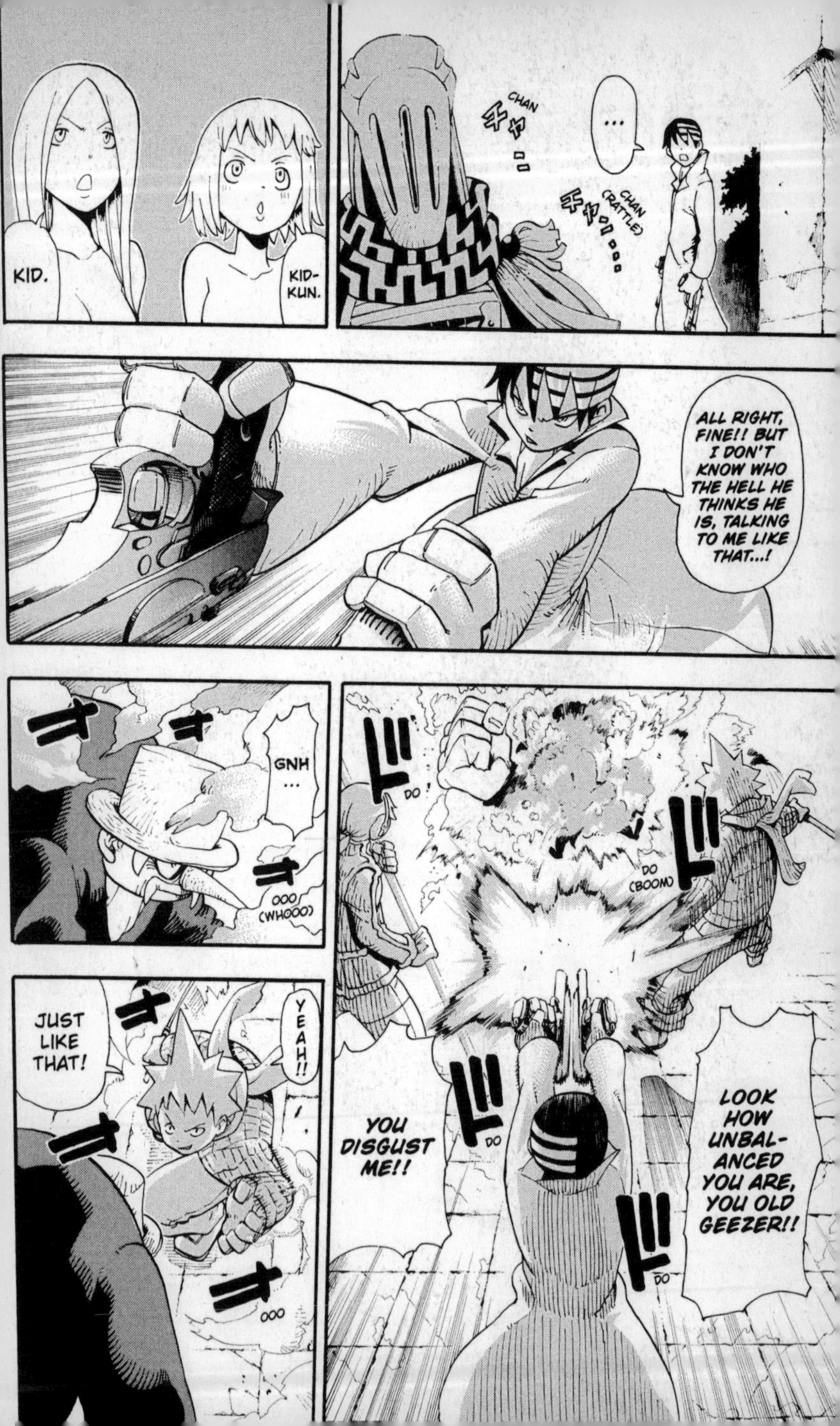

CHAN
CHAN (RATTLE)
...
KID-KUN.
KID.
ALL RIGHT, FINE!! BUT I DON'T KNOW WHO THE HELL HE THINKS HE IS, TALKING TO ME LIKE THAT...!
DO (BOOM)
DO
LOOK HOW UNBAL-ANCED YOU ARE, YOU OLD GEEZER!!
YOU DISGUST ME!!
DO
DO
GNH ...
OOO (WHOOO)
YEAH!!
JUST LIKE THAT!
OOO

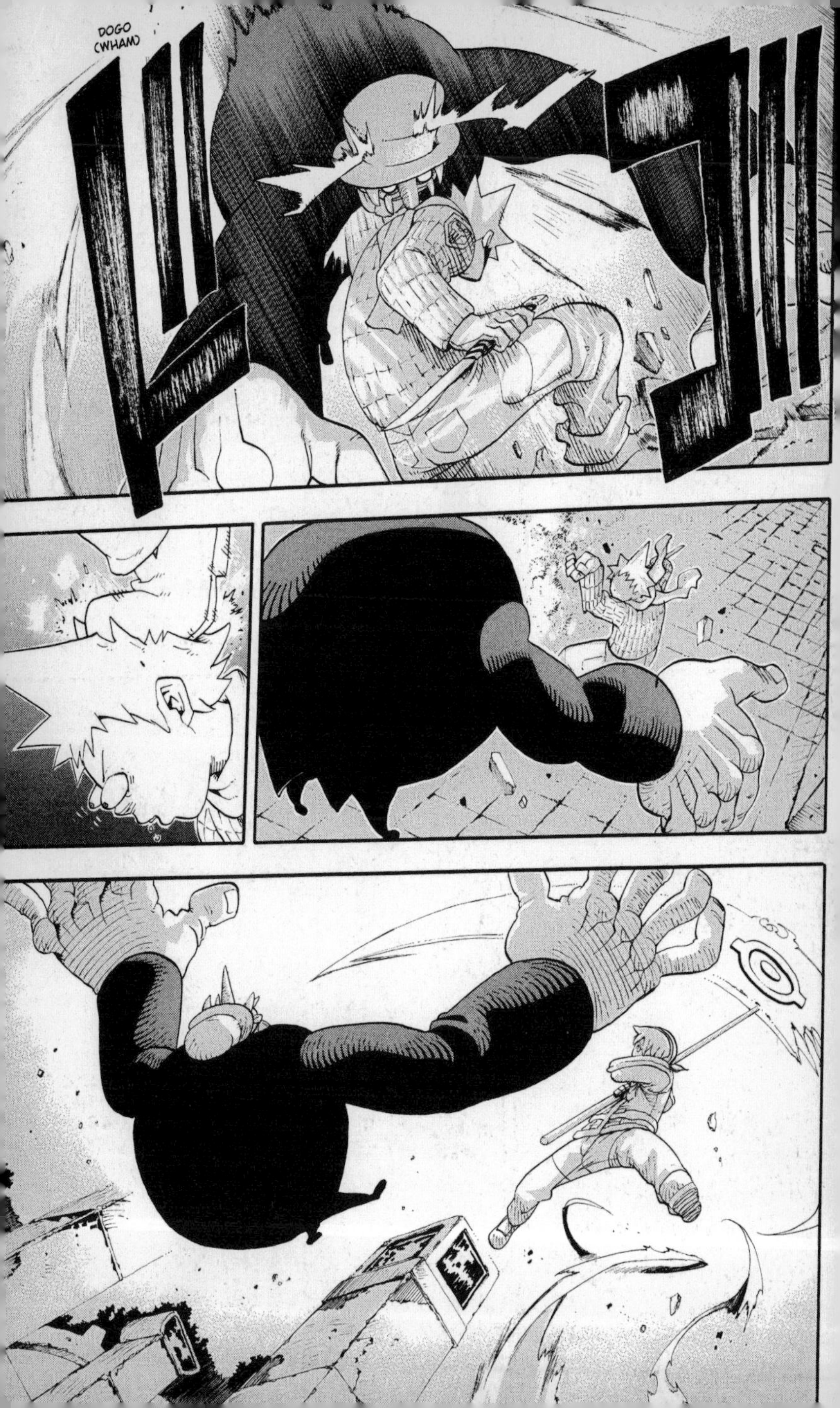
DOGO
(WHAM)

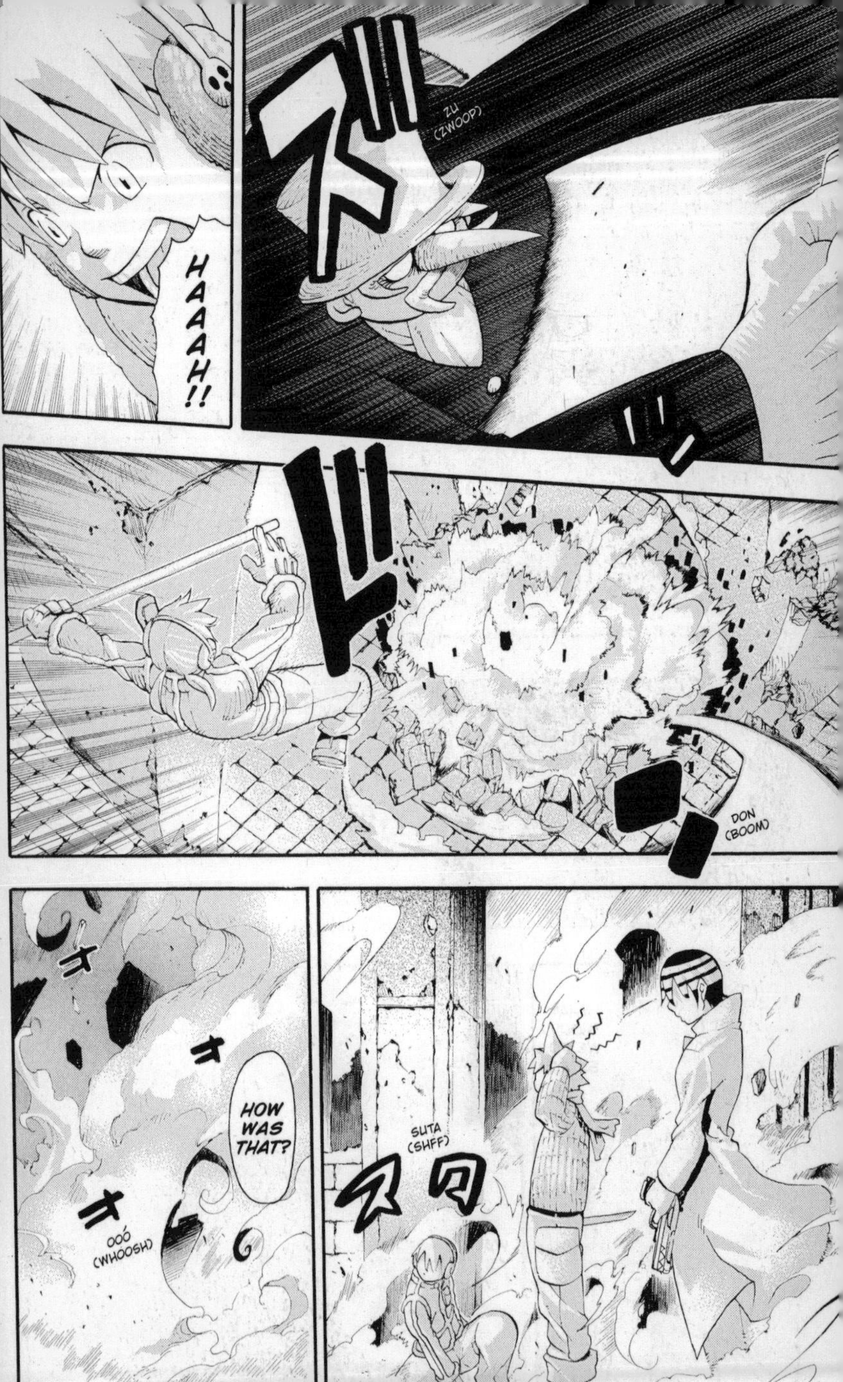

ZU
(ZWOOP)
HAAAAH!!
DON
(BOOM)
SUTA
(SHFF)
HOW WAS THAT?
OOO
(WHOOSH)

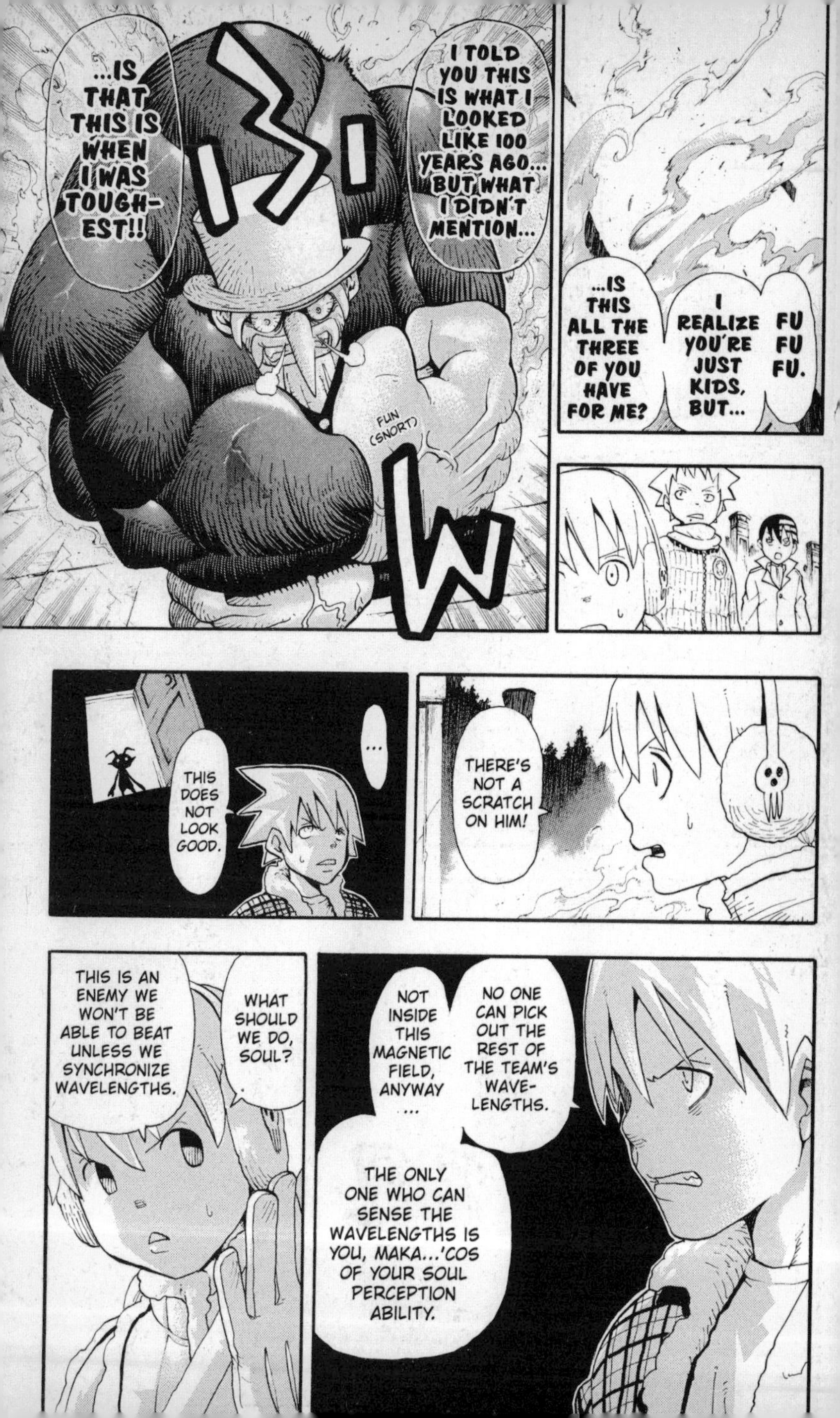
FU FU FU.
I REALIZE YOU'RE JUST KIDS, BUT...
...IS THIS ALL THE THREE OF YOU HAVE FOR ME?
I TOLD YOU THIS IS WHAT I LOOKED LIKE 100 YEARS AGO... BUT WHAT I DIDN'T MENTION...
...IS THAT THIS IS WHEN I WAS TOUGHEST!!
FUN (SNORT)
THERE'S NOT A SCRATCH ON HIM!
...
THIS DOES NOT LOOK GOOD.
NO ONE CAN PICK OUT THE REST OF THE TEAM'S WAVELENGTHS.
NOT INSIDE THIS MAGNETIC FIELD, ANYWAY...
THE ONLY ONE WHO CAN SENSE THE WAVELENGTHS IS YOU, MAKA...'COS OF YOUR SOUL PERCEPTION ABILITY.
THIS IS AN ENEMY WE WON'T BE ABLE TO BEAT UNLESS WE SYNCHRONIZE WAVELENGTHS.
WHAT SHOULD WE DO, SOUL?

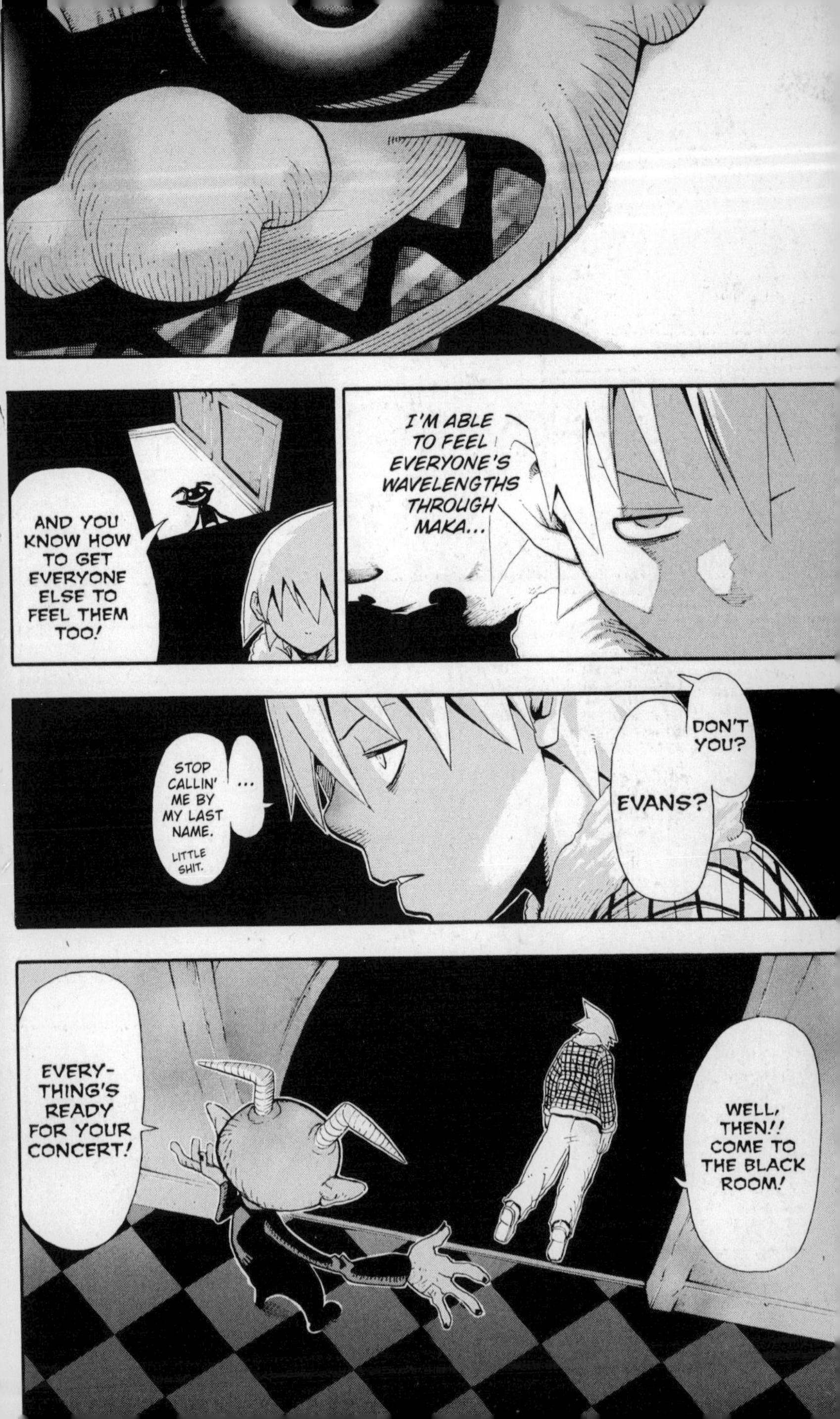
I'M ABLE TO FEEL EVERYONE'S WAVELENGTHS THROUGH MAKA...
AND YOU KNOW HOW TO GET EVERYONE ELSE TO FEEL THEM TOO!
DON'T YOU?
EVANS?
...
STOP CALLIN' ME BY MY LAST NAME.
LITTLE SHIT.
WELL, THEN!! COME TO THE BLACK ROOM!
EVERY-THING'S READY FOR YOUR CONCERT!

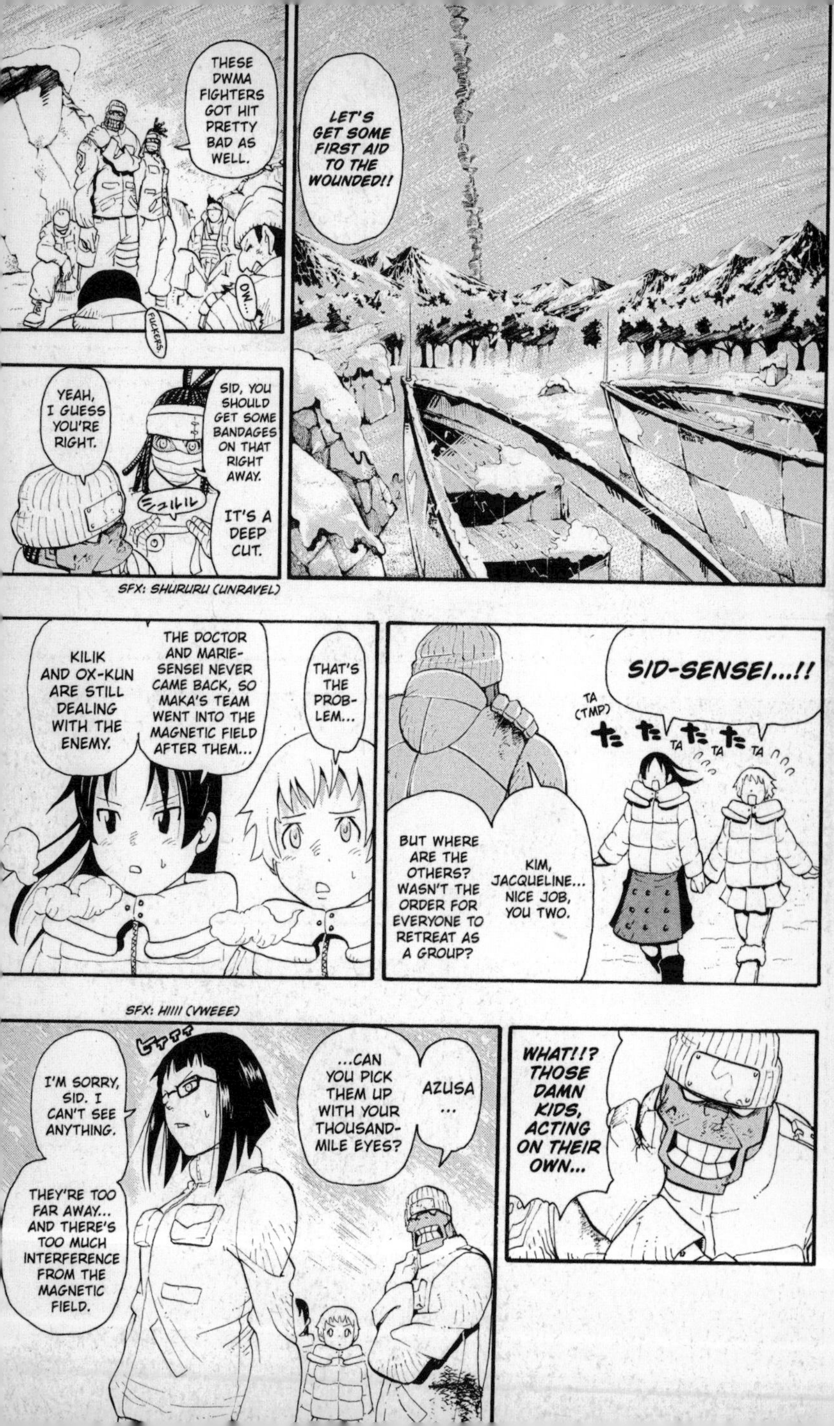
LET'S GET SOME FIRST AID TO THE WOUNDED!!
THESE DWMA FIGHTERS GOT HIT PRETTY BAD AS WELL.
OW...
FUCKERS.
SID, YOU SHOULD GET SOME BANDAGES ON THAT RIGHT AWAY.
IT'S A DEEP CUT.
シュルルル
YEAH, I GUESS YOU'RE RIGHT.
SFX: SHURURU (UNRAVEL)
SID-SENSEI...!!
TA (TMP)
た た た た
TA TA TA
KIM, JACQUELINE... NICE JOB, YOU TWO.
BUT WHERE ARE THE OTHERS? WASN'T THE ORDER FOR EVERYONE TO RETREAT AS A GROUP?
THAT'S THE PROB-LEM...
THE DOCTOR AND MARIE-SENSEI NEVER CAME BACK, SO MAKA'S TEAM WENT INTO THE MAGNETIC FIELD AFTER THEM...
KILIK AND OX-KUN ARE STILL DEALING WITH THE ENEMY.
SFX: HIIII (VWEEE)
WHAT!!? THOSE DAMN KIDS, ACTING ON THEIR OWN...
AZUSA...
...CAN YOU PICK THEM UP WITH YOUR THOUSAND-MILE EYES?
I'M SORRY, SID. I CAN'T SEE ANYTHING.
THEY'RE TOO FAR AWAY... AND THERE'S TOO MUCH INTERFERENCE FROM THE MAGNETIC FIELD.

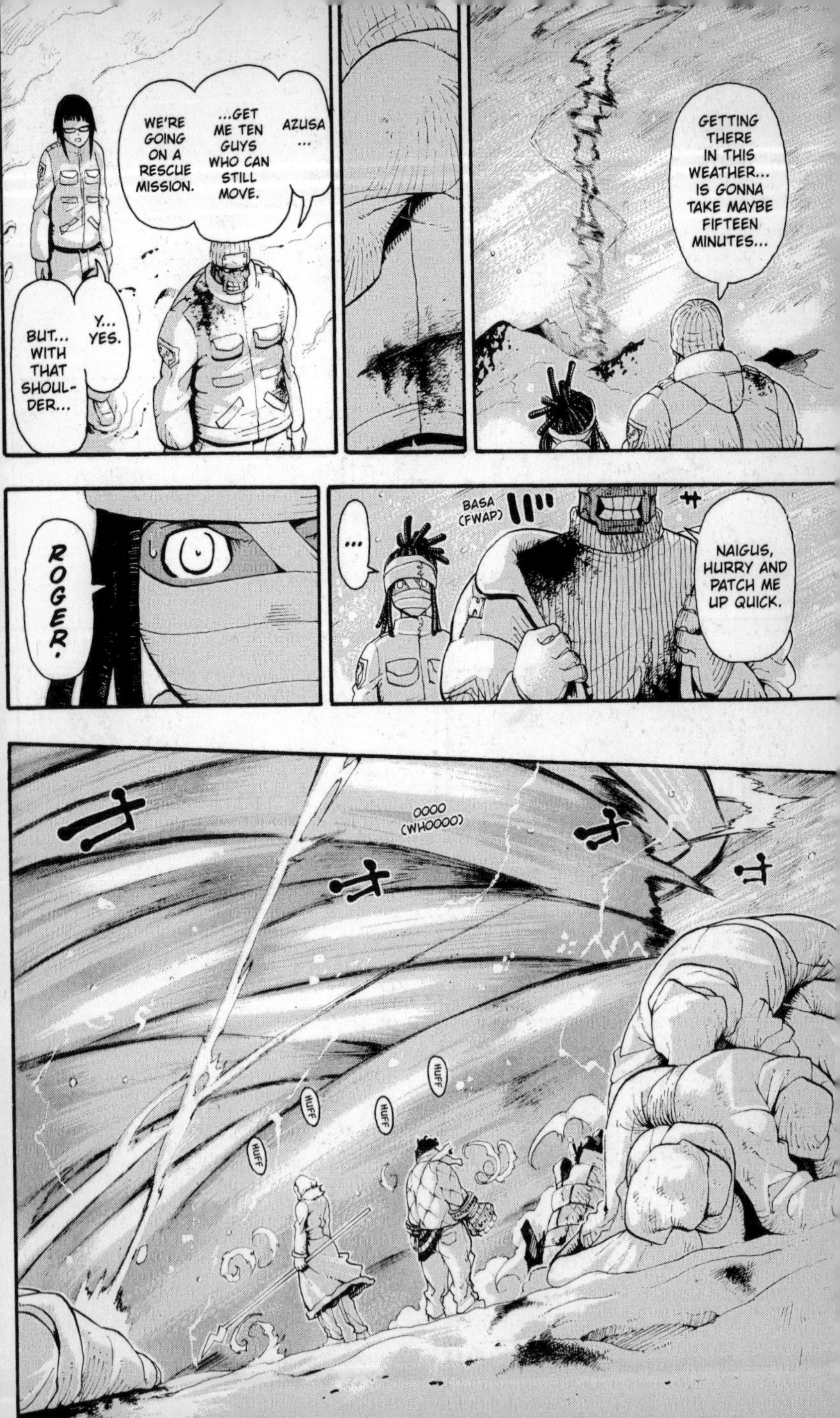
GETTING THERE IN THIS WEATHER... IS GONNA TAKE MAYBE FIFTEEN MINUTES...
AZUSA...
...GET ME TEN GUYS WHO CAN STILL MOVE.
WE'RE GOING ON A RESCUE MISSION.
Y... YES.
BUT... WITH THAT SHOULDER...
NAIGUS, HURRY AND PATCH ME UP QUICK.
BASA (FWAP)
...
ROGER.
OOOO (WHOOOO)
HUFF
HUFF
HUFF
HUFF

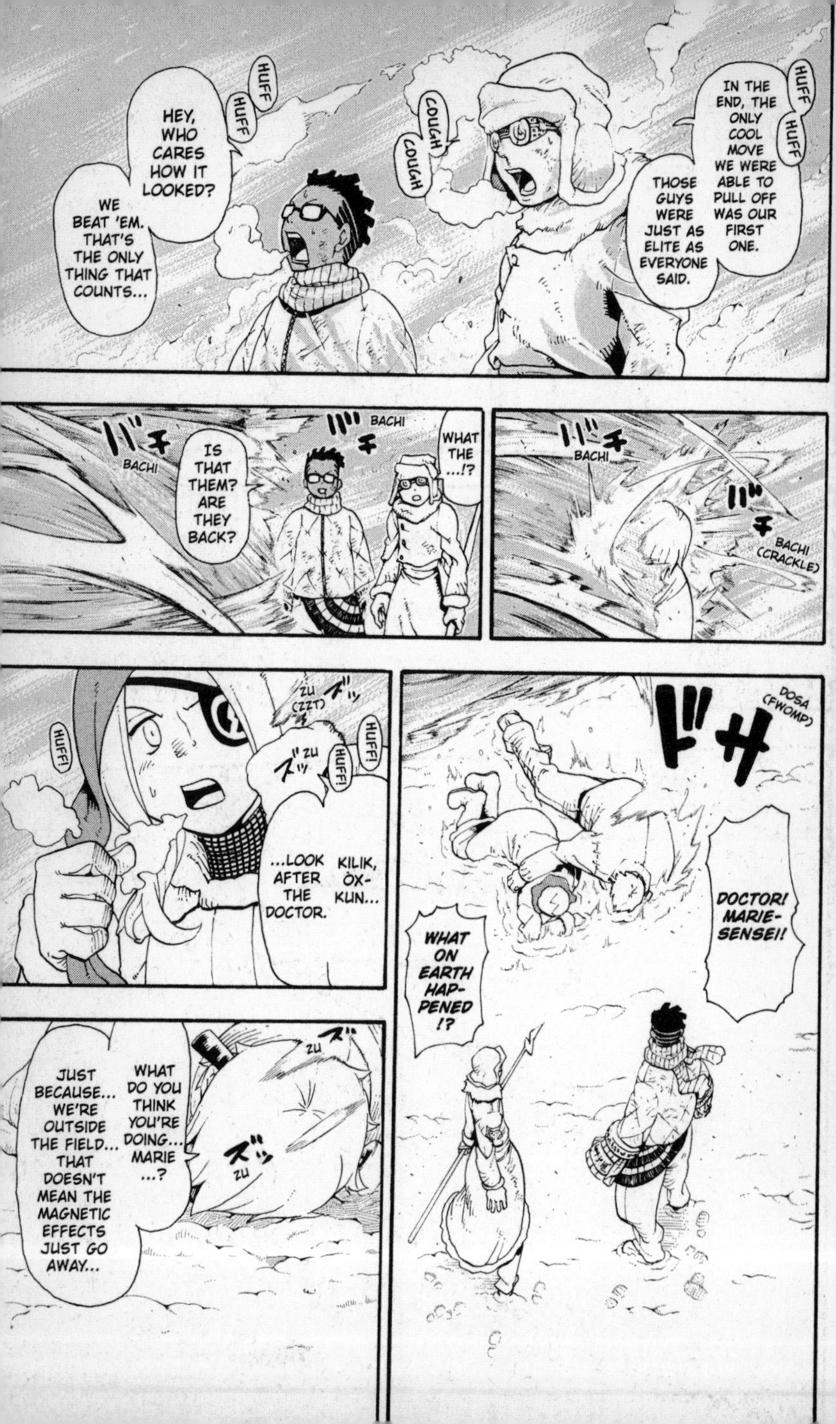
HUFF
HUFF
IN THE END, THE ONLY COOL MOVE WE WERE ABLE TO PULL OFF WAS OUR FIRST ONE.
THOSE GUYS WERE JUST AS ELITE AS EVERYONE SAID.
COUGH
COUGH
HUFF
HUFF
HEY, WHO CARES HOW IT LOOKED?
WE BEAT 'EM. THAT'S THE ONLY THING THAT COUNTS...
BACHI
BACHI (CRACKLE)
WHAT THE ...!?
BACHI
IS THAT THEM? ARE THEY BACK?
BACHI
DOSA (FWOMP)
DOCTOR! MARIE-SENSEI!
WHAT ON EARTH HAP-PENED !?
ZU (ZZT)
HUFF!
HUFF!
ZU
HUFF!
KILIK, OX-KUN...
...LOOK AFTER THE DOCTOR.
ZU
WHAT DO YOU THINK YOU'RE DOING... MARIE ...?
ZU
JUST BECAUSE... WE'RE OUTSIDE THE FIELD... THAT DOESN'T MEAN THE MAGNETIC EFFECTS JUST GO AWAY...

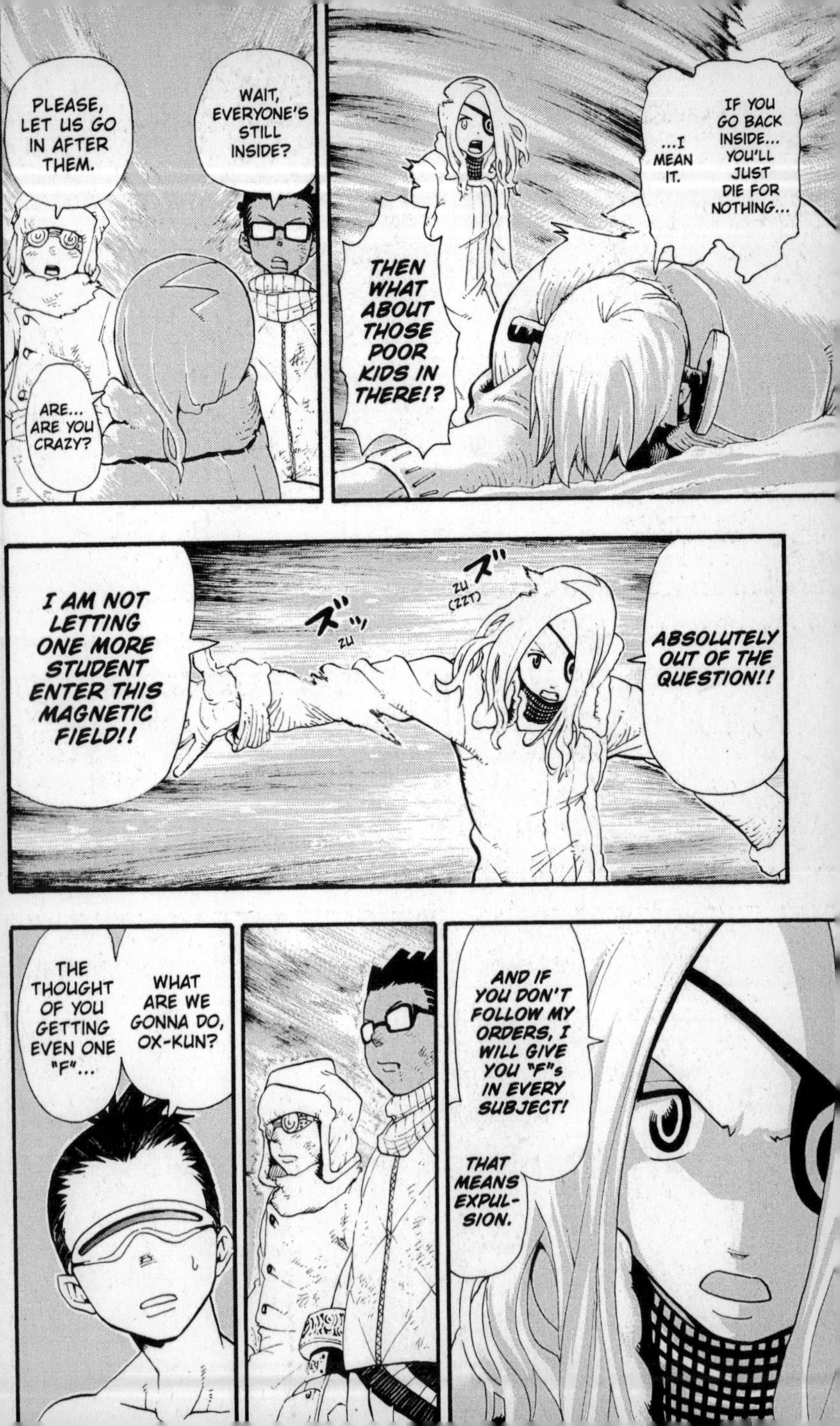
IF YOU GO BACK INSIDE... YOU'LL JUST DIE FOR NOTHING...
...I MEAN IT.
THEN WHAT ABOUT THOSE POOR KIDS IN THERE!?
WAIT, EVERYONE'S STILL INSIDE?
PLEASE, LET US GO IN AFTER THEM.
ARE... ARE YOU CRAZY?
ABSOLUTELY OUT OF THE QUESTION!!
ズ
ZU (ZZT)
ズッ
ZU
I AM NOT LETTING ONE MORE STUDENT ENTER THIS MAGNETIC FIELD!!
AND IF YOU DON'T FOLLOW MY ORDERS, I WILL GIVE YOU "F"s IN EVERY SUBJECT!
THAT MEANS EXPULSION.
WHAT ARE WE GONNA DO, OX-KUN?
THE THOUGHT OF YOU GETTING EVEN ONE "F"...

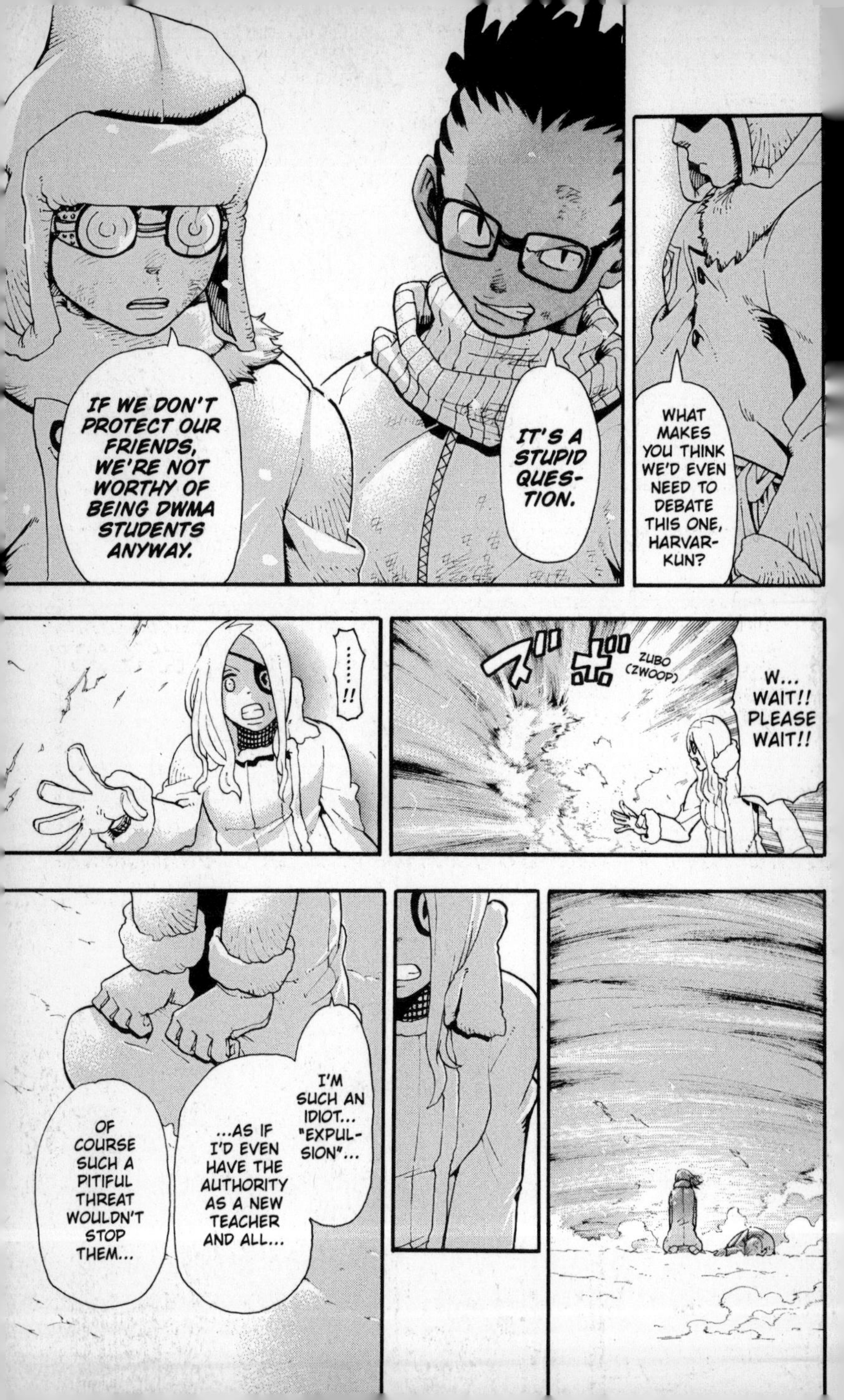
WHAT MAKES YOU THINK WE'D EVEN NEED TO DEBATE THIS ONE, HARVAR-KUN?
IT'S A STUPID QUES-TION.
IF WE DON'T PROTECT OUR FRIENDS, WE'RE NOT WORTHY OF BEING DWMA STUDENTS ANYWAY.
W... WAIT!! PLEASE WAIT!!
ZUBO (ZWOOP)
......!!
I'M SUCH AN IDIOT... "EXPUL-SION"...
...AS IF I'D EVEN HAVE THE AUTHORITY AS A NEW TEACHER AND ALL...
OF COURSE SUCH A PITIFUL THREAT WOULDN'T STOP THEM...

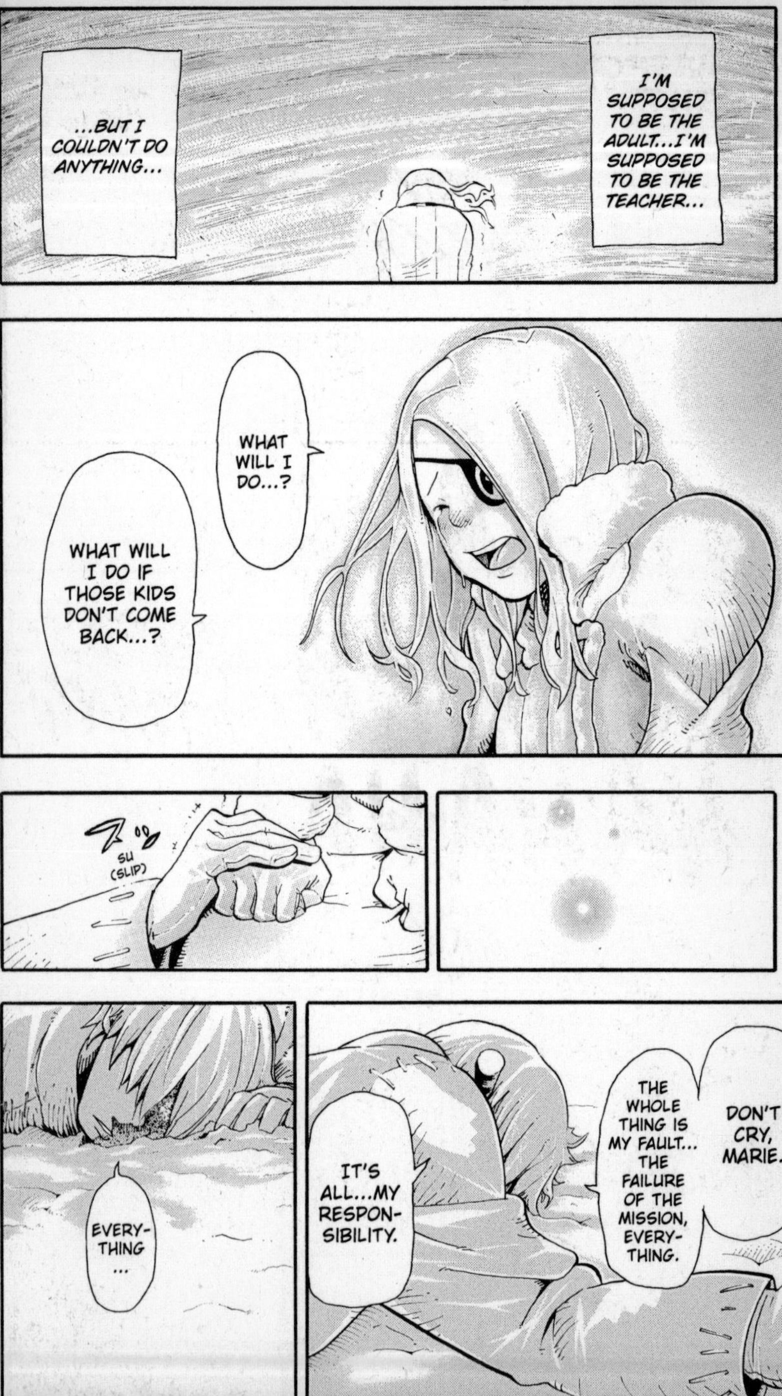
I'M SUPPOSED TO BE THE ADULT...I'M SUPPOSED TO BE THE TEACHER...
...BUT I COULDN'T DO ANYTHING...
WHAT WILL I DO...?
WHAT WILL I DO IF THOSE KIDS DON'T COME BACK...?
SU (SLIP)
DON'T CRY, MARIE.
THE WHOLE THING IS MY FAULT... THE FAILURE OF THE MISSION, EVERYTHING.
IT'S ALL...MY RESPONSIBILITY.
EVERYTHING...

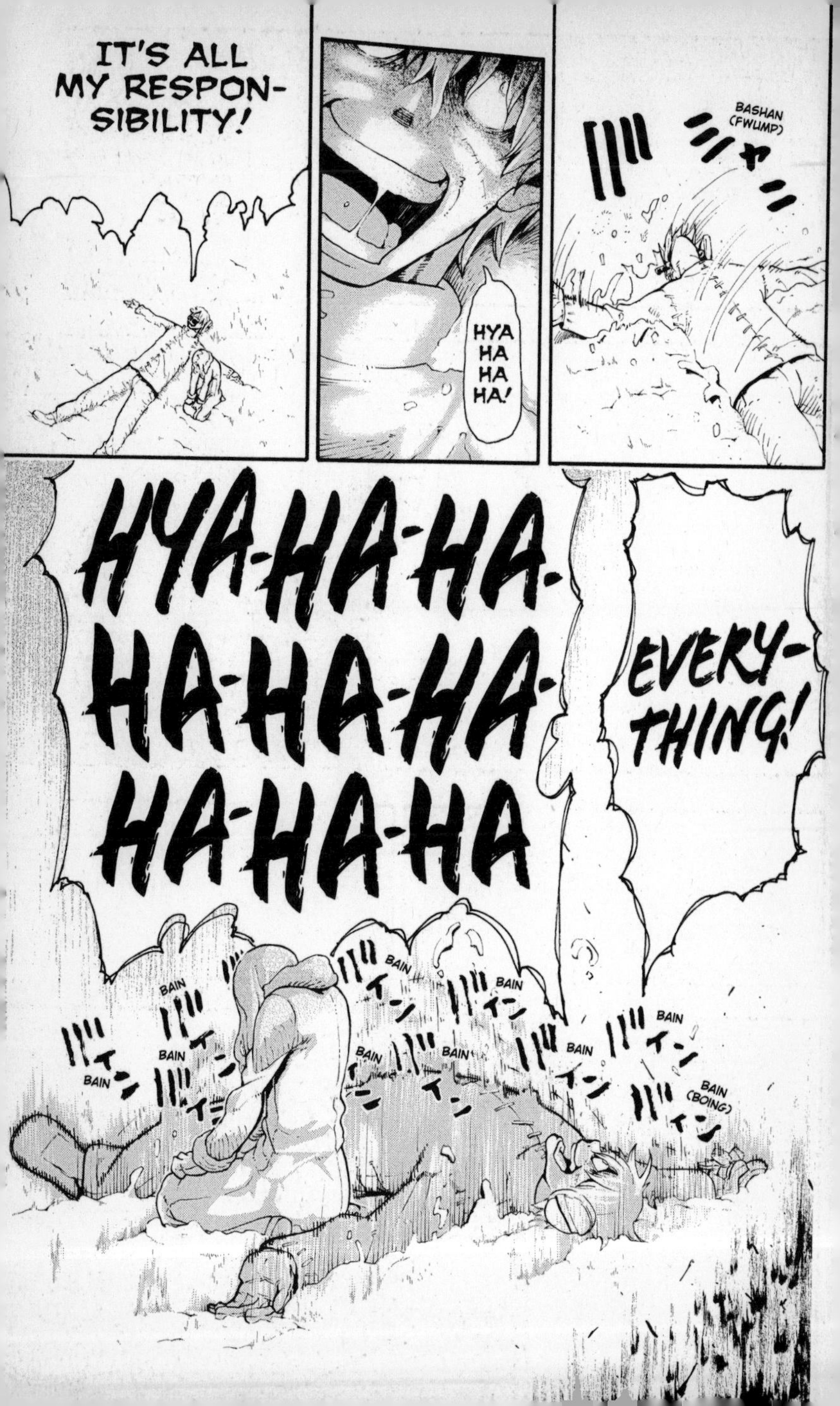
BASHAN (FWUMP)
HYA HA HA HA!
IT'S ALL MY RESPON-SIBILITY!
EVERY-THING!
HYA-HA-HA-HA-HA-HA-HA-HA-HA-HA-HA
BAIN
BAIN
BAIN
BAIN
BAIN
BAIN
BAIN
BAIN
BAIN
BAIN (BOING)

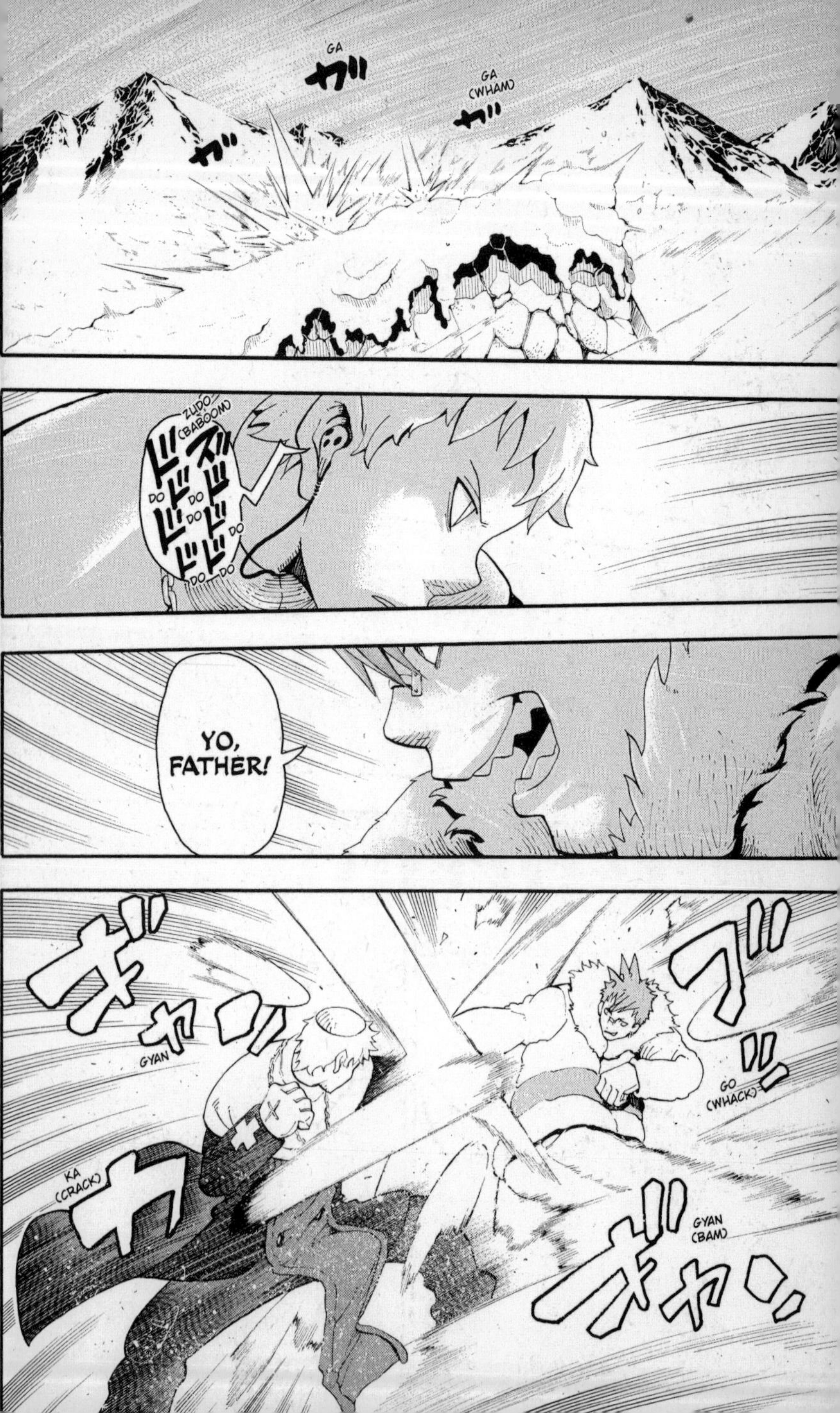
GA (WHAM)
GA
ZUDO (BABOOM)
DO DO DO DO DO DO
YO, FATHER!
GO (WHACK)
GYAN
GYAN (BAM)
KA (CRACK)

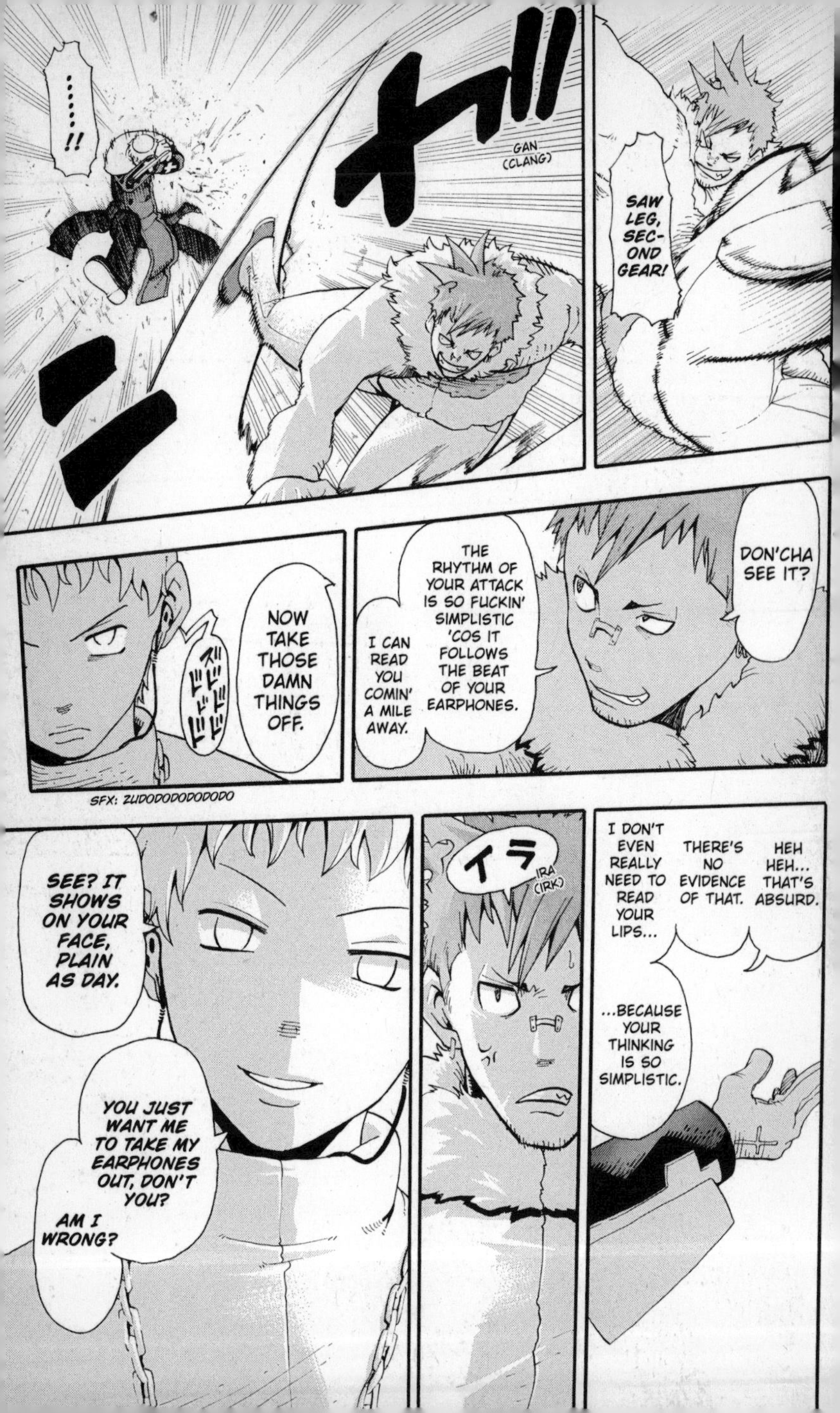
SAW LEG, SEC-OND GEAR!
GAN (CLANG)
......!!
DON'CHA SEE IT?
THE RHYTHM OF YOUR ATTACK IS SO FUCKIN' SIMPLISTIC 'COS IT FOLLOWS THE BEAT OF YOUR EARPHONES.
I CAN READ YOU COMIN' A MILE AWAY.
NOW TAKE THOSE DAMN THINGS OFF.
ズドドドドドド
SFX: ZUDODODODODODO
HEH HEH... THAT'S ABSURD.
THERE'S NO EVIDENCE OF THAT.
I DON'T EVEN REALLY NEED TO READ YOUR LIPS...
...BECAUSE YOUR THINKING IS SO SIMPLISTIC.
イラ
IRA (IRK)
SEE? IT SHOWS ON YOUR FACE, PLAIN AS DAY.
YOU JUST WANT ME TO TAKE MY EARPHONES OUT, DON'T YOU?
AM I WRONG?

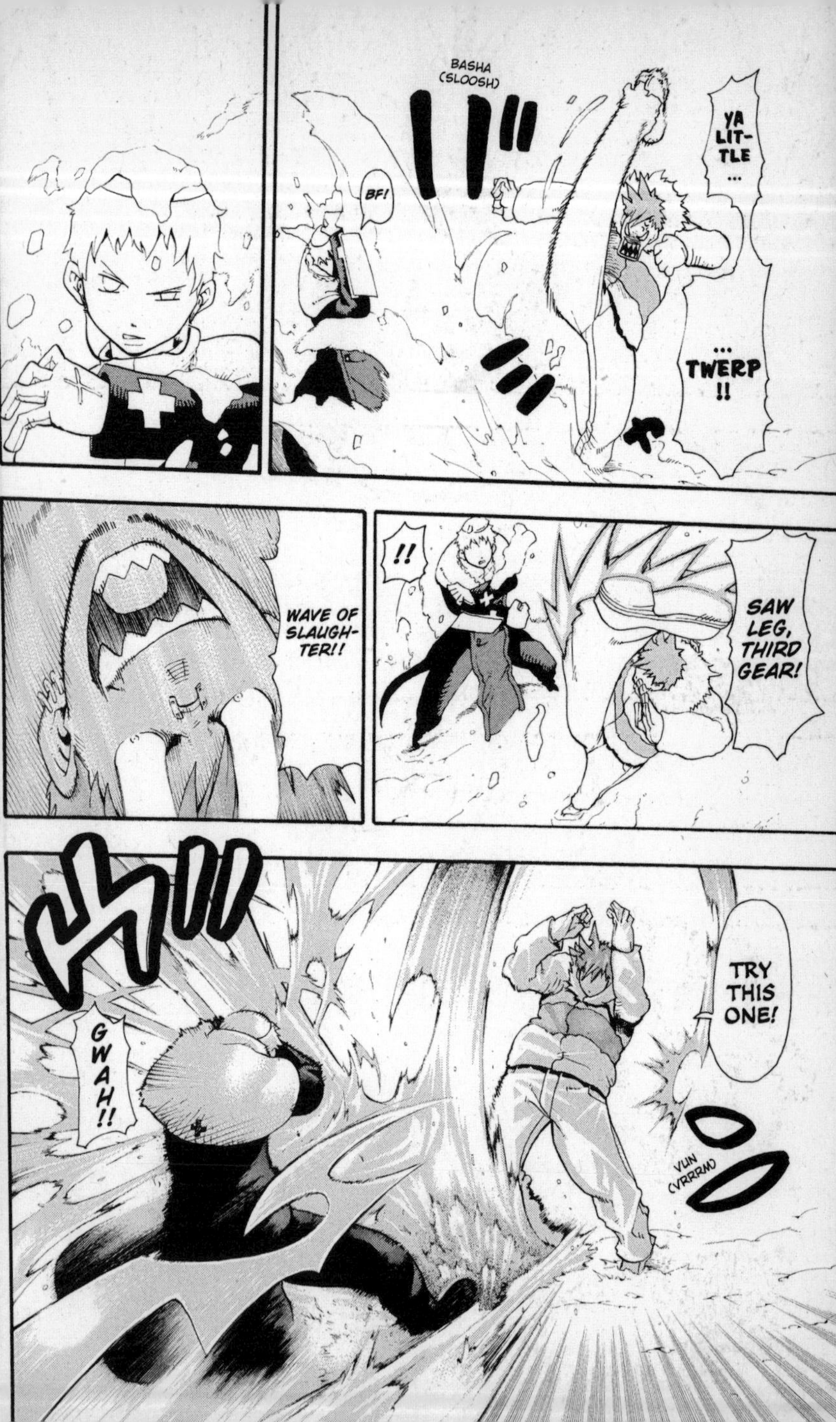
YA LITTLE ...
BASHA (SLOOSH)
BF!
... TWERP!!
SAW LEG, THIRD GEAR!
!!
WAVE OF SLAUGHTER!!
TRY THIS ONE!
VUN (VRRRM)
GWAH!!

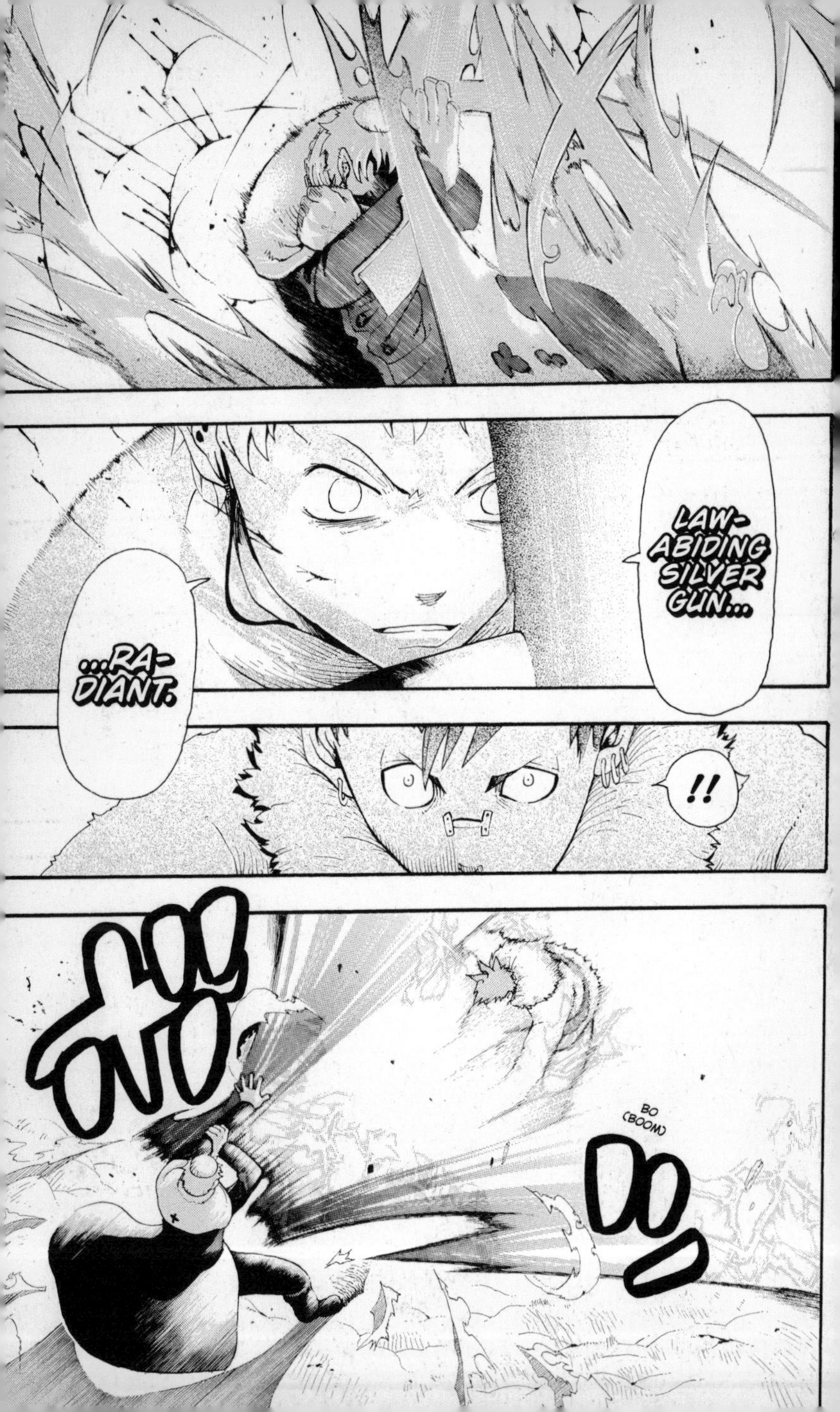

LAW-ABIDING SILVER GUN...
...RA-DIANT.
!!
BO
(BOOM)
DO

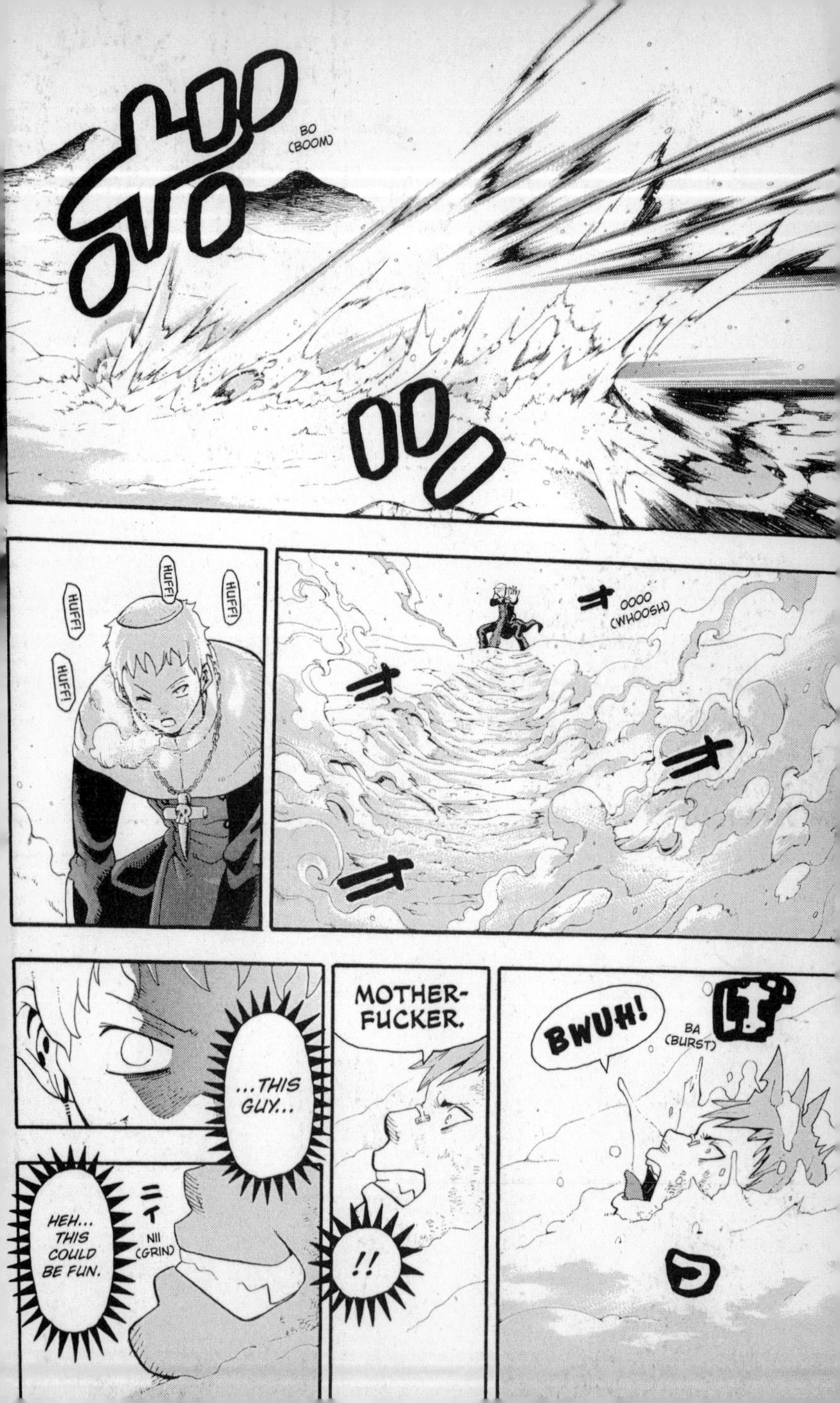
BO
(BOOM)
OOOO
(WHOOSH)
HUFF!
HUFF!
HUFF!
HUFF!
BWUH!
BA
(BURST)
MOTHER-FUCKER.
!!
...THIS GUY...
HEH... THIS COULD BE FUN.
ニィ
NII
(GRIN)

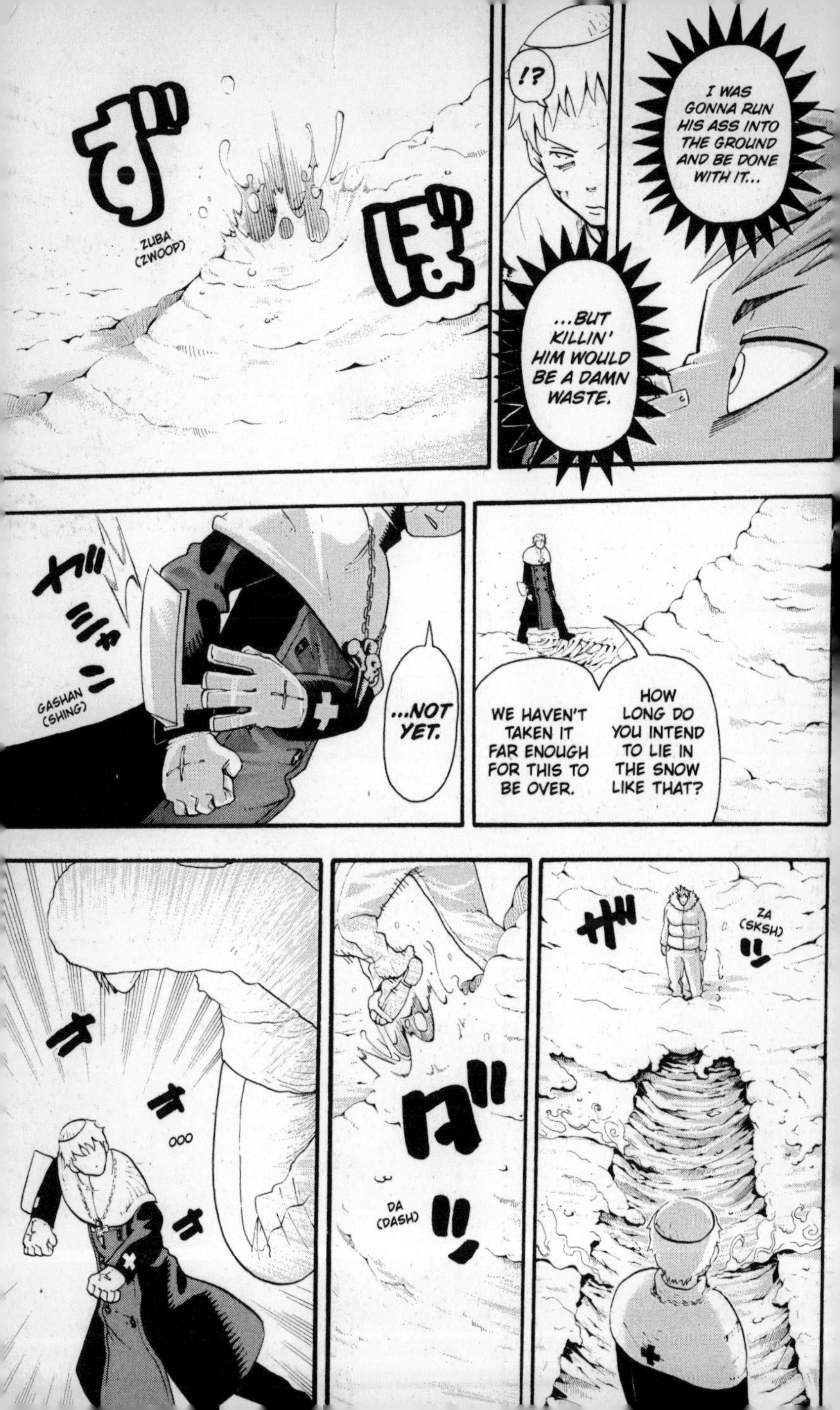
I WAS GONNA RUN HIS ASS INTO THE GROUND AND BE DONE WITH IT...
!?
...BUT KILLIN' HIM WOULD BE A DAMN WASTE.
ZUBA (ZWOOP)
HOW LONG DO YOU INTEND TO LIE IN THE SNOW LIKE THAT?
WE HAVEN'T TAKEN IT FAR ENOUGH FOR THIS TO BE OVER.
...NOT YET.
GASHAN (SHING)
ZA (SKSH)
DA (DASH)

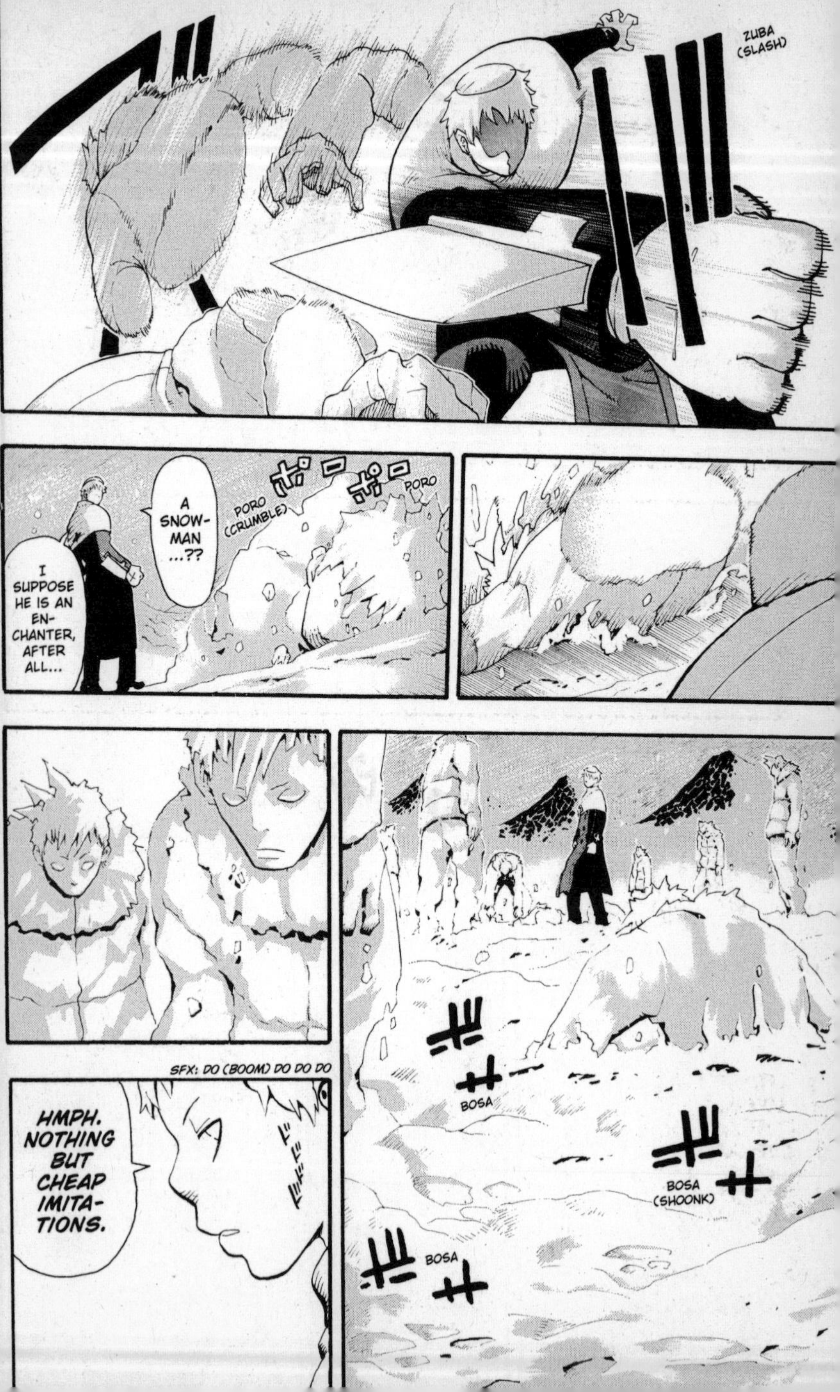
ZUBA (SLASH)
PORO
PORO (CRUMBLE)
A SNOW-MAN ...??
I SUPPOSE HE IS AN EN-CHANTER, AFTER ALL...
BOSA
BOSA (SHOONK)
BOSA
SFX: DO (BOOM) DO DO DO
HMPH. NOTHING BUT CHEAP IMITA-TIONS.

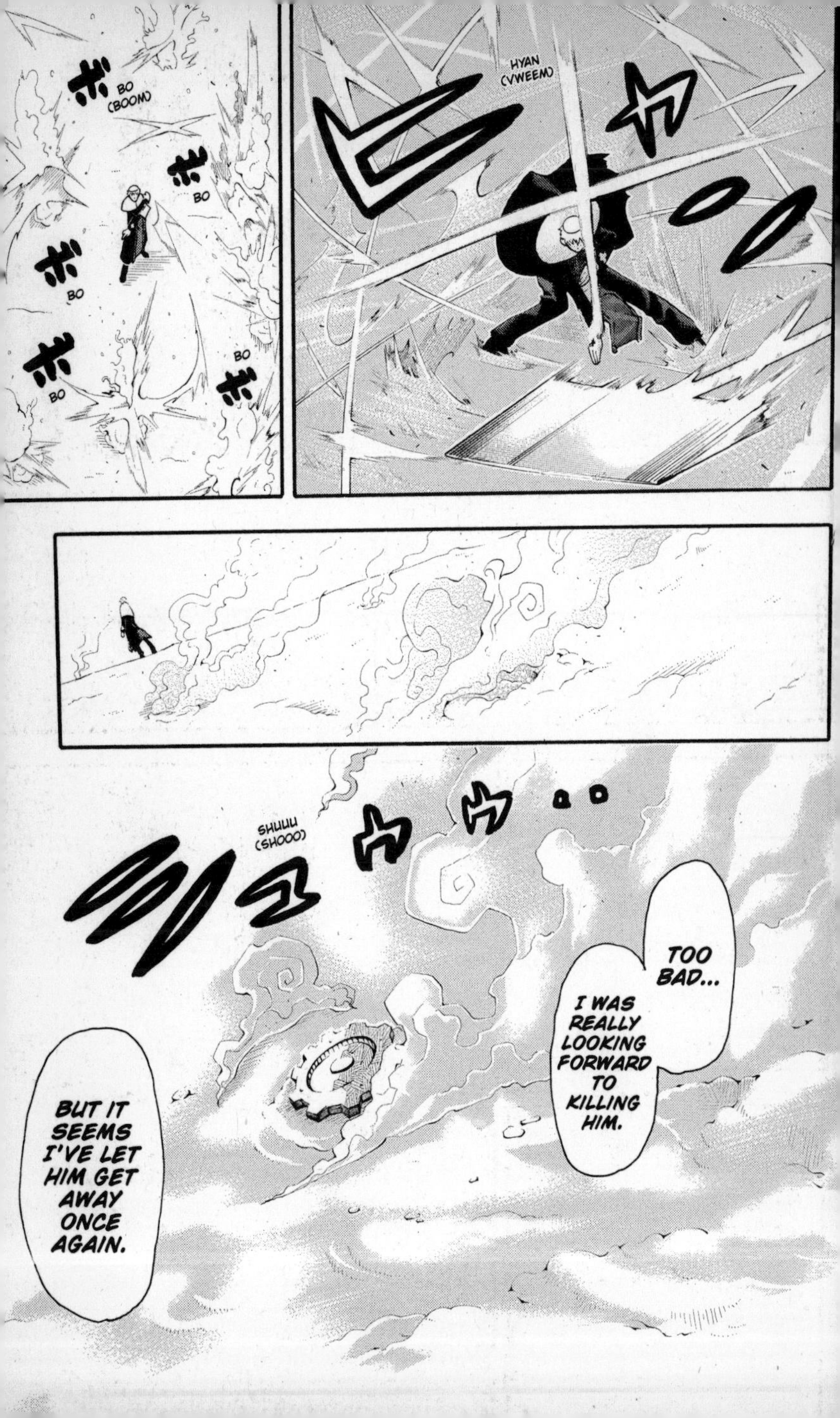
HYAN (VWEEM)
BO (BOOM)
BO
BO
BO
BO
SHUUU (SHOOO)
TOO BAD... I WAS REALLY LOOKING FORWARD TO KILLING HIM.
BUT IT SEEMS I'VE LET HIM GET AWAY ONCE AGAIN.

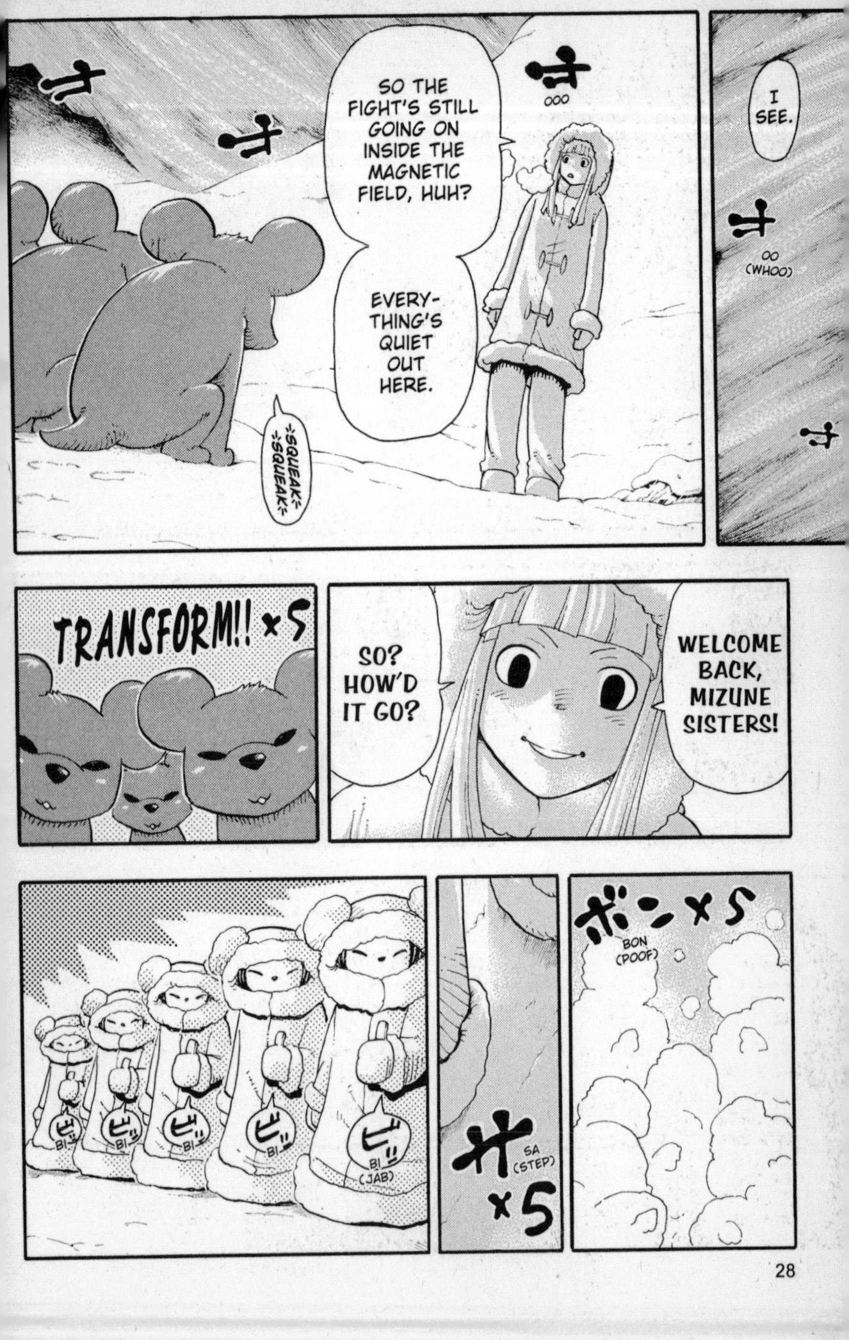
I SEE.
OO (WHOO)
OOO
SO THE FIGHT'S STILL GOING ON INSIDE THE MAGNETIC FIELD, HUH?
EVERYTHING'S QUIET OUT HERE.
SQUEAK SQUEAK
WELCOME BACK, MIZUNE SISTERS!
SO? HOW'D IT GO?
TRANSFORM!! ×5
ボン×5
BON (POOF)
×5
SA (STEP)
ビッ
BI (JAB)
BI
BI
BI
BI

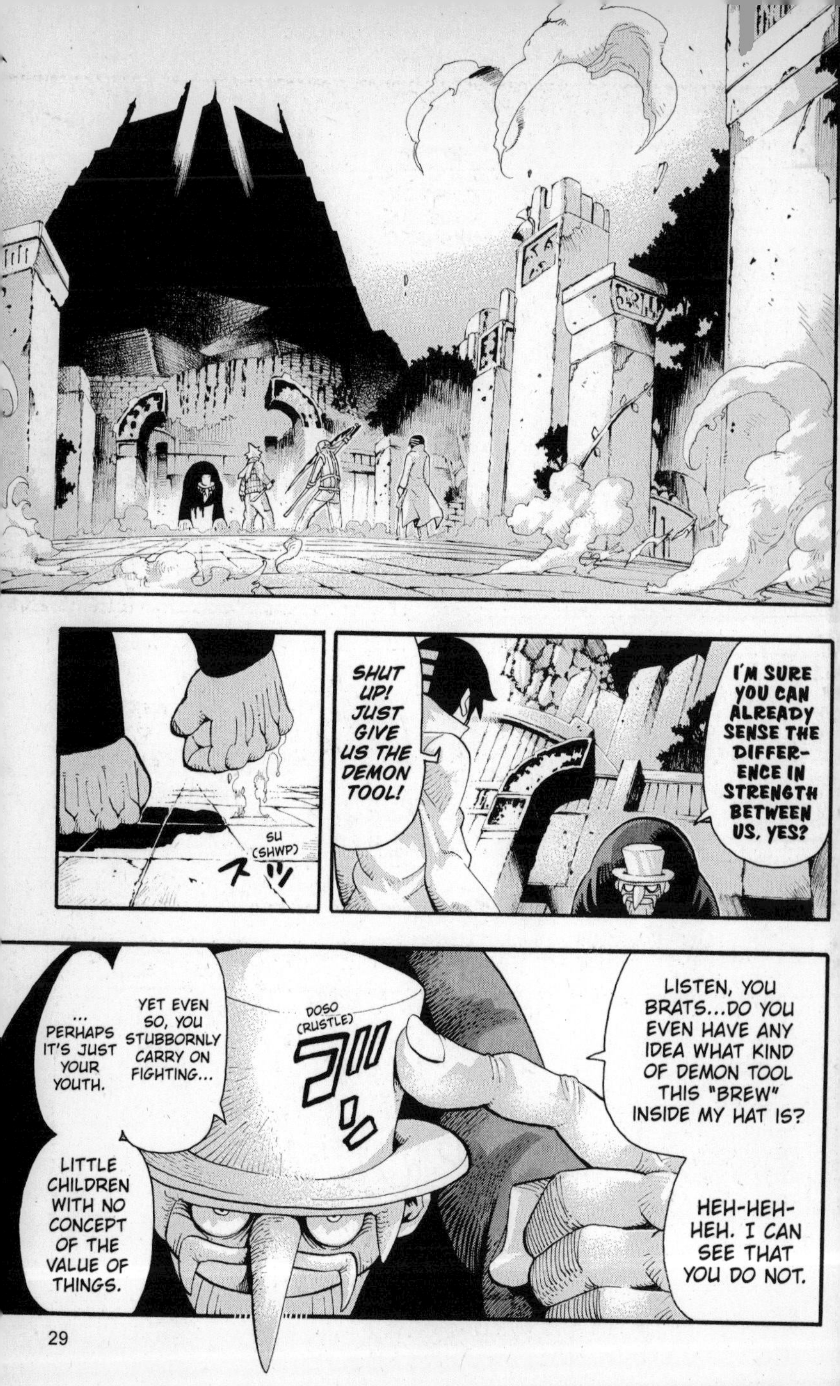

I'M SURE YOU CAN ALREADY SENSE THE DIFFERENCE IN STRENGTH BETWEEN US, YES?
SHUT UP! JUST GIVE US THE DEMON TOOL!
SU (SHWP)
LISTEN, YOU BRATS...DO YOU EVEN HAVE ANY IDEA WHAT KIND OF DEMON TOOL THIS "BREW" INSIDE MY HAT IS?
HEH-HEH-HEH. I CAN SEE THAT YOU DO NOT.
DOSO (RUSTLE)
YET EVEN SO, YOU STUBBORNLY CARRY ON FIGHTING...
...PERHAPS IT'S JUST YOUR YOUTH.
LITTLE CHILDREN WITH NO CONCEPT OF THE VALUE OF THINGS.

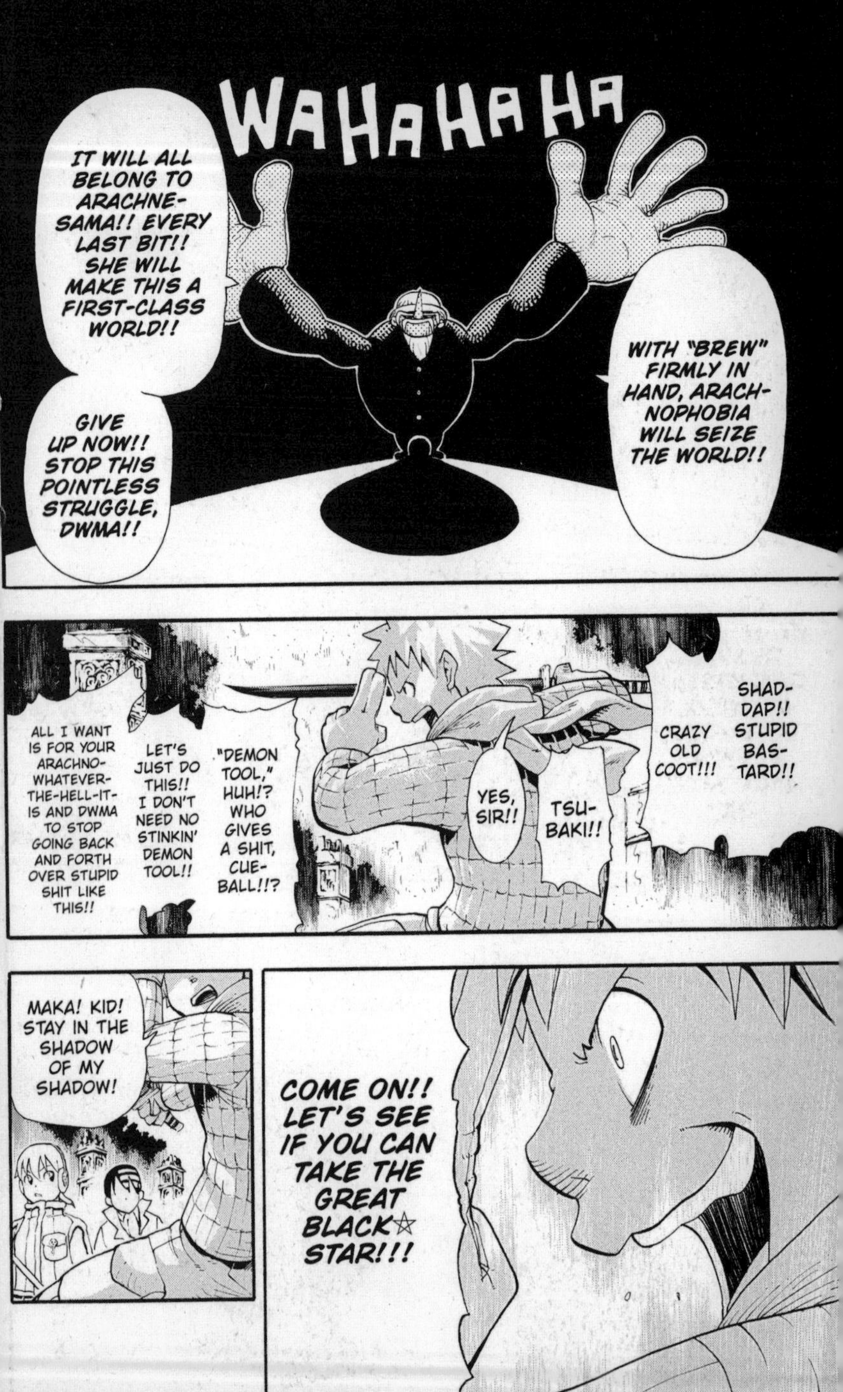

WAHAHAHA
WITH "BREW" FIRMLY IN HAND, ARACHNOPHOBIA WILL SEIZE THE WORLD!!
IT WILL ALL BELONG TO ARACHNE-SAMA!! EVERY LAST BIT!! SHE WILL MAKE THIS A FIRST-CLASS WORLD!!
GIVE UP NOW!! STOP THIS POINTLESS STRUGGLE, DWMA!!
SHAD-DAP!! STUPID BASTARD!!
CRAZY OLD COOT!!!
TSUBAKI!!
YES, SIR!!
"DEMON TOOL," HUH!? WHO GIVES A SHIT, CUEBALL!!?
LET'S JUST DO THIS!! I DON'T NEED NO STINKIN' DEMON TOOL!!
ALL I WANT IS FOR YOUR ARACHNO-WHATEVER-THE-HELL-IT-IS AND DWMA TO STOP GOING BACK AND FORTH OVER STUPID SHIT LIKE THIS!!
COME ON!! LET'S SEE IF YOU CAN TAKE THE GREAT BLACK☆STAR!!!
MAKA! KID! STAY IN THE SHADOW OF MY SHADOW!

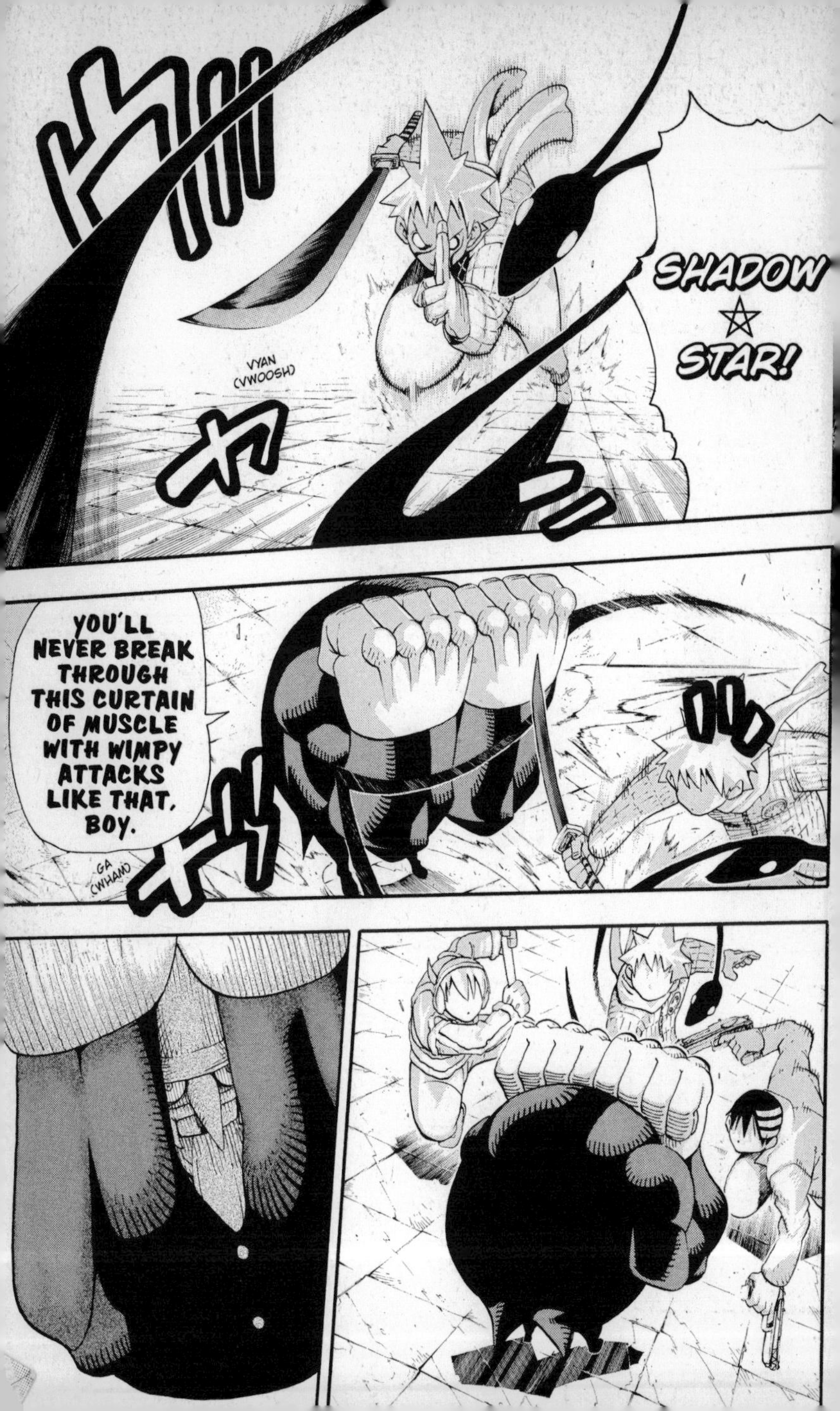
SHADOW ☆ STAR!
VYAN (VWOOSH)
YOU'LL NEVER BREAK THROUGH THIS CURTAIN OF MUSCLE WITH WIMPY ATTACKS LIKE THAT, BOY.
GA (WHAM)

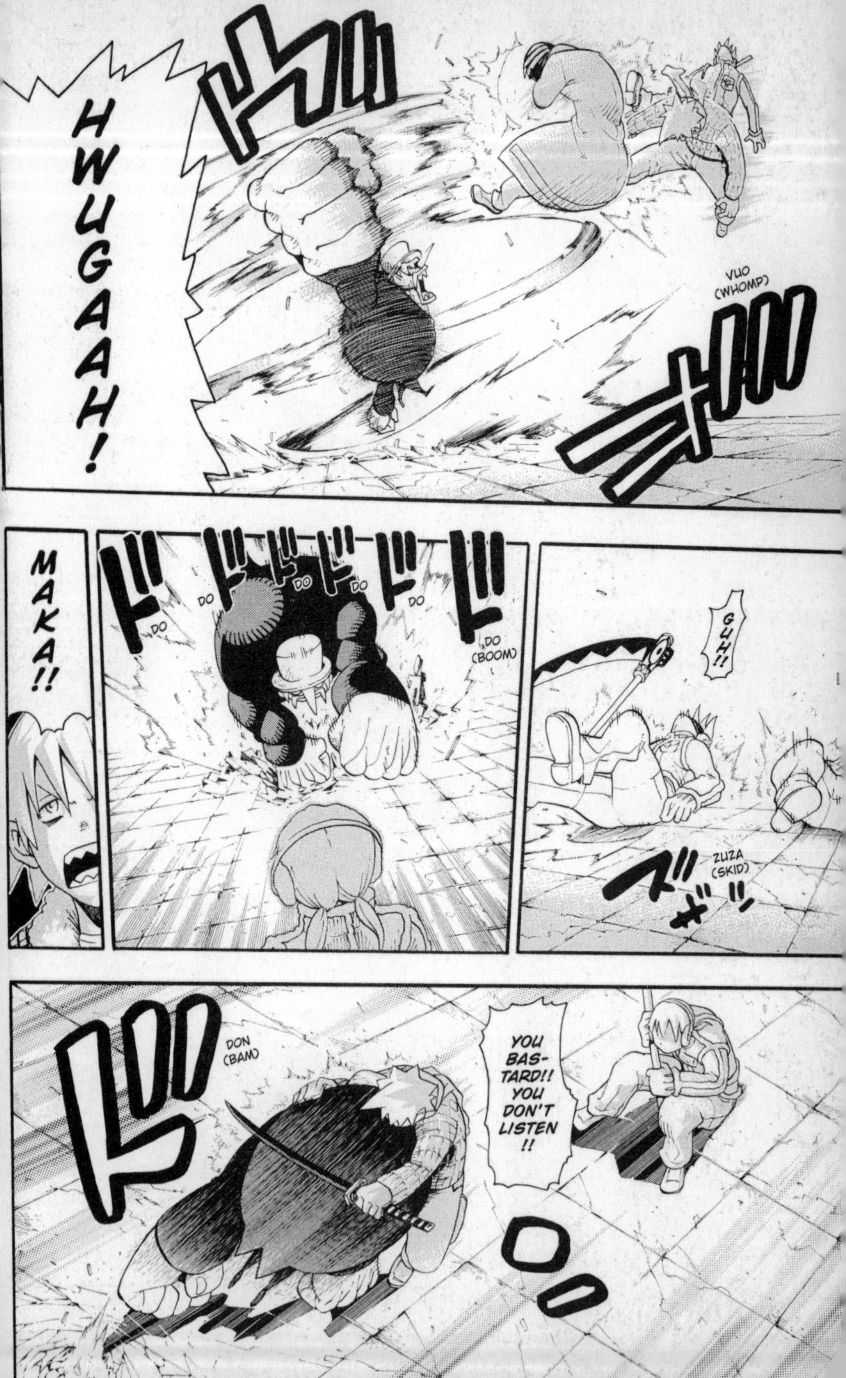
VUO (WHOMP)
HWUGAAAH!
GUH!!
ZUZA (SKID)
DO
DO
DO
DO
DO
DO (BOOM)
MAKA!!
YOU BASTARD!! YOU DON'T LISTEN!!
DON (BAM)

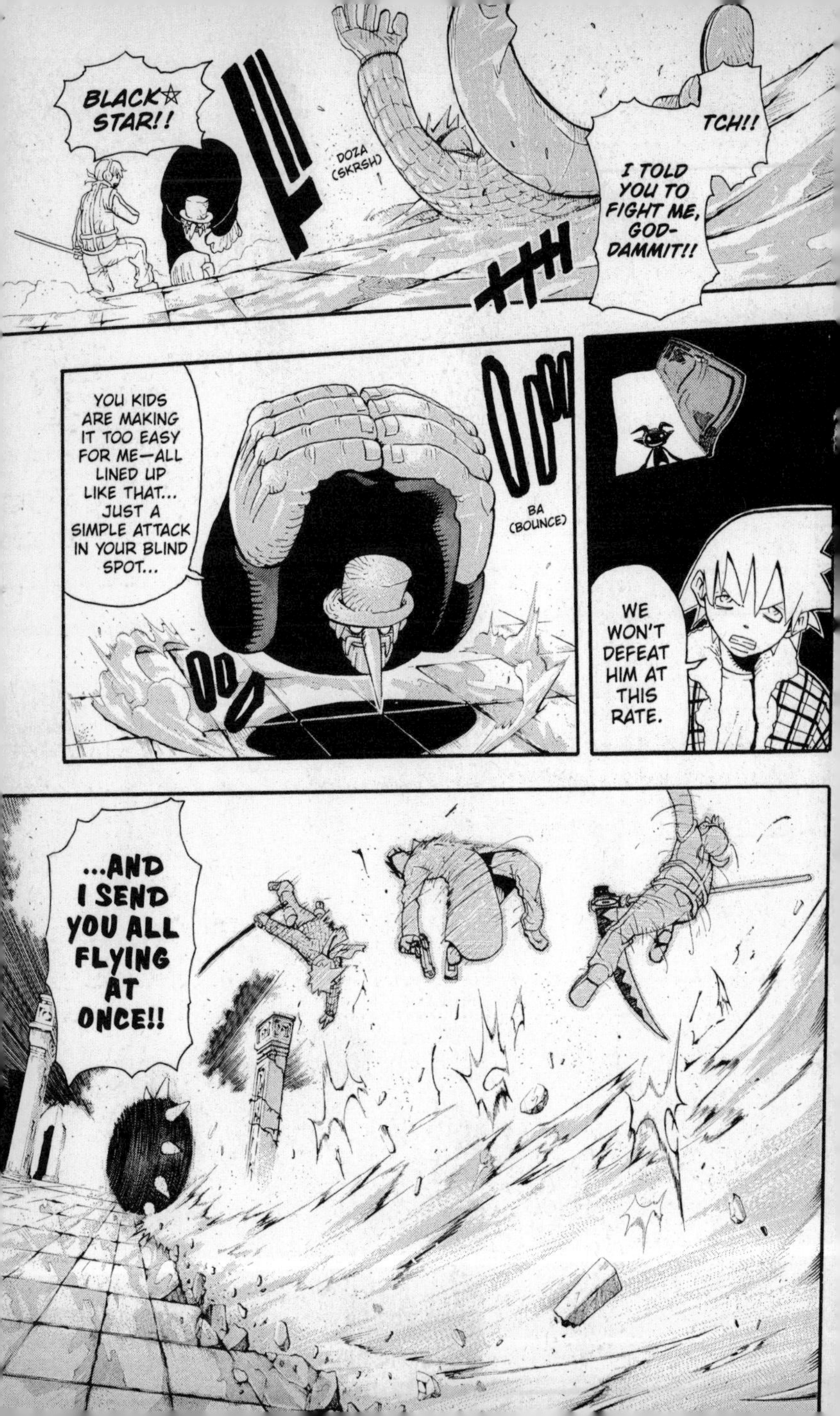
TCH!!
I TOLD YOU TO FIGHT ME, GOD-DAMMIT!!
DOZA (SKRSH)
BLACK☆STAR!!
WE WON'T DEFEAT HIM AT THIS RATE.
BA (BOUNCE)
YOU KIDS ARE MAKING IT TOO EASY FOR ME—ALL LINED UP LIKE THAT... JUST A SIMPLE ATTACK IN YOUR BLIND SPOT...
...AND I SEND YOU ALL FLYING AT ONCE!!

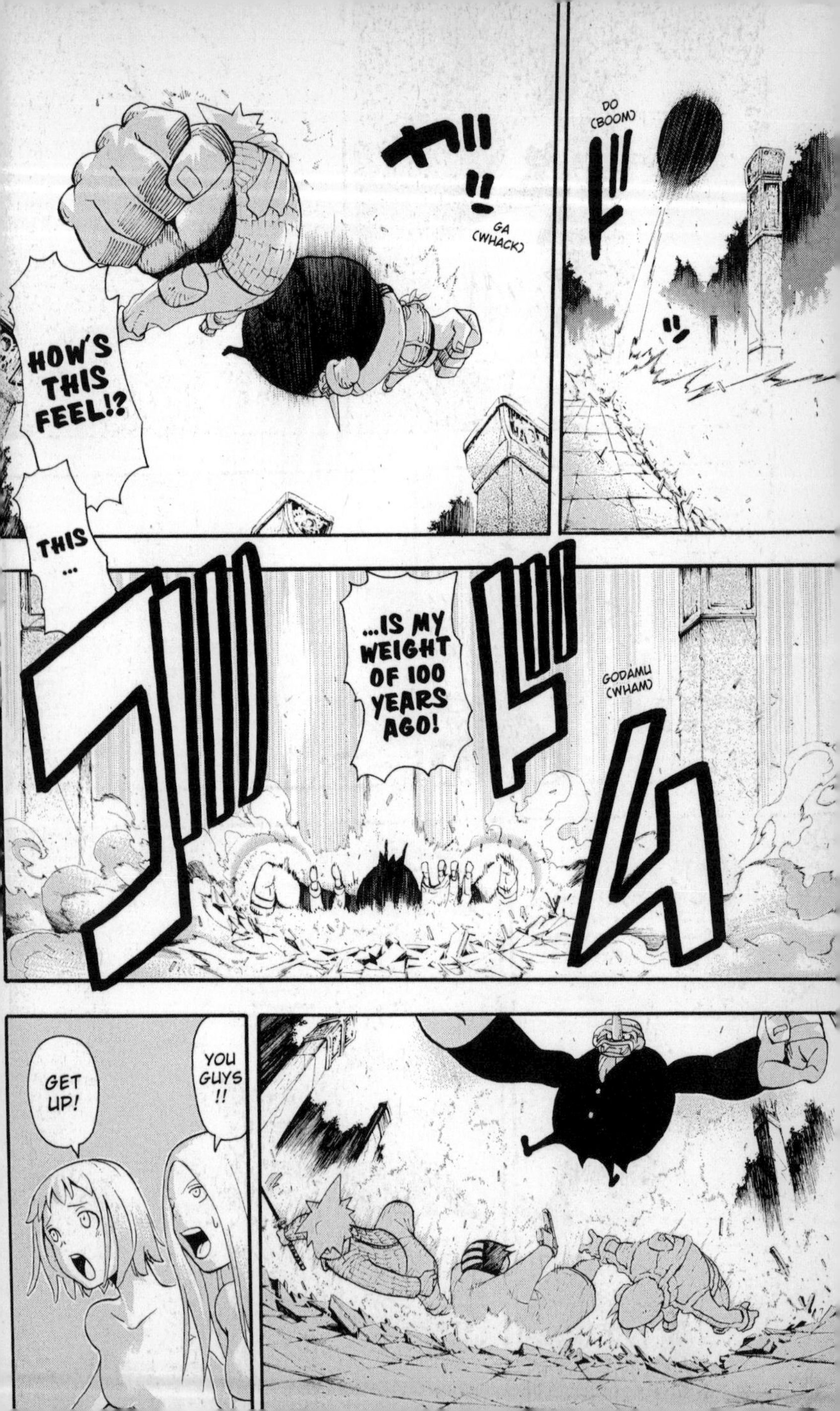
DO (BOOM)
GA (WHACK)
HOW'S THIS FEEL!?
THIS ...
...IS MY WEIGHT OF 100 YEARS AGO!
GODAMU (WHAM)
YOU GUYS !!
GET UP!

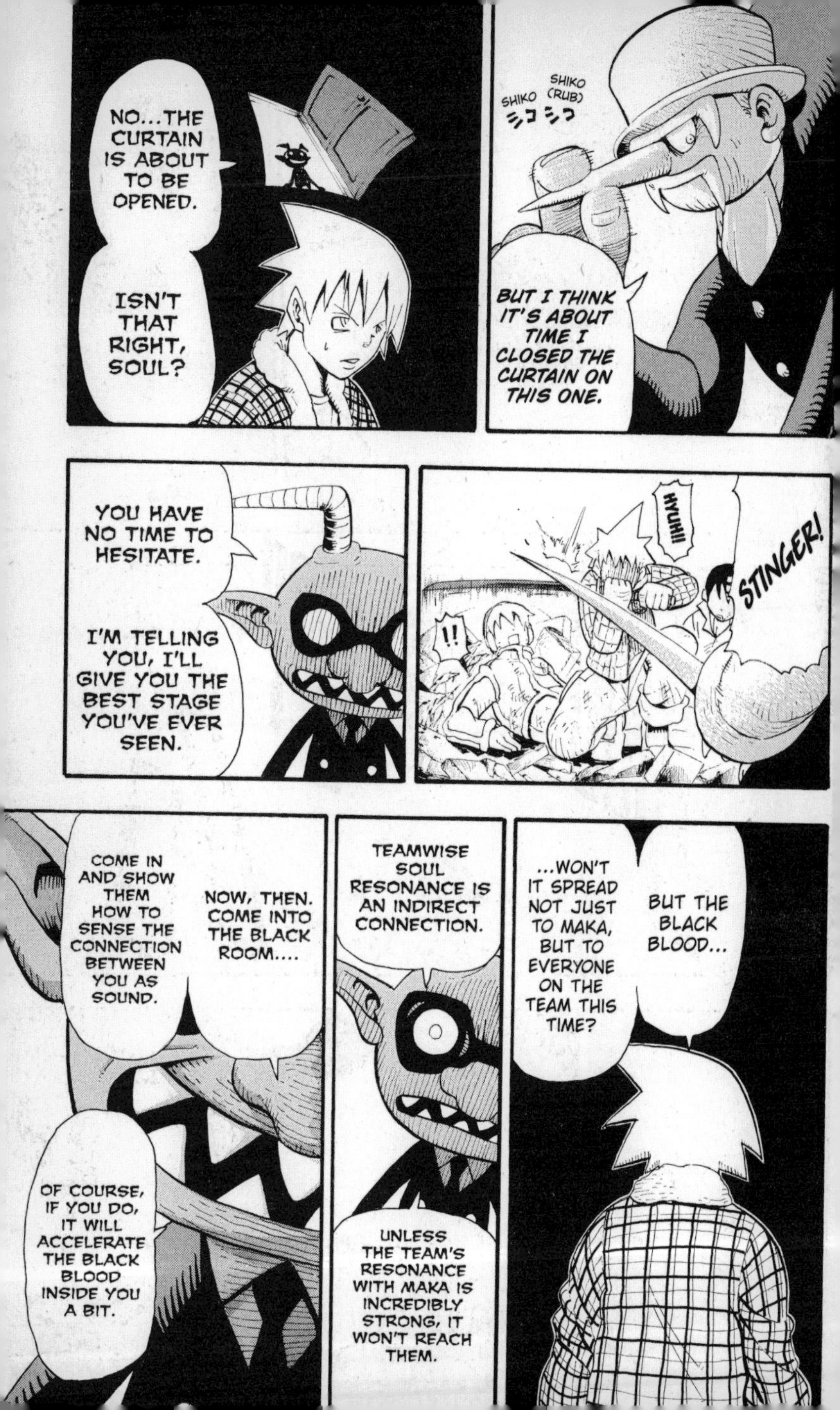
SHIKO SHIKO (RUB)
シコシコ
BUT I THINK IT'S ABOUT TIME I CLOSED THE CURTAIN ON THIS ONE.
NO...THE CURTAIN IS ABOUT TO BE OPENED.
ISN'T THAT RIGHT, SOUL?
HYUH!!
STINGER!
!!
YOU HAVE NO TIME TO HESITATE.
I'M TELLING YOU, I'LL GIVE YOU THE BEST STAGE YOU'VE EVER SEEN.
BUT THE BLACK BLOOD...
...WON'T IT SPREAD NOT JUST TO MAKA, BUT TO EVERYONE ON THE TEAM THIS TIME?
TEAMWISE SOUL RESONANCE IS AN INDIRECT CONNECTION.
UNLESS THE TEAM'S RESONANCE WITH MAKA IS INCREDIBLY STRONG, IT WON'T REACH THEM.
NOW, THEN. COME INTO THE BLACK ROOM....
COME IN AND SHOW THEM HOW TO SENSE THE CONNECTION BETWEEN YOU AS SOUND.
OF COURSE, IF YOU DO, IT WILL ACCELERATE THE BLACK BLOOD INSIDE YOU A BIT.

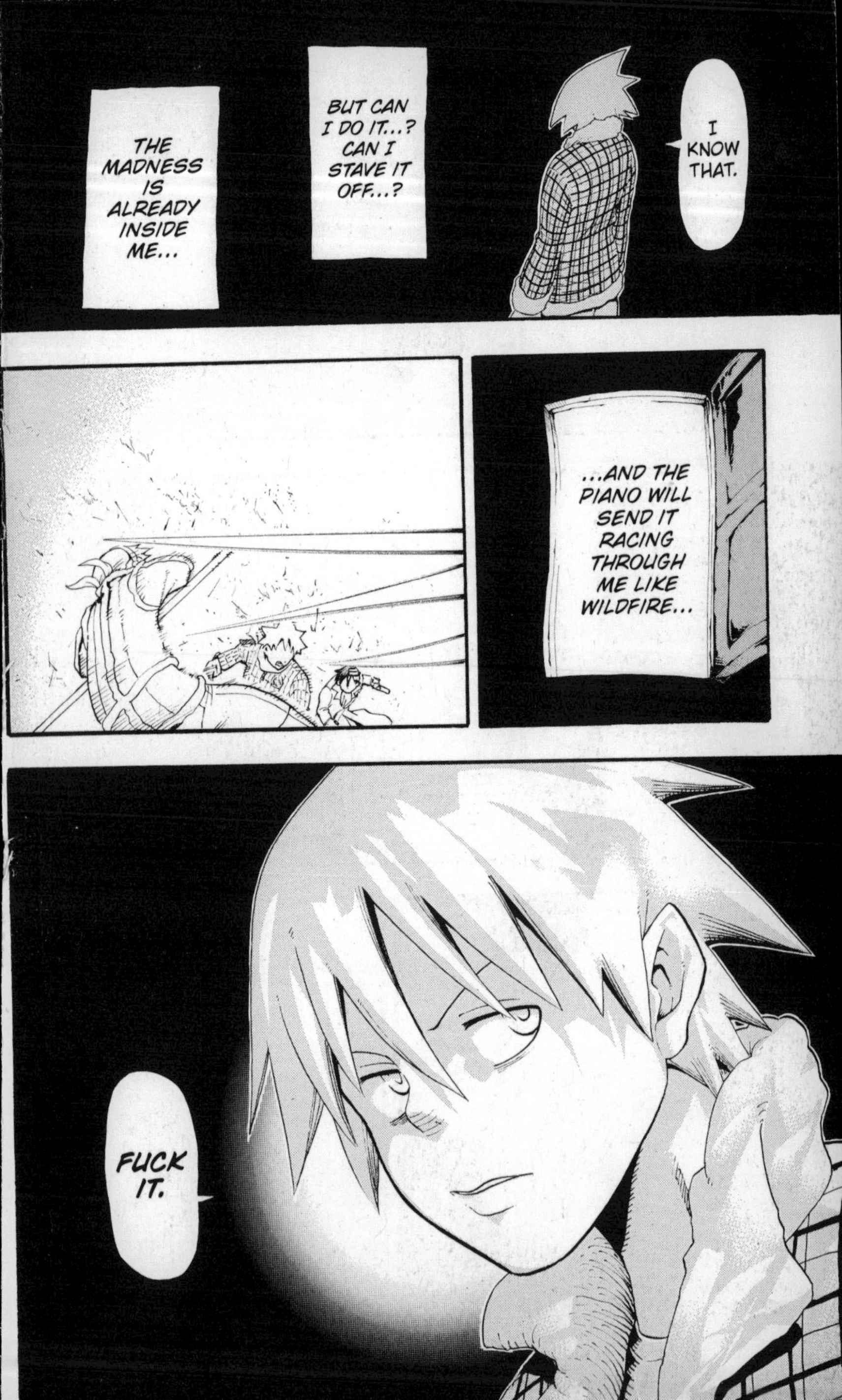
I KNOW THAT.
BUT CAN I DO IT...? CAN I STAVE IT OFF...?
THE MADNESS IS ALREADY INSIDE ME...
...AND THE PIANO WILL SEND IT RACING THROUGH ME LIKE WILDFIRE...
FUCK IT.

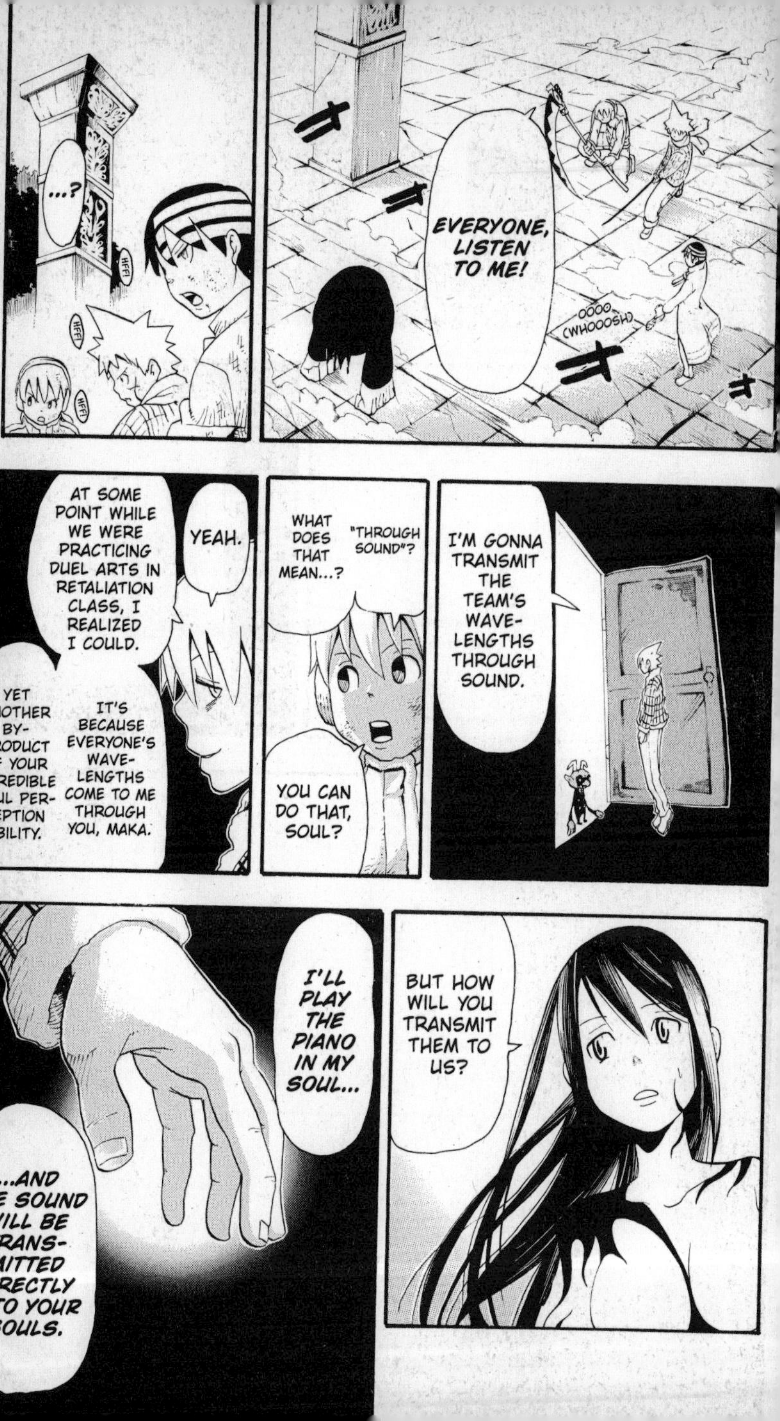
EVERYONE, LISTEN TO ME!
OOOO (WHOOOSH)
...?
HFF!
HFF!
HFF!
I'M GONNA TRANSMIT THE TEAM'S WAVE-LENGTHS THROUGH SOUND.
WHAT DOES THAT MEAN...?
"THROUGH SOUND"?
YOU CAN DO THAT, SOUL?
YEAH.
AT SOME POINT WHILE WE WERE PRACTICING DUEL ARTS IN RETALIATION CLASS, I REALIZED I COULD.
IT'S BECAUSE EVERYONE'S WAVE-LENGTHS COME TO ME THROUGH YOU, MAKA.
YET ANOTHER BY-PRODUCT OF YOUR INCREDIBLE SOUL PER-CEPTION ABILITY.
BUT HOW WILL YOU TRANSMIT THEM TO US?
I'LL PLAY THE PIANO IN MY SOUL...
...AND THE SOUND WILL BE TRANS-MITTED DIRECTLY INTO YOUR SOULS.

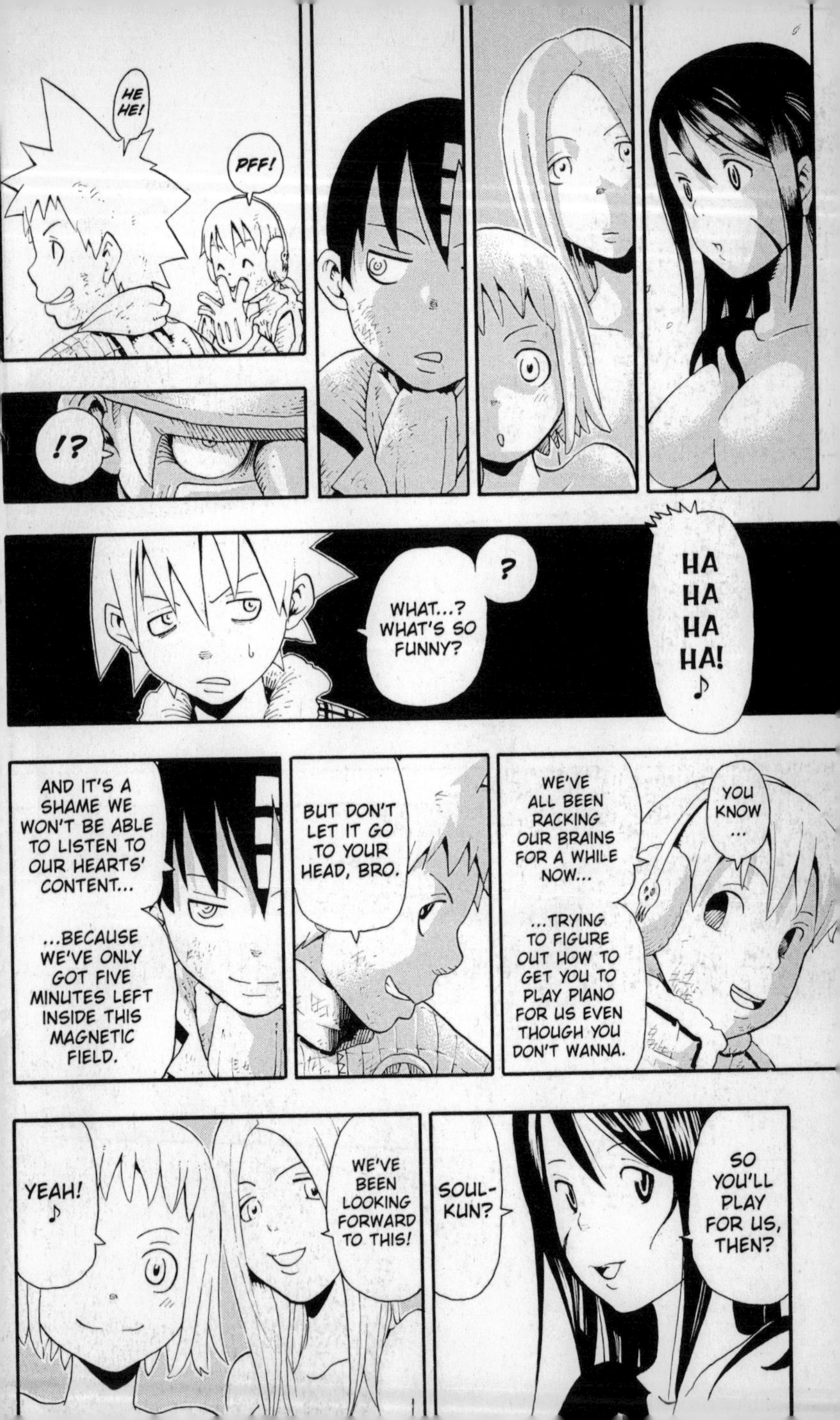
HE HE!
PFF!
!?
HA HA HA HA! ♪
?
WHAT...? WHAT'S SO FUNNY?
YOU KNOW...
WE'VE ALL BEEN RACKING OUR BRAINS FOR A WHILE NOW...
...TRYING TO FIGURE OUT HOW TO GET YOU TO PLAY PIANO FOR US EVEN THOUGH YOU DON'T WANNA.
BUT DON'T LET IT GO TO YOUR HEAD, BRO.
AND IT'S A SHAME WE WON'T BE ABLE TO LISTEN TO OUR HEARTS' CONTENT...
...BECAUSE WE'VE ONLY GOT FIVE MINUTES LEFT INSIDE THIS MAGNETIC FIELD.
SO YOU'LL PLAY FOR US, THEN?
SOUL-KUN?
WE'VE BEEN LOOKING FORWARD TO THIS!
YEAH! ♪

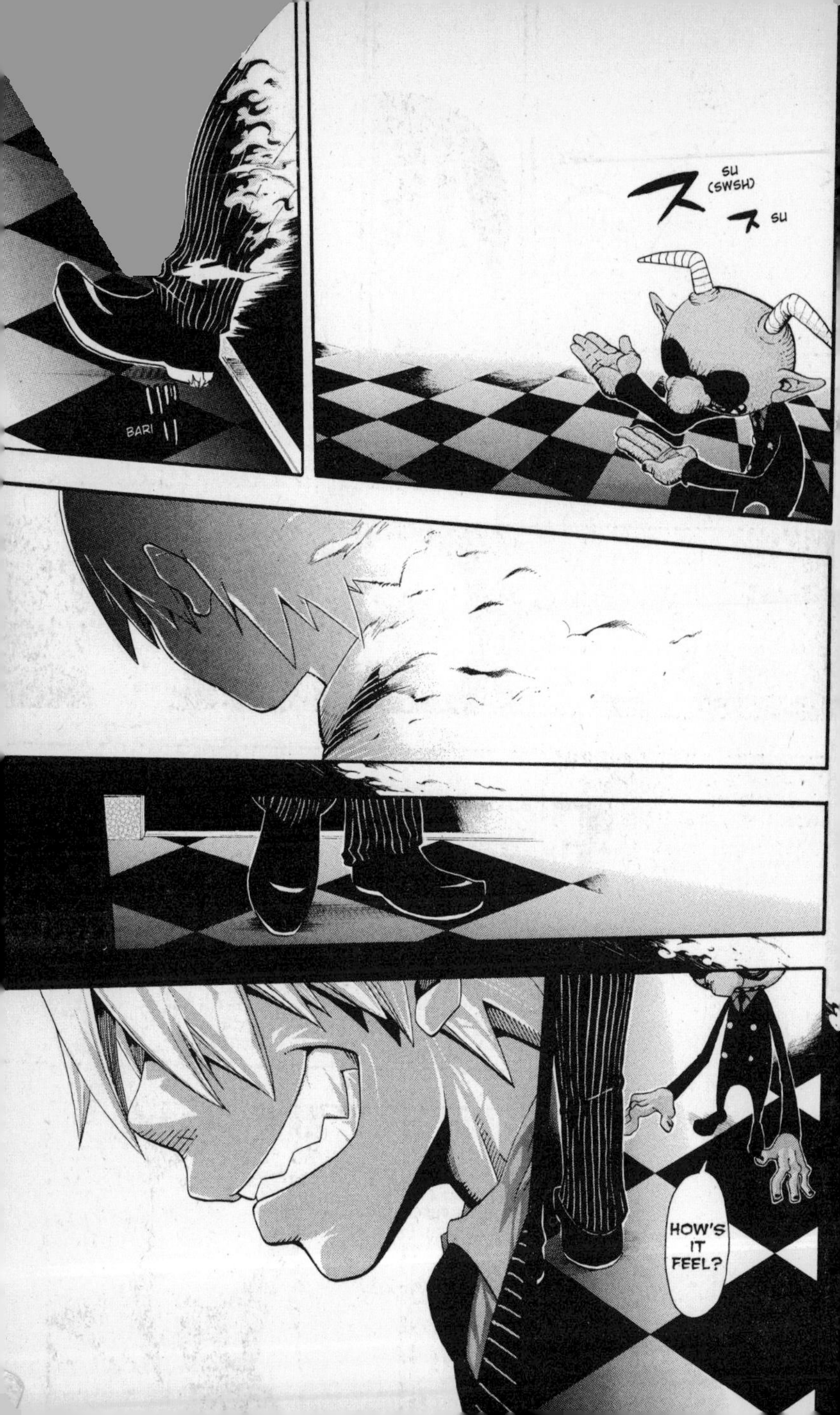
ス SU (SWSH)
ス SU
BARI
HOW'S IT FEEL?

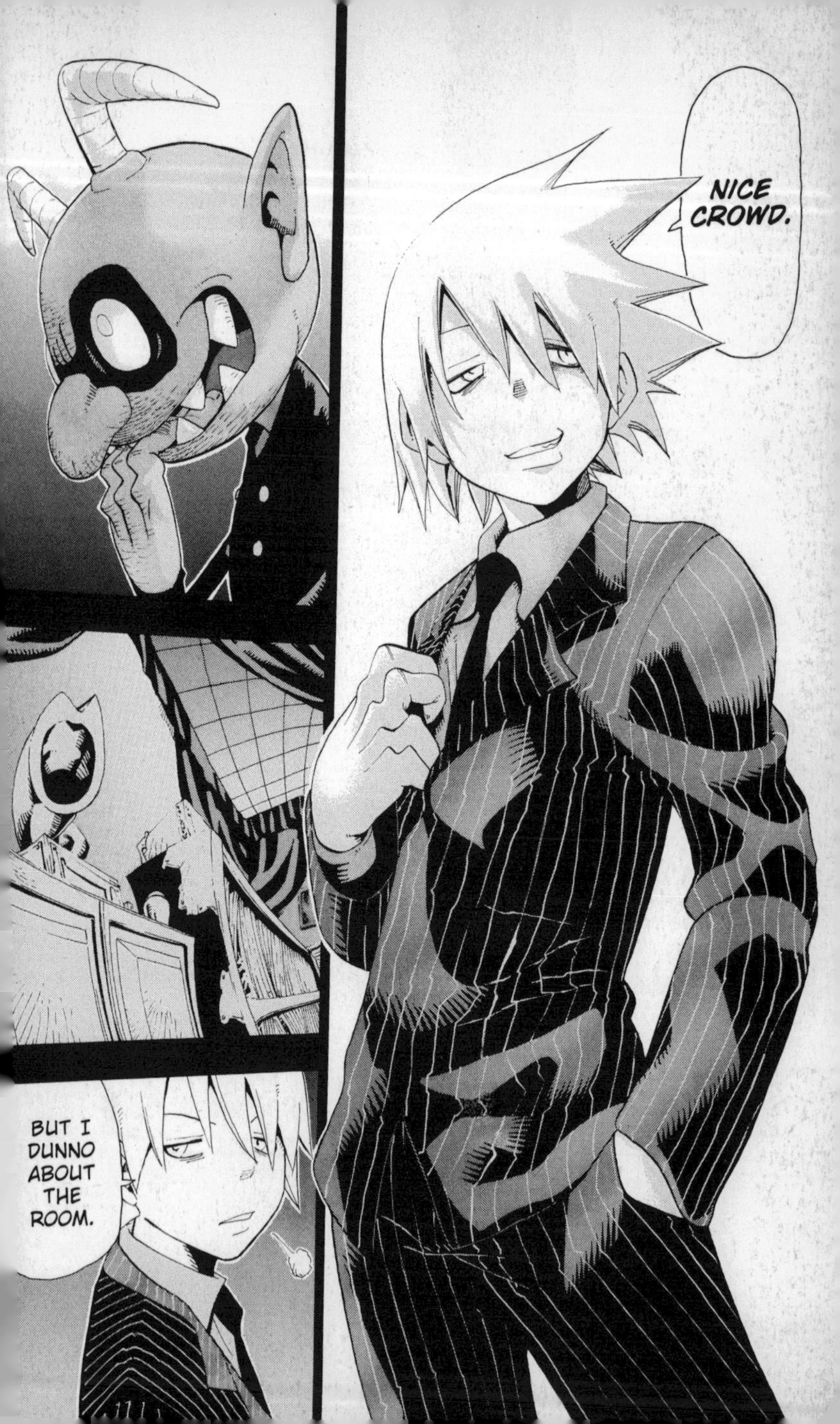
NICE CROWD.
BUT I DUNNO ABOUT THE ROOM.

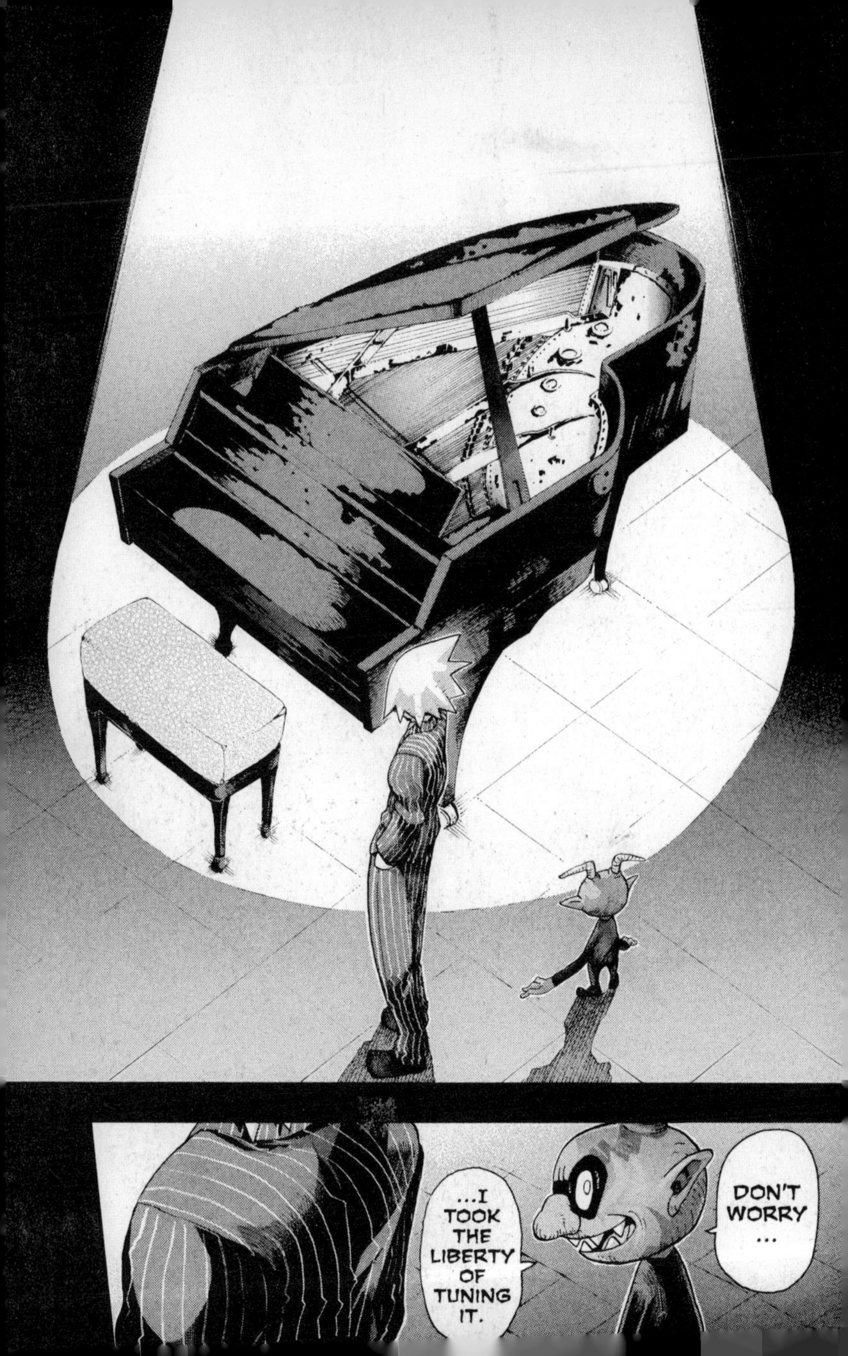
DON'T WORRY ...
...I TOOK THE LIBERTY OF TUNING IT.

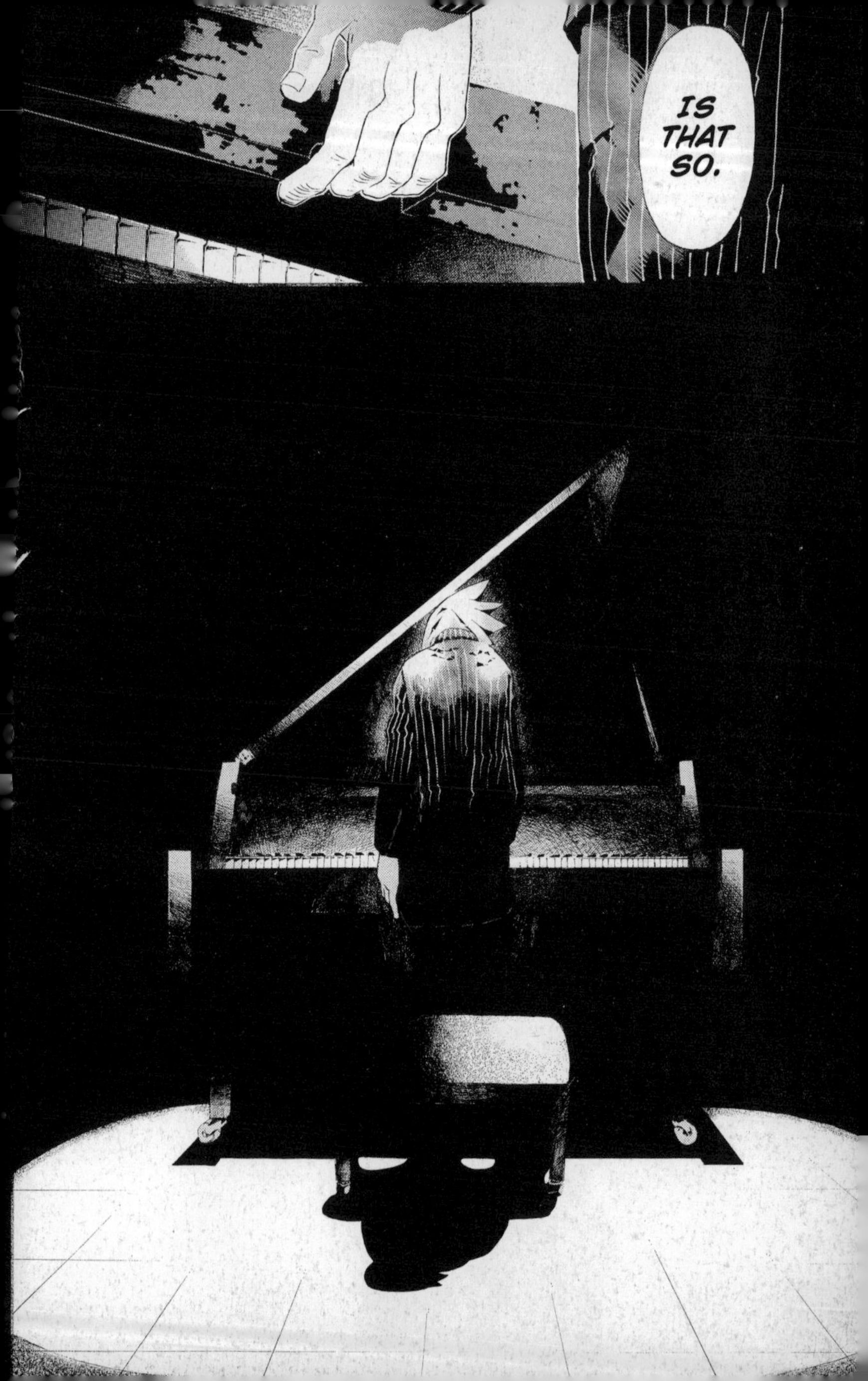
IS THAT SO.

SOUL EATER

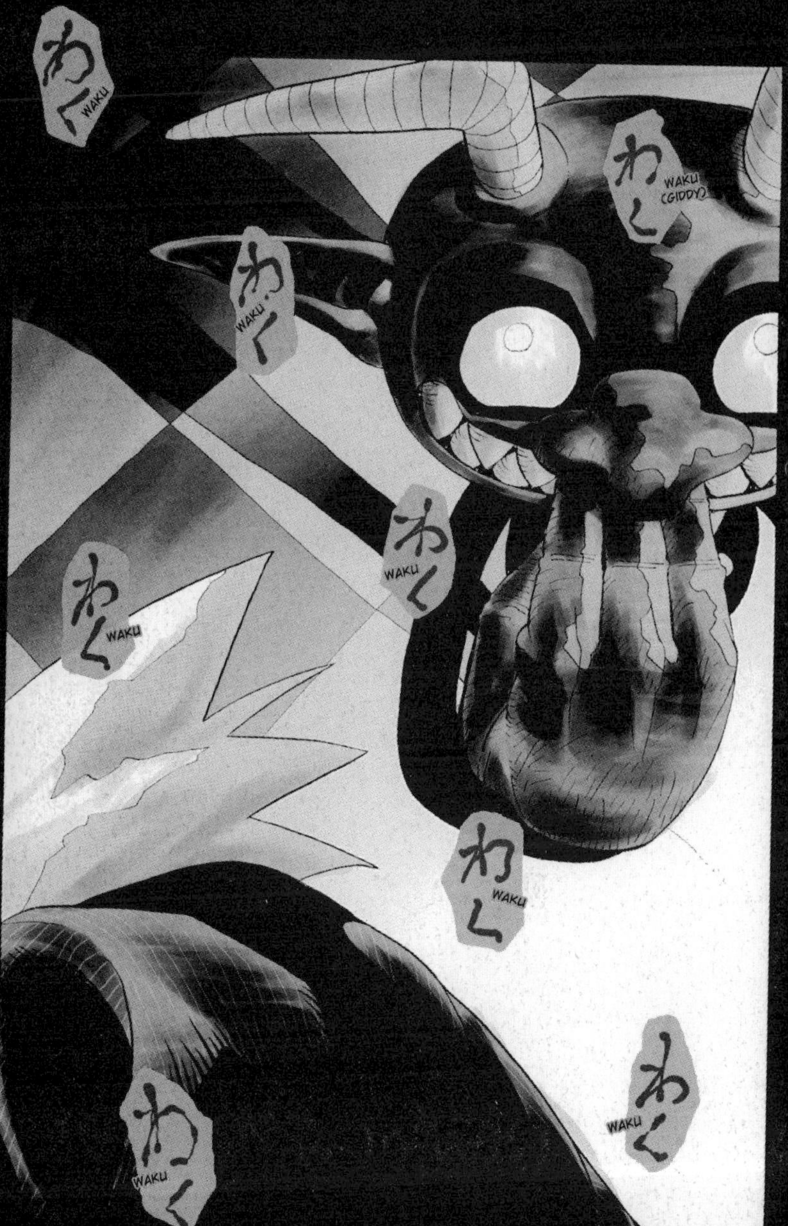
わく WAKU (GIDDY)
わく WAKU
わく WAKU
わく WAKU
わく WAKU
わく WAKU
わく WAKU
わく WAKU

CHAPTER 37: "BREW"—THE TEMPEST (PART 4)

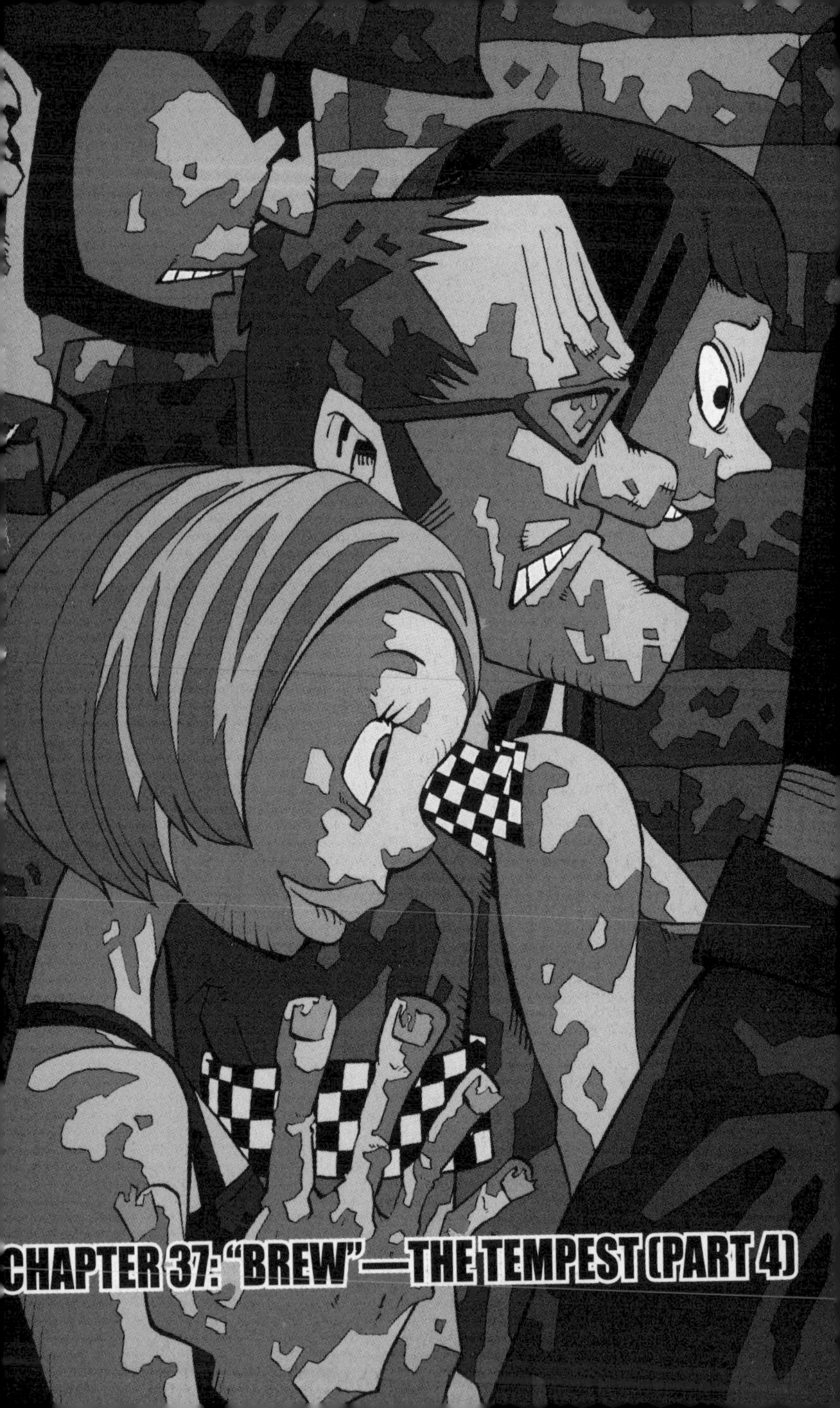

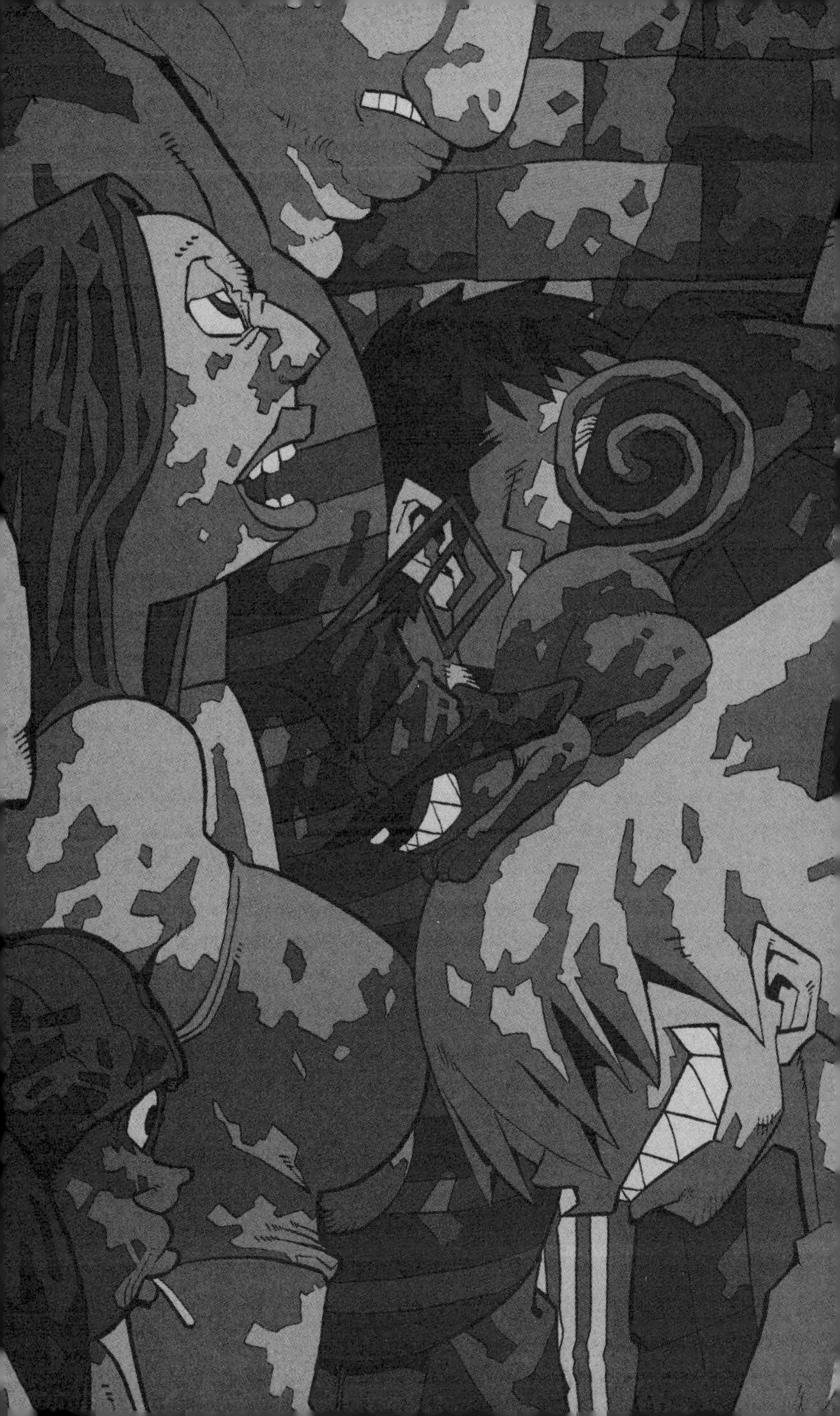

SOUL EATER

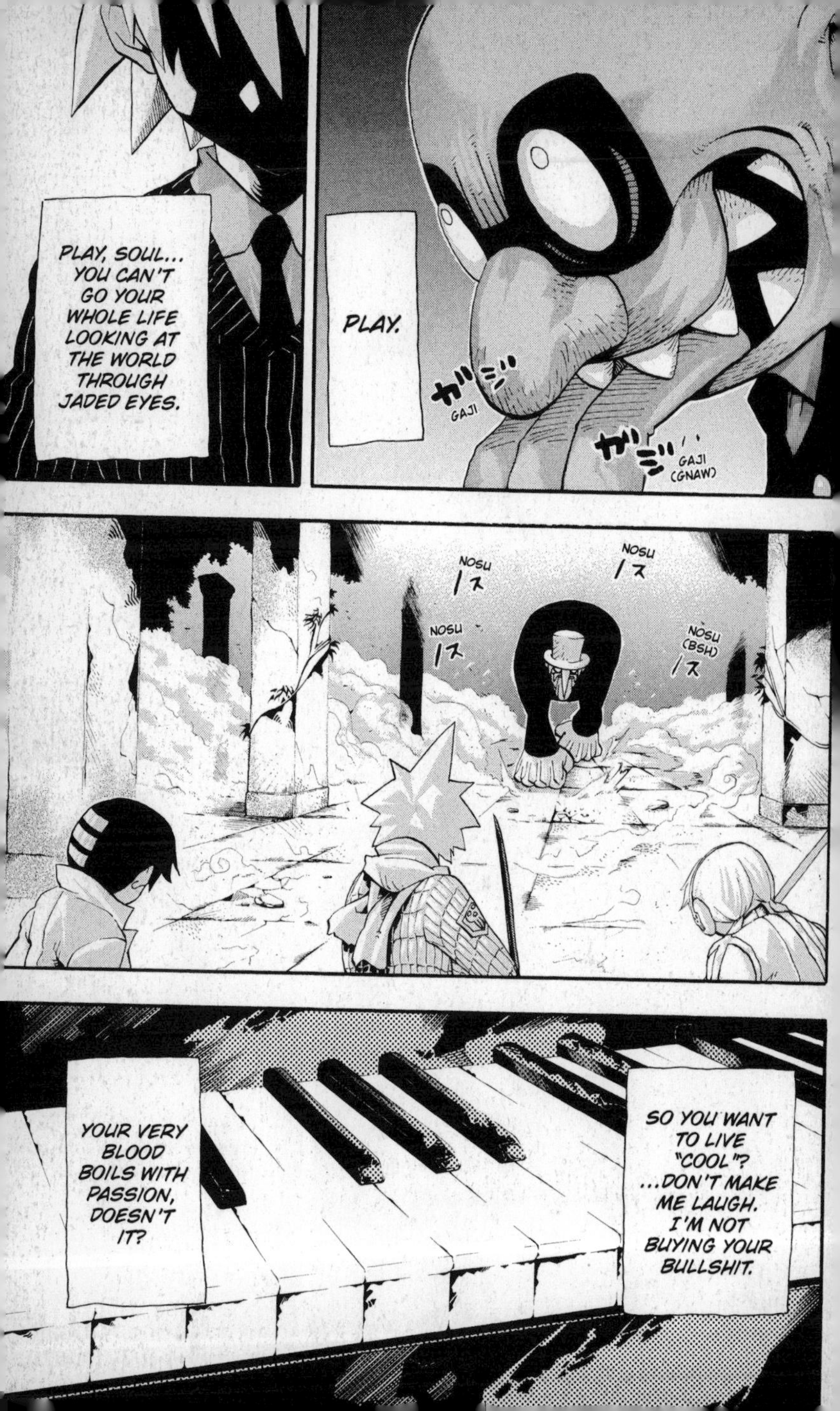
PLAY.
ガジ
GAJI
ガジ
GAJI (GNAW)
PLAY, SOUL... YOU CAN'T GO YOUR WHOLE LIFE LOOKING AT THE WORLD THROUGH JADED EYES.
NOSU
ノス
NOSU
ノス
NOSU (BSH)
ノス
NOSU
ノス
SO YOU WANT TO LIVE "COOL"? ...DON'T MAKE ME LAUGH. I'M NOT BUYING YOUR BULLSHIT.
YOUR VERY BLOOD BOILS WITH PASSION, DOESN'T IT?

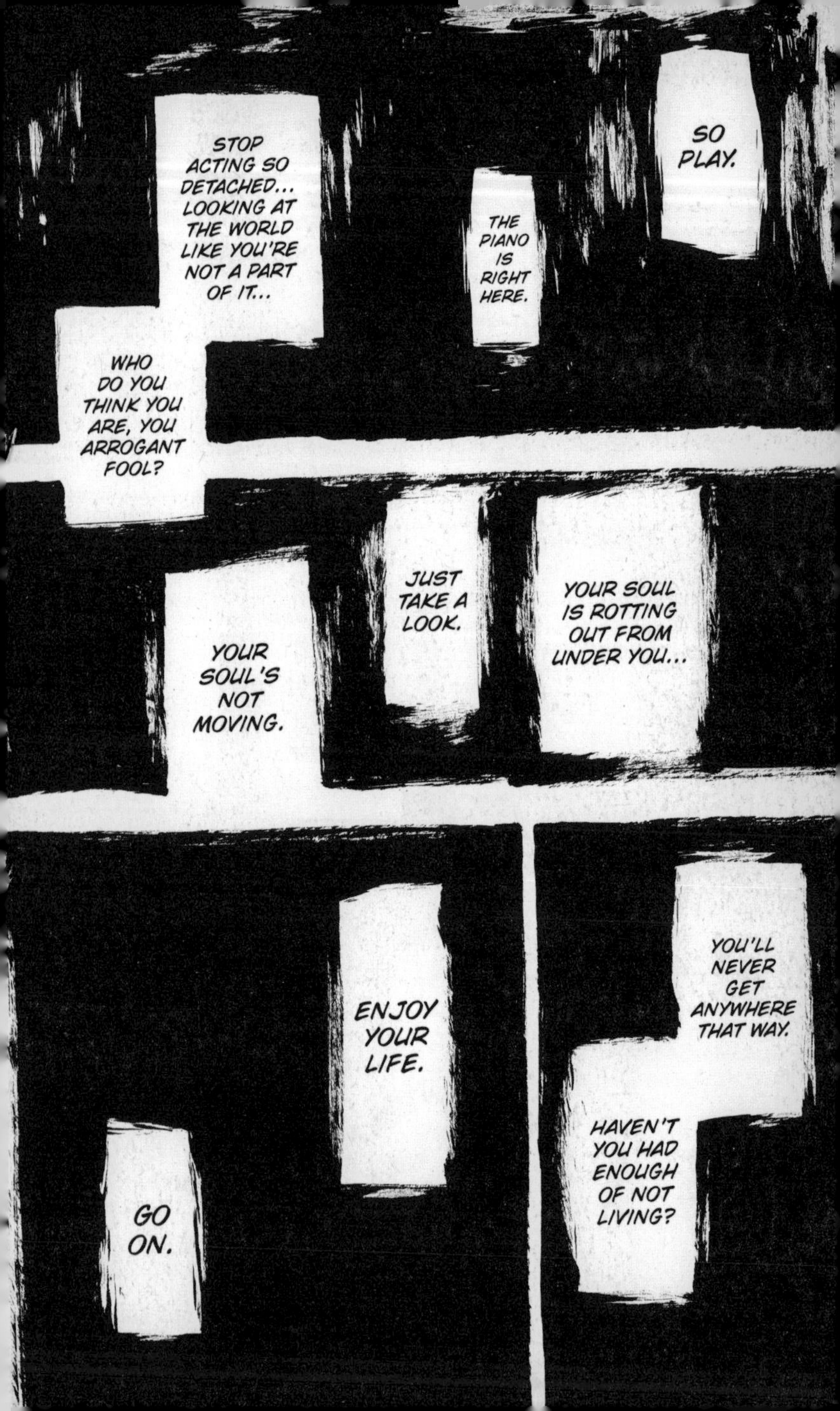
SO PLAY.
THE PIANO IS RIGHT HERE.
STOP ACTING SO DETACHED... LOOKING AT THE WORLD LIKE YOU'RE NOT A PART OF IT...
WHO DO YOU THINK YOU ARE, YOU ARROGANT FOOL?
YOUR SOUL IS ROTTING OUT FROM UNDER YOU...
JUST TAKE A LOOK.
YOUR SOUL'S NOT MOVING.
YOU'LL NEVER GET ANYWHERE THAT WAY.
HAVEN'T YOU HAD ENOUGH OF NOT LIVING?
ENJOY YOUR LIFE.
GO ON.

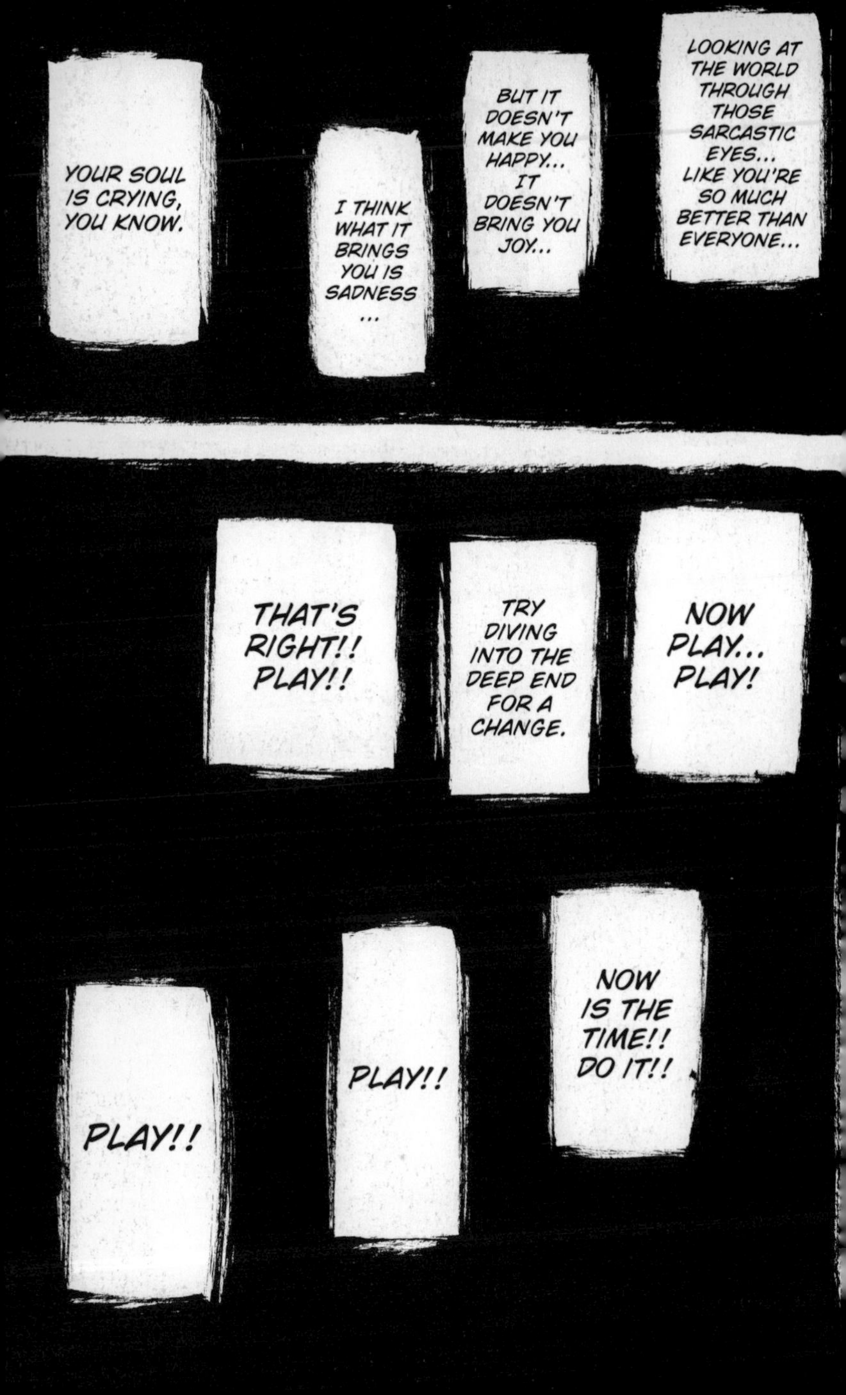
LOOKING AT THE WORLD THROUGH THOSE SARCASTIC EYES... LIKE YOU'RE SO MUCH BETTER THAN EVERYONE...
BUT IT DOESN'T MAKE YOU HAPPY... IT DOESN'T BRING YOU JOY...
I THINK WHAT IT BRINGS YOU IS SADNESS...
YOUR SOUL IS CRYING, YOU KNOW.
NOW PLAY... PLAY!
TRY DIVING INTO THE DEEP END FOR A CHANGE.
THAT'S RIGHT!! PLAY!!
NOW IS THE TIME!! DO IT!!
PLAY!!
PLAY!!

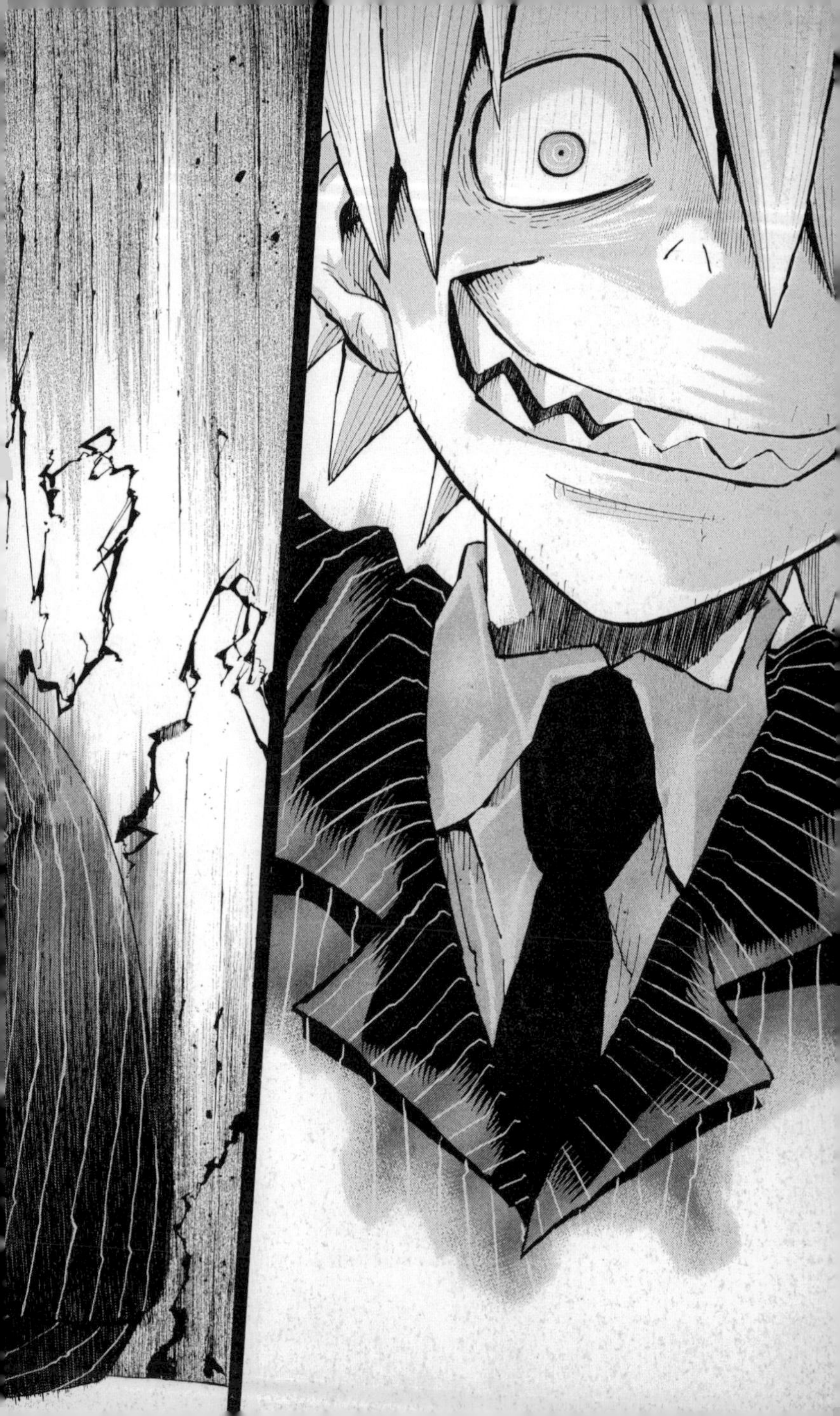

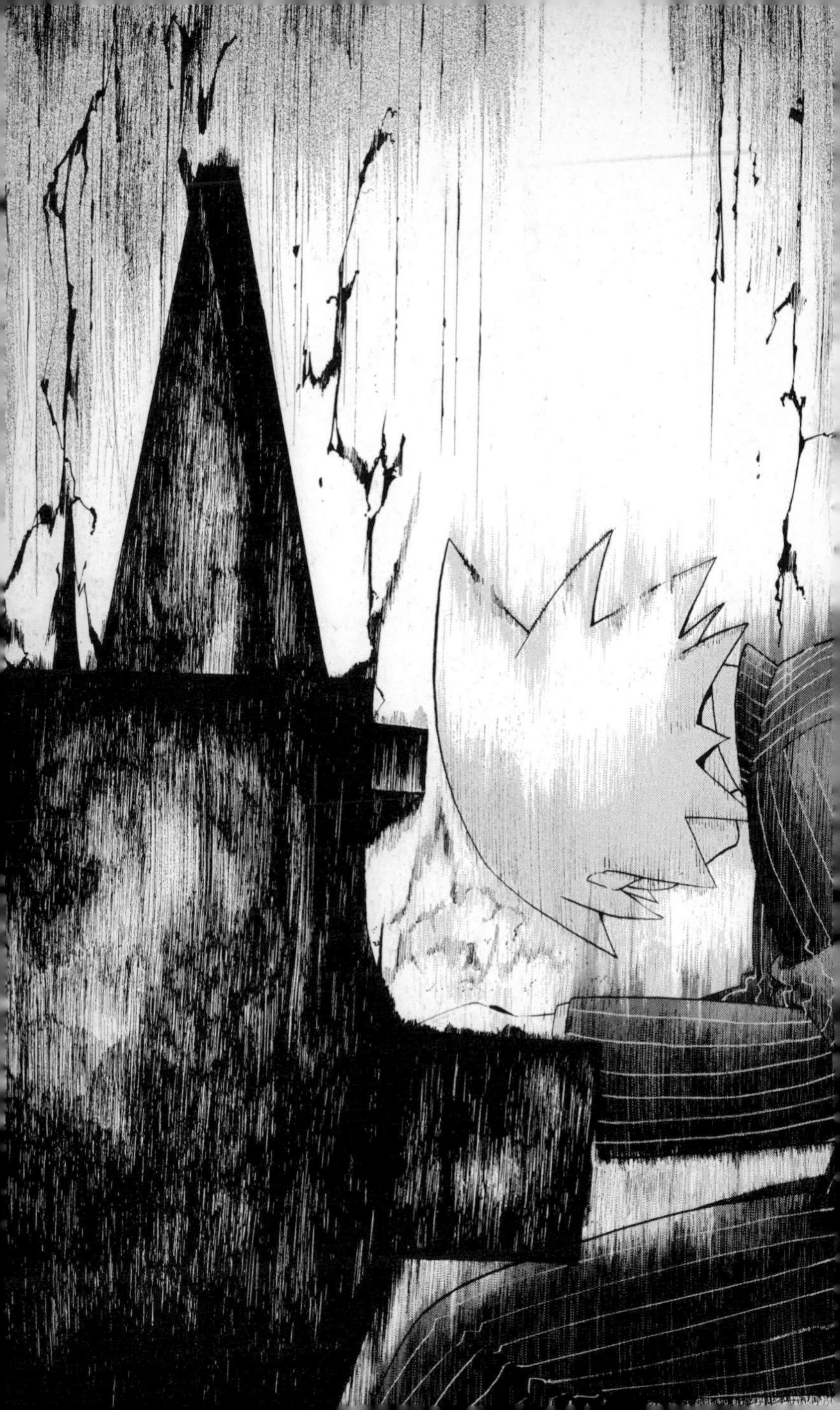

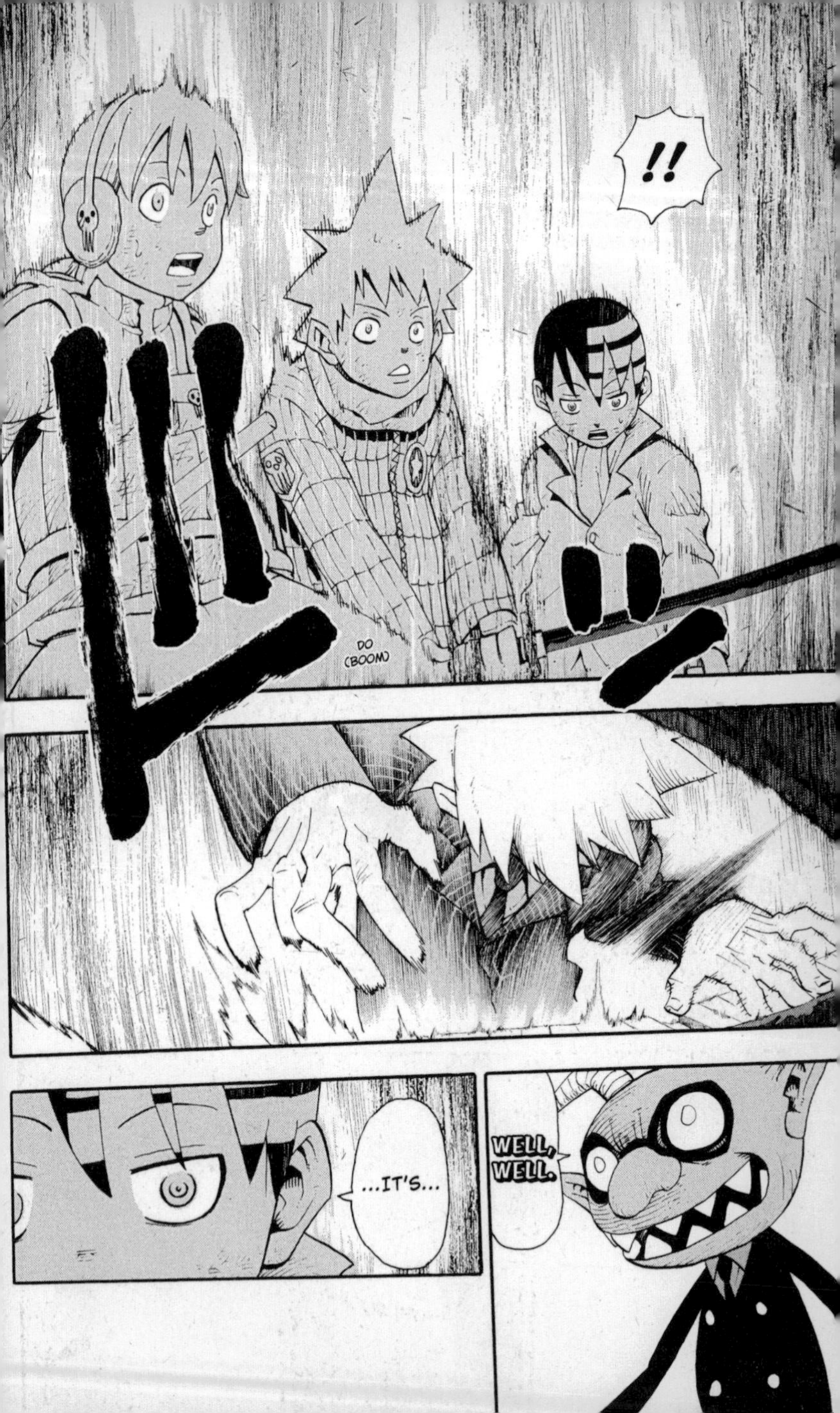
!!
DO (BOOM)
WELL, WELL.
...IT'S...

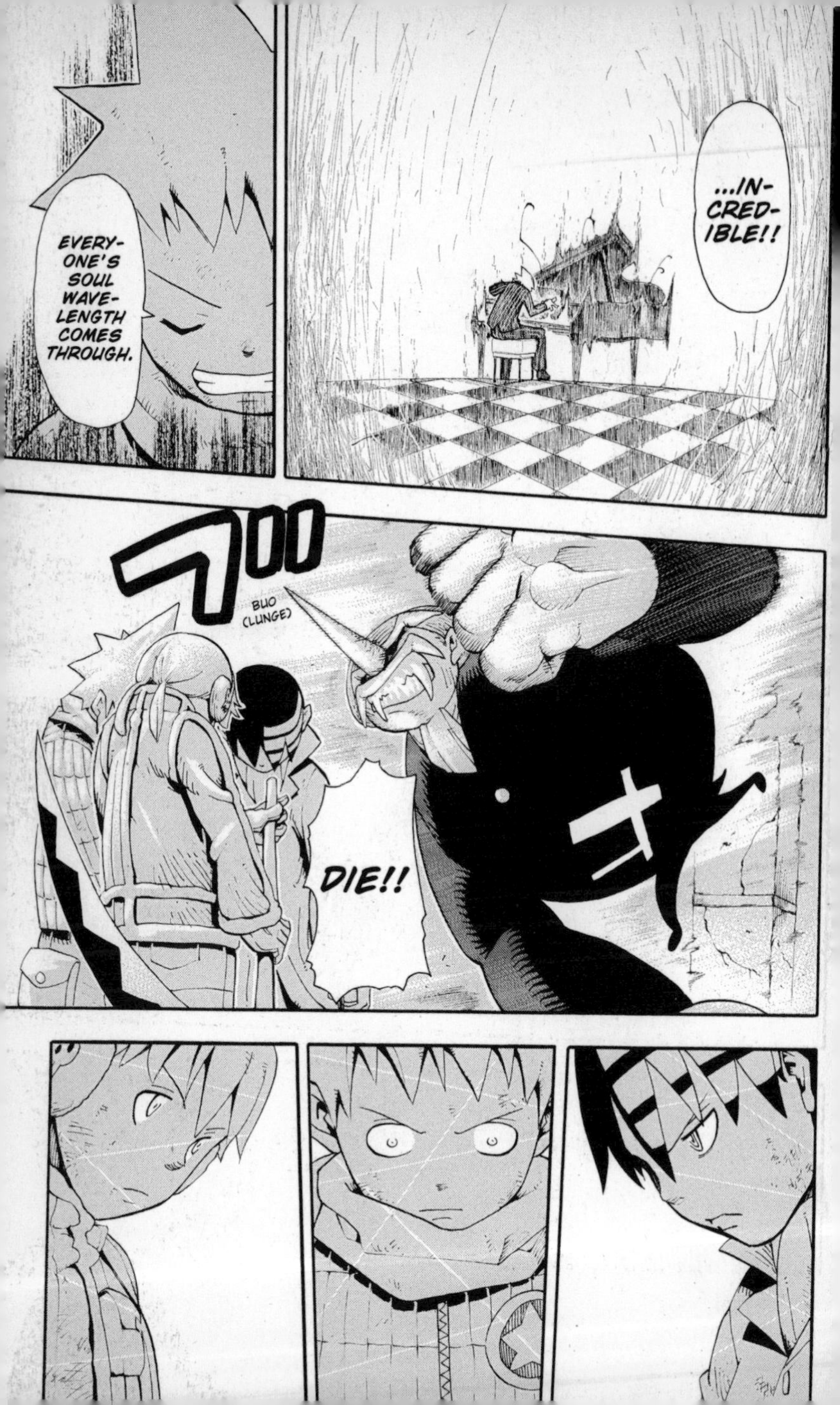

...INCREDIBLE!!
EVERYONE'S SOUL WAVELENGTH COMES THROUGH.
BUO (LUNGE)
DIE!!

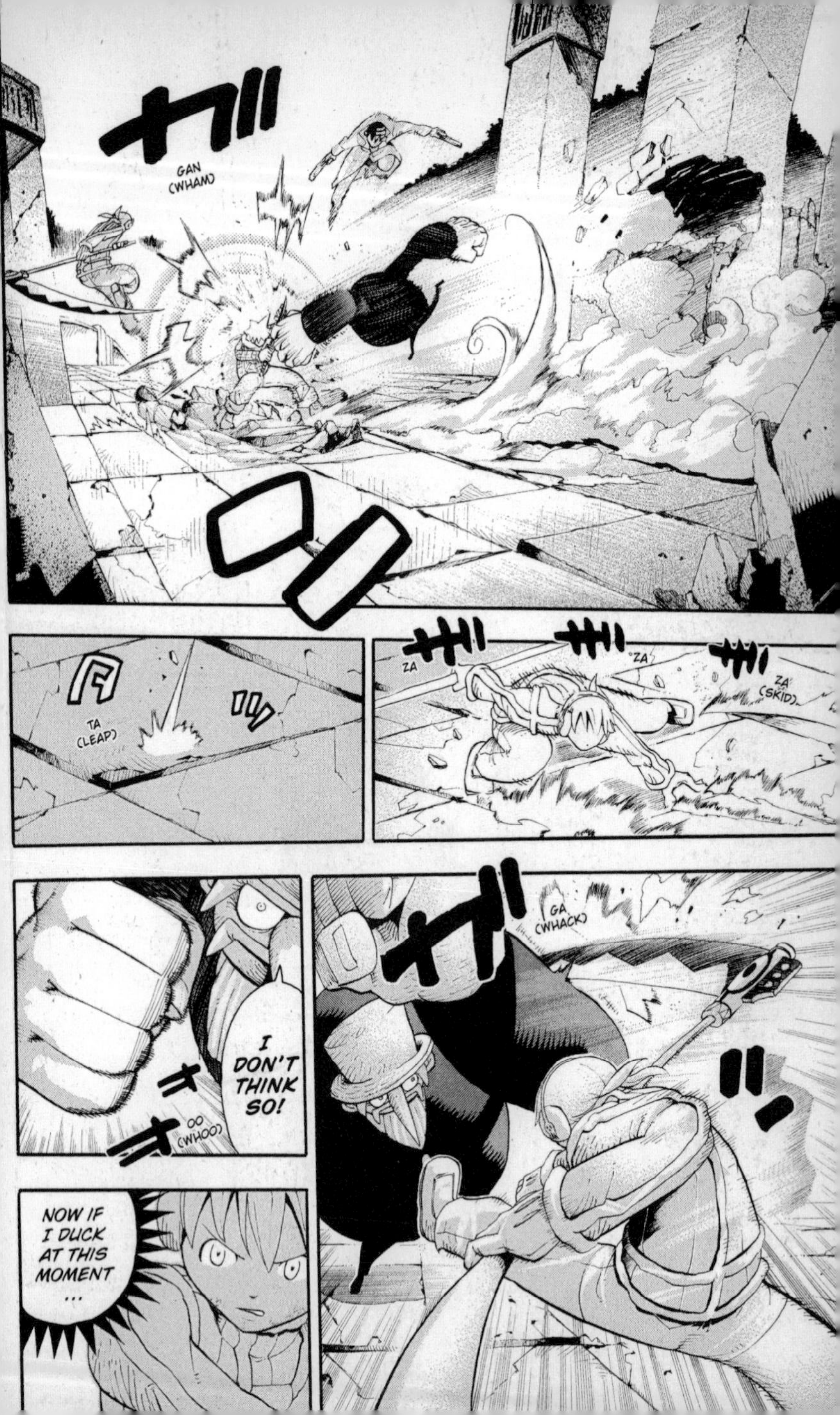
GAN (WHAM)
ZA
ZA
ZA (SKID)
TA (LEAP)
GA (WHACK)
I DON'T THINK SO!
OO (WHOO)
NOW IF I DUCK AT THIS MOMENT...

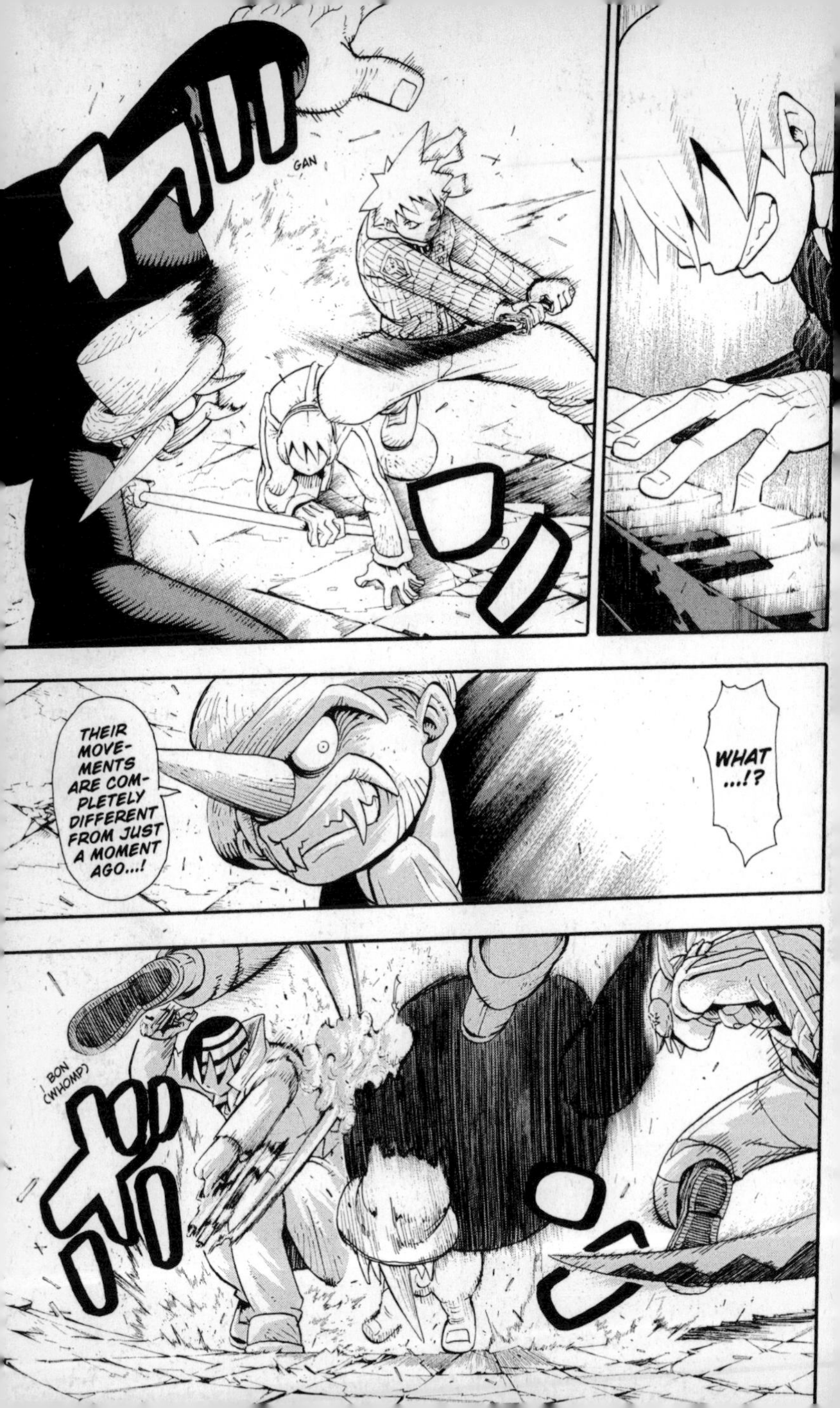
GAN
WHAT ...!?
THEIR MOVEMENTS ARE COMPLETELY DIFFERENT FROM JUST A MOMENT AGO...!
BON (WHOMP)

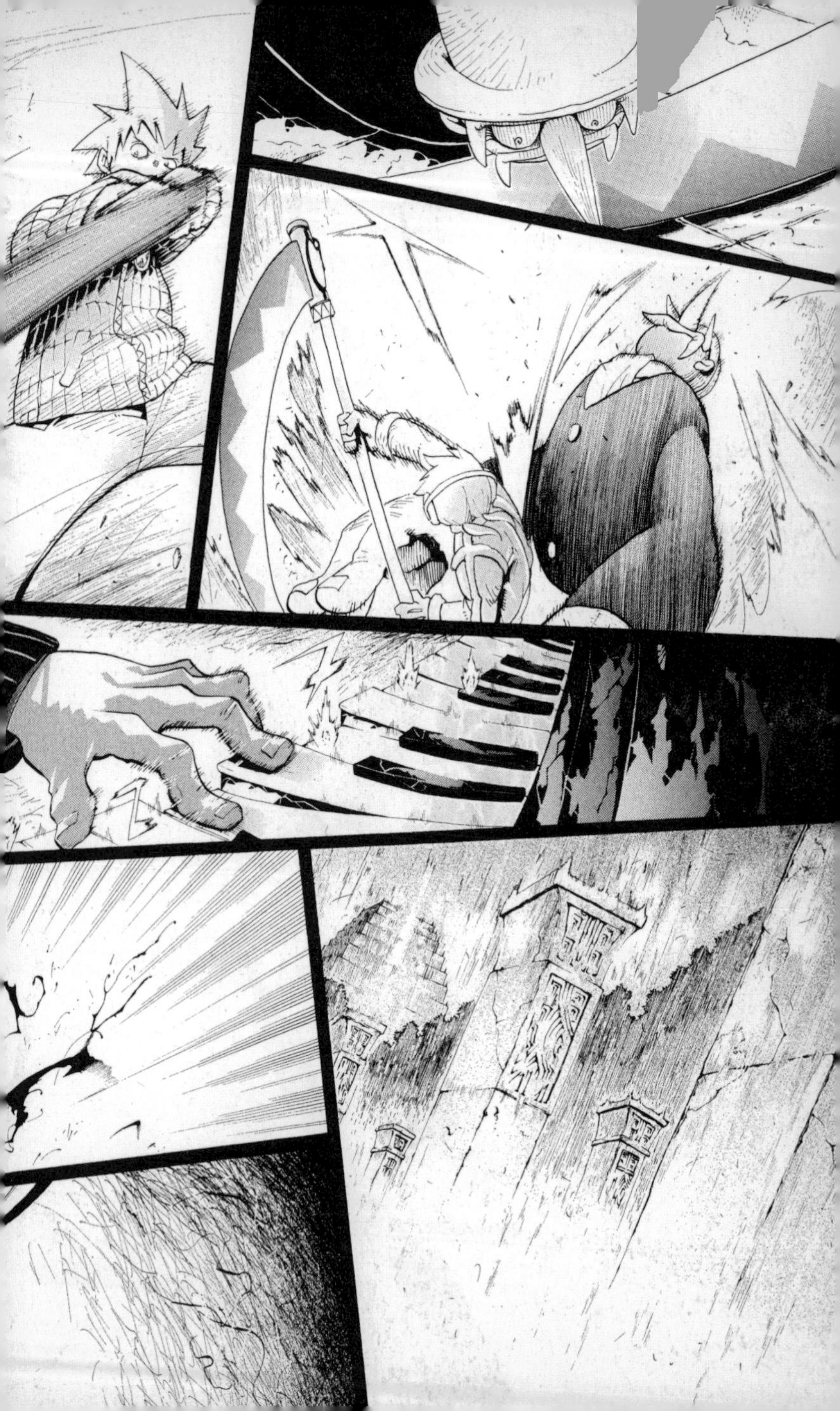

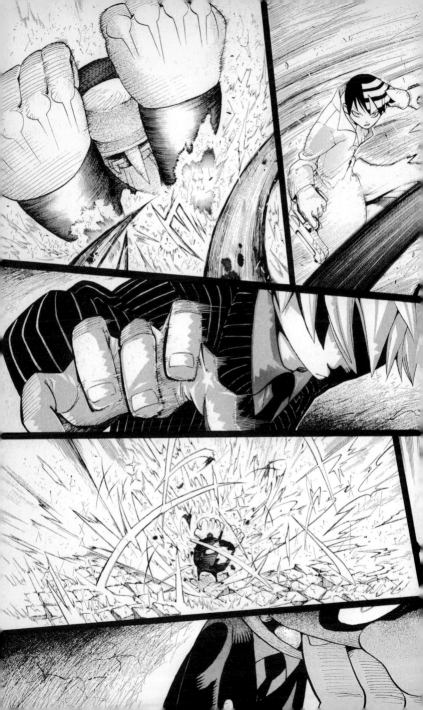

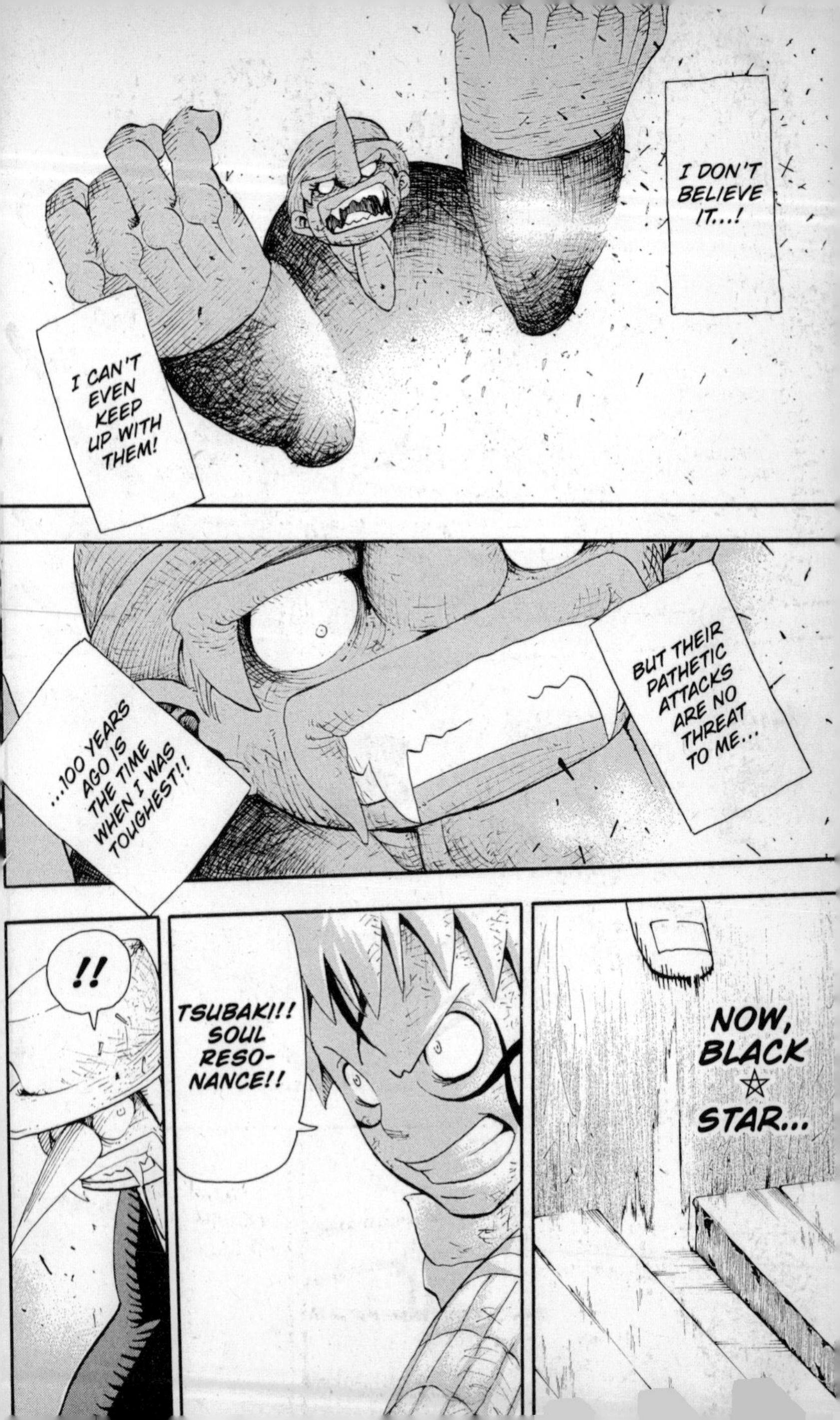
I DON'T BELIEVE IT...!
I CAN'T EVEN KEEP UP WITH THEM!
BUT THEIR PATHETIC ATTACKS ARE NO THREAT TO ME...
...100 YEARS AGO IS THE TIME WHEN I WAS TOUGHEST!!
NOW, BLACK☆STAR...
TSUBAKI!! SOUL RESO-NANCE!!
!!

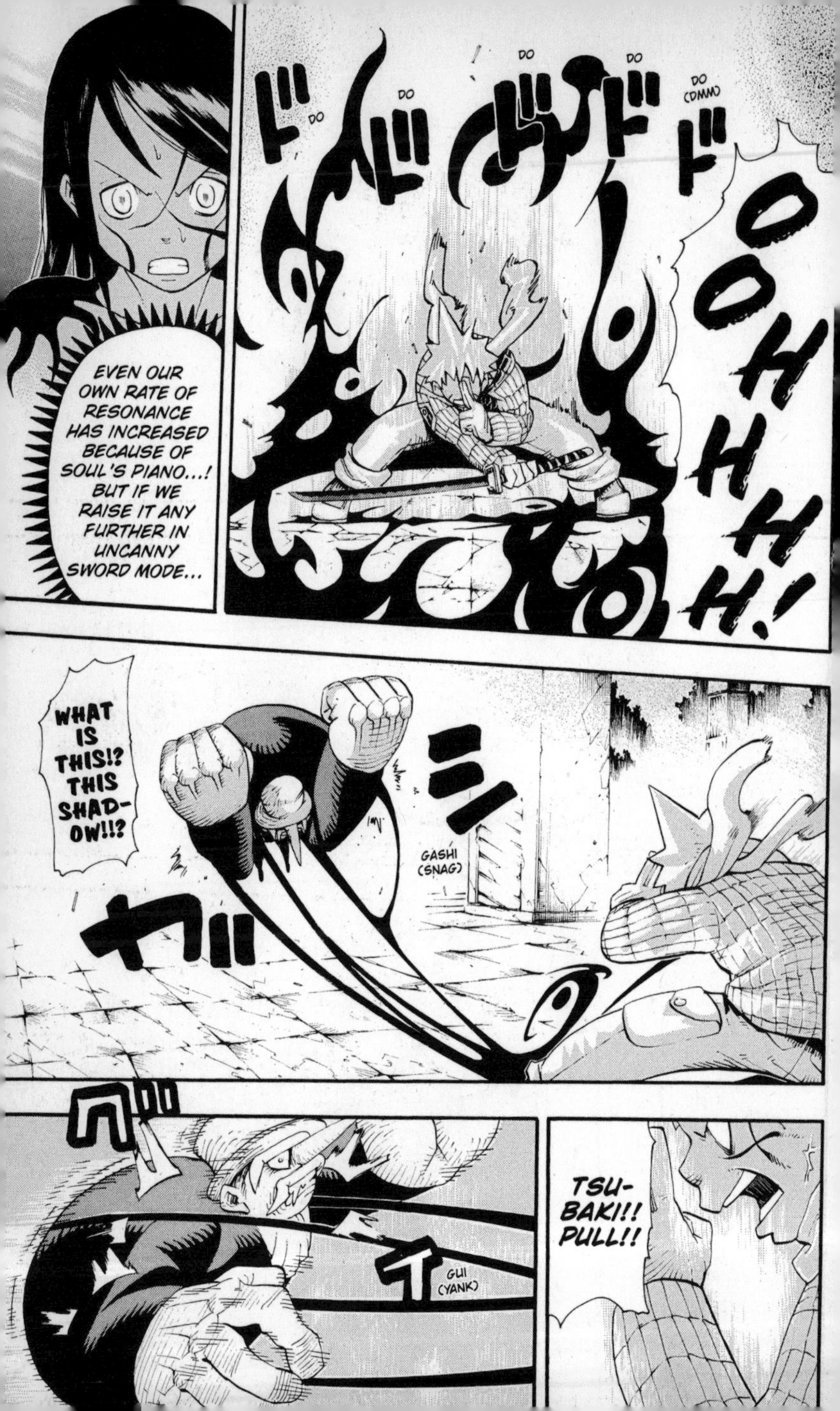
DO
DO
DO
DO
DO (DMM)
OOOHHHHH!
EVEN OUR OWN RATE OF RESONANCE HAS INCREASED BECAUSE OF SOUL'S PIANO...! BUT IF WE RAISE IT ANY FURTHER IN UNCANNY SWORD MODE...
GASHI (SNAG)
WHAT IS THIS!? THIS SHAD-OW!!?
TSU-BAKI!! PULL!!
GUI (YANK)

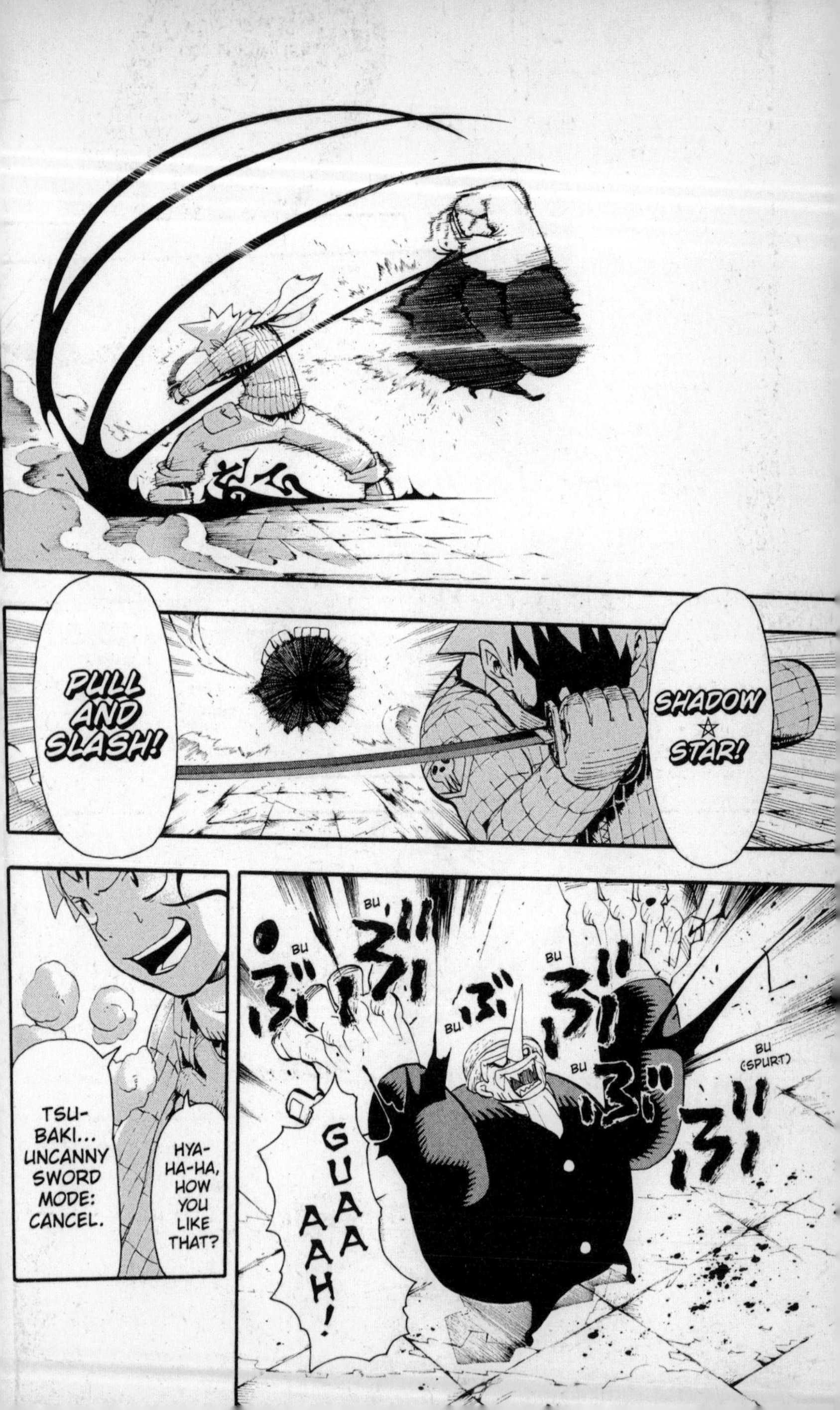
SHADOW ☆ STAR!
PULL AND SLASH!
ぶ BU (SPURT)
ぶ BU
ぶ BU
ぶ BU
ぶ BU
ぶ BU
GUAAAAAH!
HYA-HA-HA, HOW YOU LIKE THAT?
TSU-BAKI... UNCANNY SWORD MODE: CANCEL.

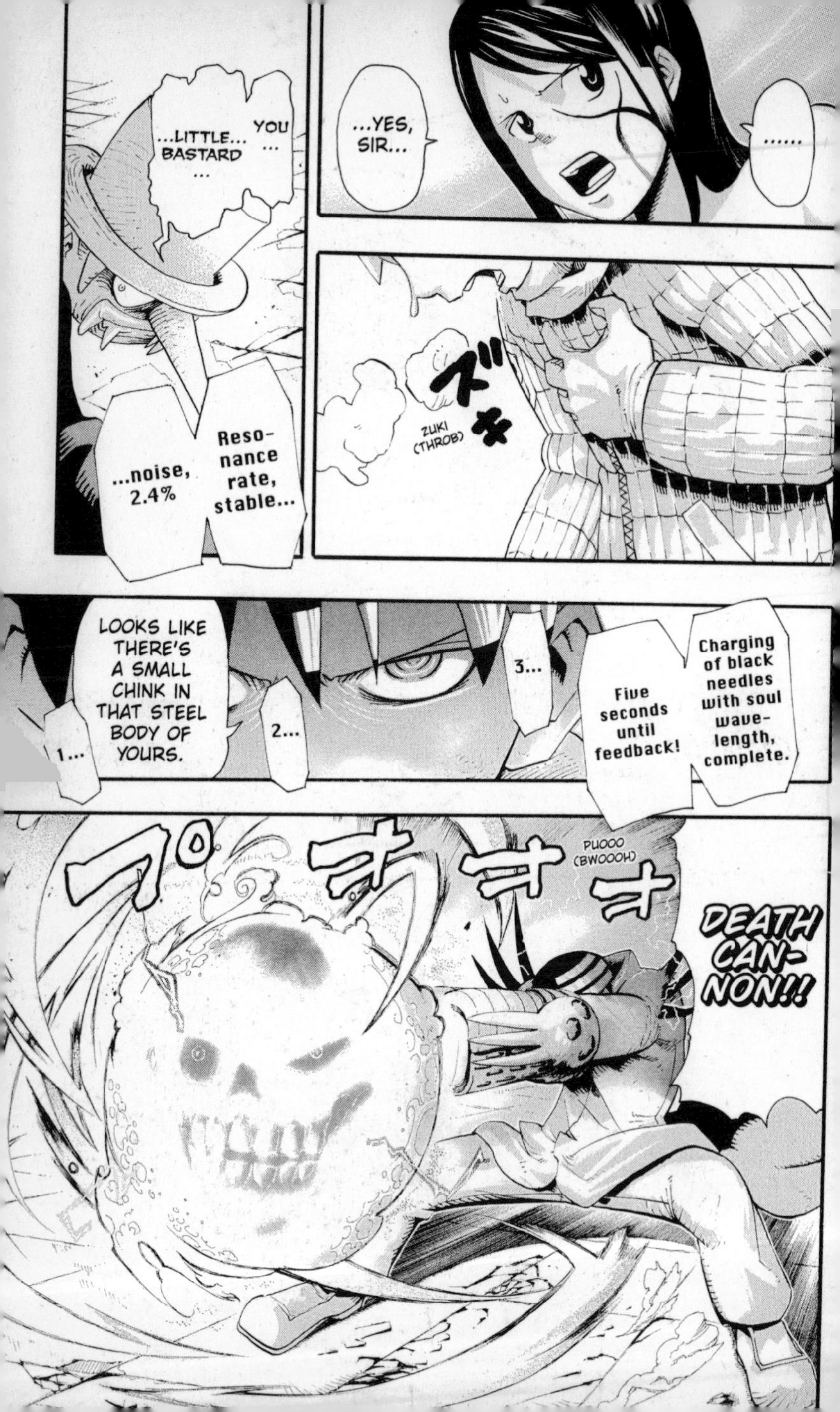
......
...YES, SIR...
ズキ
ZUKI (THROB)
YOU ...
...LITTLE... BASTARD ...
Reso-nance rate, stable...
...noise, 2.4%
Charging of black needles with soul wave-length, complete.
Five seconds until feedback!
3...
2...
LOOKS LIKE THERE'S A SMALL CHINK IN THAT STEEL BODY OF YOURS.
1...
DEATH CAN-NON!!
プオオオ
PUOOO (BWOOOH)

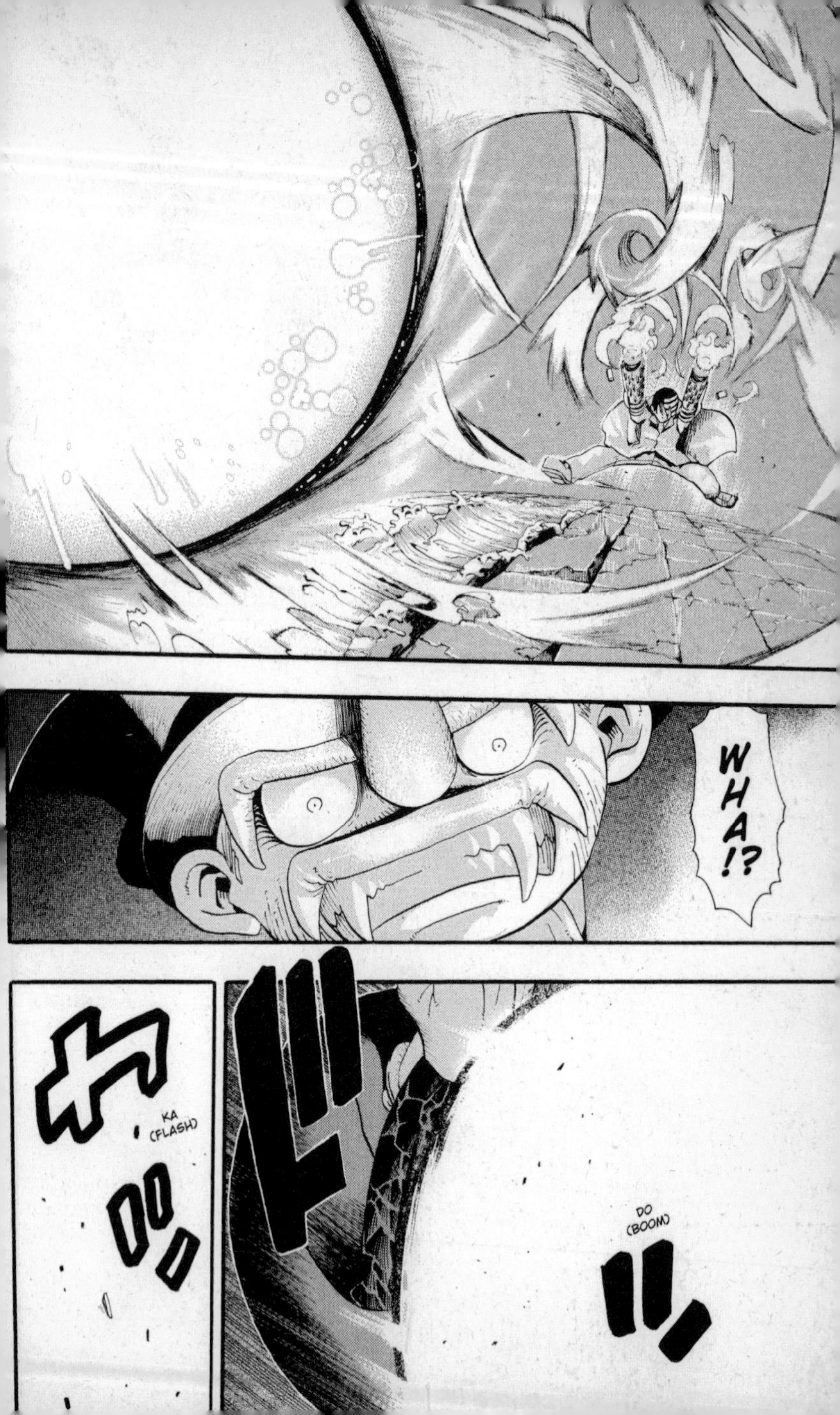
WHA!?
ドッ
DO (BOOM)
カッ
KA (FLASH)

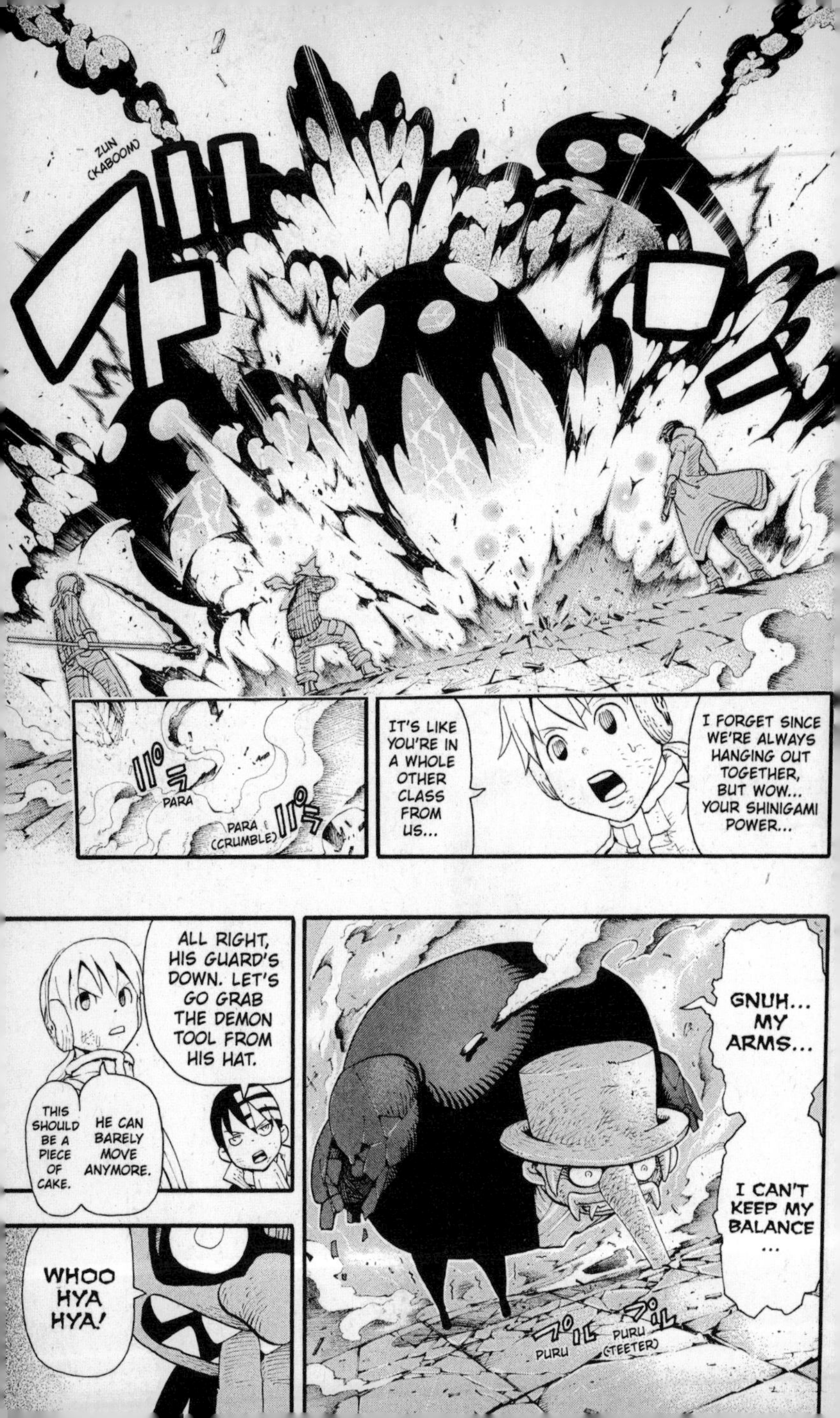
ZUN (KABOOM)
I FORGET SINCE WE'RE ALWAYS HANGING OUT TOGETHER, BUT WOW... YOUR SHINIGAMI POWER...
IT'S LIKE YOU'RE IN A WHOLE OTHER CLASS FROM US...
PARA
PARA (CRUMBLE)
GNUH... MY ARMS...
I CAN'T KEEP MY BALANCE ...
PURU
PURU (TEETER)
ALL RIGHT, HIS GUARD'S DOWN. LET'S GO GRAB THE DEMON TOOL FROM HIS HAT.
HE CAN BARELY MOVE ANYMORE.
THIS SHOULD BE A PIECE OF CAKE.
WHOO HYA HYA!

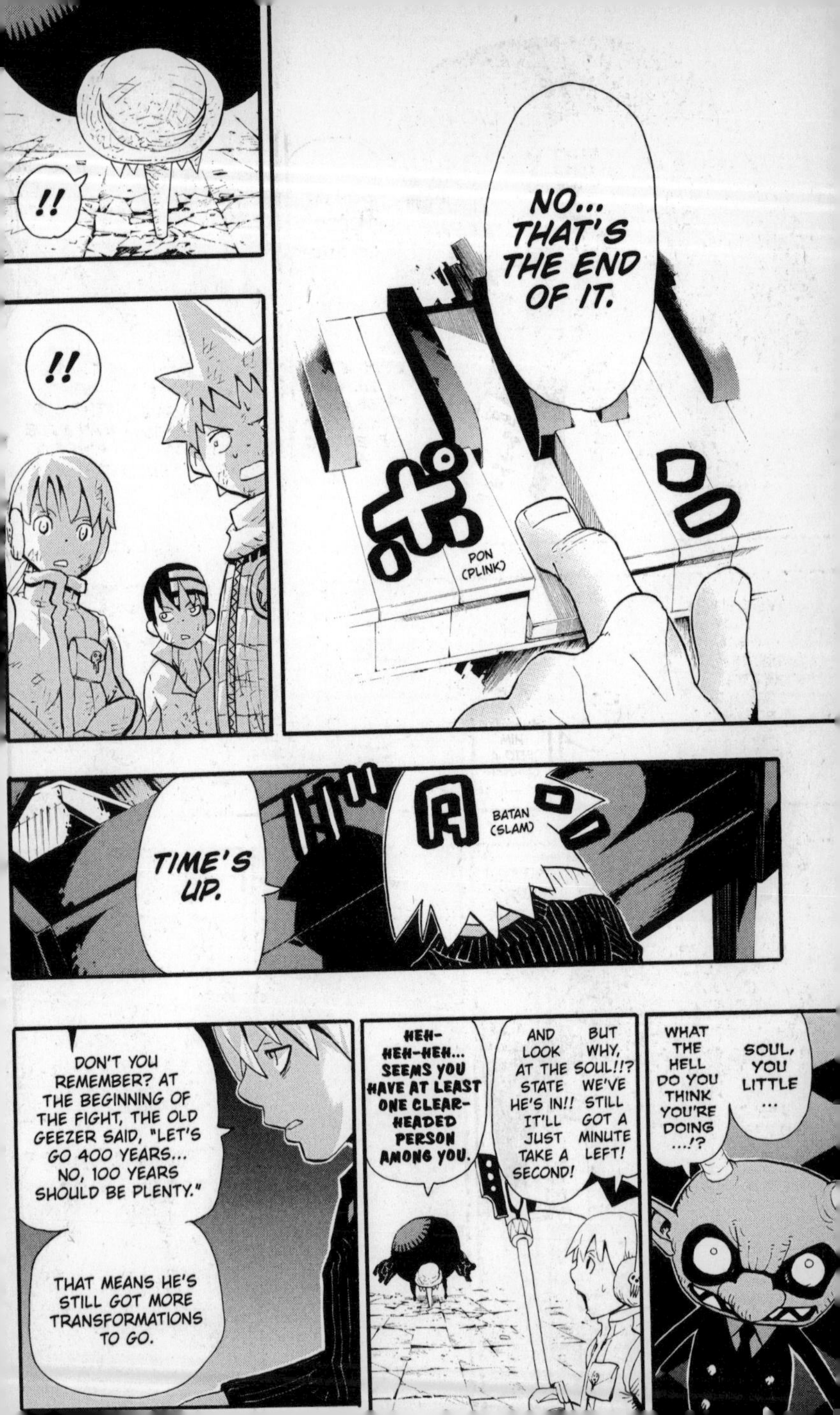
NO... THAT'S THE END OF IT.
PON (PLINK)
!!
!!
BATAN (SLAM)
TIME'S UP.
SOUL, YOU LITTLE ...
WHAT THE HELL DO YOU THINK YOU'RE DOING ...!?
BUT WHY, SOUL!!? WE'VE STILL GOT A MINUTE LEFT!
AND LOOK AT THE STATE HE'S IN!! IT'LL JUST TAKE A SECOND!
HEH-HEH-HEH... SEEMS YOU HAVE AT LEAST ONE CLEAR-HEADED PERSON AMONG YOU.
DON'T YOU REMEMBER? AT THE BEGINNING OF THE FIGHT, THE OLD GEEZER SAID, "LET'S GO 400 YEARS... NO, 100 YEARS SHOULD BE PLENTY."
THAT MEANS HE'S STILL GOT MORE TRANSFORMATIONS TO GO.

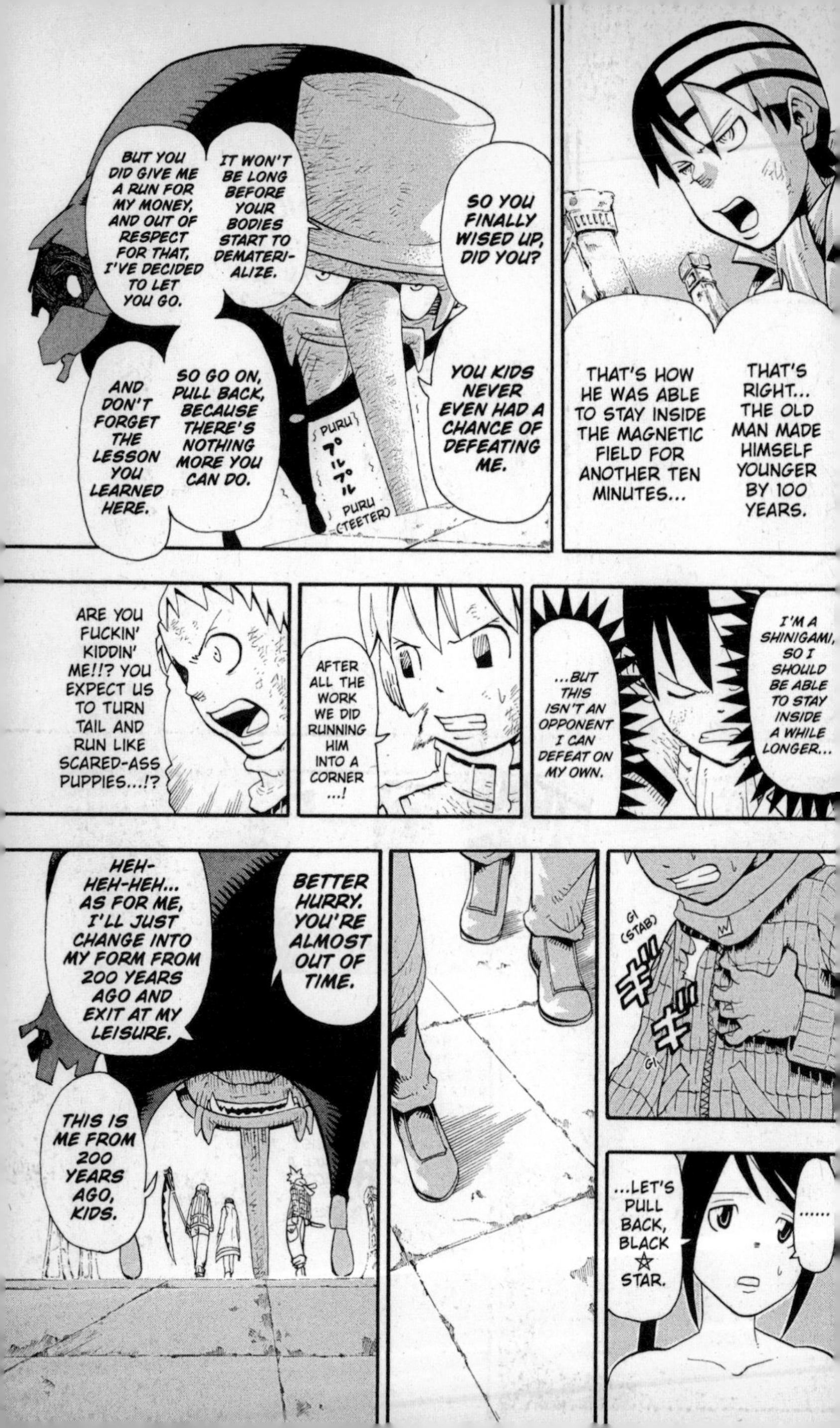
THAT'S RIGHT... THE OLD MAN MADE HIMSELF YOUNGER BY 100 YEARS.
THAT'S HOW HE WAS ABLE TO STAY INSIDE THE MAGNETIC FIELD FOR ANOTHER TEN MINUTES...
SO YOU FINALLY WISED UP, DID YOU?
IT WON'T BE LONG BEFORE YOUR BODIES START TO DEMATERI-ALIZE.
BUT YOU DID GIVE ME A RUN FOR MY MONEY, AND OUT OF RESPECT FOR THAT, I'VE DECIDED TO LET YOU GO.
YOU KIDS NEVER EVEN HAD A CHANCE OF DEFEATING ME.
PURU プルプル PURU (TEETER)
SO GO ON, PULL BACK, BECAUSE THERE'S NOTHING MORE YOU CAN DO.
AND DON'T FORGET THE LESSON YOU LEARNED HERE.
I'M A SHINIGAMI, SO I SHOULD BE ABLE TO STAY INSIDE A WHILE LONGER...
...BUT THIS ISN'T AN OPPONENT I CAN DEFEAT ON MY OWN.
AFTER ALL THE WORK WE DID RUNNING HIM INTO A CORNER...!
ARE YOU FUCKIN' KIDDIN' ME!!? YOU EXPECT US TO TURN TAIL AND RUN LIKE SCARED-ASS PUPPIES...!?
GI (STAB) ギ ギ GI
......
...LET'S PULL BACK, BLACK☆STAR.
BETTER HURRY. YOU'RE ALMOST OUT OF TIME.
HEH-HEH-HEH... AS FOR ME, I'LL JUST CHANGE INTO MY FORM FROM 200 YEARS AGO AND EXIT AT MY LEISURE.
THIS IS ME FROM 200 YEARS AGO, KIDS.

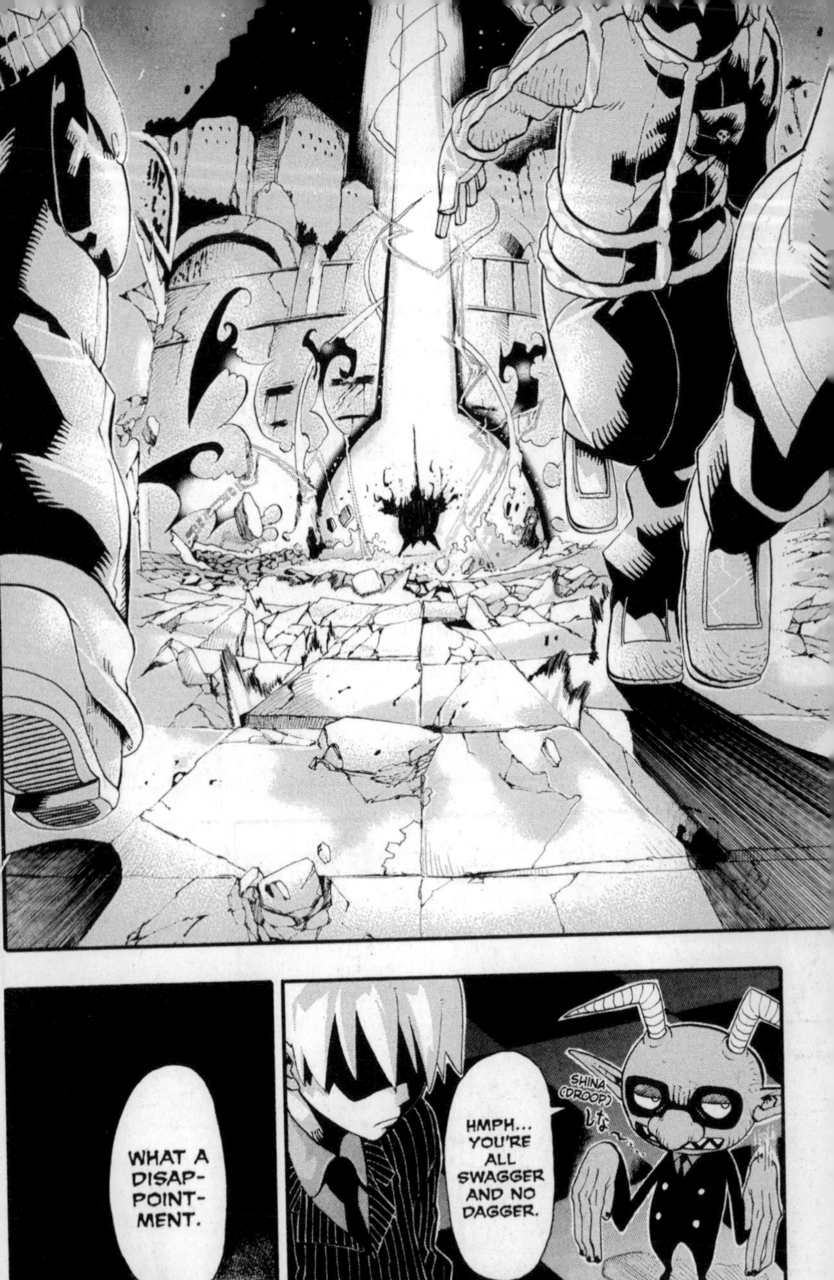
SHINA (DROOP) しな～
HMPH... YOU'RE ALL SWAGGER AND NO DAGGER.
WHAT A DISAPPOINTMENT.

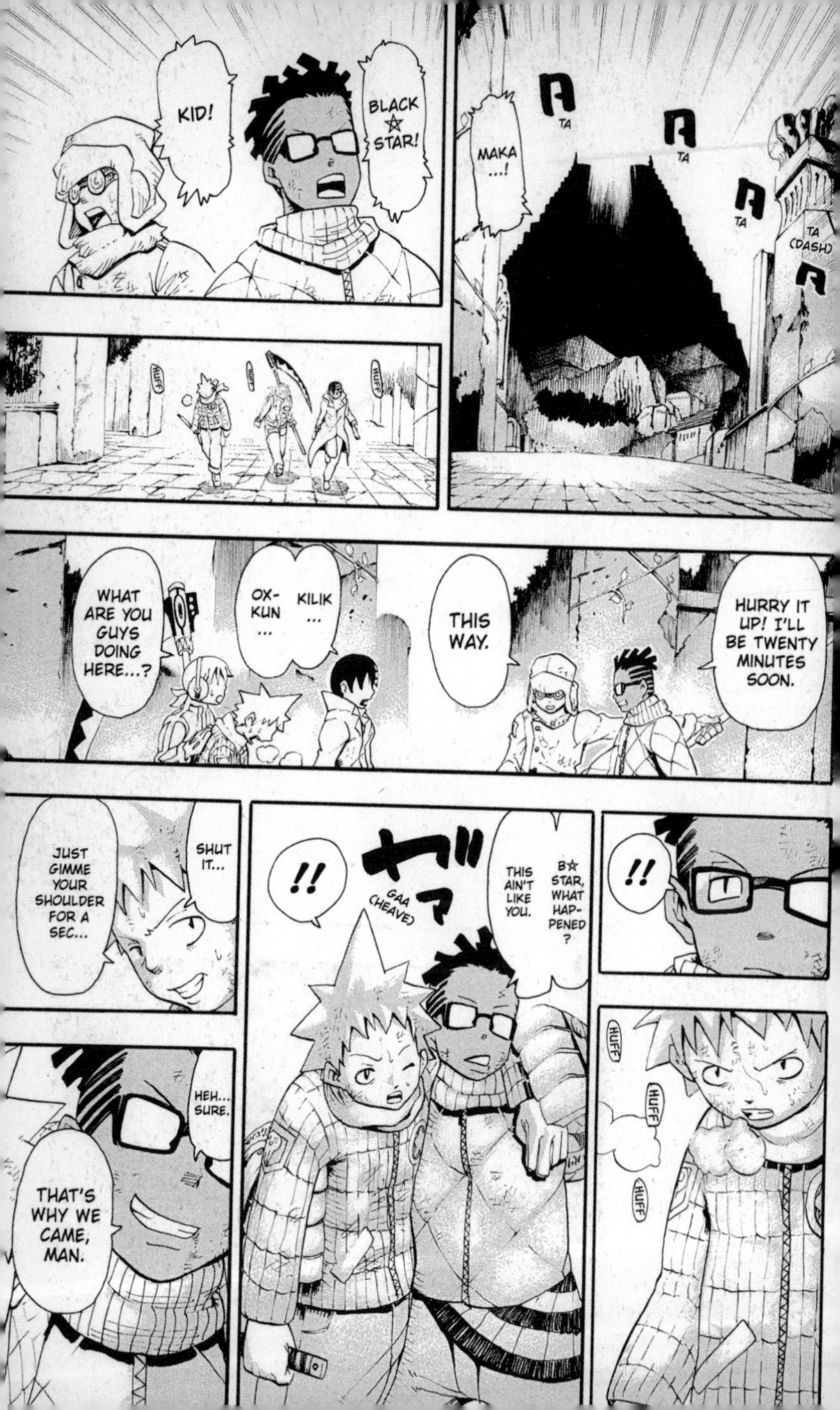
TA
TA
TA
TA (DASH)
MAKA ...!
BLACK ☆ STAR!
KID!
HUFF
HUFF
HUFF
HURRY IT UP! I'LL BE TWENTY MINUTES SOON.
THIS WAY.
KILIK ...
OX-KUN ...
WHAT ARE YOU GUYS DOING HERE...?
!!
HUFF
HUFF
HUFF
B☆STAR, WHAT HAPPENED?
THIS AIN'T LIKE YOU.
GAA (HEAVE)
!!
SHUT IT...
JUST GIMME YOUR SHOULDER FOR A SEC...
HEH... SURE.
THAT'S WHY WE CAME, MAN.

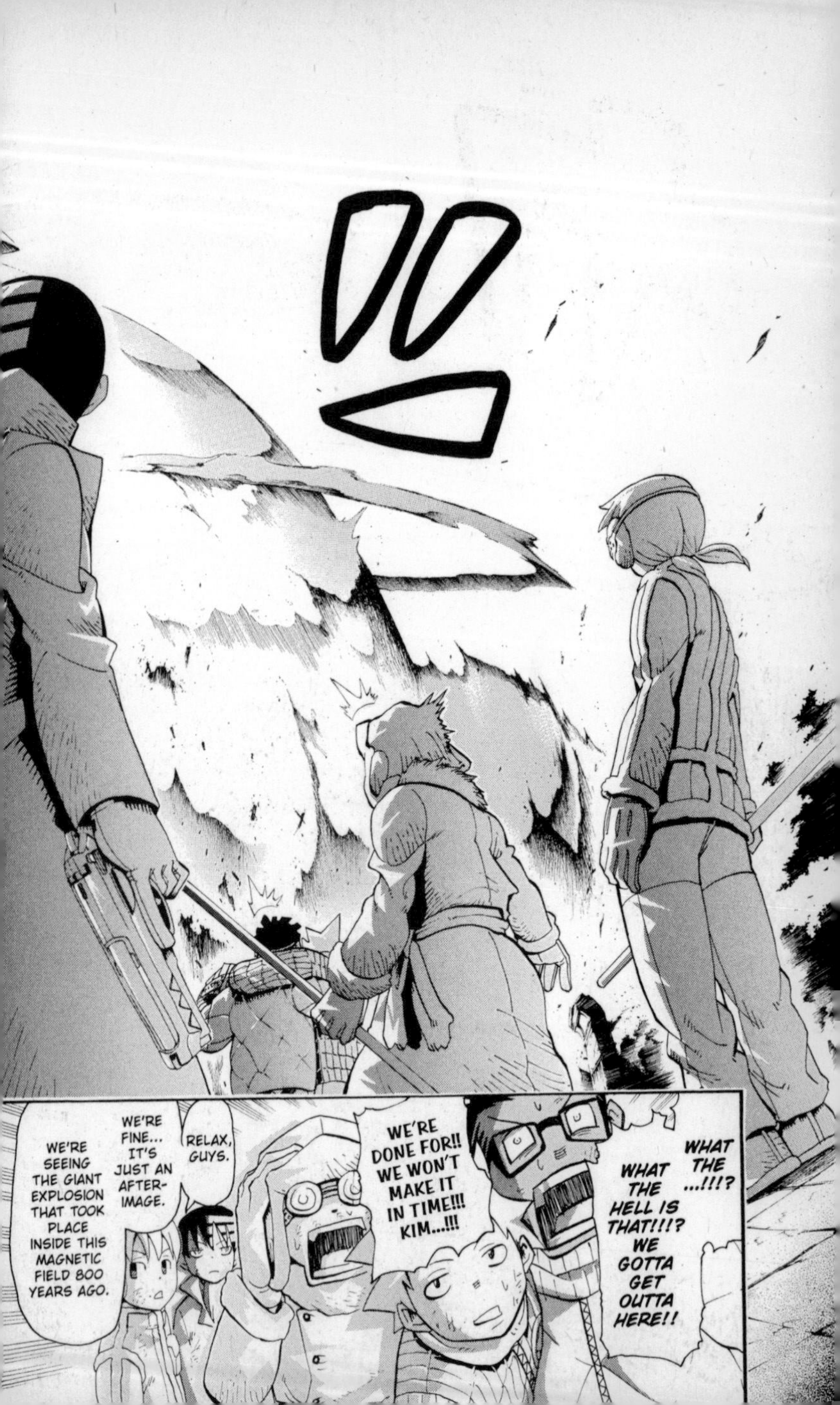
WHAT THE ...!!!?
WHAT THE HELL IS THAT!!!? WE GOTTA GET OUTTA HERE!!
WE'RE DONE FOR!! WE WON'T MAKE IT IN TIME!!! KIM...!!!
RELAX, GUYS.
WE'RE FINE... IT'S JUST AN AFTER-IMAGE.
WE'RE SEEING THE GIANT EXPLOSION THAT TOOK PLACE INSIDE THIS MAGNETIC FIELD 800 YEARS AGO.

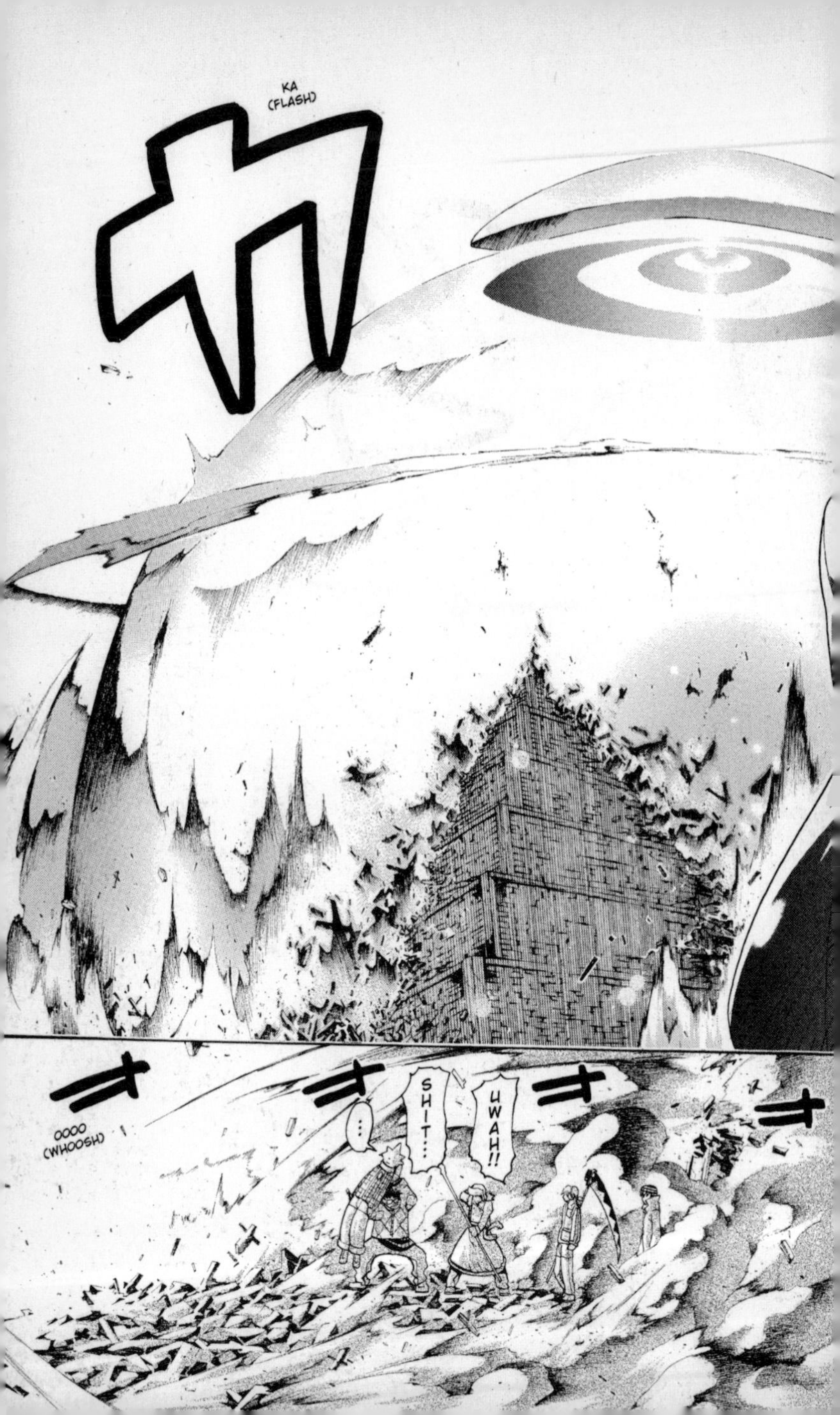
KA (FLASH)
UWAH!!
SHIT...
...
OOOO (WHOOSH)

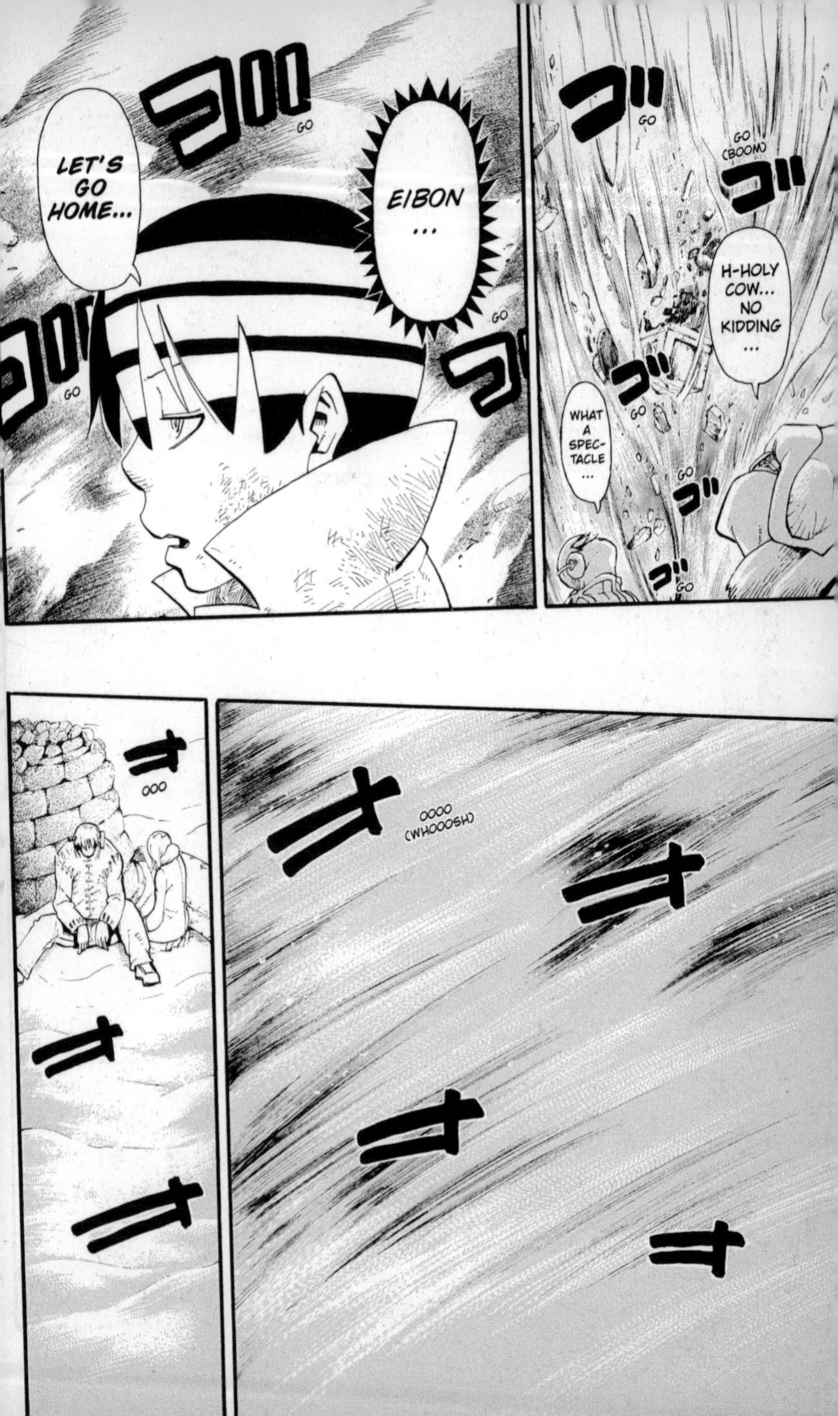
GO
GO
(BOOM)
H-HOLY COW... NO KIDDING...
WHAT A SPECTACLE...
GO
GO
GO
GO
LET'S GO HOME...
EIBON...
GO
GO
OOOO
(WHOOOSH)
OOO

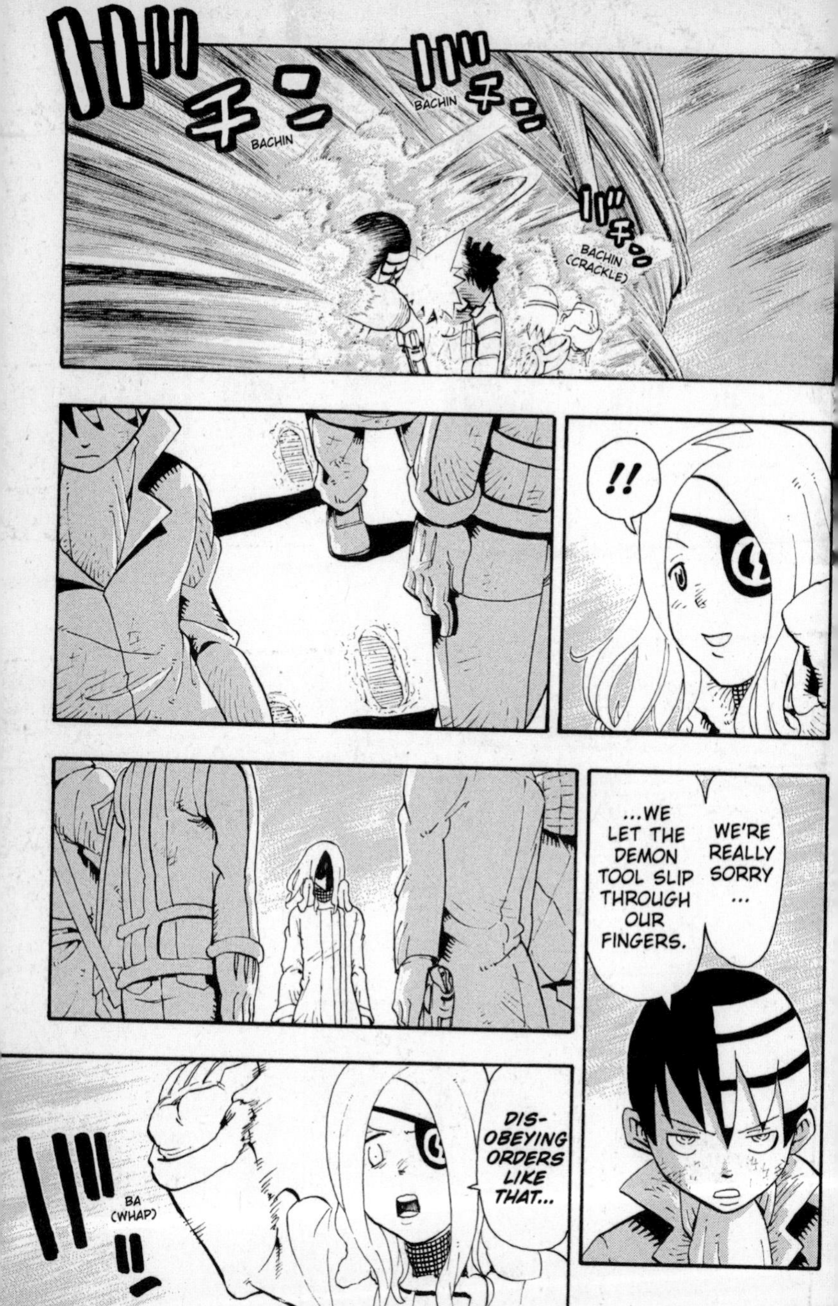
BACHIN
BACHIN (CRACKLE)
BACHIN
!!
WE'RE REALLY SORRY ...
...WE LET THE DEMON TOOL SLIP THROUGH OUR FINGERS.
DIS-OBEYING ORDERS LIKE THAT...
BA (WHAP)

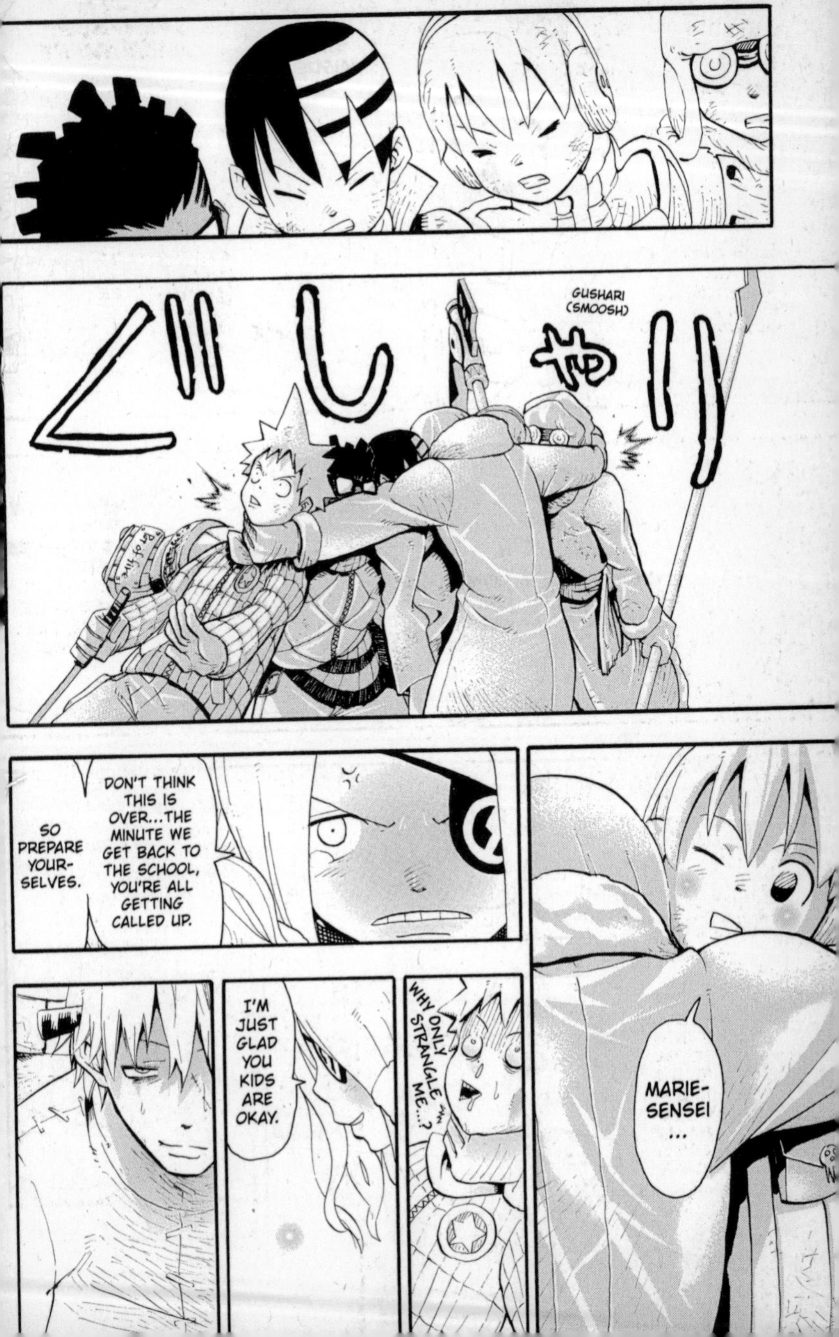
ぐしゃり
GUSHARI (SMOOSH)
MARIE-SENSEI ...
DON'T THINK THIS IS OVER...THE MINUTE WE GET BACK TO THE SCHOOL, YOU'RE ALL GETTING CALLED UP.
SO PREPARE YOUR-SELVES.
WHY ONLY STRANGLE ME...?
I'M JUST GLAD YOU KIDS ARE OKAY.

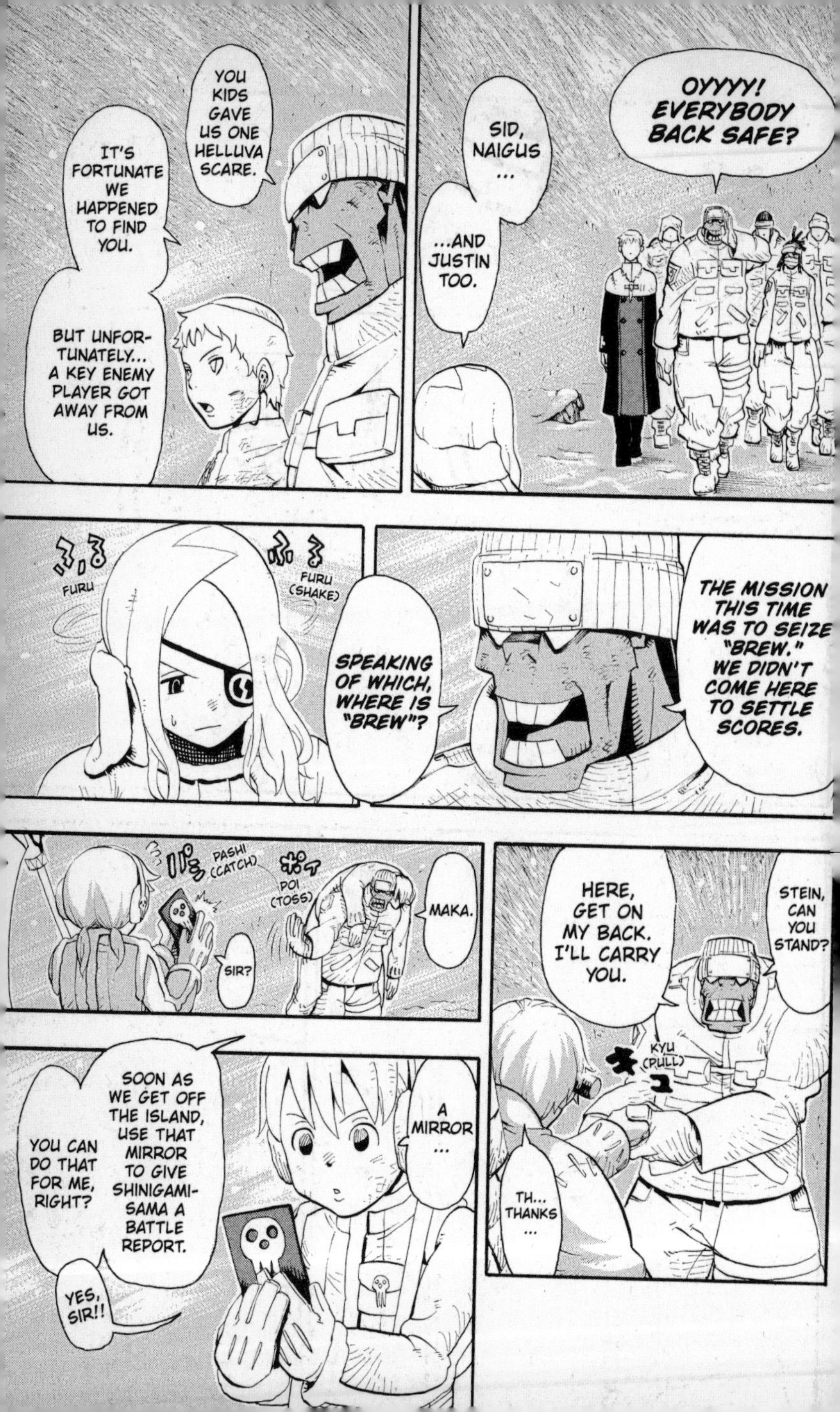
OYYYY! EVERYBODY BACK SAFE?
SID, NAIGUS ...
...AND JUSTIN TOO.
YOU KIDS GAVE US ONE HELLUVA SCARE.
IT'S FORTUNATE WE HAPPENED TO FIND YOU.
BUT UNFOR-TUNATELY... A KEY ENEMY PLAYER GOT AWAY FROM US.
THE MISSION THIS TIME WAS TO SEIZE "BREW." WE DIDN'T COME HERE TO SETTLE SCORES.
SPEAKING OF WHICH, WHERE IS "BREW"?
FURU (SHAKE)
FURU
STEIN, CAN YOU STAND?
HERE, GET ON MY BACK. I'LL CARRY YOU.
KYU (PULL)
TH... THANKS ...
MAKA.
POI (TOSS)
PASHI (CATCH)
SIR?
A MIRROR ...
SOON AS WE GET OFF THE ISLAND, USE THAT MIRROR TO GIVE SHINIGAMI-SAMA A BATTLE REPORT.
YOU CAN DO THAT FOR ME, RIGHT?
YES, SIR!!

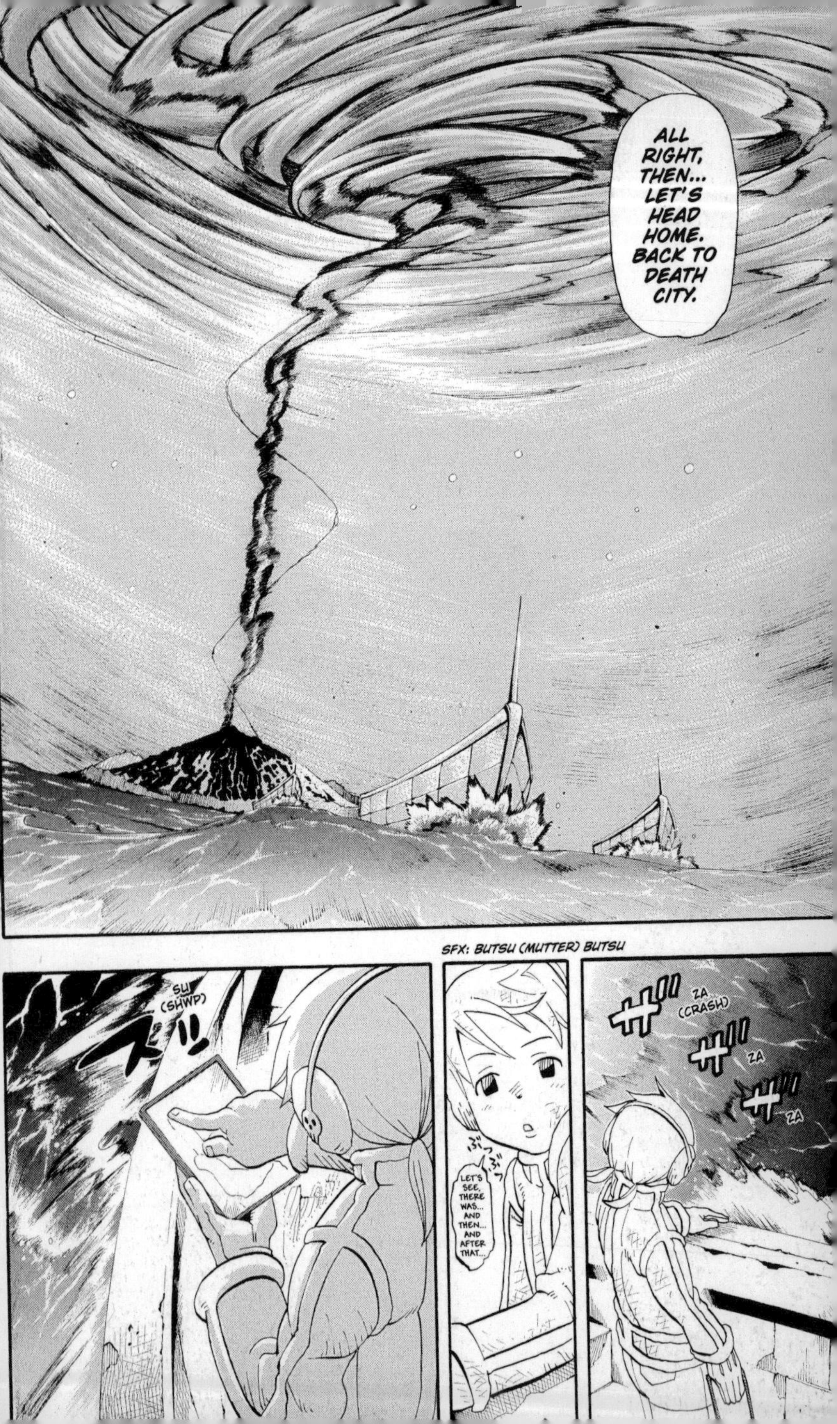
ALL RIGHT, THEN... LET'S HEAD HOME. BACK TO DEATH CITY.
SFX: BUTSU (MUTTER) BUTSU
ZA (CRASH)
ZA
ZA
LET'S SEE, THERE WAS... AND THEN... AND AFTER THAT...
SU (SHWP)

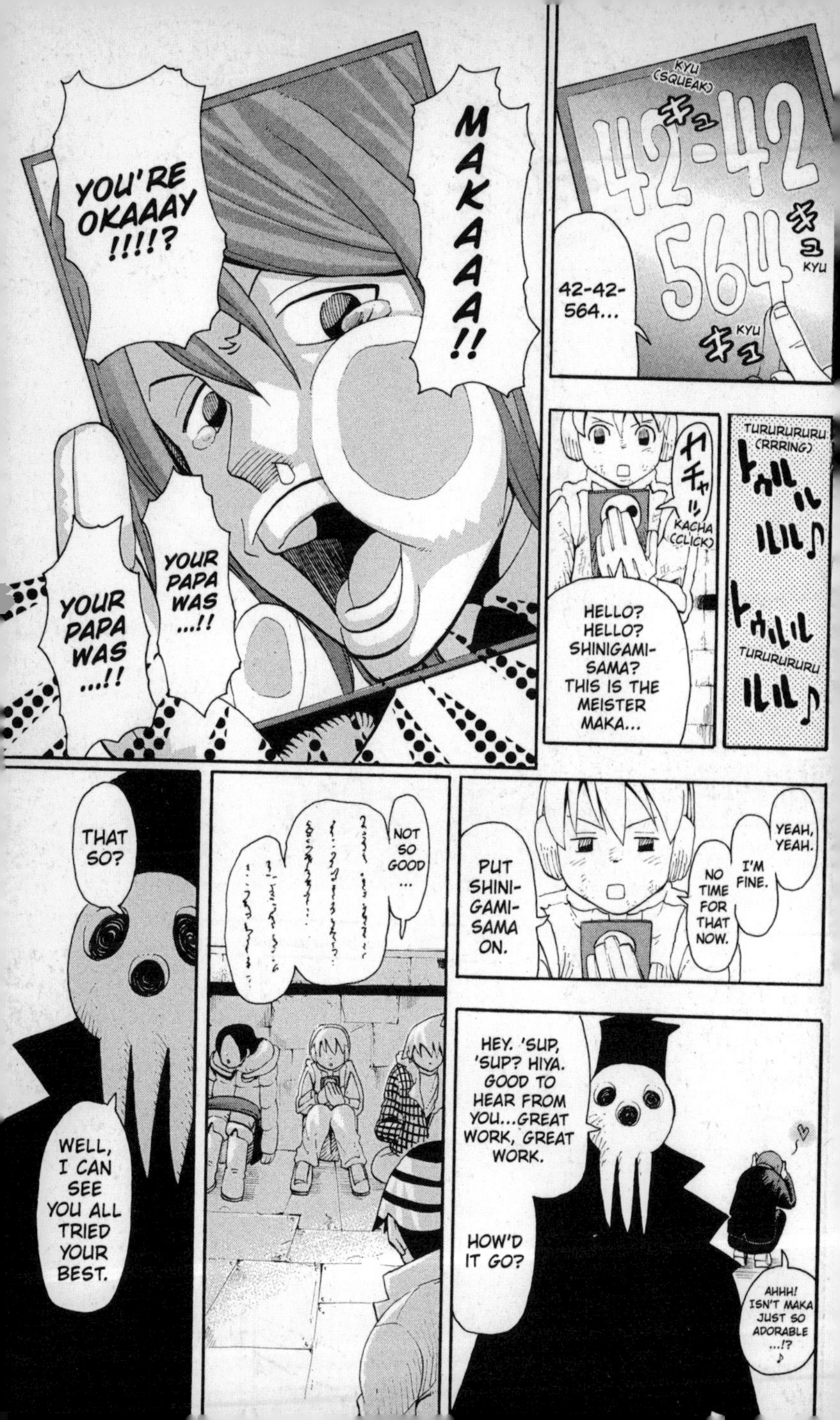
KYU (SQUEAK)
KYU
KYU
42-42-564...
TURURURURU (RRRING)
TURURURURU
KACHA (CLICK)
HELLO? HELLO? SHINIGAMI-SAMA? THIS IS THE MEISTER MAKA...
MAKAAAAA!!
YOU'RE OKAAAY!!!!?
YOUR PAPA WAS...!!
YOUR PAPA WAS...!!
YEAH, YEAH.
I'M FINE.
NO TIME FOR THAT NOW.
PUT SHINIGAMI-SAMA ON.
HEY. 'SUP, 'SUP? HIYA. GOOD TO HEAR FROM YOU...GREAT WORK, GREAT WORK.
HOW'D IT GO?
AHHH! ISN'T MAKA JUST SO ADORABLE...!? ♪
NOT SO GOOD...
THAT SO?
WELL, I CAN SEE YOU ALL TRIED YOUR BEST.

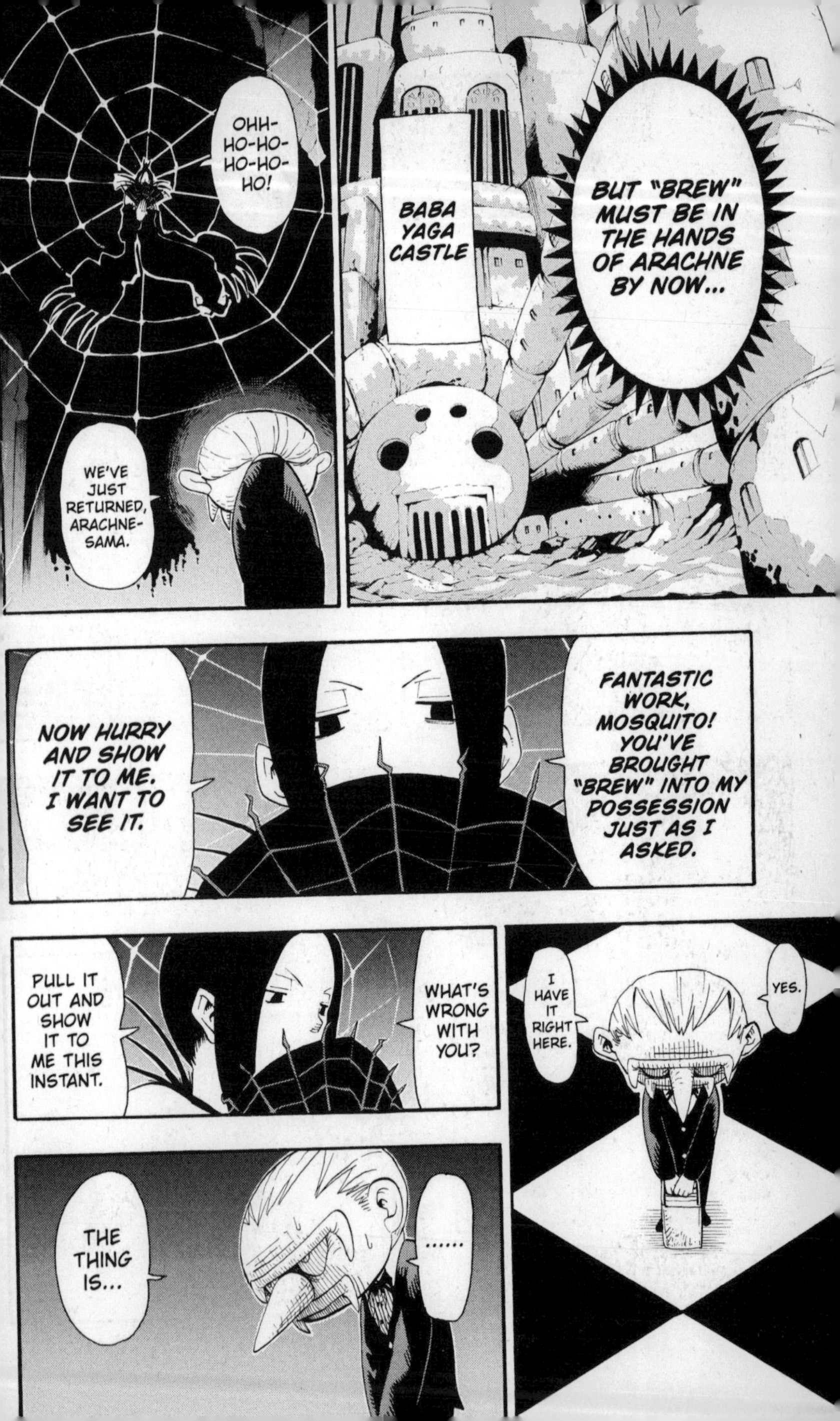

BUT "BREW" MUST BE IN THE HANDS OF ARACHNE BY NOW...
BABA YAGA CASTLE
OHH-HO-HO-HO-HO-HO!
WE'VE JUST RETURNED, ARACHNE-SAMA.
FANTASTIC WORK, MOSQUITO! YOU'VE BROUGHT "BREW" INTO MY POSSESSION JUST AS I ASKED.
NOW HURRY AND SHOW IT TO ME. I WANT TO SEE IT.
YES.
I HAVE IT RIGHT HERE.
WHAT'S WRONG WITH YOU?
PULL IT OUT AND SHOW IT TO ME THIS INSTANT.
......
THE THING IS...

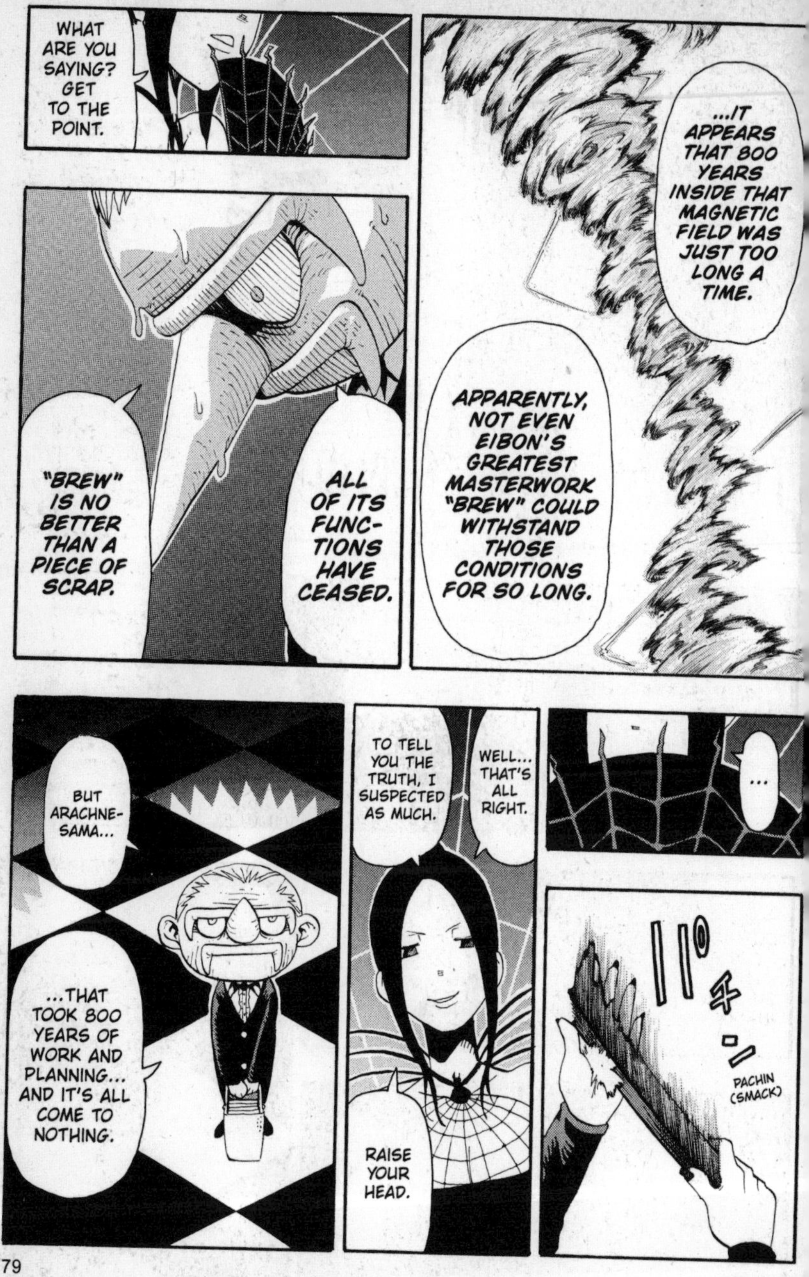
...IT APPEARS THAT 800 YEARS INSIDE THAT MAGNETIC FIELD WAS JUST TOO LONG A TIME.
APPARENTLY, NOT EVEN EIBON'S GREATEST MASTERWORK "BREW" COULD WITHSTAND THOSE CONDITIONS FOR SO LONG.
WHAT ARE YOU SAYING? GET TO THE POINT.
ALL OF ITS FUNC-TIONS HAVE CEASED.
"BREW" IS NO BETTER THAN A PIECE OF SCRAP.
...
PACHIN (SMACK)
WELL... THAT'S ALL RIGHT.
TO TELL YOU THE TRUTH, I SUSPECTED AS MUCH.
RAISE YOUR HEAD.
BUT ARACHNE-SAMA...
...THAT TOOK 800 YEARS OF WORK AND PLANNING... AND IT'S ALL COME TO NOTHING.

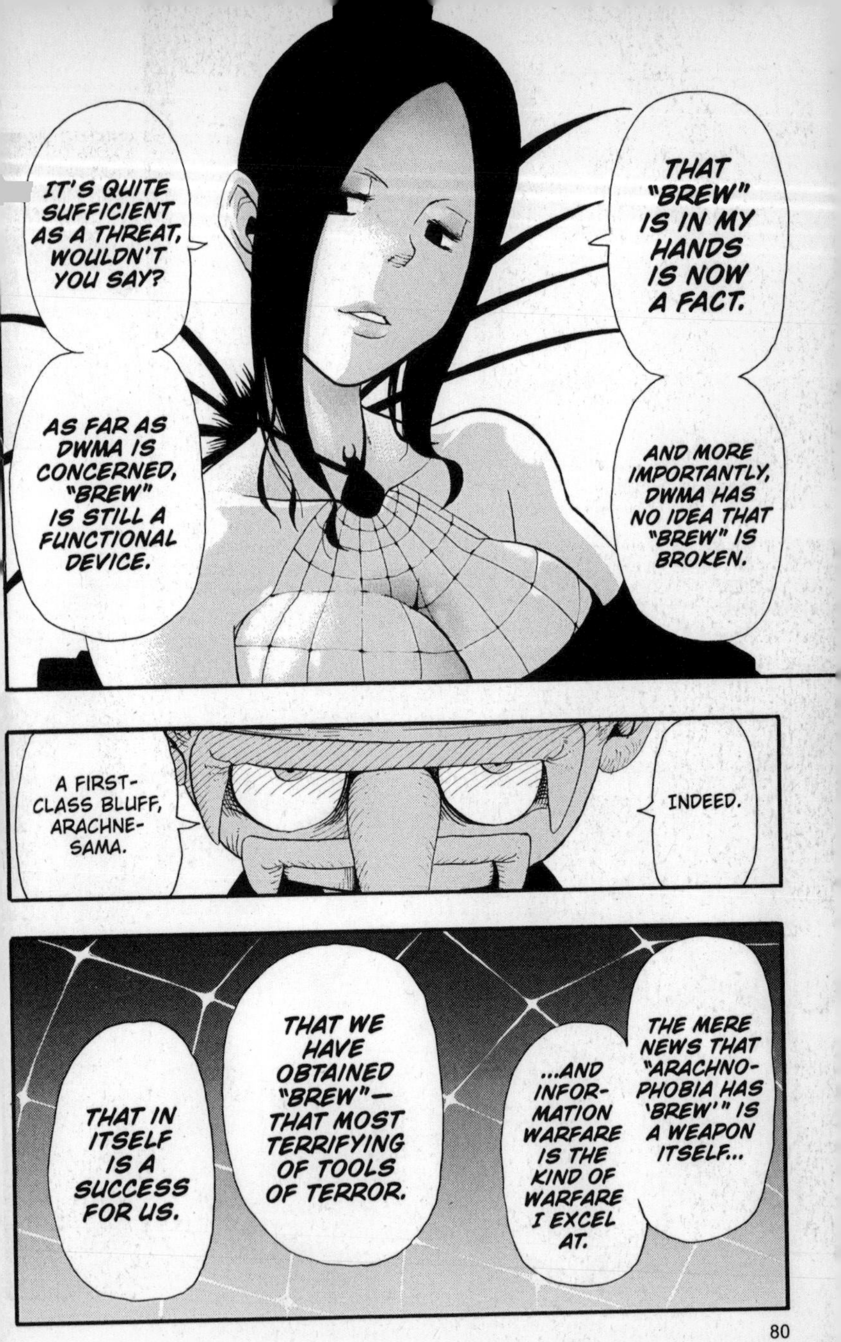
THAT "BREW" IS IN MY HANDS IS NOW A FACT.
AND MORE IMPORTANTLY, DWMA HAS NO IDEA THAT "BREW" IS BROKEN.
IT'S QUITE SUFFICIENT AS A THREAT, WOULDN'T YOU SAY?
AS FAR AS DWMA IS CONCERNED, "BREW" IS STILL A FUNCTIONAL DEVICE.
INDEED.
A FIRST-CLASS BLUFF, ARACHNE-SAMA.
THE MERE NEWS THAT "ARACHNOPHOBIA HAS 'BREW'" IS A WEAPON ITSELF...
...AND INFORMATION WARFARE IS THE KIND OF WARFARE I EXCEL AT.
THAT WE HAVE OBTAINED "BREW"—THAT MOST TERRIFYING OF TOOLS OF TERROR.
THAT IN ITSELF IS A SUCCESS FOR US.

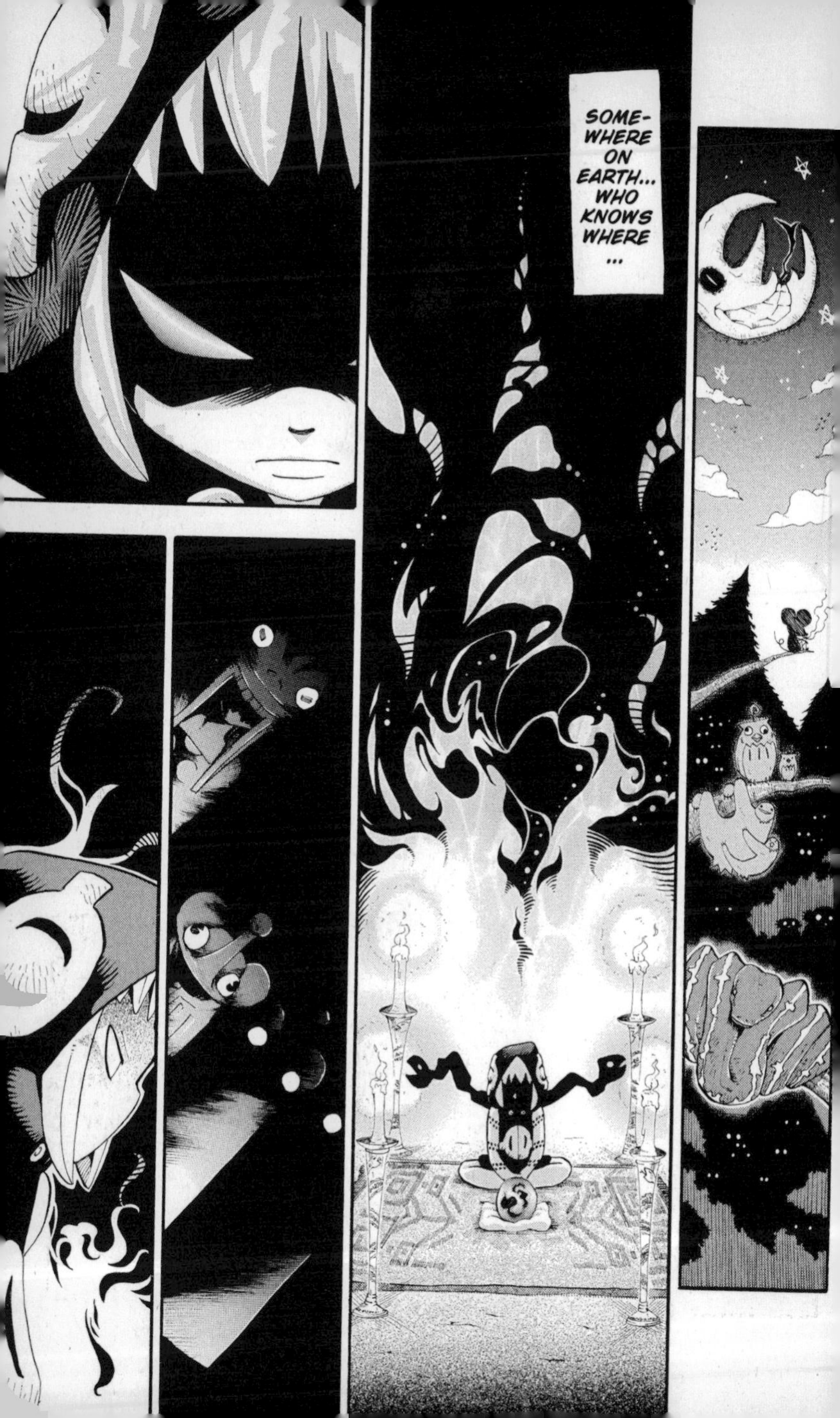
SOME-WHERE ON EARTH... WHO KNOWS WHERE ...

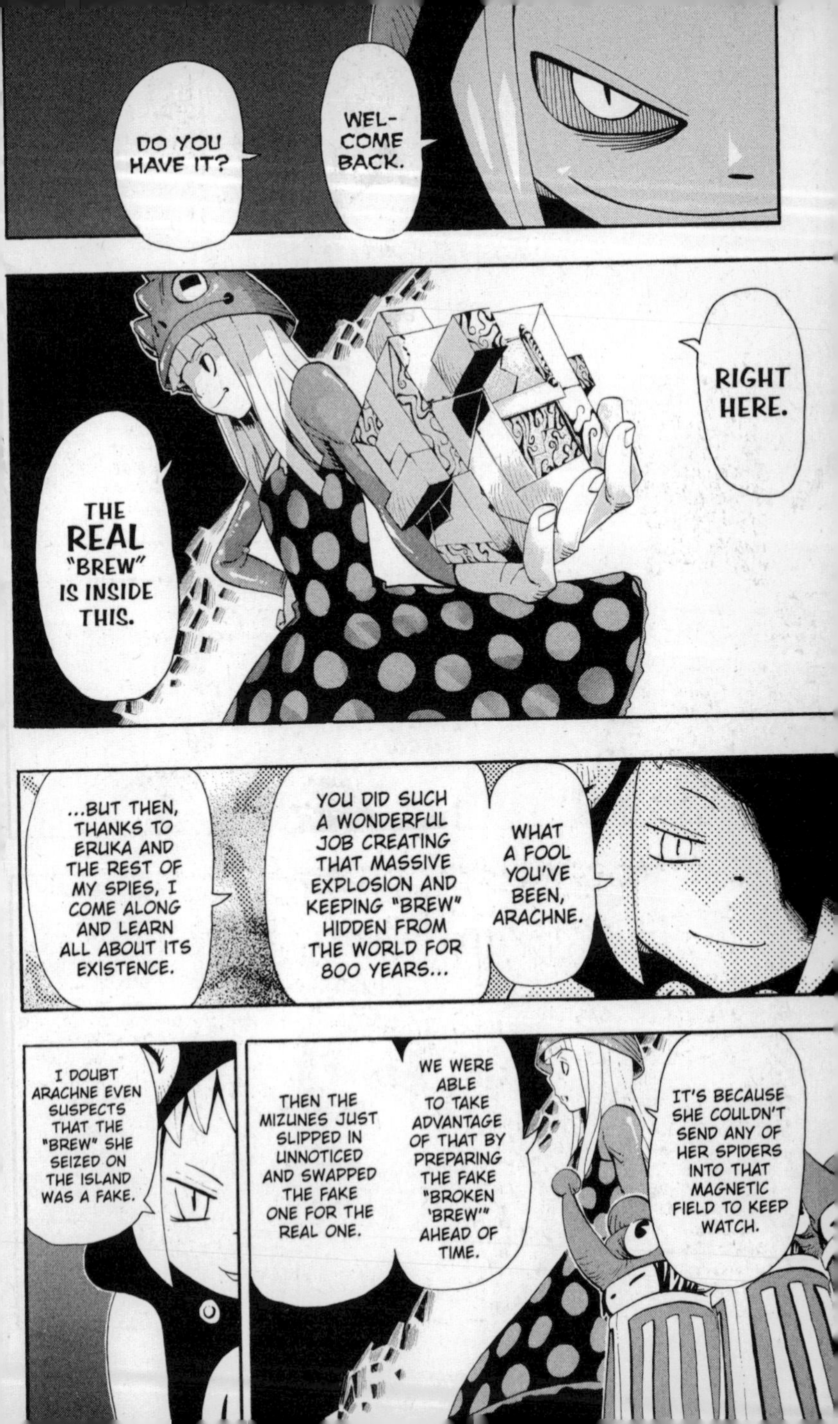
WEL-COME BACK.
DO YOU HAVE IT?
RIGHT HERE.
THE REAL "BREW" IS INSIDE THIS.
WHAT A FOOL YOU'VE BEEN, ARACHNE.
YOU DID SUCH A WONDERFUL JOB CREATING THAT MASSIVE EXPLOSION AND KEEPING "BREW" HIDDEN FROM THE WORLD FOR 800 YEARS...
...BUT THEN, THANKS TO ERUKA AND THE REST OF MY SPIES, I COME ALONG AND LEARN ALL ABOUT ITS EXISTENCE.
IT'S BECAUSE SHE COULDN'T SEND ANY OF HER SPIDERS INTO THAT MAGNETIC FIELD TO KEEP WATCH.
WE WERE ABLE TO TAKE ADVANTAGE OF THAT BY PREPARING THE FAKE "BROKEN 'BREW'" AHEAD OF TIME.
THEN THE MIZUNES JUST SLIPPED IN UNNOTICED AND SWAPPED THE FAKE ONE FOR THE REAL ONE.
I DOUBT ARACHNE EVEN SUSPECTS THAT THE "BREW" SHE SEIZED ON THE ISLAND WAS A FAKE.

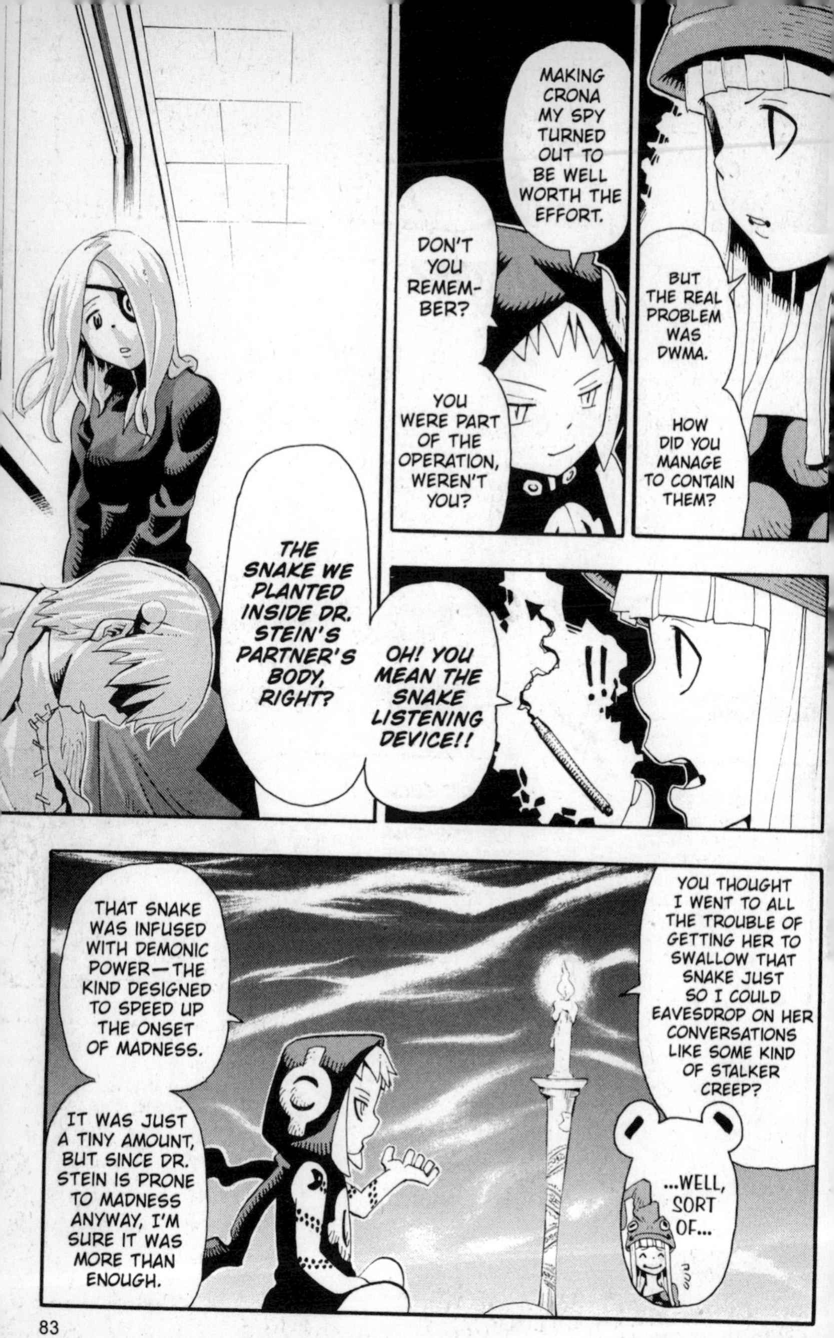
MAKING CRONA MY SPY TURNED OUT TO BE WELL WORTH THE EFFORT.
BUT THE REAL PROBLEM WAS DWMA.
HOW DID YOU MANAGE TO CONTAIN THEM?
DON'T YOU REMEMBER?
YOU WERE PART OF THE OPERATION, WEREN'T YOU?
!!
OH! YOU MEAN THE SNAKE LISTENING DEVICE!!
THE SNAKE WE PLANTED INSIDE DR. STEIN'S PARTNER'S BODY, RIGHT?
YOU THOUGHT I WENT TO ALL THE TROUBLE OF GETTING HER TO SWALLOW THAT SNAKE JUST SO I COULD EAVESDROP ON HER CONVERSATIONS LIKE SOME KIND OF STALKER CREEP?
...WELL, SORT OF...
THAT SNAKE WAS INFUSED WITH DEMONIC POWER—THE KIND DESIGNED TO SPEED UP THE ONSET OF MADNESS.
IT WAS JUST A TINY AMOUNT, BUT SINCE DR. STEIN IS PRONE TO MADNESS ANYWAY, I'M SURE IT WAS MORE THAN ENOUGH.

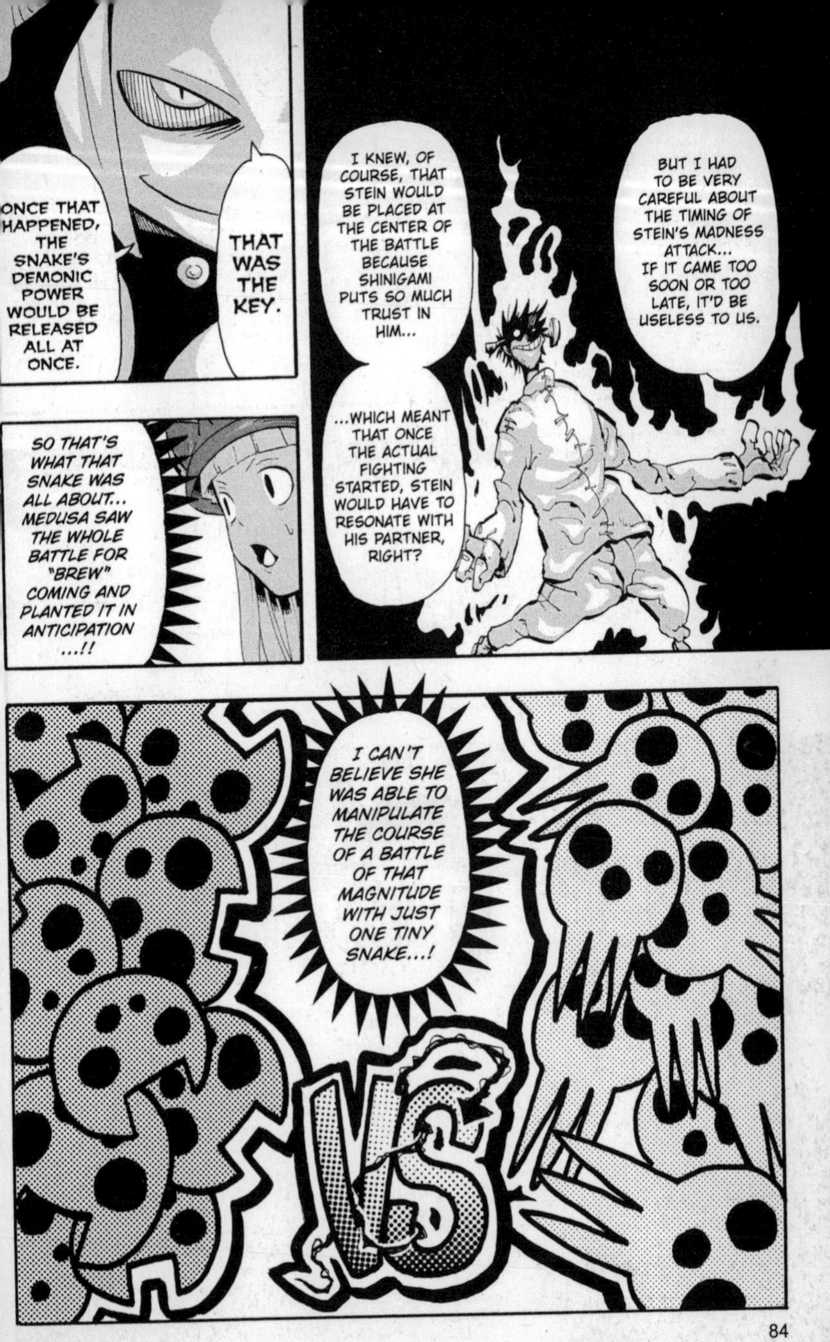
I KNEW, OF COURSE, THAT STEIN WOULD BE PLACED AT THE CENTER OF THE BATTLE BECAUSE SHINIGAMI PUTS SO MUCH TRUST IN HIM...
...WHICH MEANT THAT ONCE THE ACTUAL FIGHTING STARTED, STEIN WOULD HAVE TO RESONATE WITH HIS PARTNER, RIGHT?
BUT I HAD TO BE VERY CAREFUL ABOUT THE TIMING OF STEIN'S MADNESS ATTACK... IF IT CAME TOO SOON OR TOO LATE, IT'D BE USELESS TO US.
THAT WAS THE KEY.
ONCE THAT HAPPENED, THE SNAKE'S DEMONIC POWER WOULD BE RELEASED ALL AT ONCE.
SO THAT'S WHAT THAT SNAKE WAS ALL ABOUT... MEDUSA SAW THE WHOLE BATTLE FOR "BREW" COMING AND PLANTED IT IN ANTICIPATION ...!!
I CAN'T BELIEVE SHE WAS ABLE TO MANIPULATE THE COURSE OF A BATTLE OF THAT MAGNITUDE WITH JUST ONE TINY SNAKE...!
VS

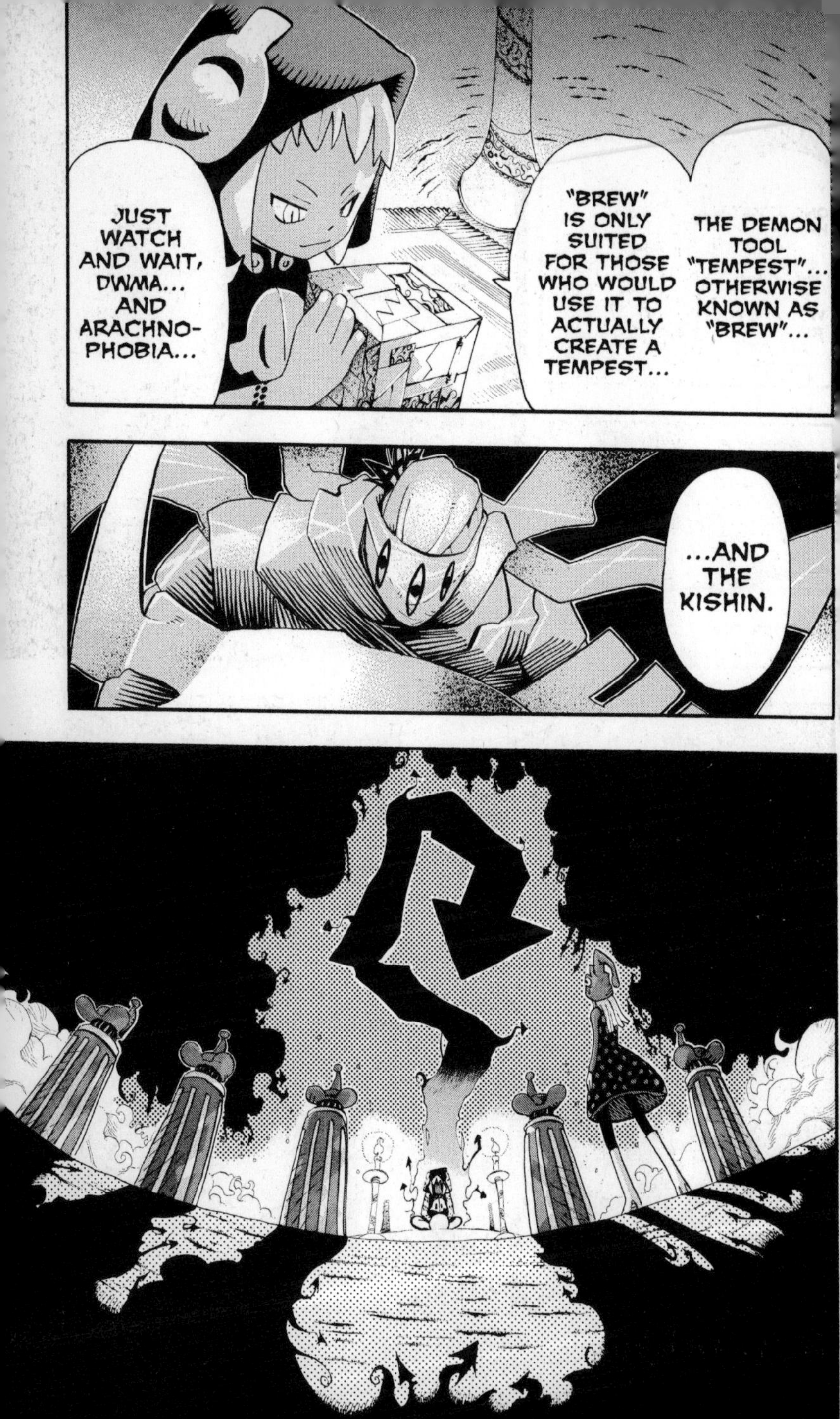
THE DEMON TOOL "TEMPEST"... OTHERWISE KNOWN AS "BREW"...
"BREW" IS ONLY SUITED FOR THOSE WHO WOULD USE IT TO ACTUALLY CREATE A TEMPEST...
JUST WATCH AND WAIT, DWMA... AND ARACHNO-PHOBIA...
...AND THE KISHIN.

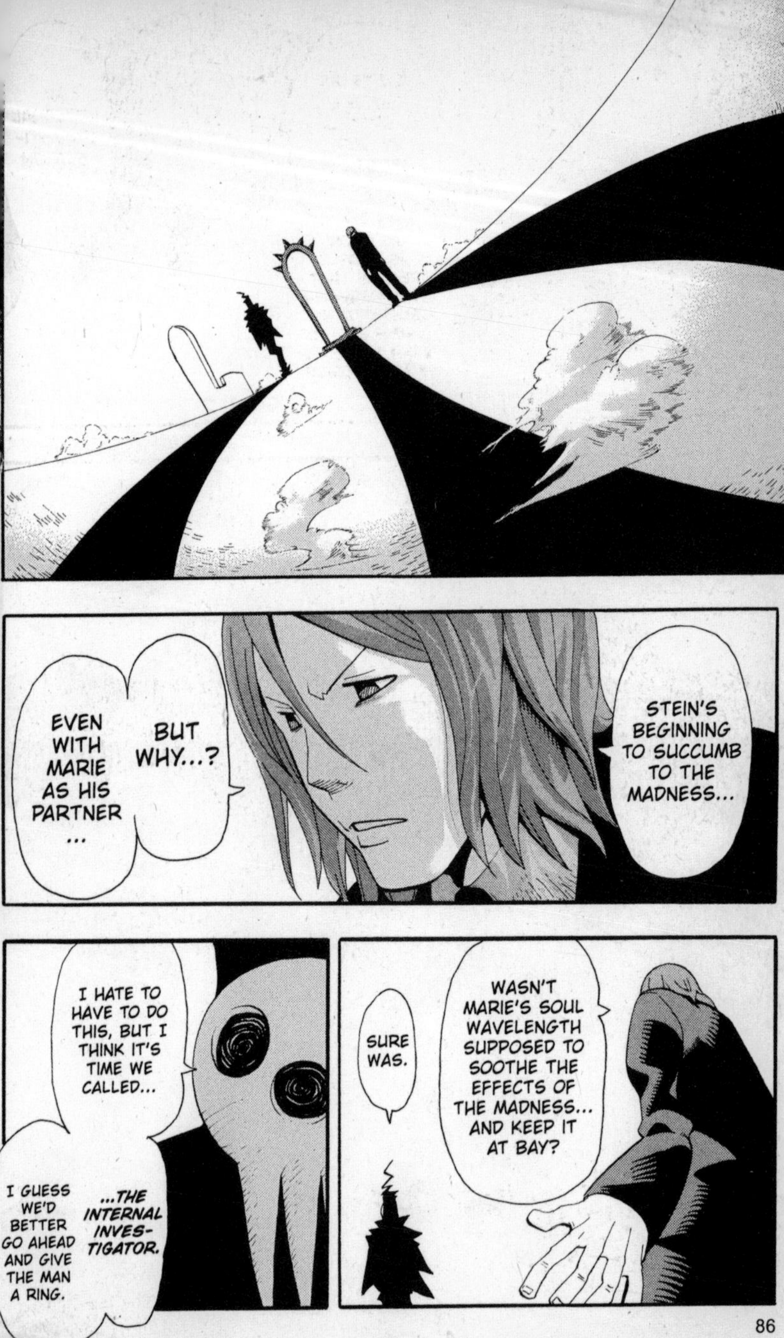
STEIN'S BEGINNING TO SUCCUMB TO THE MADNESS...
BUT WHY...?
EVEN WITH MARIE AS HIS PARTNER...
WASN'T MARIE'S SOUL WAVELENGTH SUPPOSED TO SOOTHE THE EFFECTS OF THE MADNESS... AND KEEP IT AT BAY?
SURE WAS.
I HATE TO HAVE TO DO THIS, BUT I THINK IT'S TIME WE CALLED...
...THE INTERNAL INVES-TIGATOR.
I GUESS WE'D BETTER GO AHEAD AND GIVE THE MAN A RING.

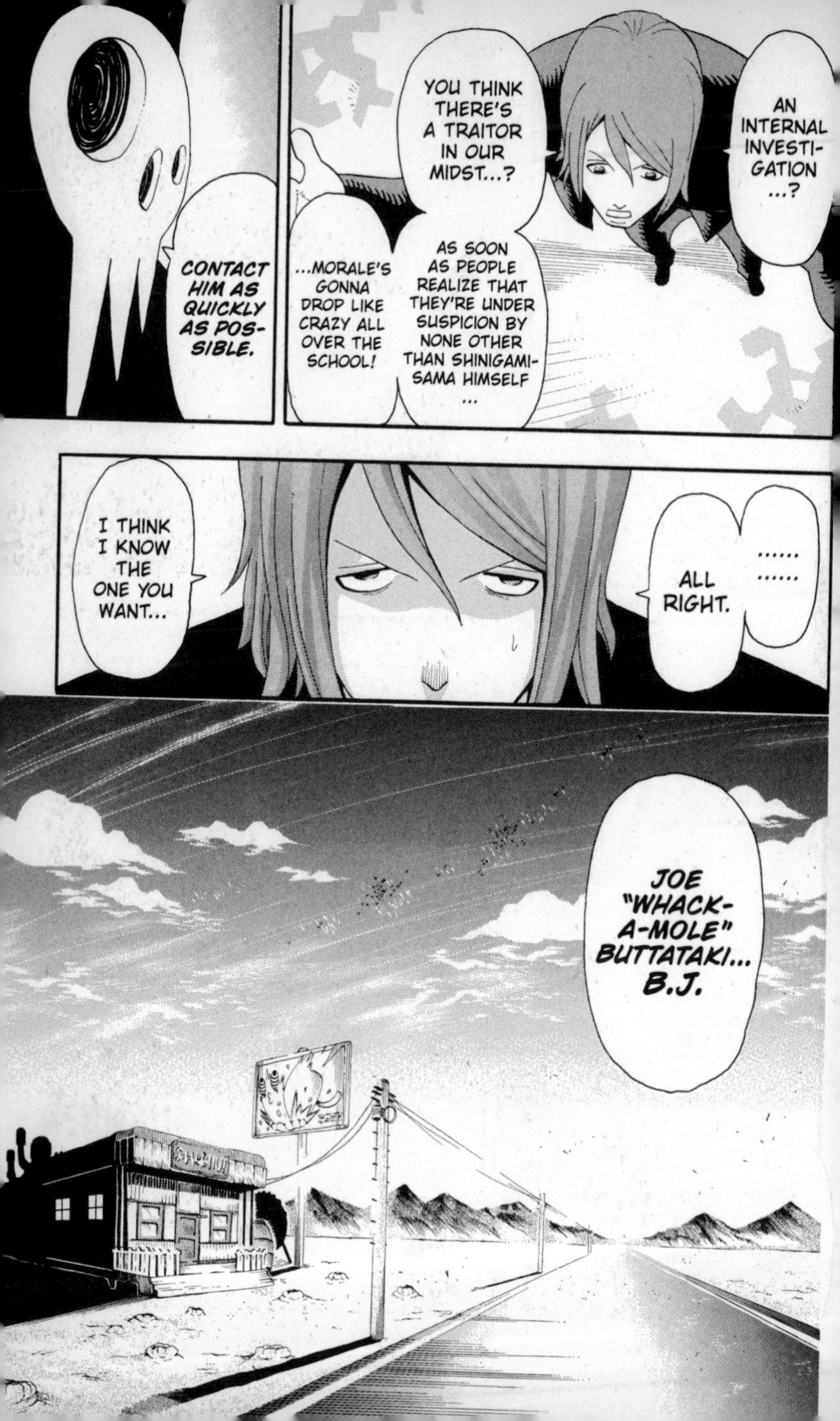
AN INTERNAL INVESTI-GATION ...?
YOU THINK THERE'S A TRAITOR IN OUR MIDST...?
AS SOON AS PEOPLE REALIZE THAT THEY'RE UNDER SUSPICION BY NONE OTHER THAN SHINIGAMI-SAMA HIMSELF ...
...MORALE'S GONNA DROP LIKE CRAZY ALL OVER THE SCHOOL!
CONTACT HIM AS QUICKLY AS POS-SIBLE.
....
ALL RIGHT.
I THINK I KNOW THE ONE YOU WANT...
JOE "WHACK-A-MOLE" BUTTATAKI... B.J.

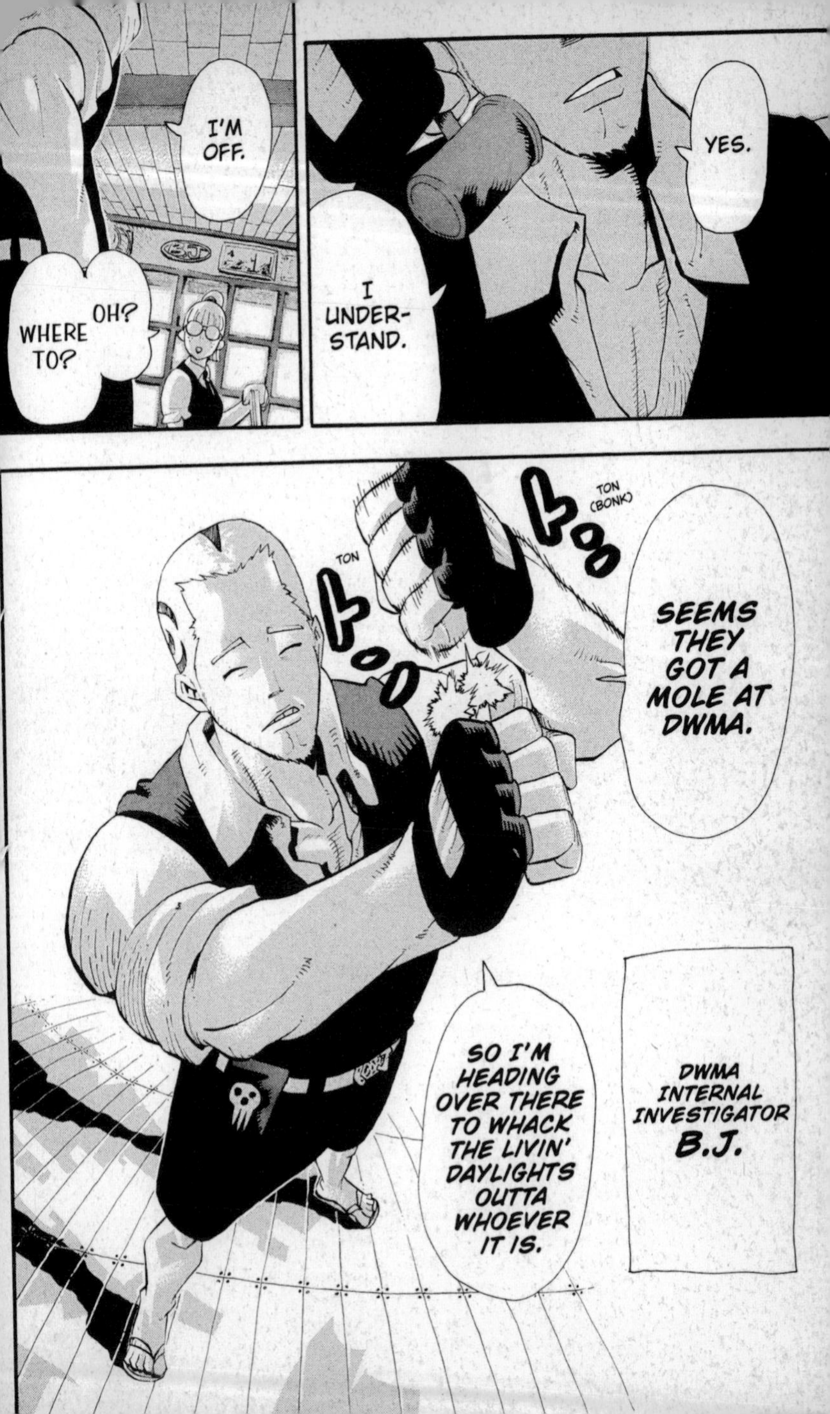
YES.
I UNDERSTAND.
I'M OFF.
OH? WHERE TO?
TON (BONK)
SEEMS THEY GOT A MOLE AT DWMA.
TON
SO I'M HEADING OVER THERE TO WHACK THE LIVIN' DAYLIGHTS OUTTA WHOEVER IT IS.
DWMA INTERNAL INVESTIGATOR B.J.

SOUL EATER

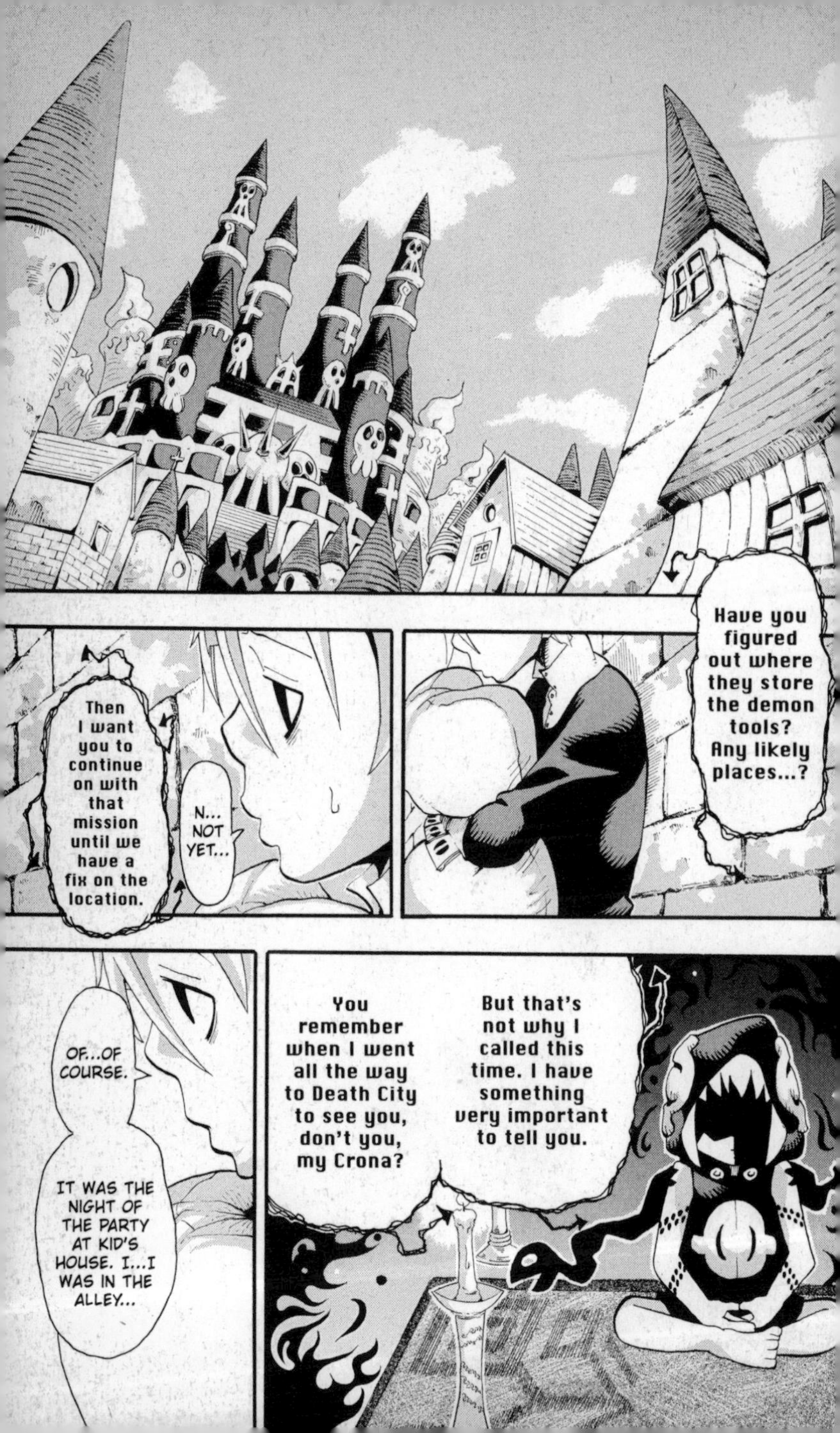
Have you figured out where they store the demon tools? Any likely places...?
N... NOT YET...
Then I want you to continue on with that mission until we have a fix on the location.
But that's not why I called this time. I have something very important to tell you.
You remember when I went all the way to Death City to see you, don't you, my Crona?
OF...OF COURSE.
IT WAS THE NIGHT OF THE PARTY AT KID'S HOUSE. I...I WAS IN THE ALLEY...

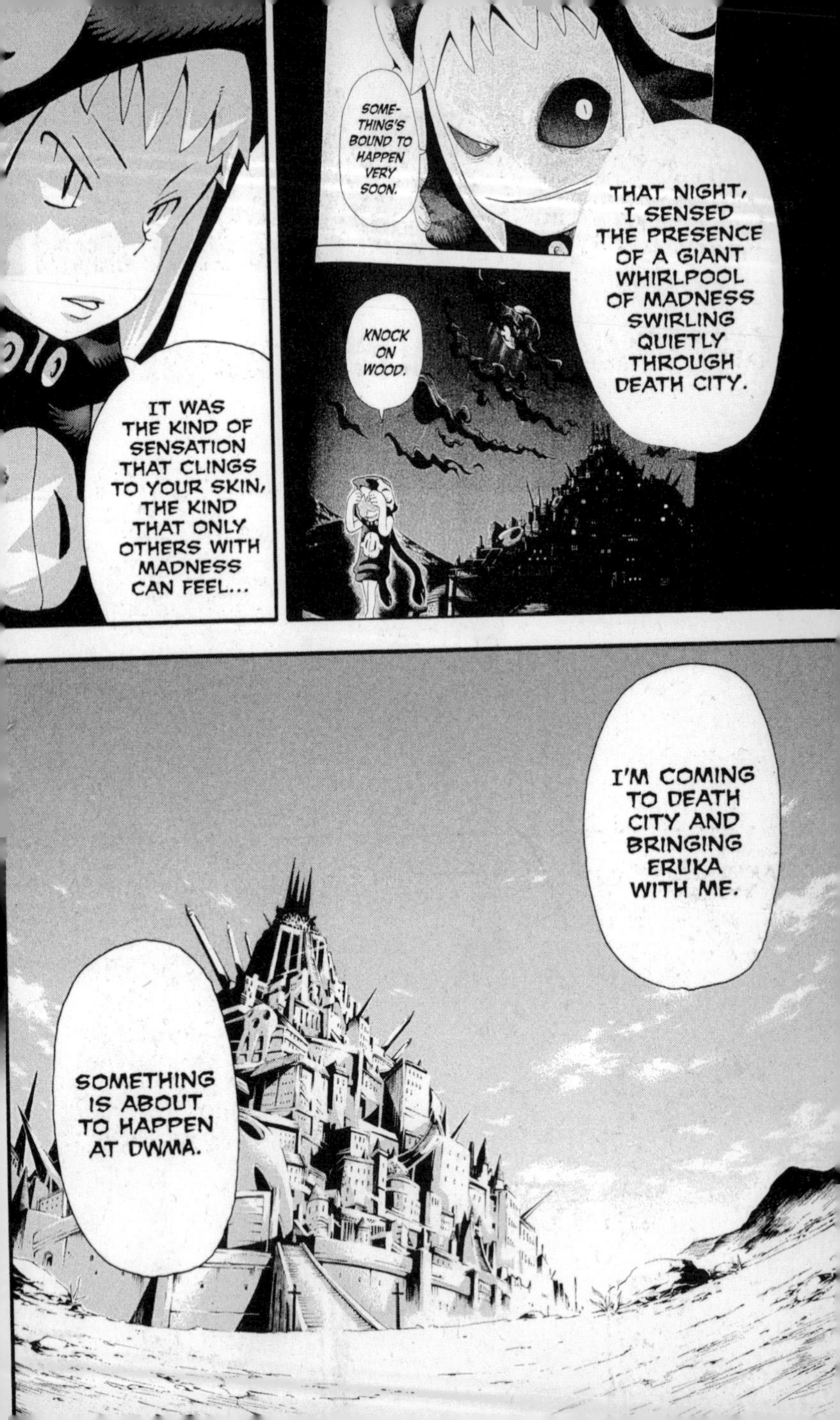
THAT NIGHT, I SENSED THE PRESENCE OF A GIANT WHIRLPOOL OF MADNESS SWIRLING QUIETLY THROUGH DEATH CITY.
SOME-THING'S BOUND TO HAPPEN VERY SOON.
KNOCK ON WOOD.
IT WAS THE KIND OF SENSATION THAT CLINGS TO YOUR SKIN, THE KIND THAT ONLY OTHERS WITH MADNESS CAN FEEL...
I'M COMING TO DEATH CITY AND BRINGING ERUKA WITH ME.
SOMETHING IS ABOUT TO HAPPEN AT DWMA.

SOUL EATER

CHAPTER 38: INTERNAL INVESTIGATION (PART 1

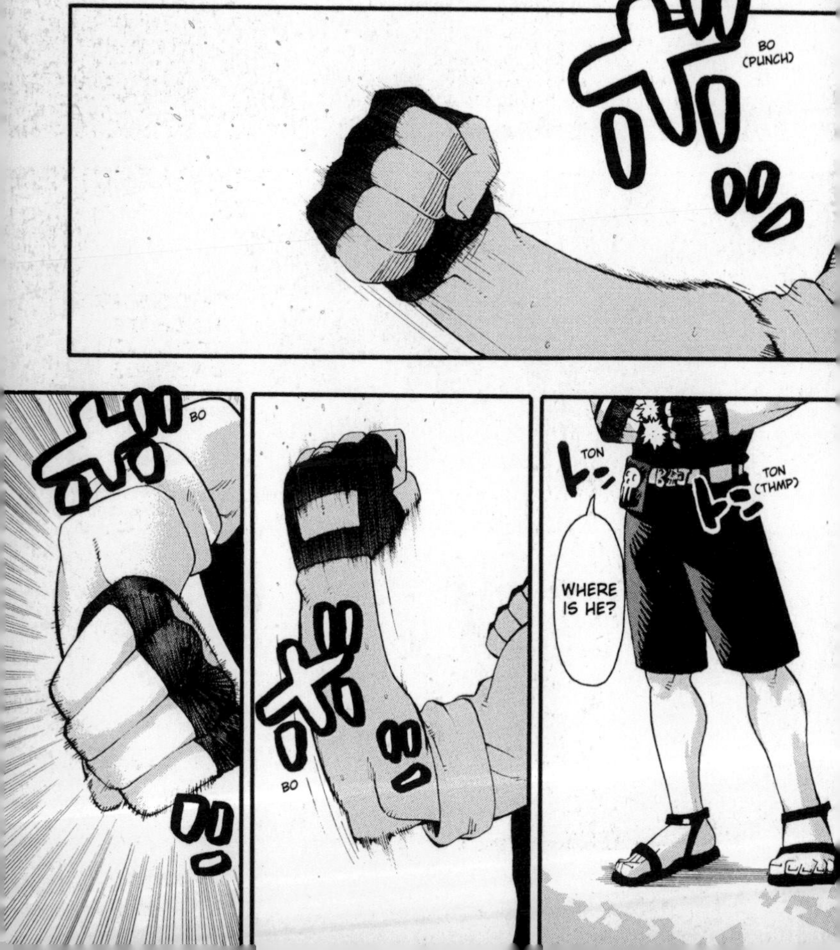

BO (PUNCH)
TON (THMP)
TON
WHERE IS HE?
BO
BO

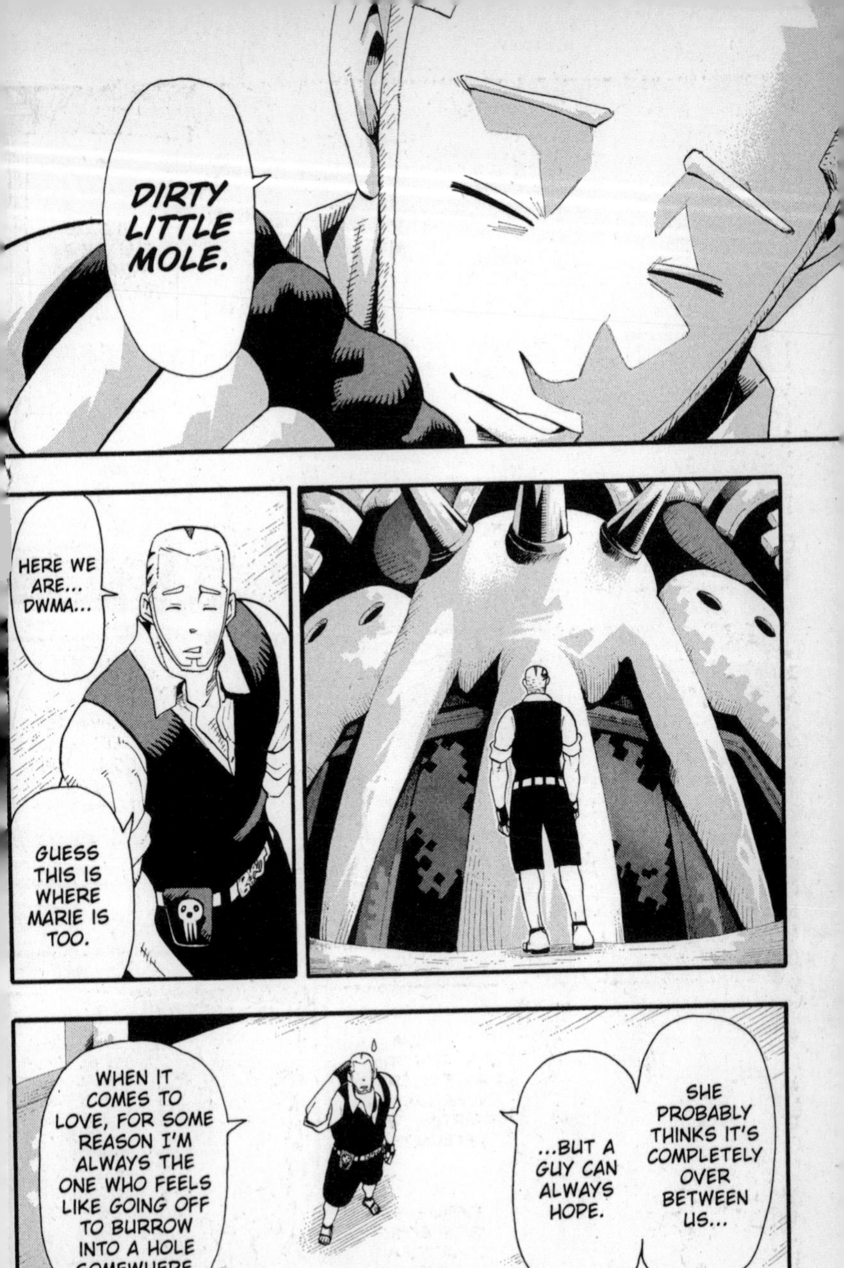
DIRTY LITTLE MOLE.
HERE WE ARE... DWMA...
GUESS THIS IS WHERE MARIE IS TOO.
SHE PROBABLY THINKS IT'S COMPLETELY OVER BETWEEN US...
...BUT A GUY CAN ALWAYS HOPE.
WHEN IT COMES TO LOVE, FOR SOME REASON I'M ALWAYS THE ONE WHO FEELS LIKE GOING OFF TO BURROW INTO A HOLE SOMEWHERE.

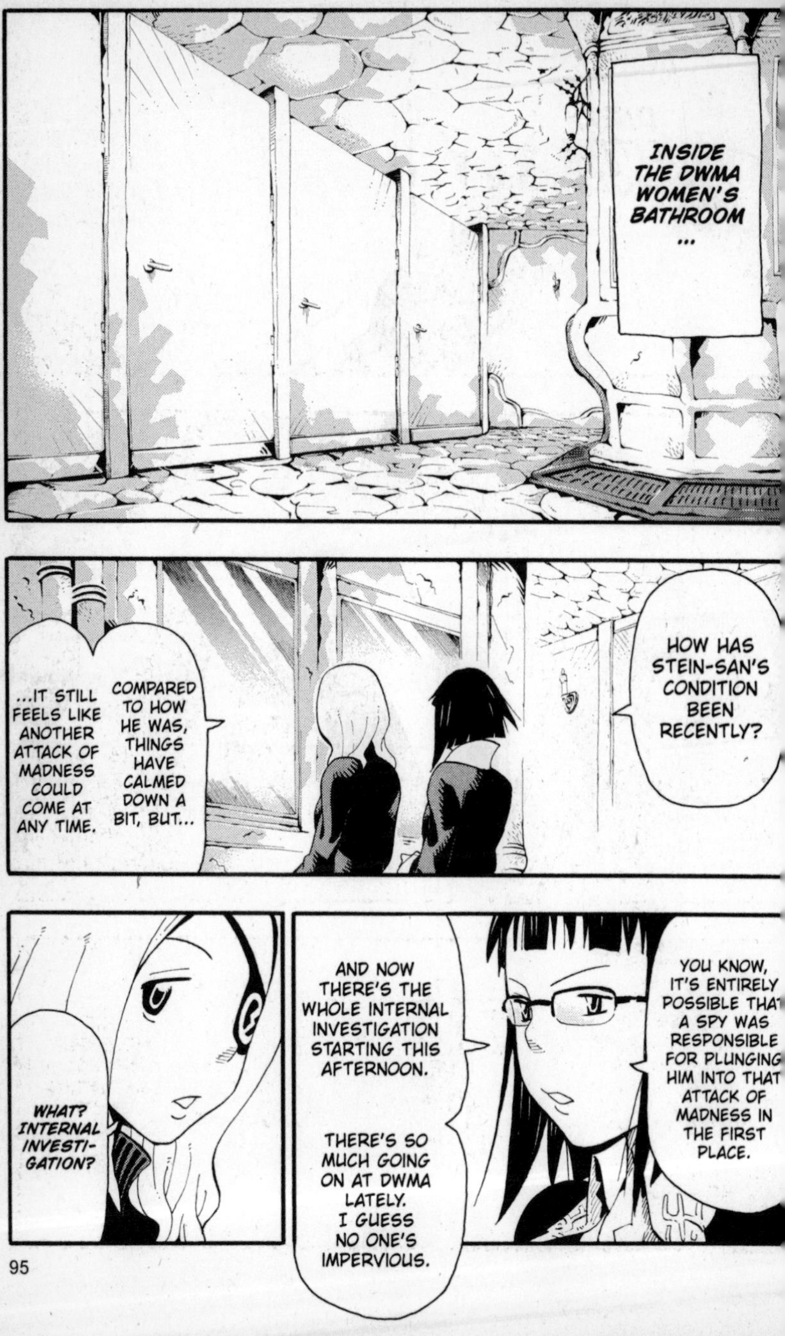
INSIDE THE DWMA WOMEN'S BATHROOM ...
HOW HAS STEIN-SAN'S CONDITION BEEN RECENTLY?
COMPARED TO HOW HE WAS, THINGS HAVE CALMED DOWN A BIT, BUT...
...IT STILL FEELS LIKE ANOTHER ATTACK OF MADNESS COULD COME AT ANY TIME.
YOU KNOW, IT'S ENTIRELY POSSIBLE THAT A SPY WAS RESPONSIBLE FOR PLUNGING HIM INTO THAT ATTACK OF MADNESS IN THE FIRST PLACE.
AND NOW THERE'S THE WHOLE INTERNAL INVESTIGATION STARTING THIS AFTERNOON.
THERE'S SO MUCH GOING ON AT DWMA LATELY. I GUESS NO ONE'S IMPERVIOUS.
WHAT? INTERNAL INVESTI-GATION?

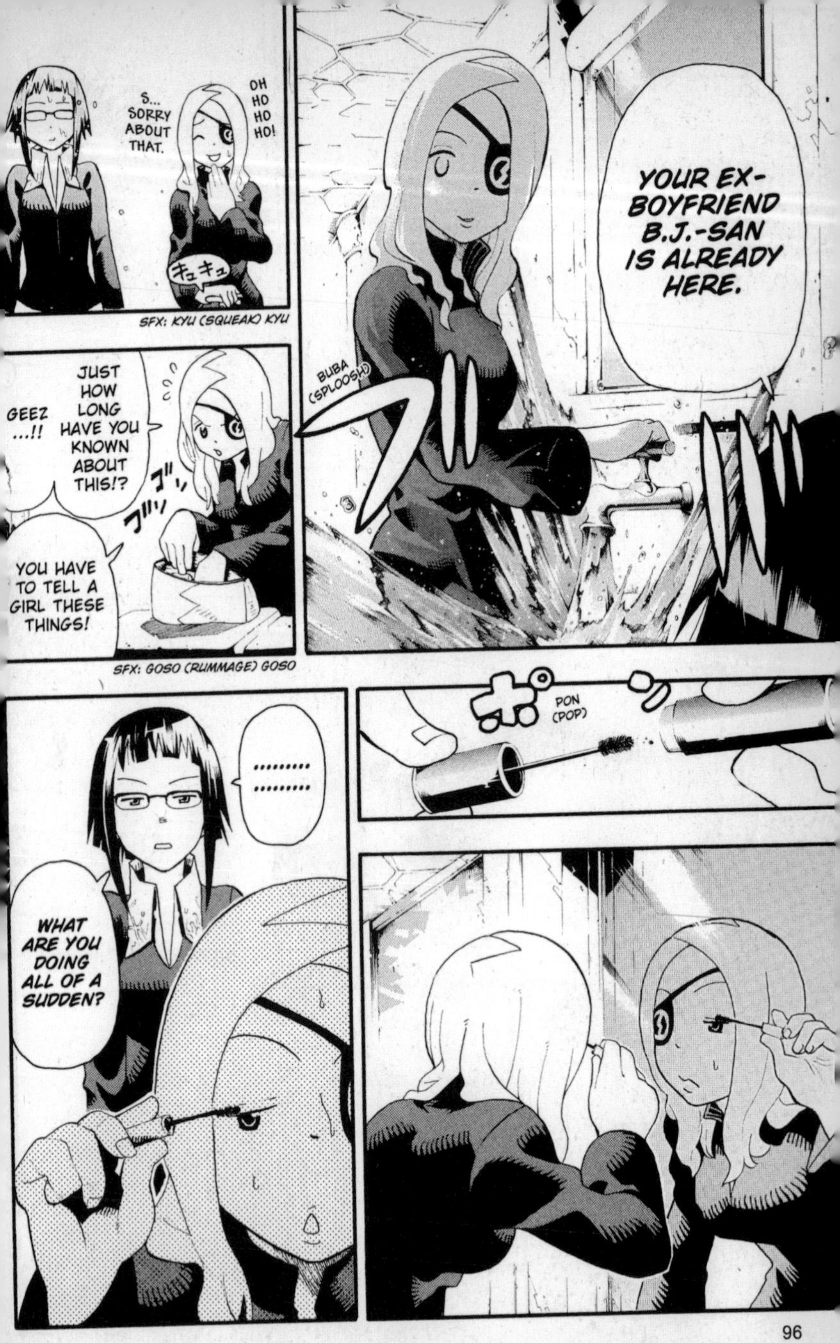
YOUR EX-BOYFRIEND B.J.-SAN IS ALREADY HERE.
BUBA (SPLOOSH)
OH HO HO HO!
S... SORRY ABOUT THAT.
キュキュ
SFX: KYU (SQUEAK) KYU
JUST HOW LONG HAVE YOU KNOWN ABOUT THIS!?
GEEZ ...!!
ゴソゴソ
YOU HAVE TO TELL A GIRL THESE THINGS!
SFX: GOSO (RUMMAGE) GOSO
ポン
PON (POP)
....
WHAT ARE YOU DOING ALL OF A SUDDEN?

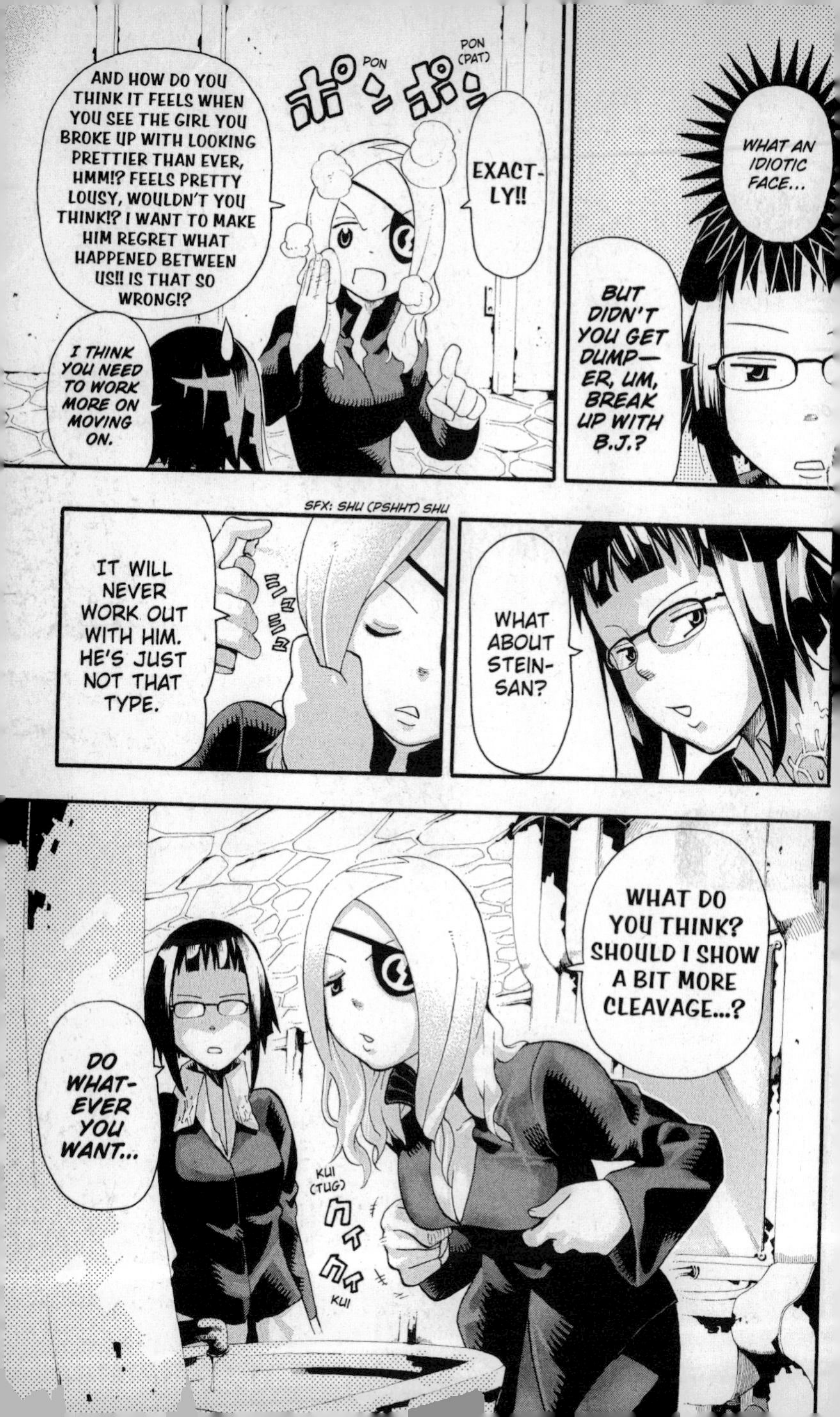
WHAT AN IDIOTIC FACE...
BUT DIDN'T YOU GET DUMP— ER, UM, BREAK UP WITH B.J.?
PON (PAT) PON
EXACT-LY!!
AND HOW DO YOU THINK IT FEELS WHEN YOU SEE THE GIRL YOU BROKE UP WITH LOOKING PRETTIER THAN EVER, HMM!? FEELS PRETTY LOUSY, WOULDN'T YOU THINK!? I WANT TO MAKE HIM REGRET WHAT HAPPENED BETWEEN US!! IS THAT SO WRONG!?
I THINK YOU NEED TO WORK MORE ON MOVING ON.
WHAT ABOUT STEIN-SAN?
SFX: SHU (PSHHT) SHU
IT WILL NEVER WORK OUT WITH HIM. HE'S JUST NOT THAT TYPE.
WHAT DO YOU THINK? SHOULD I SHOW A BIT MORE CLEAVAGE...?
KUI (TUG) KUI
DO WHAT-EVER YOU WANT...

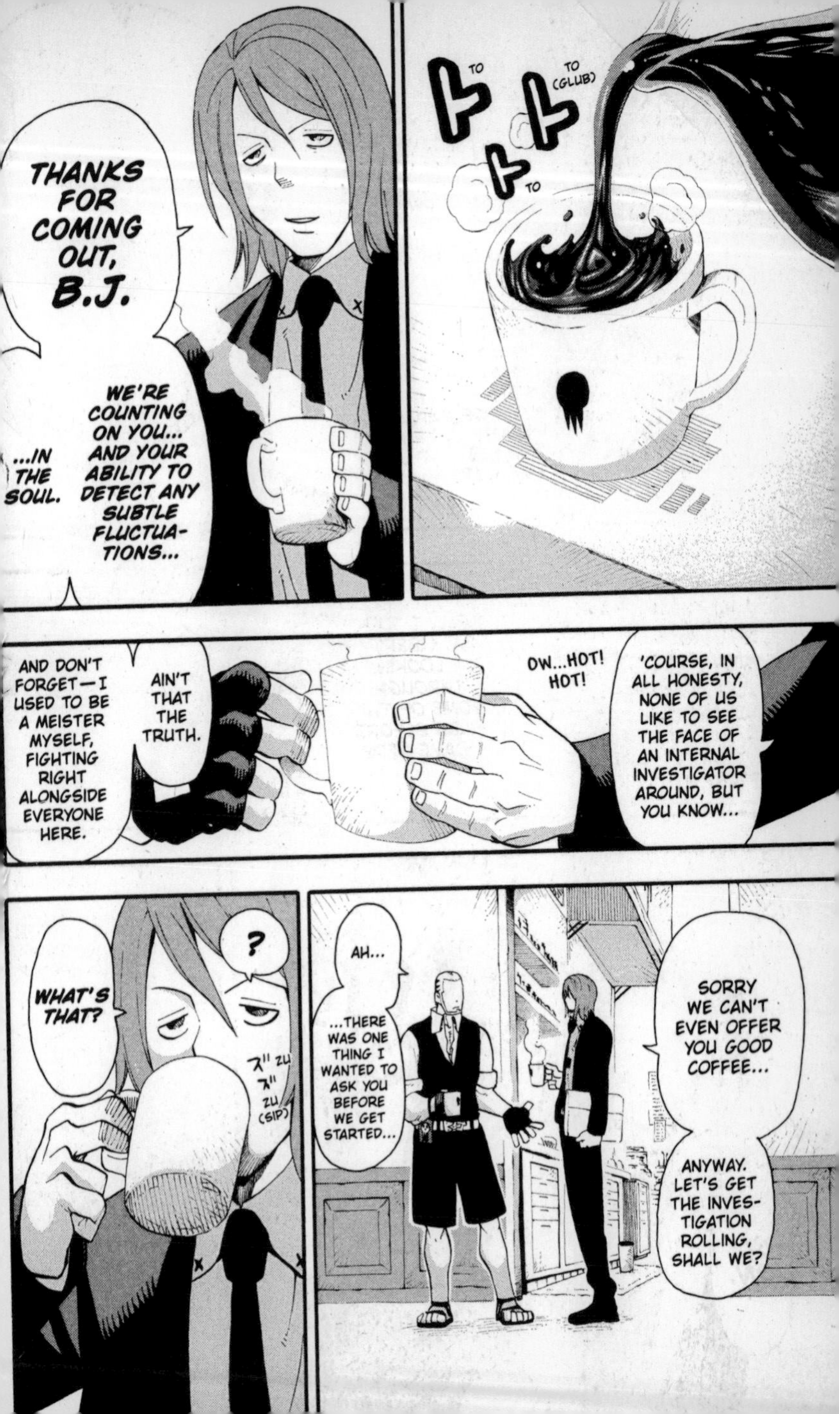

ト TO
ト TO (GLUB)
ト TO
THANKS FOR COMING OUT, B.J.
WE'RE COUNTING ON YOU... AND YOUR ABILITY TO DETECT ANY SUBTLE FLUCTUATIONS...
...IN THE SOUL.
'COURSE, IN ALL HONESTY, NONE OF US LIKE TO SEE THE FACE OF AN INTERNAL INVESTIGATOR AROUND, BUT YOU KNOW...
OW...HOT! HOT!
AIN'T THAT THE TRUTH.
AND DON'T FORGET—I USED TO BE A MEISTER MYSELF, FIGHTING RIGHT ALONGSIDE EVERYONE HERE.
SORRY WE CAN'T EVEN OFFER YOU GOOD COFFEE...
ANYWAY. LET'S GET THE INVESTIGATION ROLLING, SHALL WE?
AH...
...THERE WAS ONE THING I WANTED TO ASK YOU BEFORE WE GET STARTED...
?
WHAT'S THAT?
ズ ZU
ズ ZU (SIP)

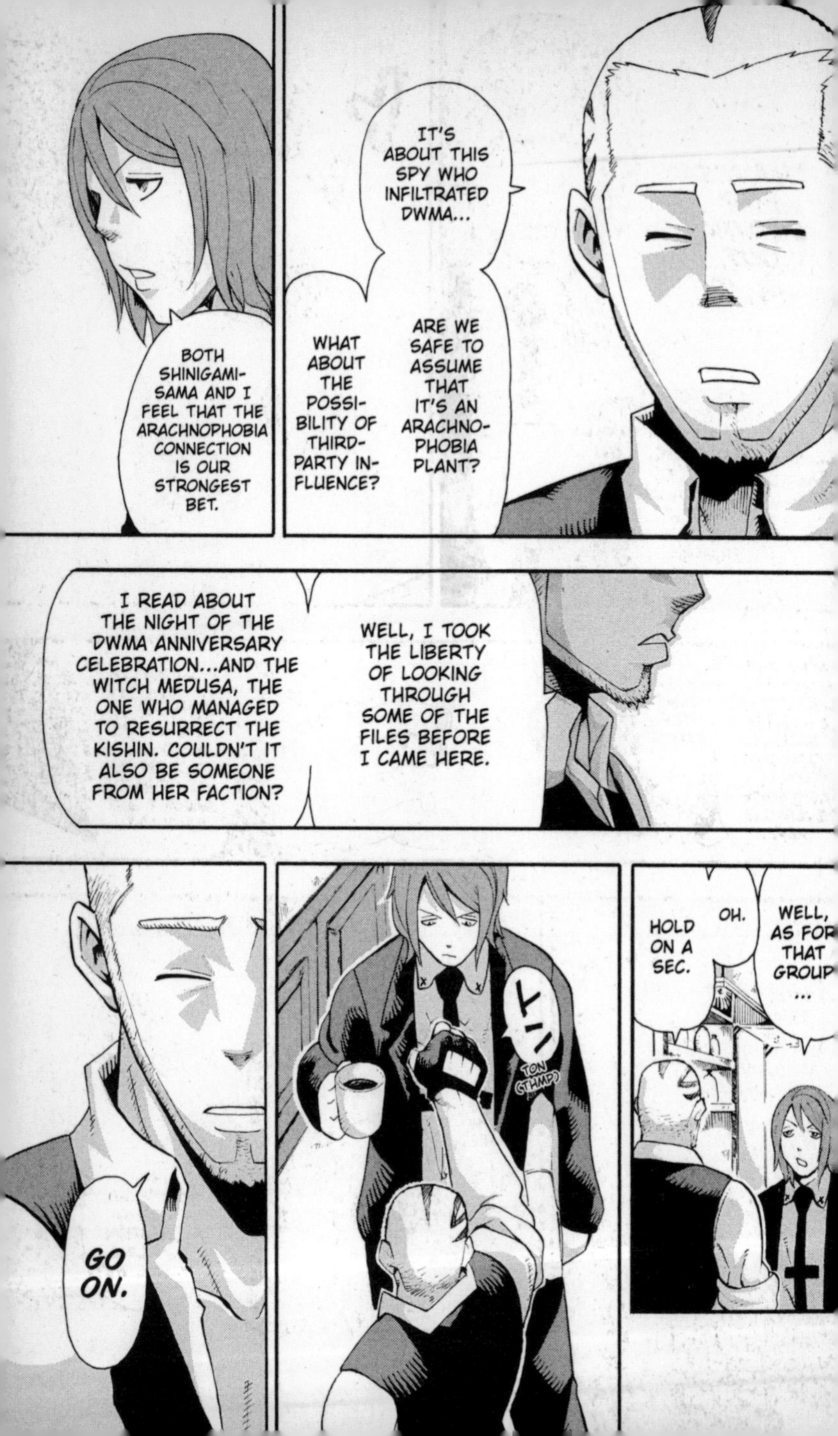
IT'S ABOUT THIS SPY WHO INFILTRATED DWMA...
ARE WE SAFE TO ASSUME THAT IT'S AN ARACHNO-PHOBIA PLANT?
WHAT ABOUT THE POSSI-BILITY OF THIRD-PARTY IN-FLUENCE?
BOTH SHINIGAMI-SAMA AND I FEEL THAT THE ARACHNOPHOBIA CONNECTION IS OUR STRONGEST BET.
WELL, I TOOK THE LIBERTY OF LOOKING THROUGH SOME OF THE FILES BEFORE I CAME HERE.
I READ ABOUT THE NIGHT OF THE DWMA ANNIVERSARY CELEBRATION...AND THE WITCH MEDUSA, THE ONE WHO MANAGED TO RESURRECT THE KISHIN. COULDN'T IT ALSO BE SOMEONE FROM HER FACTION?
WELL, AS FOR THAT GROUP...
OH.
HOLD ON A SEC.
トン
TON (THMP)
GO ON.

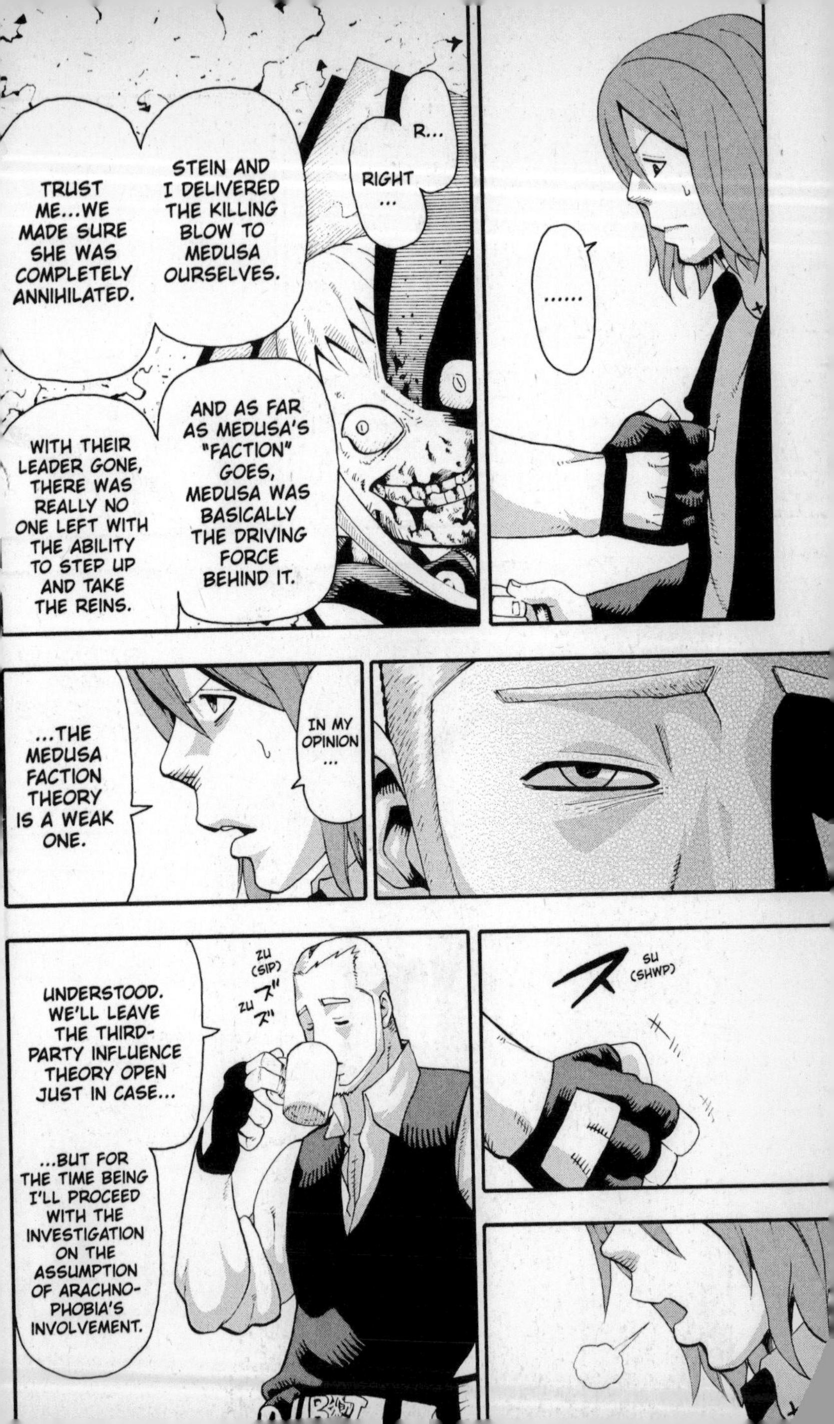
......
R...
RIGHT...
STEIN AND I DELIVERED THE KILLING BLOW TO MEDUSA OURSELVES.
TRUST ME...WE MADE SURE SHE WAS COMPLETELY ANNIHILATED.
AND AS FAR AS MEDUSA'S "FACTION" GOES, MEDUSA WAS BASICALLY THE DRIVING FORCE BEHIND IT.
WITH THEIR LEADER GONE, THERE WAS REALLY NO ONE LEFT WITH THE ABILITY TO STEP UP AND TAKE THE REINS.
IN MY OPINION...
...THE MEDUSA FACTION THEORY IS A WEAK ONE.
ス
SU (SHWP)
ズズ
ZU (SIP)
ZU
UNDERSTOOD. WE'LL LEAVE THE THIRD-PARTY INFLUENCE THEORY OPEN JUST IN CASE...
...BUT FOR THE TIME BEING I'LL PROCEED WITH THE INVESTIGATION ON THE ASSUMPTION OF ARACHNOPHOBIA'S INVOLVEMENT.

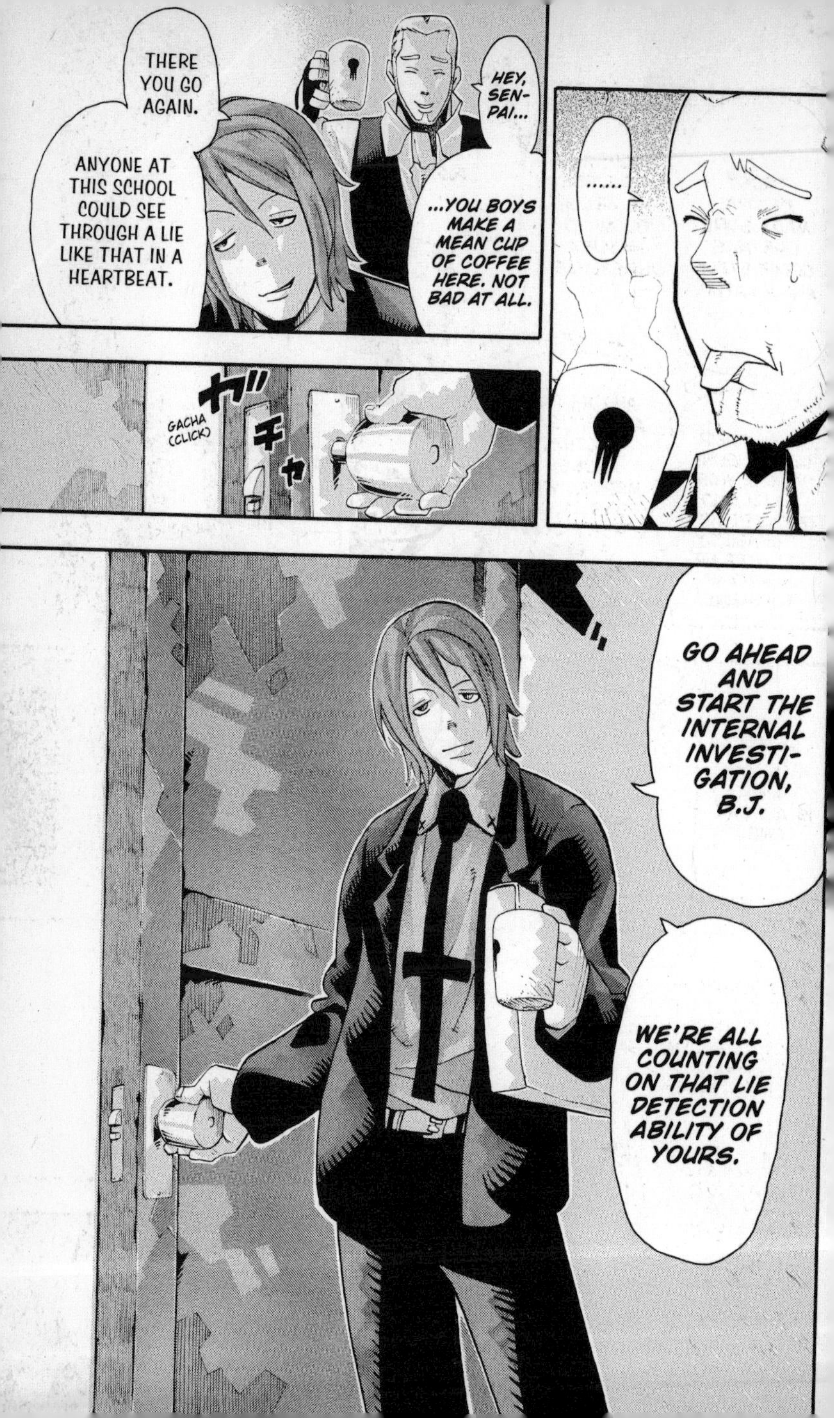
......
HEY, SEN-PAI...
...YOU BOYS MAKE A MEAN CUP OF COFFEE HERE. NOT BAD AT ALL.
THERE YOU GO AGAIN.
ANYONE AT THIS SCHOOL COULD SEE THROUGH A LIE LIKE THAT IN A HEARTBEAT.
ガチャ
GACHA (CLICK)
GO AHEAD AND START THE INTERNAL INVESTI-GATION, B.J.
WE'RE ALL COUNTING ON THAT LIE DETECTION ABILITY OF YOURS.

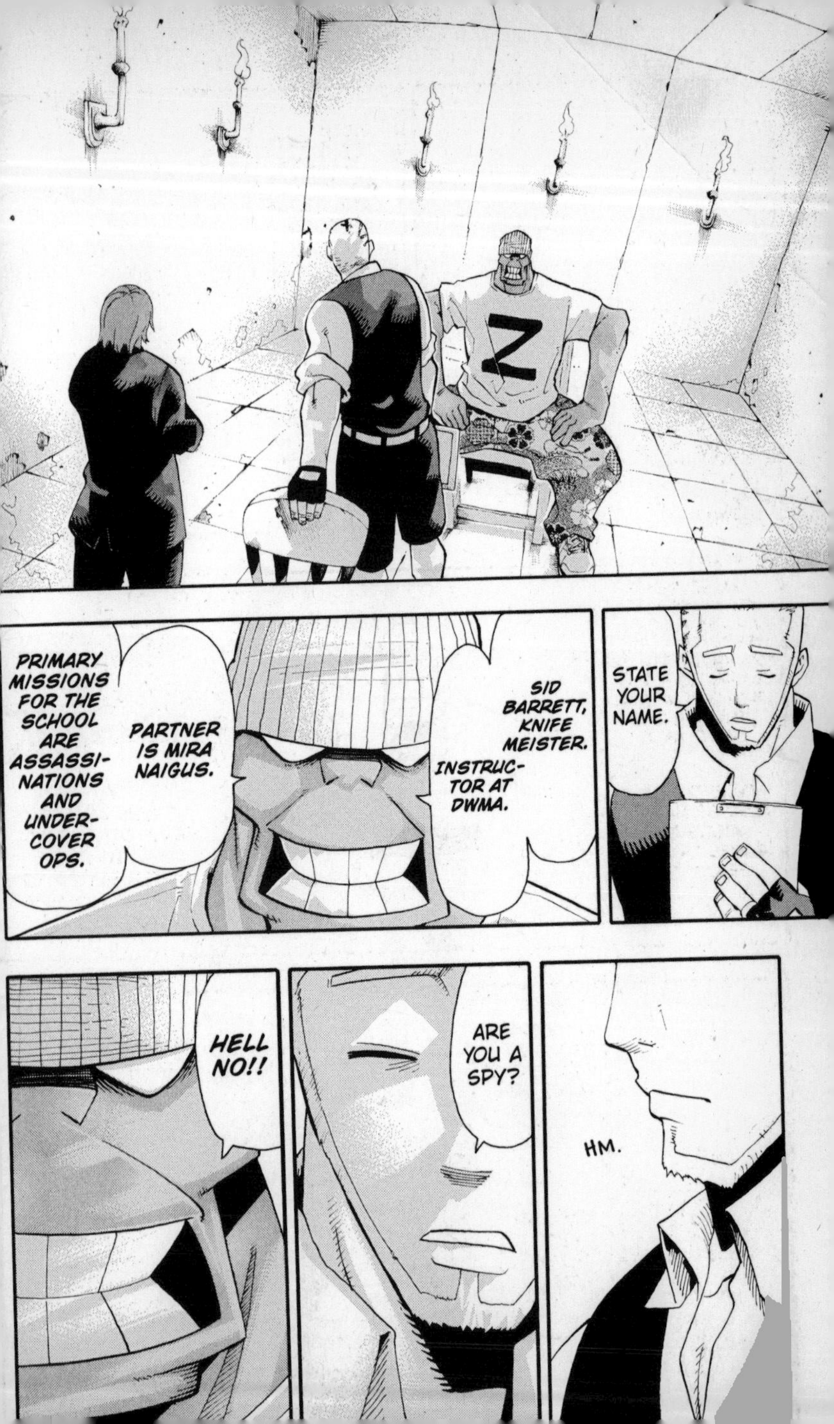
STATE YOUR NAME.
SID BARRETT, KNIFE MEISTER.
INSTRUCTOR AT DWMA.
PARTNER IS MIRA NAIGUS.
PRIMARY MISSIONS FOR THE SCHOOL ARE ASSASSINATIONS AND UNDERCOVER OPS.
HM.
ARE YOU A SPY?
HELL NO!!

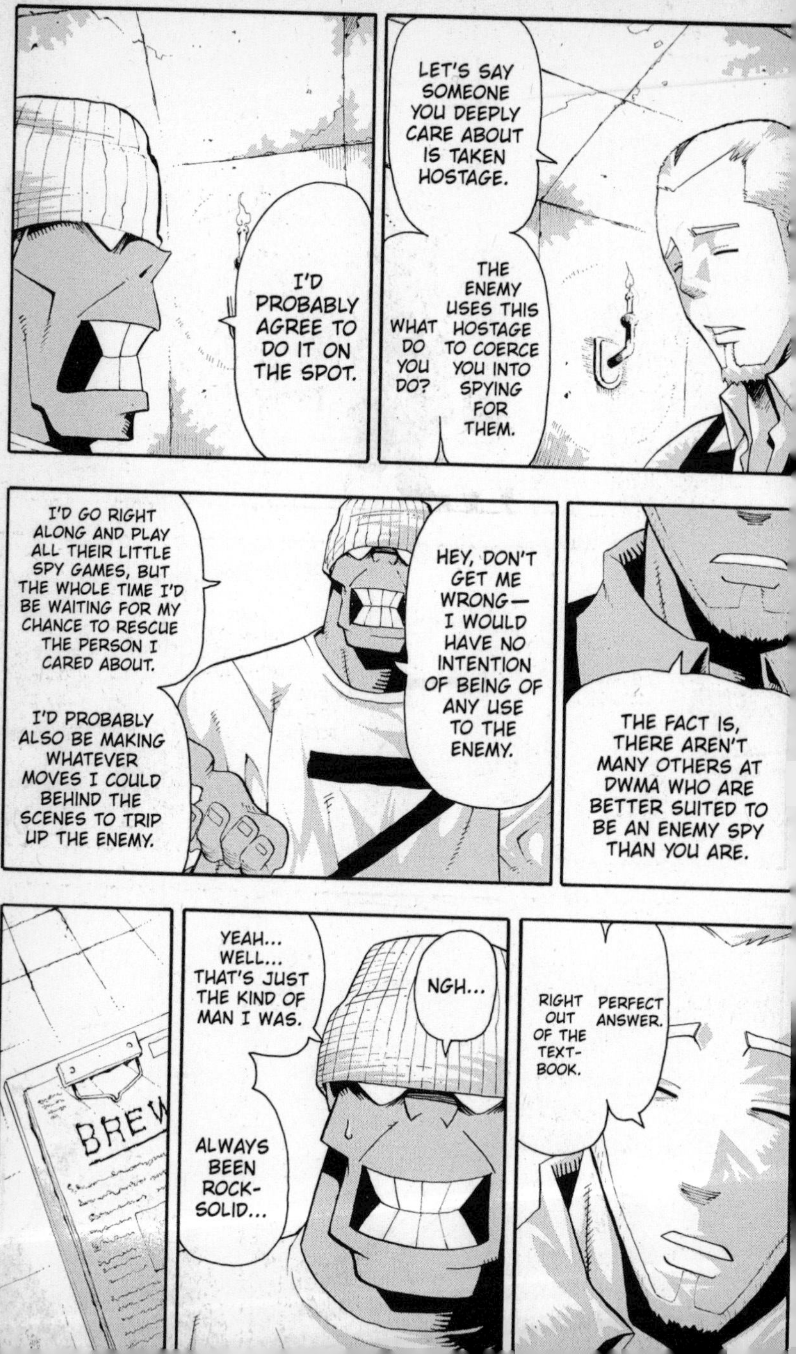
LET'S SAY SOMEONE YOU DEEPLY CARE ABOUT IS TAKEN HOSTAGE.
THE ENEMY USES THIS HOSTAGE TO COERCE YOU INTO SPYING FOR THEM.
WHAT DO YOU DO?
I'D PROBABLY AGREE TO DO IT ON THE SPOT.
THE FACT IS, THERE AREN'T MANY OTHERS AT DWMA WHO ARE BETTER SUITED TO BE AN ENEMY SPY THAN YOU ARE.
HEY, DON'T GET ME WRONG— I WOULD HAVE NO INTENTION OF BEING OF ANY USE TO THE ENEMY.
I'D GO RIGHT ALONG AND PLAY ALL THEIR LITTLE SPY GAMES, BUT THE WHOLE TIME I'D BE WAITING FOR MY CHANCE TO RESCUE THE PERSON I CARED ABOUT.
I'D PROBABLY ALSO BE MAKING WHATEVER MOVES I COULD BEHIND THE SCENES TO TRIP UP THE ENEMY.
PERFECT ANSWER.
RIGHT OUT OF THE TEXT-BOOK.
NGH...
YEAH... WELL... THAT'S JUST THE KIND OF MAN I WAS.
ALWAYS BEEN ROCK-SOLID...
BREW

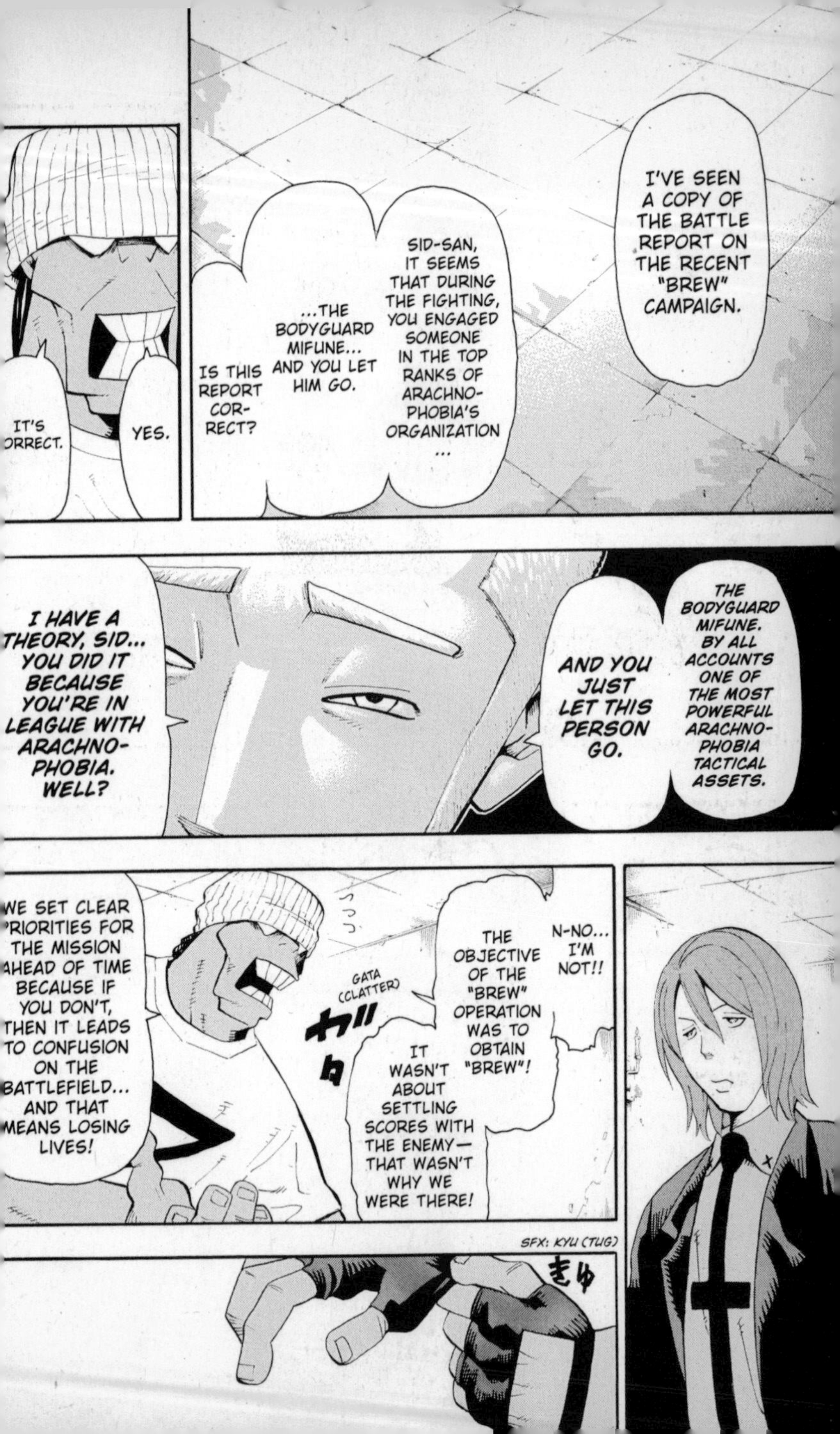
I'VE SEEN A COPY OF THE BATTLE REPORT ON THE RECENT "BREW" CAMPAIGN.
SID-SAN, IT SEEMS THAT DURING THE FIGHTING, YOU ENGAGED SOMEONE IN THE TOP RANKS OF ARACHNO-PHOBIA'S ORGANIZATION ...
...THE BODYGUARD MIFUNE... AND YOU LET HIM GO.
IS THIS REPORT COR-RECT?
YES.
IT'S ORRECT.
THE BODYGUARD MIFUNE. BY ALL ACCOUNTS ONE OF THE MOST POWERFUL ARACHNO-PHOBIA TACTICAL ASSETS.
AND YOU JUST LET THIS PERSON GO.
I HAVE A THEORY, SID... YOU DID IT BECAUSE YOU'RE IN LEAGUE WITH ARACHNO-PHOBIA. WELL?
N-NO... I'M NOT!!
THE OBJECTIVE OF THE "BREW" OPERATION WAS TO OBTAIN "BREW"!
IT WASN'T ABOUT SETTLING SCORES WITH THE ENEMY— THAT WASN'T WHY WE WERE THERE!
GATA (CLATTER)
WE SET CLEAR RIORITIES FOR THE MISSION HEAD OF TIME BECAUSE IF YOU DON'T, THEN IT LEADS TO CONFUSION ON THE BATTLEFIELD... AND THAT MEANS LOSING LIVES!
SFX: KYU (TUG)

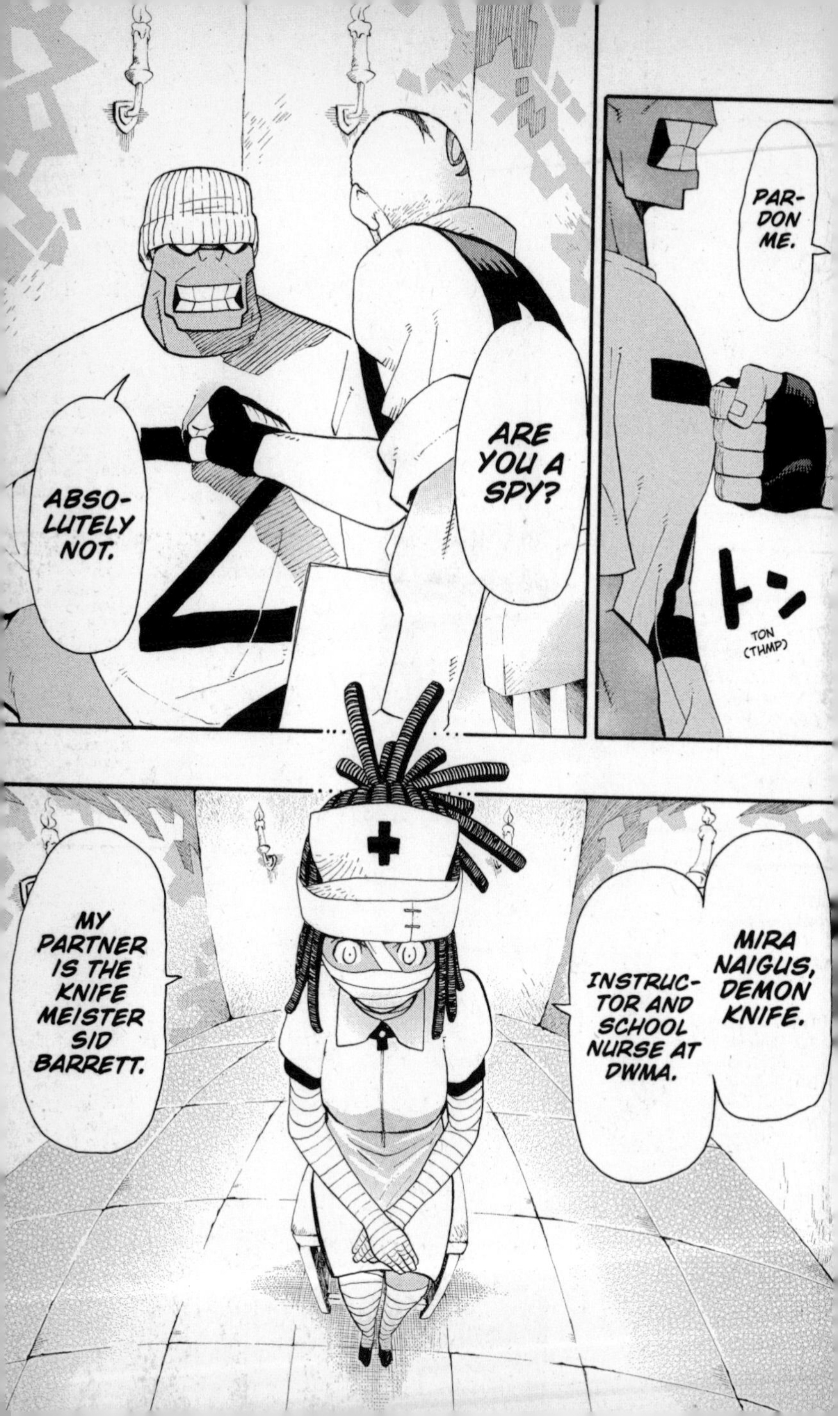
PAR-DON ME.
トン
TON (THMP)
ARE YOU A SPY?
ABSO-LUTELY NOT.
MIRA NAIGUS, DEMON KNIFE.
INSTRUC-TOR AND SCHOOL NURSE AT DWMA.
MY PARTNER IS THE KNIFE MEISTER SID BARRETT.

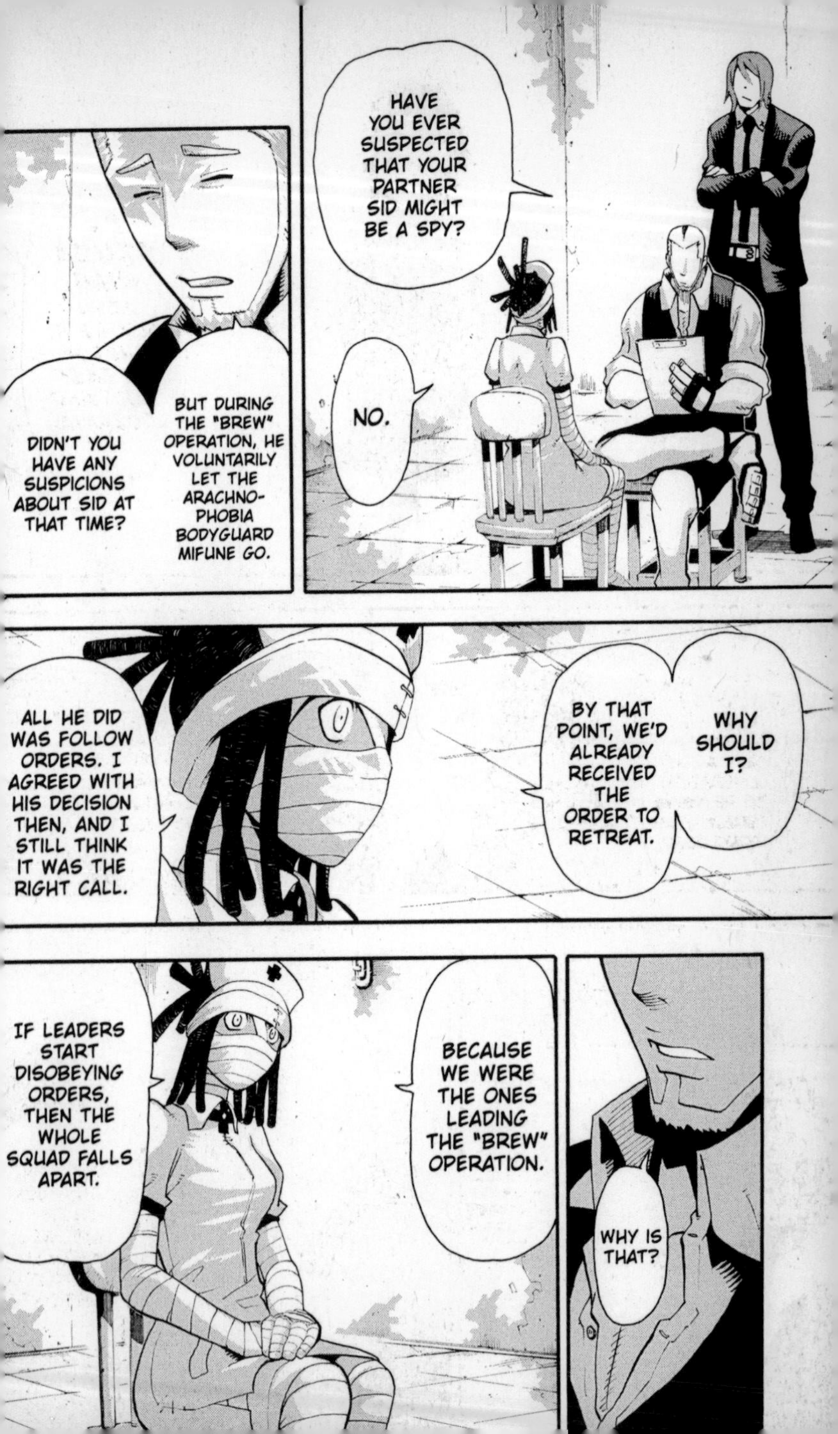
HAVE YOU EVER SUSPECTED THAT YOUR PARTNER SID MIGHT BE A SPY?
NO.
BUT DURING THE "BREW" OPERATION, HE VOLUNTARILY LET THE ARACHNO-PHOBIA BODYGUARD MIFUNE GO.
DIDN'T YOU HAVE ANY SUSPICIONS ABOUT SID AT THAT TIME?
WHY SHOULD I?
BY THAT POINT, WE'D ALREADY RECEIVED THE ORDER TO RETREAT.
ALL HE DID WAS FOLLOW ORDERS. I AGREED WITH HIS DECISION THEN, AND I STILL THINK IT WAS THE RIGHT CALL.
WHY IS THAT?
BECAUSE WE WERE THE ONES LEADING THE "BREW" OPERATION.
IF LEADERS START DISOBEYING ORDERS, THEN THE WHOLE SQUAD FALLS APART.

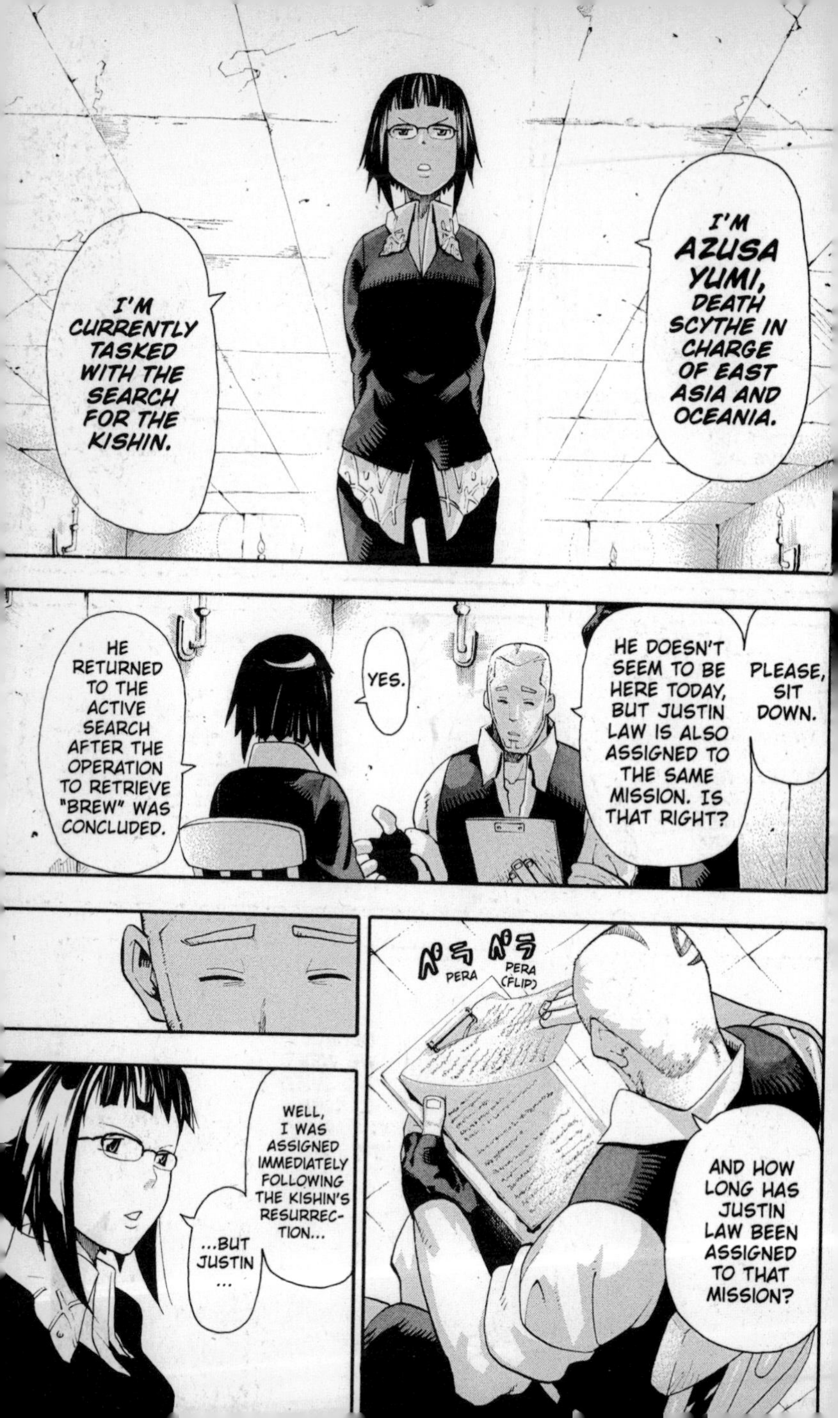
I'M AZUSA YUMI, DEATH SCYTHE IN CHARGE OF EAST ASIA AND OCEANIA.
I'M CURRENTLY TASKED WITH THE SEARCH FOR THE KISHIN.
PLEASE, SIT DOWN.
HE DOESN'T SEEM TO BE HERE TODAY, BUT JUSTIN LAW IS ALSO ASSIGNED TO THE SAME MISSION. IS THAT RIGHT?
YES.
HE RETURNED TO THE ACTIVE SEARCH AFTER THE OPERATION TO RETRIEVE "BREW" WAS CONCLUDED.
ペラ ペラ
PERA PERA (FLIP)
AND HOW LONG HAS JUSTIN LAW BEEN ASSIGNED TO THAT MISSION?
WELL, I WAS ASSIGNED IMMEDIATELY FOLLOWING THE KISHIN'S RESURREC-TION...
...BUT JUSTIN ...

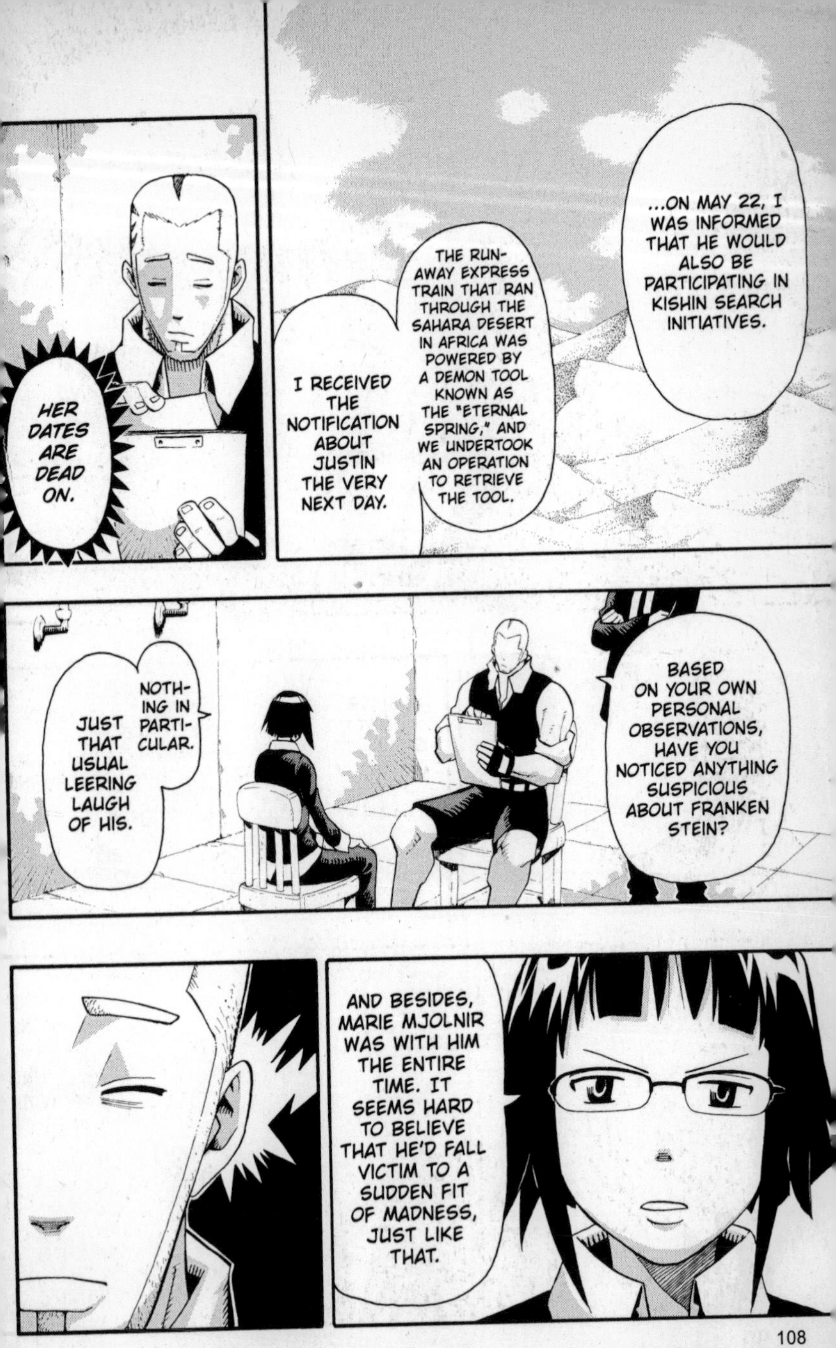
...ON MAY 22, I WAS INFORMED THAT HE WOULD ALSO BE PARTICIPATING IN KISHIN SEARCH INITIATIVES.
THE RUN-AWAY EXPRESS TRAIN THAT RAN THROUGH THE SAHARA DESERT IN AFRICA WAS POWERED BY A DEMON TOOL KNOWN AS THE "ETERNAL SPRING," AND WE UNDERTOOK AN OPERATION TO RETRIEVE THE TOOL.
I RECEIVED THE NOTIFICATION ABOUT JUSTIN THE VERY NEXT DAY.
HER DATES ARE DEAD ON.
BASED ON YOUR OWN PERSONAL OBSERVATIONS, HAVE YOU NOTICED ANYTHING SUSPICIOUS ABOUT FRANKEN STEIN?
NOTHING IN PARTICULAR.
JUST THAT USUAL LEERING LAUGH OF HIS.
AND BESIDES, MARIE MJOLNIR WAS WITH HIM THE ENTIRE TIME. IT SEEMS HARD TO BELIEVE THAT HE'D FALL VICTIM TO A SUDDEN FIT OF MADNESS, JUST LIKE THAT.

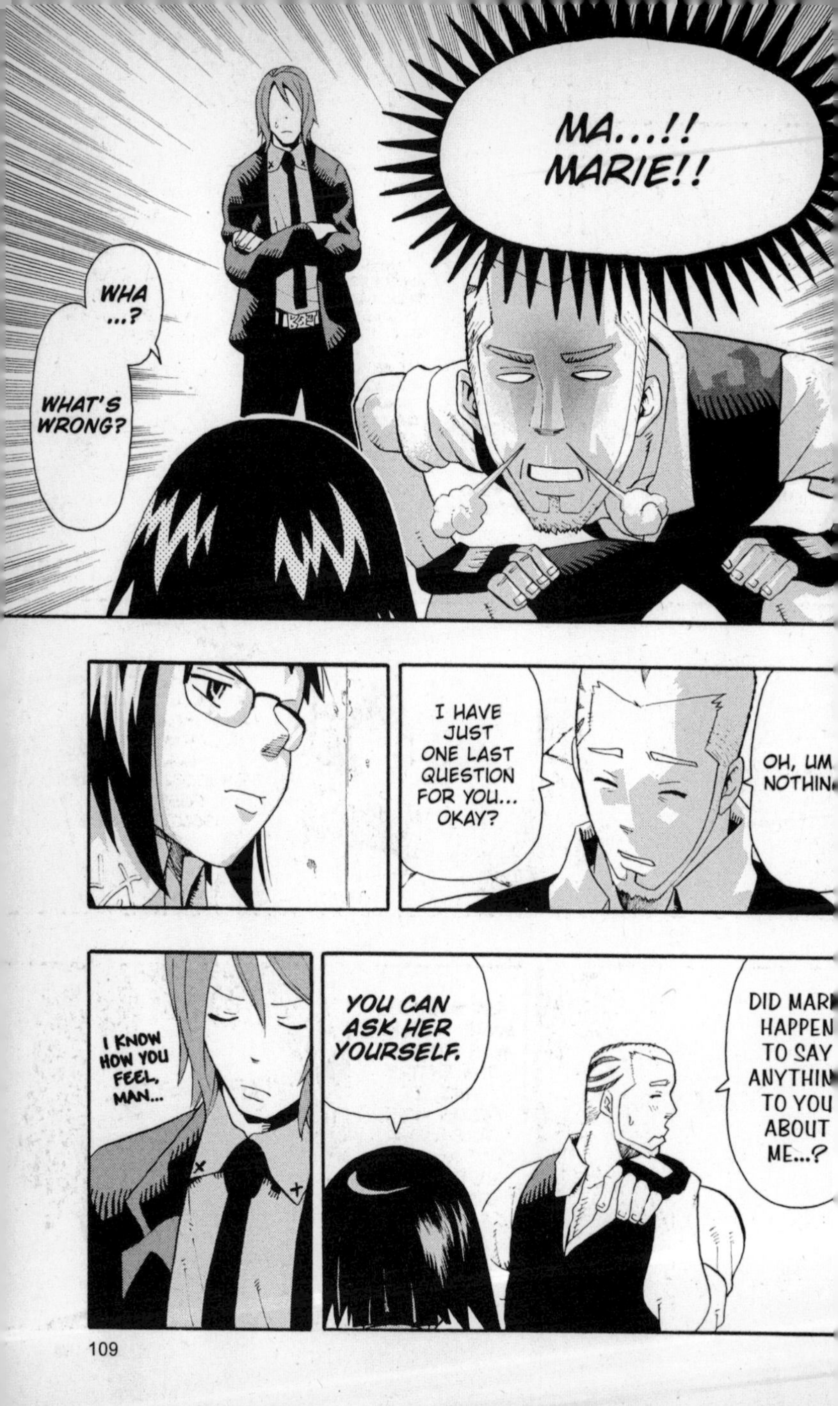
MA...!! MARIE!!
WHA...?
WHAT'S WRONG?
OH, UM NOTHIN
I HAVE JUST ONE LAST QUESTION FOR YOU... OKAY?
DID MAR HAPPEN TO SAY ANYTHIN TO YOU ABOUT ME...?
YOU CAN ASK HER YOURSELF.
I KNOW HOW YOU FEEL, MAN...

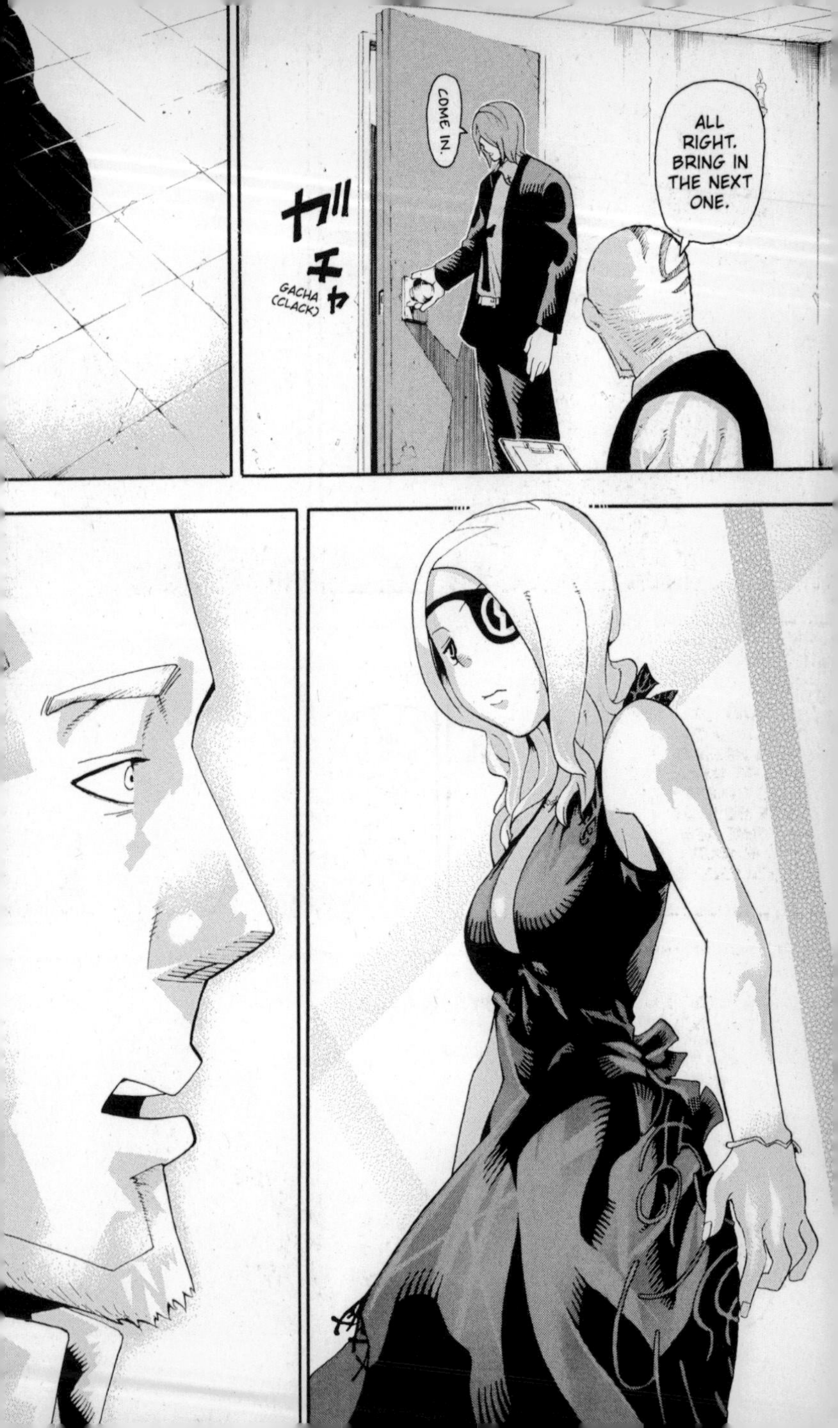
ALL RIGHT. BRING IN THE NEXT ONE.
COME IN.
ガチャ
GACHA (CLACK)

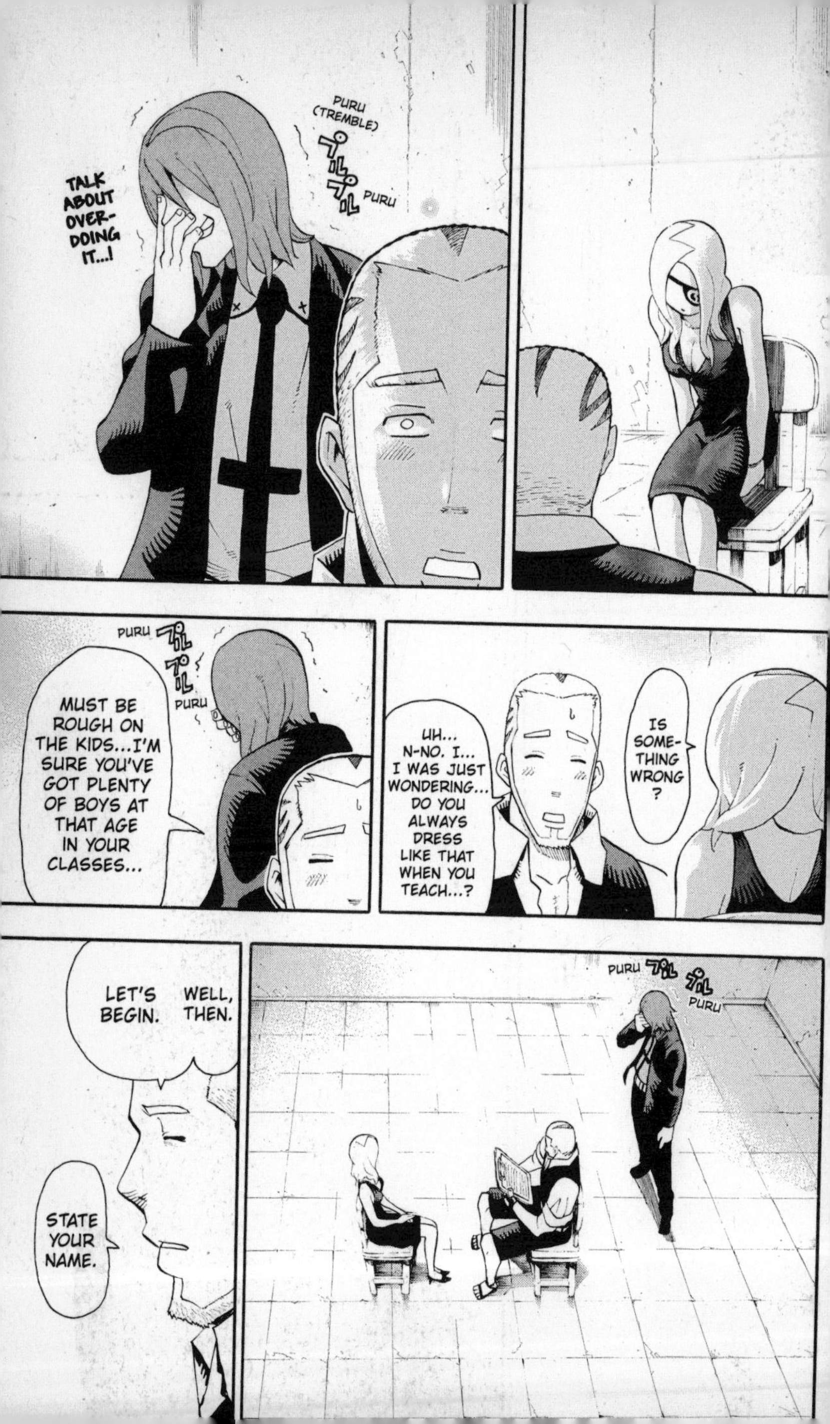
PURU (TREMBLE)
プルプル
PURU
TALK ABOUT OVER-DOING IT...!
IS SOME-THING WRONG?
UH... N-NO. I... I WAS JUST WONDERING... DO YOU ALWAYS DRESS LIKE THAT WHEN YOU TEACH...?
PURU
プルプル
PURU
MUST BE ROUGH ON THE KIDS...I'M SURE YOU'VE GOT PLENTY OF BOYS AT THAT AGE IN YOUR CLASSES...
PURU
プルプル
PURU
WELL, THEN.
LET'S BEGIN.
STATE YOUR NAME.

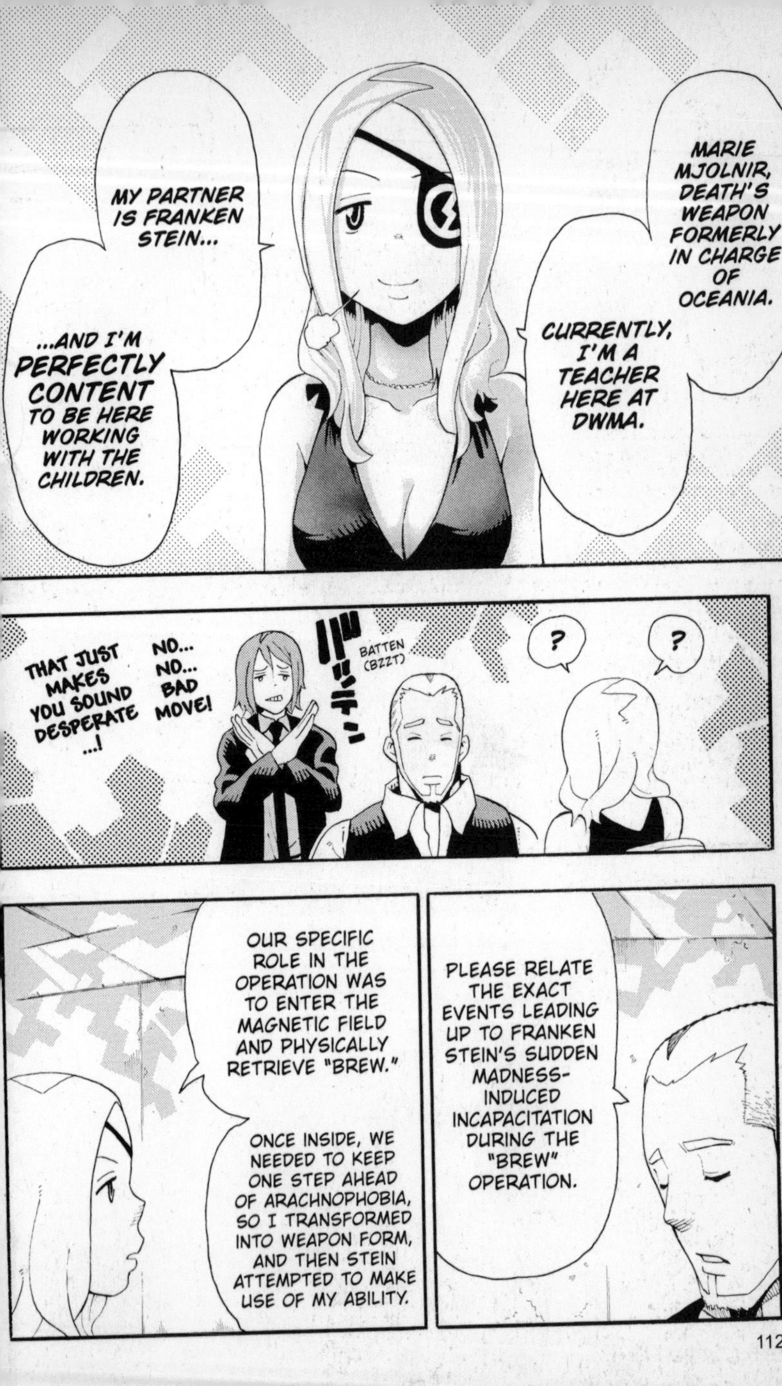
MARIE MJOLNIR, DEATH'S WEAPON FORMERLY IN CHARGE OF OCEANIA.
CURRENTLY, I'M A TEACHER HERE AT DWMA.
MY PARTNER IS FRANKEN STEIN...
...AND I'M **PERFECTLY CONTENT** TO BE HERE WORKING WITH THE CHILDREN.
?
?
BATTEN (BZZT)
NO... NO... BAD MOVE!
THAT JUST MAKES YOU SOUND DESPERATE ...!
PLEASE RELATE THE EXACT EVENTS LEADING UP TO FRANKEN STEIN'S SUDDEN MADNESS-INDUCED INCAPACITATION DURING THE "BREW" OPERATION.
OUR SPECIFIC ROLE IN THE OPERATION WAS TO ENTER THE MAGNETIC FIELD AND PHYSICALLY RETRIEVE "BREW."
ONCE INSIDE, WE NEEDED TO KEEP ONE STEP AHEAD OF ARACHNOPHOBIA, SO I TRANSFORMED INTO WEAPON FORM, AND THEN STEIN ATTEMPTED TO MAKE USE OF MY ABILITY.

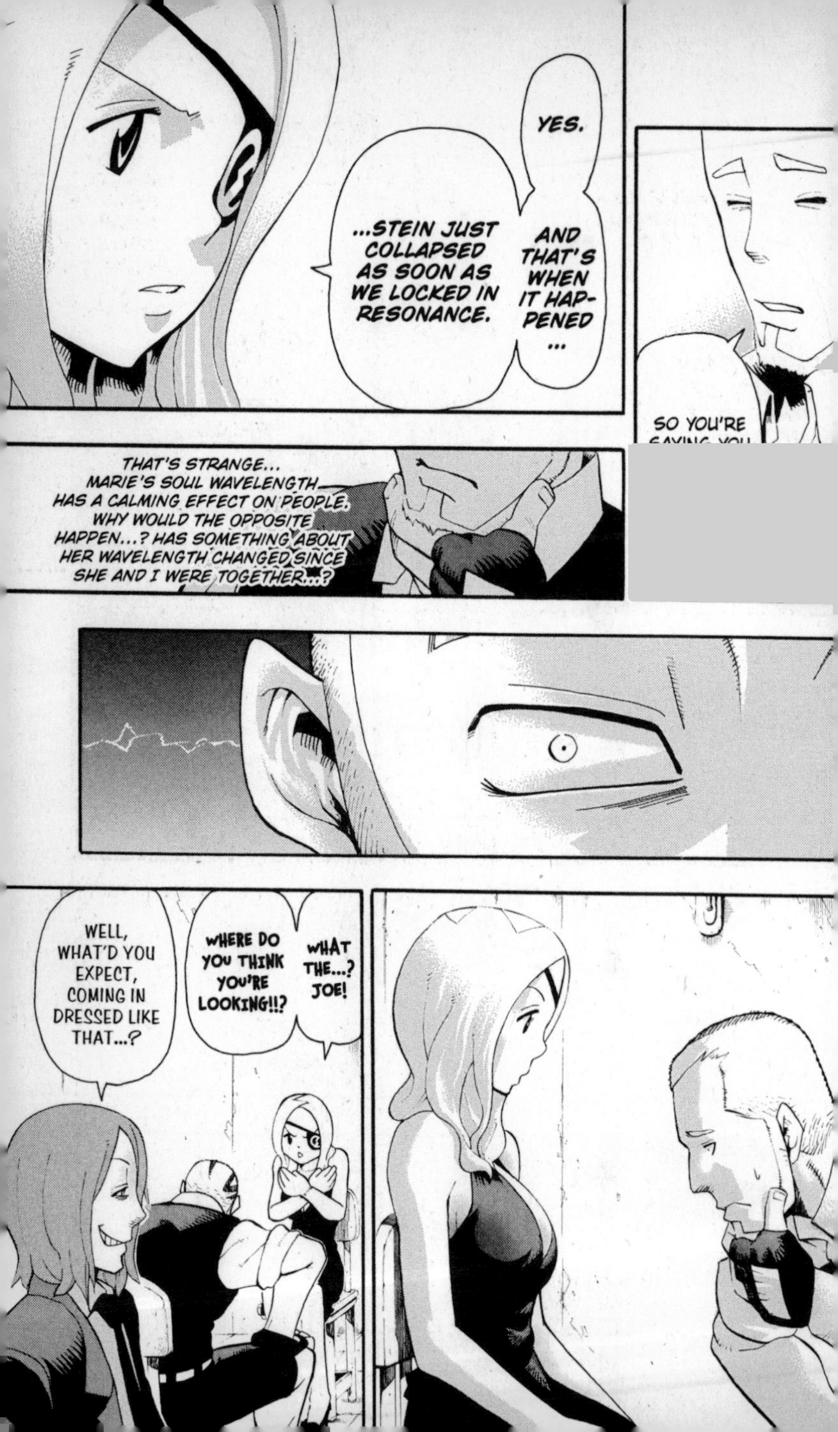
SO YOU'RE
YES.
AND THAT'S WHEN IT HAPPENED...
...STEIN JUST COLLAPSED AS SOON AS WE LOCKED IN RESONANCE.
THAT'S STRANGE... MARIE'S SOUL WAVELENGTH HAS A CALMING EFFECT ON PEOPLE. WHY WOULD THE OPPOSITE HAPPEN...? HAS SOMETHING ABOUT HER WAVELENGTH CHANGED SINCE SHE AND I WERE TOGETHER...?
WHAT THE...? JOE!
WHERE DO YOU THINK YOU'RE LOOKING!!?
WELL, WHAT'D YOU EXPECT, COMING IN DRESSED LIKE THAT...?

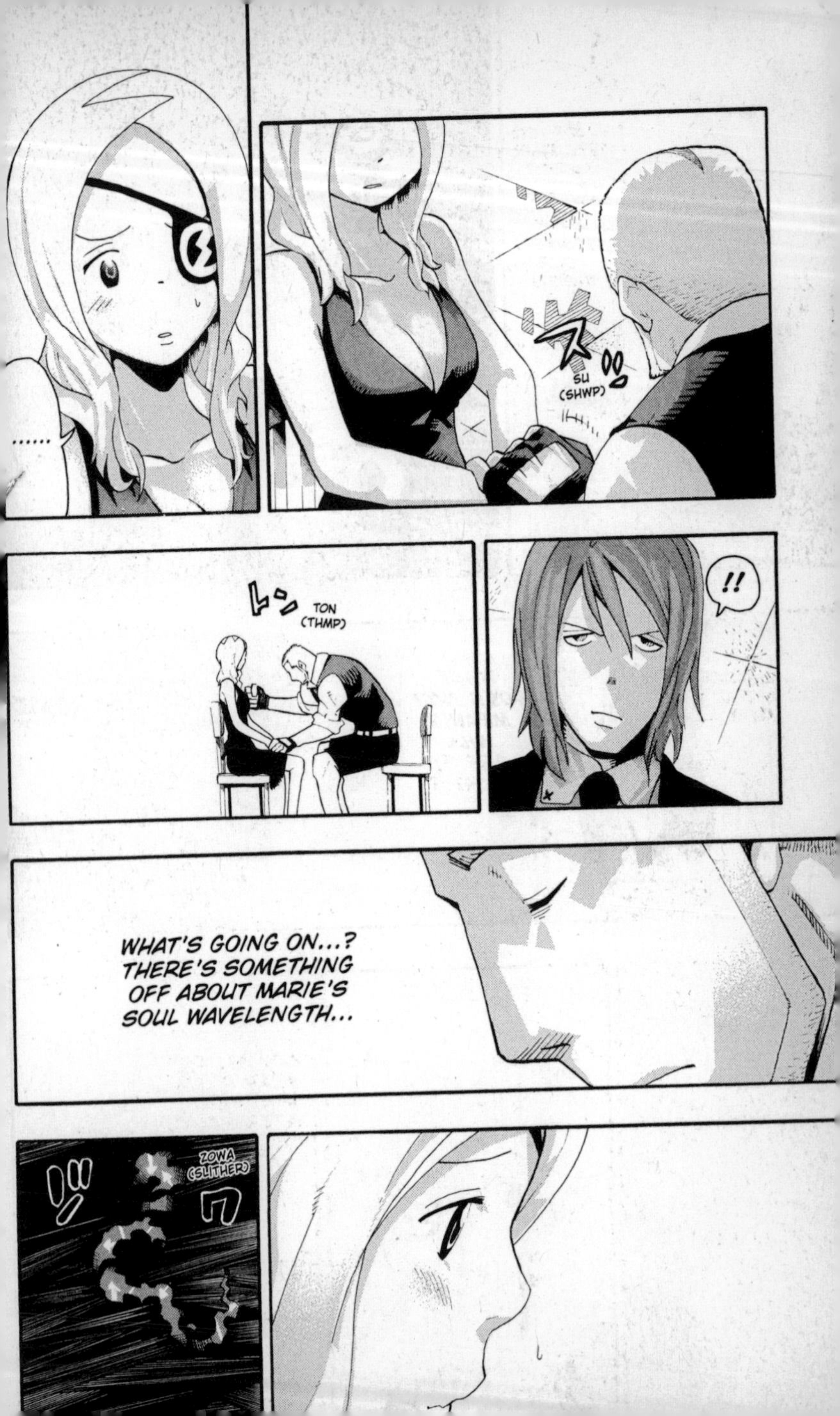

SU (SHWP)
......
!!
TON (THMP)
WHAT'S GOING ON...? THERE'S SOMETHING OFF ABOUT MARIE'S SOUL WAVELENGTH...
ZOWA (SLITHER)

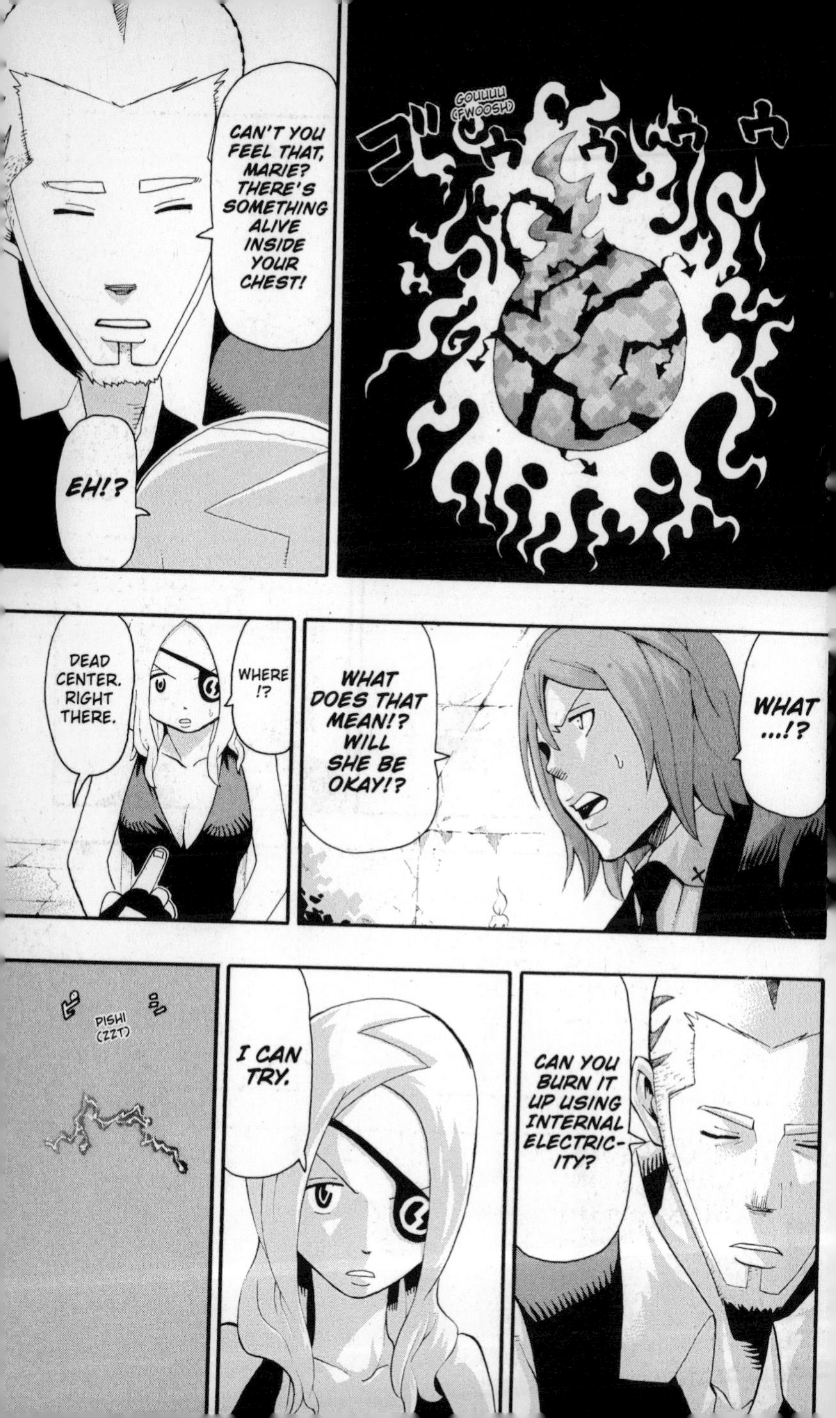
GOUUUU (FWOOSH)
CAN'T YOU FEEL THAT, MARIE? THERE'S SOMETHING ALIVE INSIDE YOUR CHEST!
EH!?
WHAT ...!?
WHAT DOES THAT MEAN!? WILL SHE BE OKAY!?
WHERE !?
DEAD CENTER. RIGHT THERE.
CAN YOU BURN IT UP USING INTERNAL ELECTRIC-ITY?
I CAN TRY.
PISHI (ZZT)

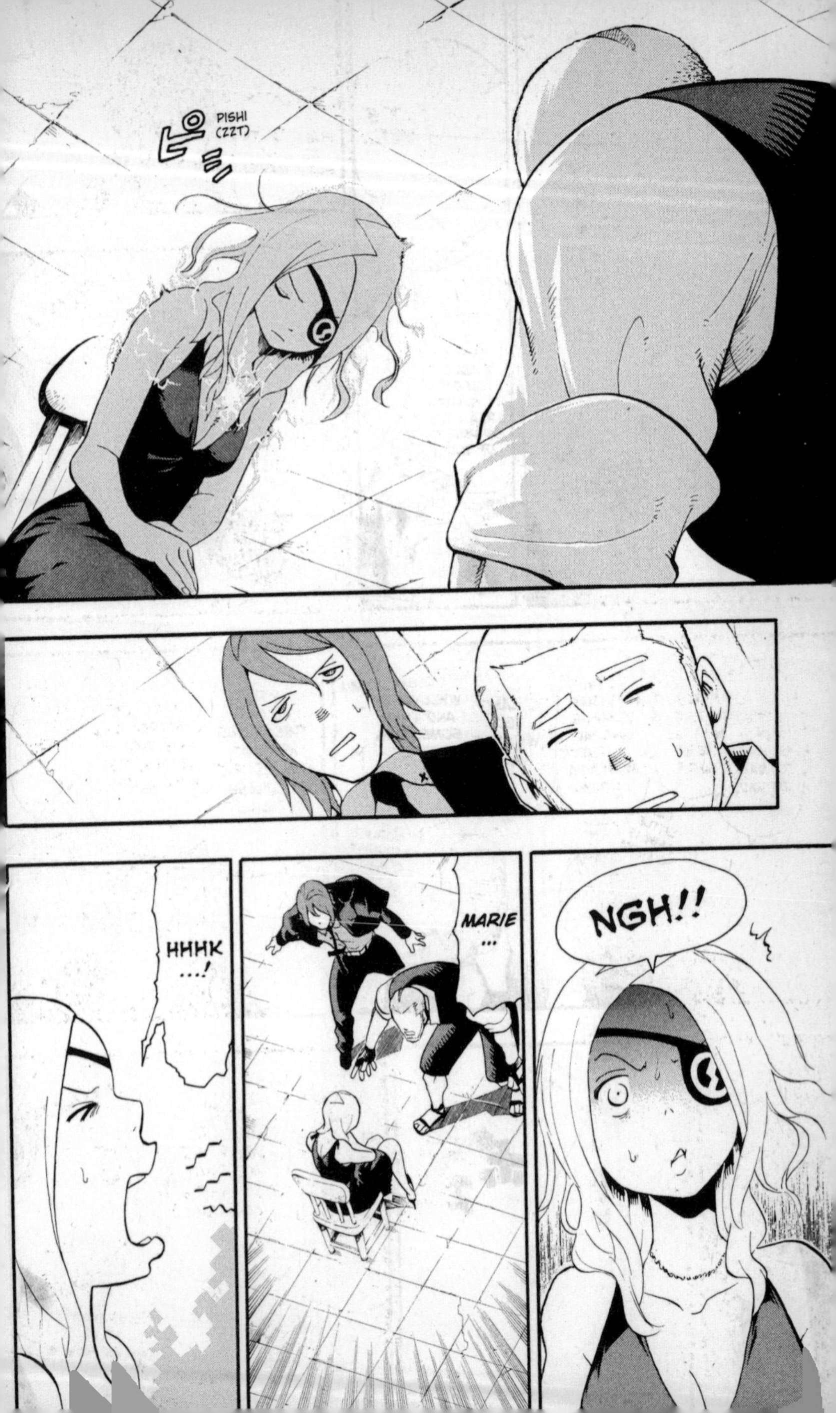
PISHI (ZZT)
NGH!!
MARIE ...
HHHK ...!

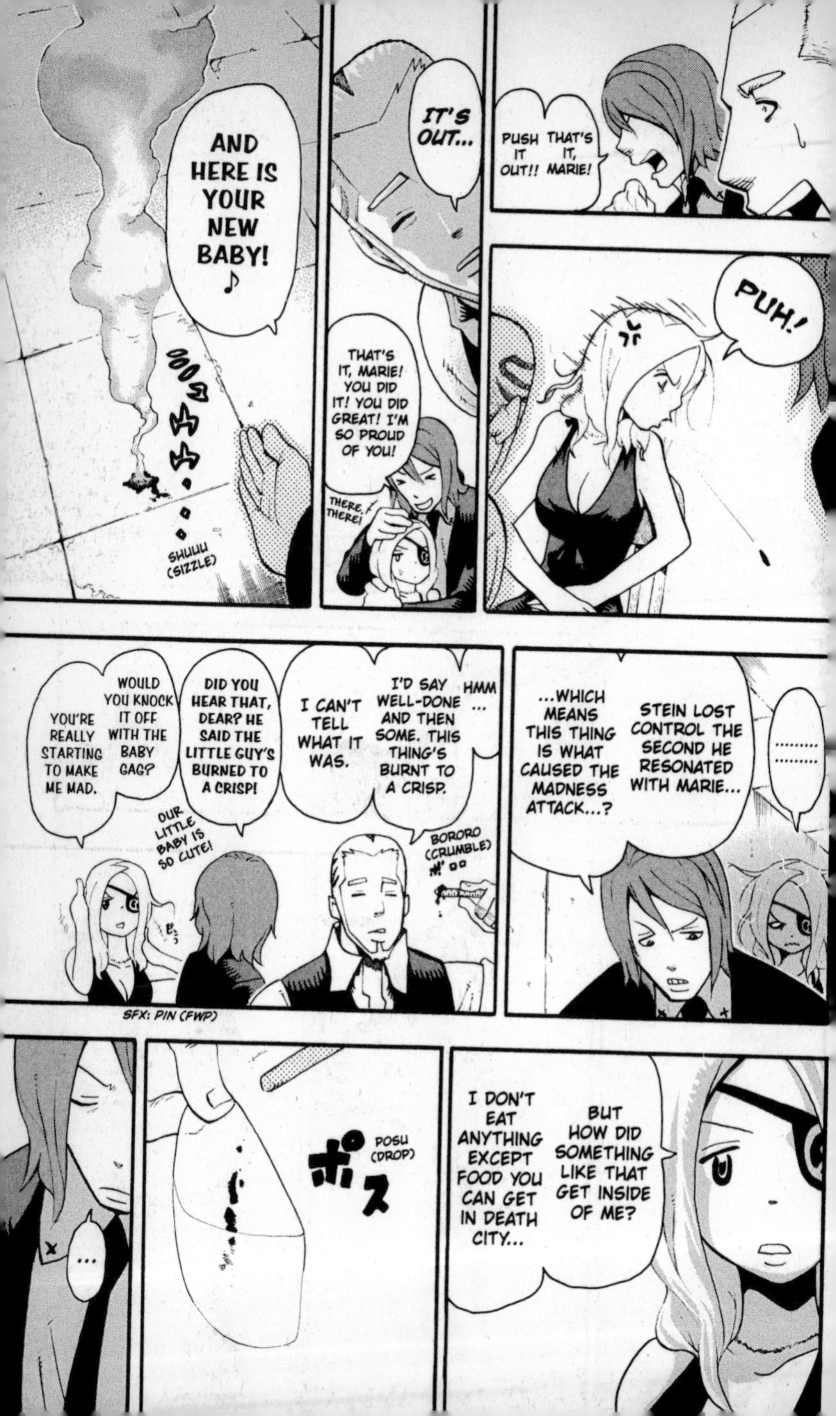
THAT'S IT, MARIE!
PUSH IT OUT!!
PUH!
IT'S OUT...
THAT'S IT, MARIE! YOU DID IT! YOU DID GREAT! I'M SO PROUD OF YOU!
THERE, THERE!
AND HERE IS YOUR NEW BABY! ♪
SHUUU (SIZZLE)
....
STEIN LOST CONTROL THE SECOND HE RESONATED WITH MARIE...
...WHICH MEANS THIS THING IS WHAT CAUSED THE MADNESS ATTACK...?
HMM ...
I'D SAY WELL-DONE AND THEN SOME. THIS THING'S BURNT TO A CRISP.
I CAN'T TELL WHAT IT WAS.
BORORO (CRUMBLE)
DID YOU HEAR THAT, DEAR? HE SAID THE LITTLE GUY'S BURNED TO A CRISP!
OUR LITTLE BABY IS SO CUTE!
WOULD YOU KNOCK IT OFF WITH THE BABY GAG?
YOU'RE REALLY STARTING TO MAKE ME MAD.
SFX: PIN (FWP)
BUT HOW DID SOMETHING LIKE THAT GET INSIDE OF ME?
I DON'T EAT ANYTHING EXCEPT FOOD YOU CAN GET IN DEATH CITY...
POSU (DROP)
...

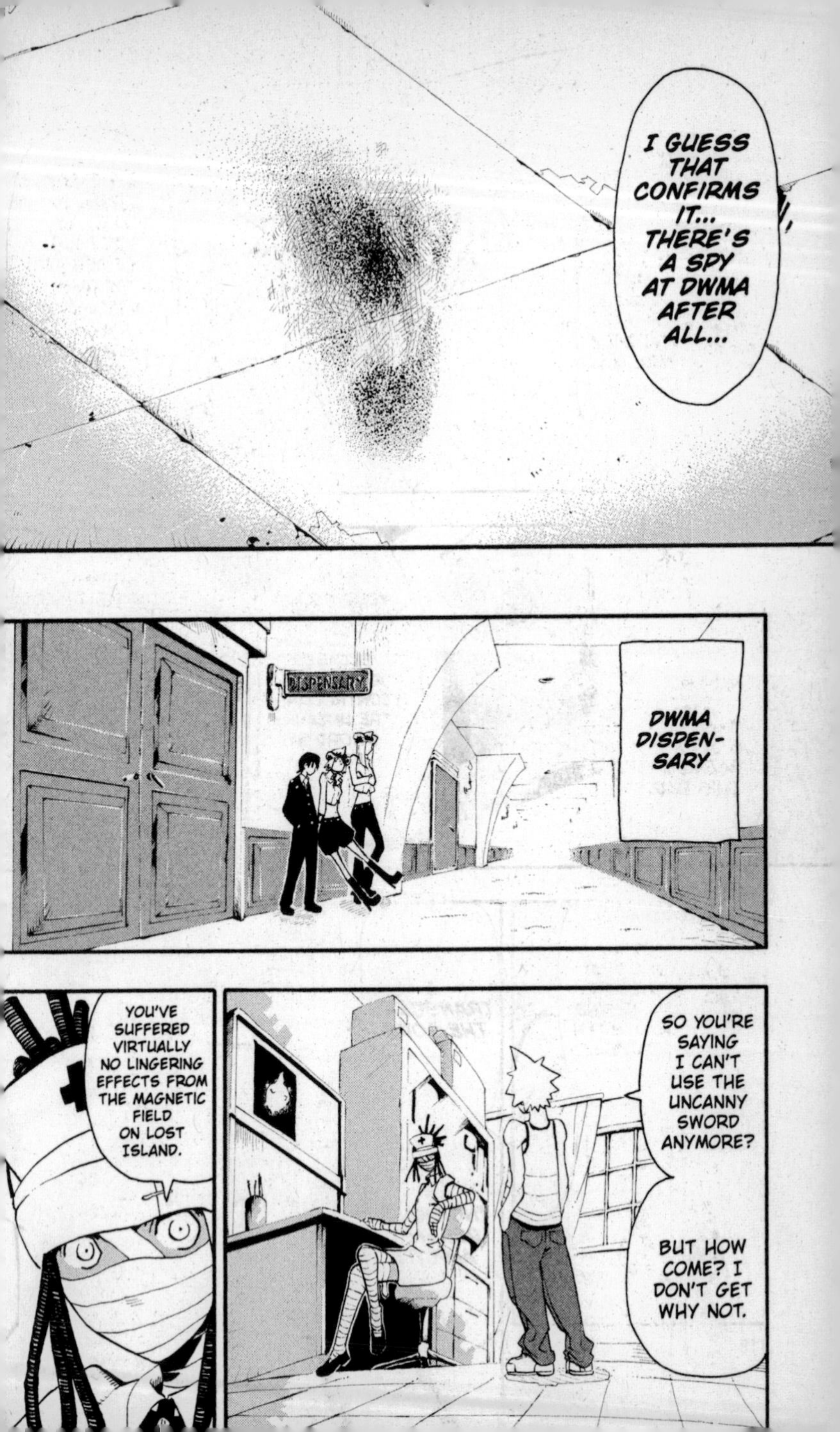
I GUESS THAT CONFIRMS IT... THERE'S A SPY AT DWMA AFTER ALL...
DWMA DISPEN-SARY
DISPENSARY
SO YOU'RE SAYING I CAN'T USE THE UNCANNY SWORD ANYMORE?
BUT HOW COME? I DON'T GET WHY NOT.
YOU'VE SUFFERED VIRTUALLY NO LINGERING EFFECTS FROM THE MAGNETIC FIELD ON LOST ISLAND.

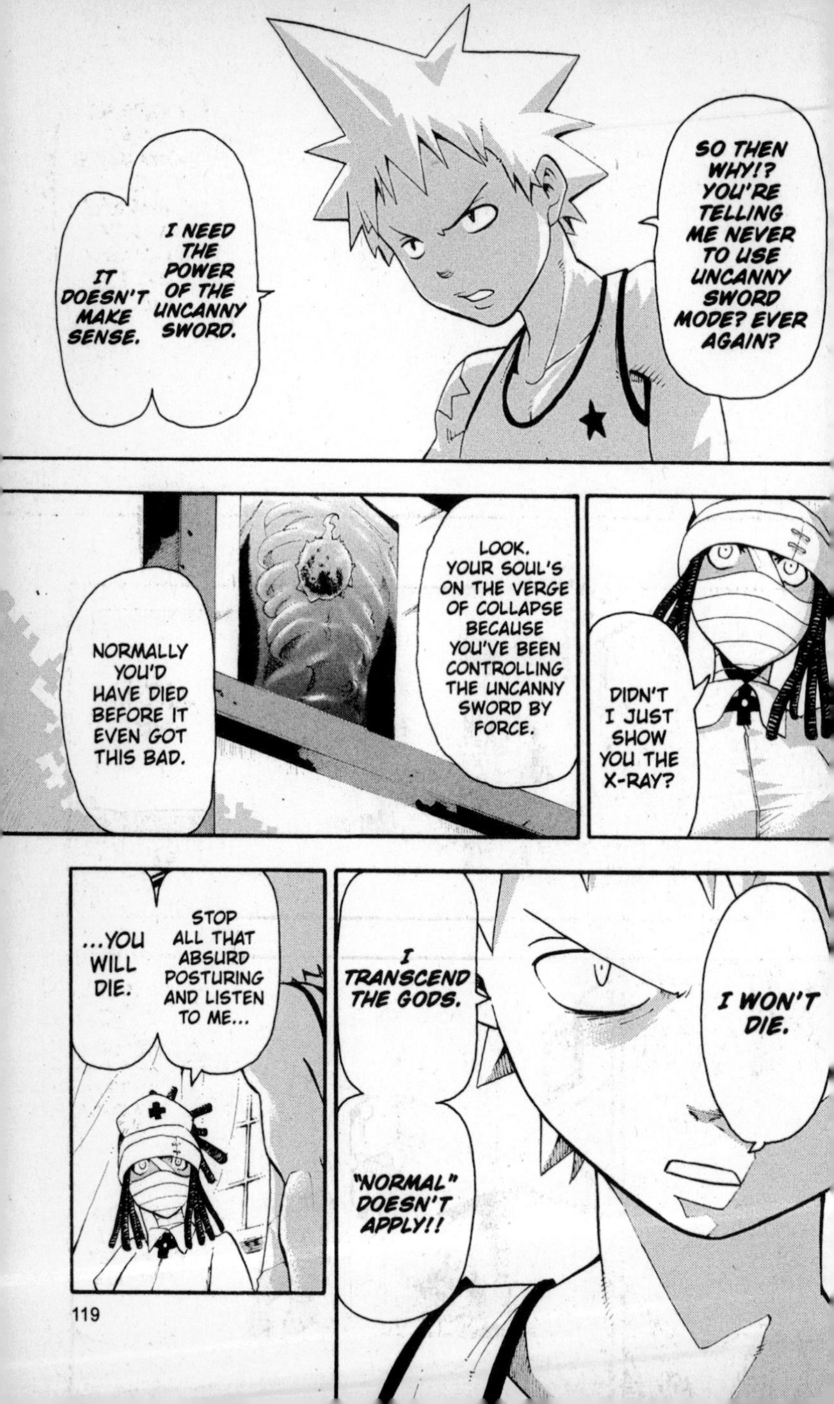
SO THEN WHY!? YOU'RE TELLING ME NEVER TO USE UNCANNY SWORD MODE? EVER AGAIN?
I NEED THE POWER OF THE UNCANNY SWORD.
IT DOESN'T MAKE SENSE.
DIDN'T I JUST SHOW YOU THE X-RAY?
LOOK. YOUR SOUL'S ON THE VERGE OF COLLAPSE BECAUSE YOU'VE BEEN CONTROLLING THE UNCANNY SWORD BY FORCE.
NORMALLY YOU'D HAVE DIED BEFORE IT EVEN GOT THIS BAD.
I WON'T DIE.
I TRANSCEND THE GODS.
"NORMAL" DOESN'T APPLY!!
STOP ALL THAT ABSURD POSTURING AND LISTEN TO ME...
...YOU WILL DIE.

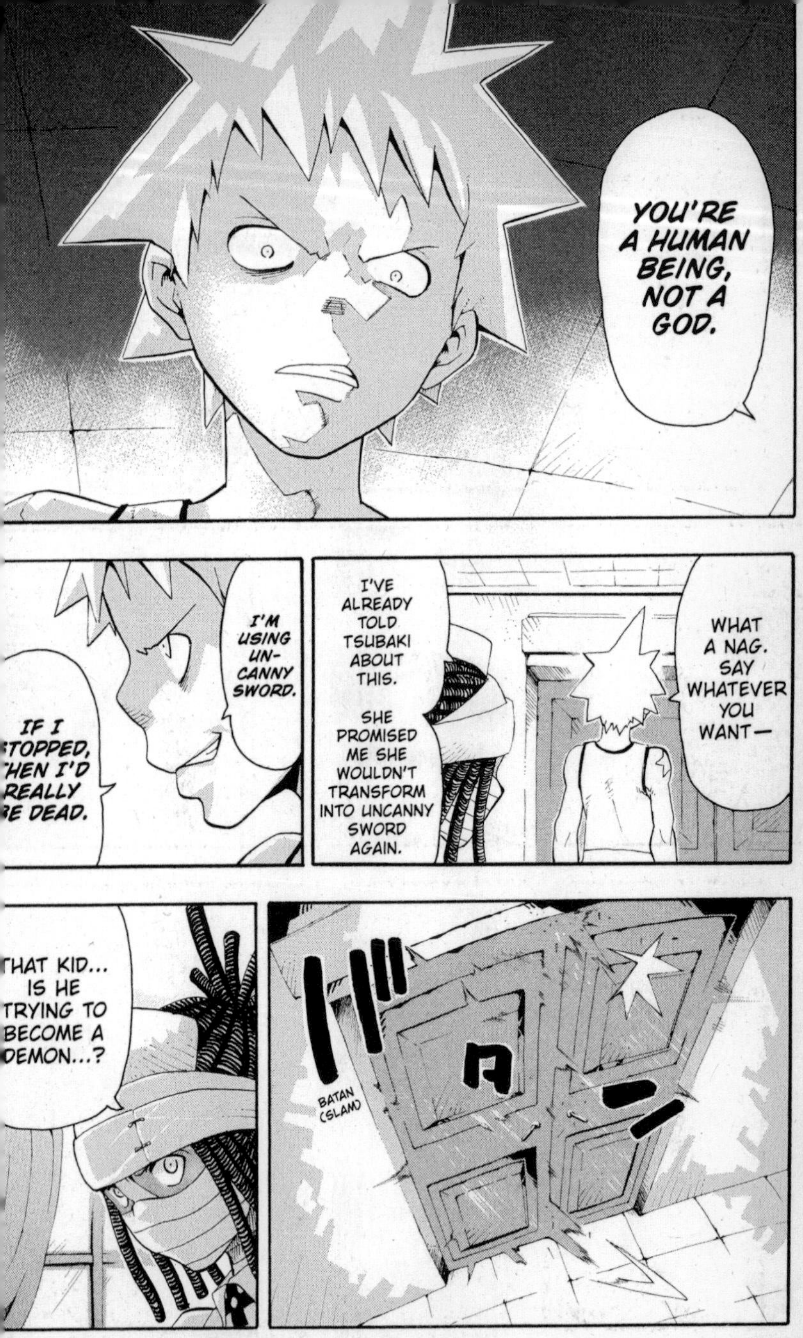
YOU'RE A HUMAN BEING, NOT A GOD.
WHAT A NAG. SAY WHATEVER YOU WANT—
I'VE ALREADY TOLD TSUBAKI ABOUT THIS.
SHE PROMISED ME SHE WOULDN'T TRANSFORM INTO UNCANNY SWORD AGAIN.
I'M USING UNCANNY SWORD.
IF I STOPPED, THEN I'D REALLY BE DEAD.
BATAN (SLAM)
THAT KID... IS HE TRYING TO BECOME A DEMON...?

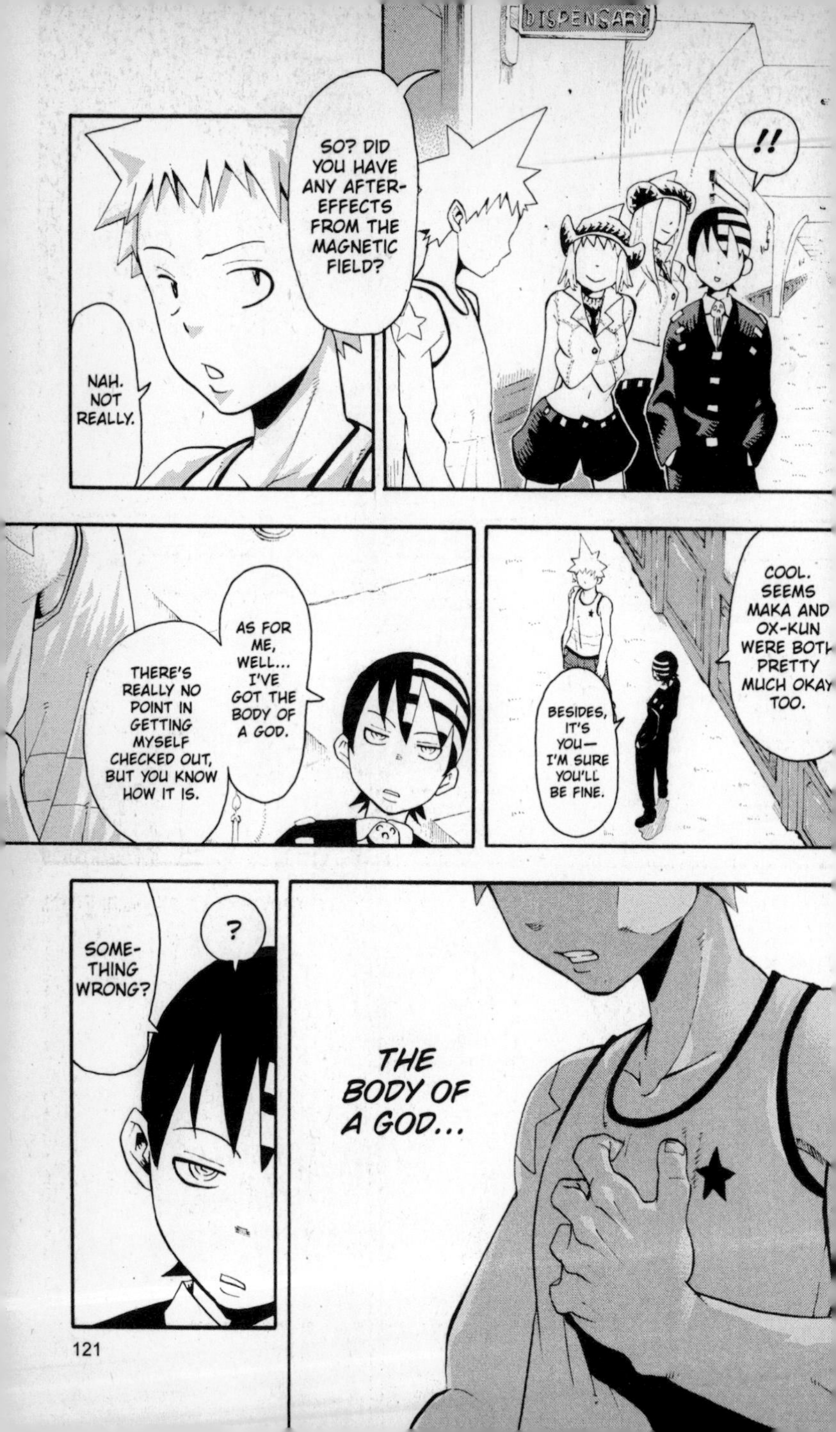
DISPENSARY
SO? DID YOU HAVE ANY AFTER-EFFECTS FROM THE MAGNETIC FIELD?
!!
NAH. NOT REALLY.
COOL. SEEMS MAKA AND OX-KUN WERE BOTH PRETTY MUCH OKAY TOO.
BESIDES, IT'S YOU— I'M SURE YOU'LL BE FINE.
AS FOR ME, WELL... I'VE GOT THE BODY OF A GOD.
THERE'S REALLY NO POINT IN GETTING MYSELF CHECKED OUT, BUT YOU KNOW HOW IT IS.
THE BODY OF A GOD...
?
SOME-THING WRONG?

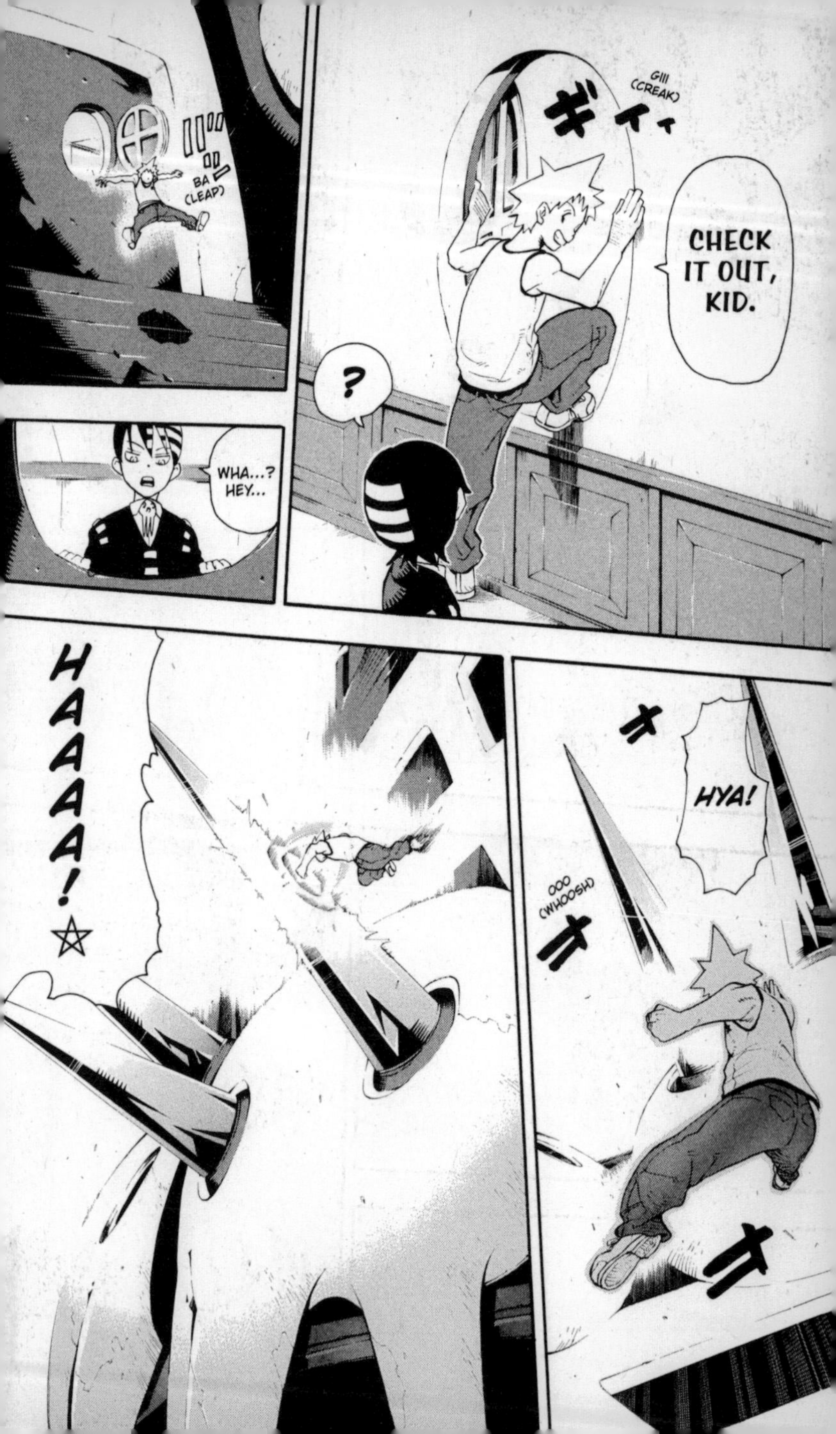
GIII (CREAK)
CHECK IT OUT, KID.
?
BA (LEAP)
WHA...? HEY...
HYA!
OOO (WHOOSH)
HAAAAA!☆

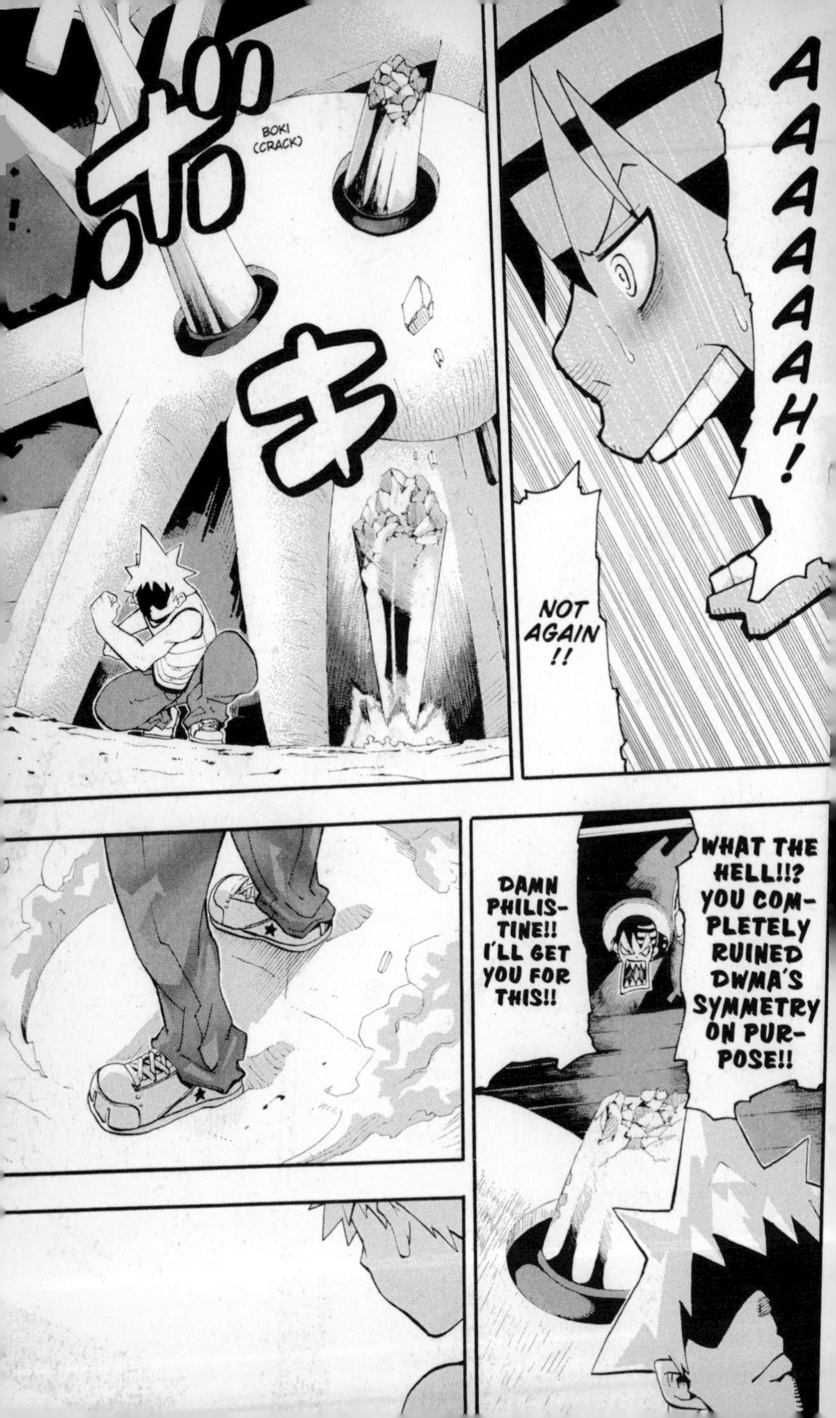
AAAAAAAH!
NOT AGAIN!!
BOKI (CRACK)
WHAT THE HELL!!? YOU COMPLETELY RUINED DWMA'S SYMMETRY ON PURPOSE!!
DAMN PHILISTINE!! I'LL GET YOU FOR THIS!!

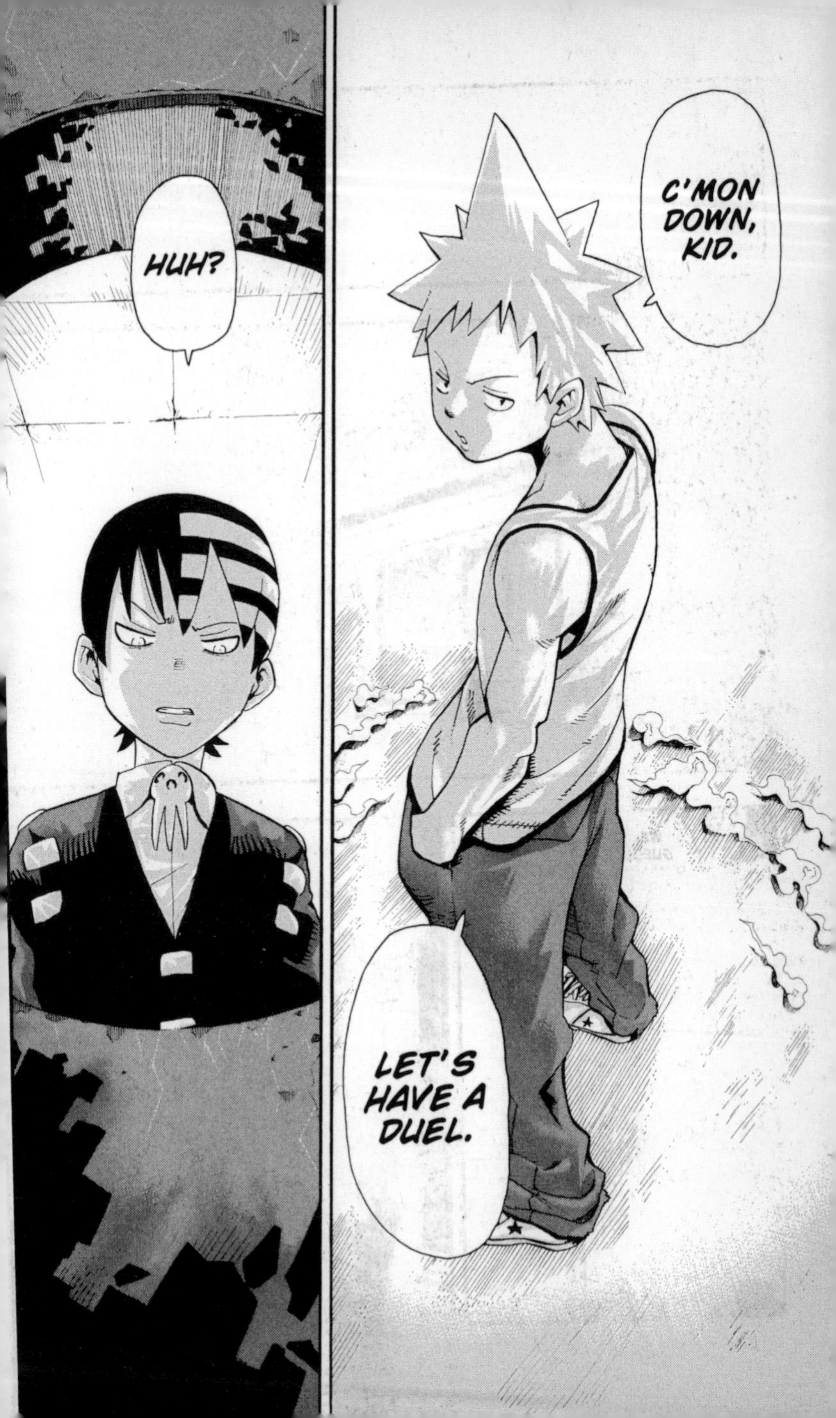
C'MON DOWN, KID.
LET'S HAVE A DUEL.
HUH?

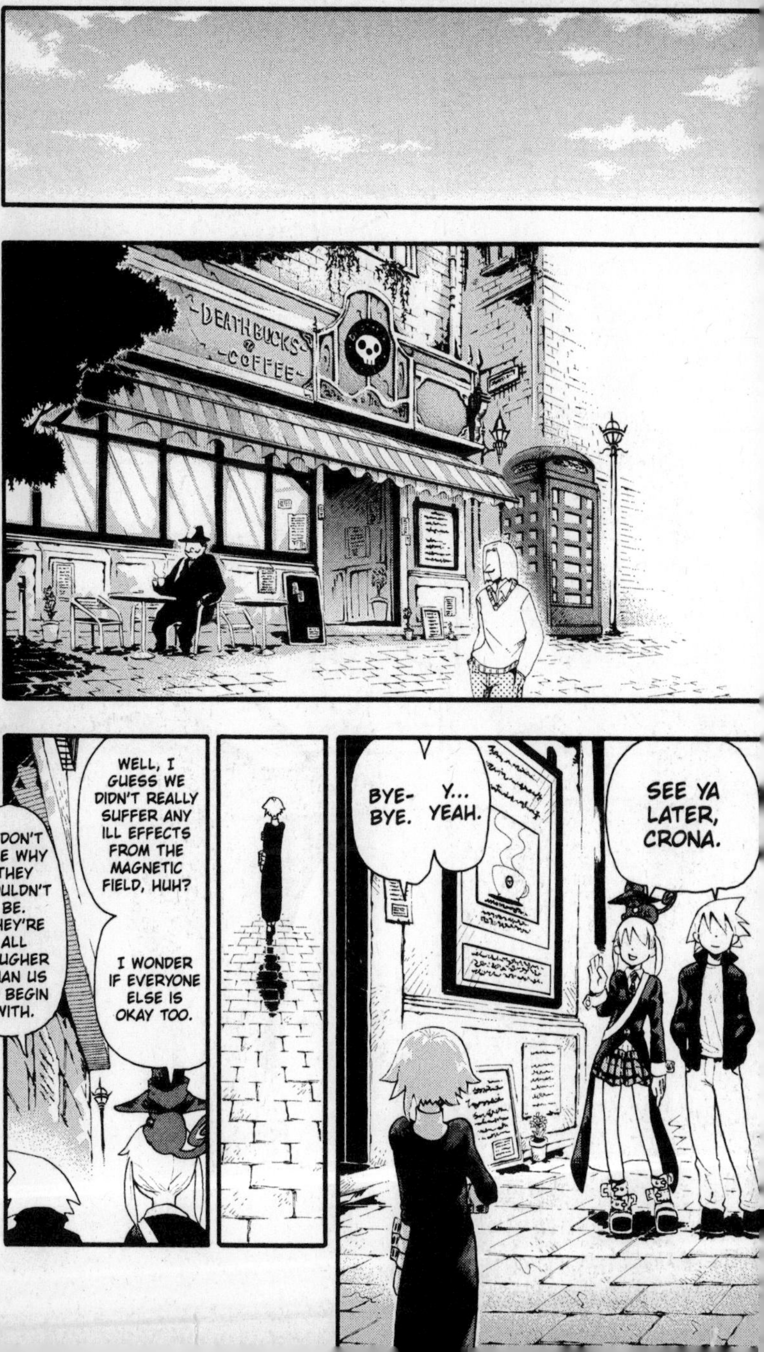
DEATHBUCKS COFFEE
SEE YA LATER, CRONA.
Y... YEAH.
BYE-BYE.
WELL, I GUESS WE DIDN'T REALLY SUFFER ANY ILL EFFECTS FROM THE MAGNETIC FIELD, HUH?
I WONDER IF EVERYONE ELSE IS OKAY TOO.
I DON'T SEE WHY THEY WOULDN'T BE. THEY'RE ALL TOUGHER THAN US TO BEGIN WITH.

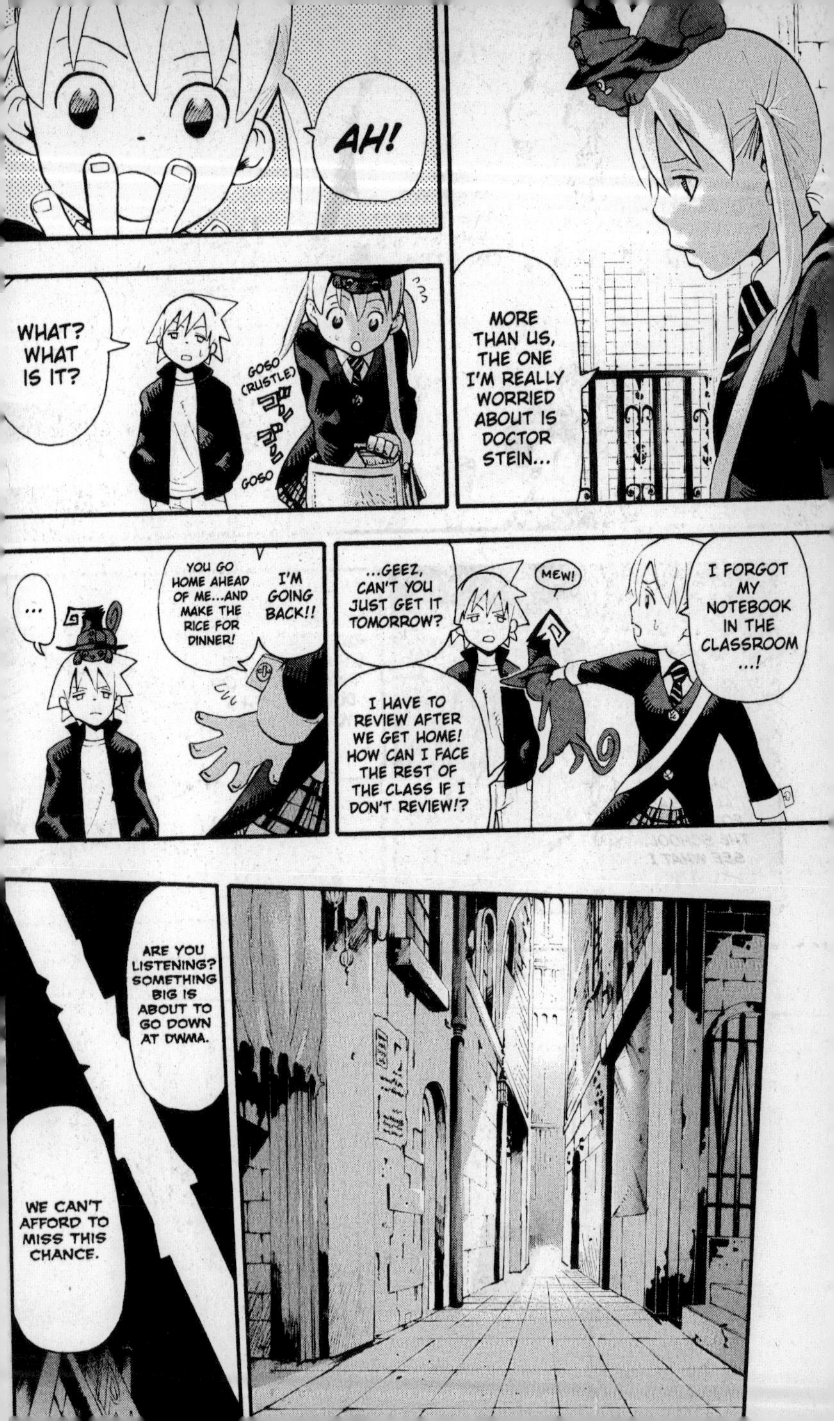
MORE THAN US, THE ONE I'M REALLY WORRIED ABOUT IS DOCTOR STEIN...
AH!
WHAT? WHAT IS IT?
GOSO (RUSTLE)
GOSO
I FORGOT MY NOTEBOOK IN THE CLASSROOM ...!
MEW!
...GEEZ, CAN'T YOU JUST GET IT TOMORROW?
I HAVE TO REVIEW AFTER WE GET HOME! HOW CAN I FACE THE REST OF THE CLASS IF I DON'T REVIEW!?
I'M GOING BACK!!
YOU GO HOME AHEAD OF ME...AND MAKE THE RICE FOR DINNER!
...
ARE YOU LISTENING? SOMETHING BIG IS ABOUT TO GO DOWN AT DWMA.
WE CAN'T AFFORD TO MISS THIS CHANCE.

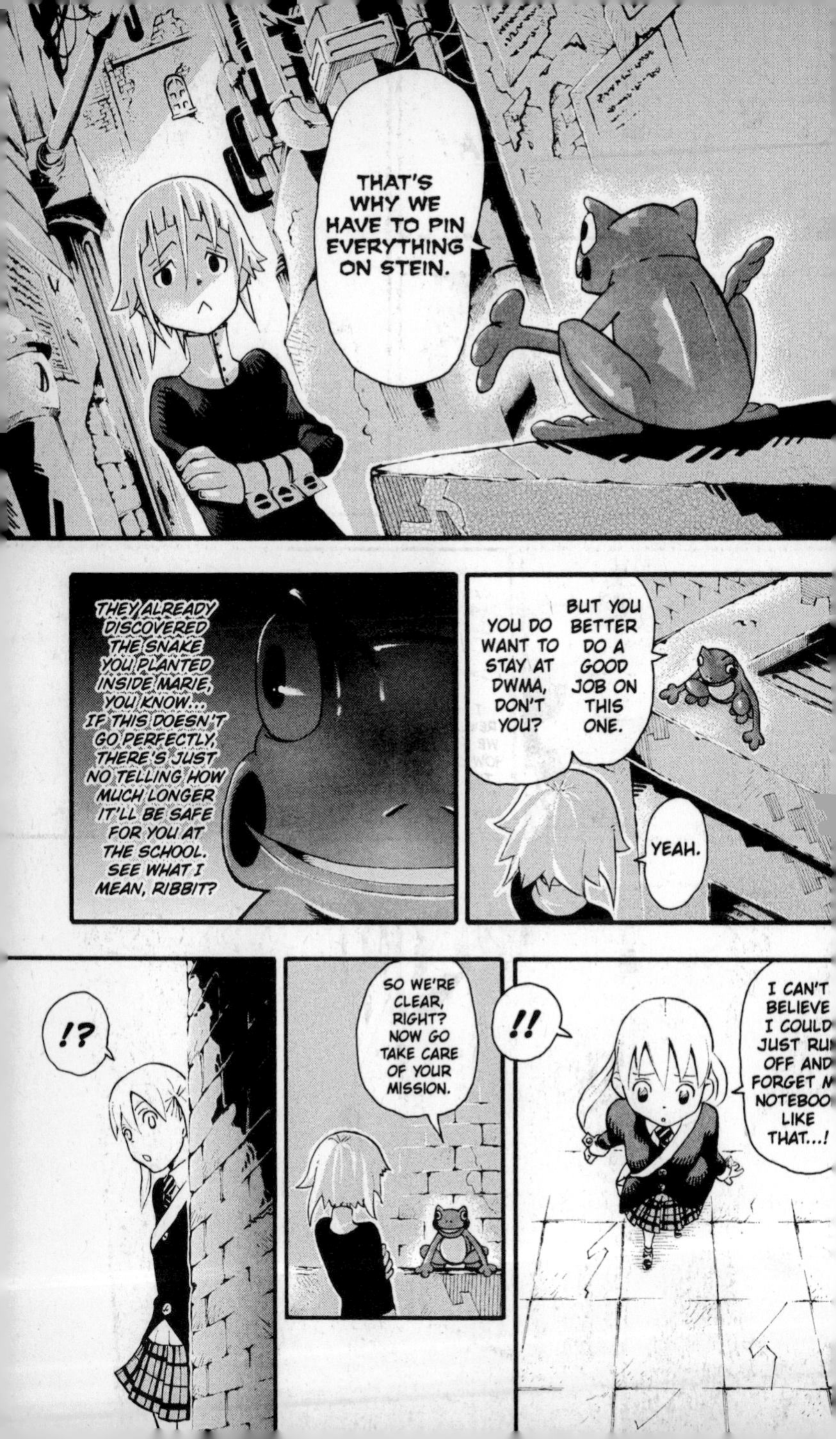
THAT'S WHY WE HAVE TO PIN EVERYTHING ON STEIN.
YOU DO WANT TO STAY AT DWMA, DON'T YOU? BUT YOU BETTER DO A GOOD JOB ON THIS ONE.
YEAH.
THEY ALREADY DISCOVERED THE SNAKE YOU PLANTED INSIDE MARIE, YOU KNOW... IF THIS DOESN'T GO PERFECTLY, THERE'S JUST NO TELLING HOW MUCH LONGER IT'LL BE SAFE FOR YOU AT THE SCHOOL. SEE WHAT I MEAN, RIBBIT?
I CAN'T BELIEVE I COULD JUST RU OFF AND FORGET M NOTEBOO LIKE THAT...!
!!
SO WE'RE CLEAR, RIGHT? NOW GO TAKE CARE OF YOUR MISSION.
!?

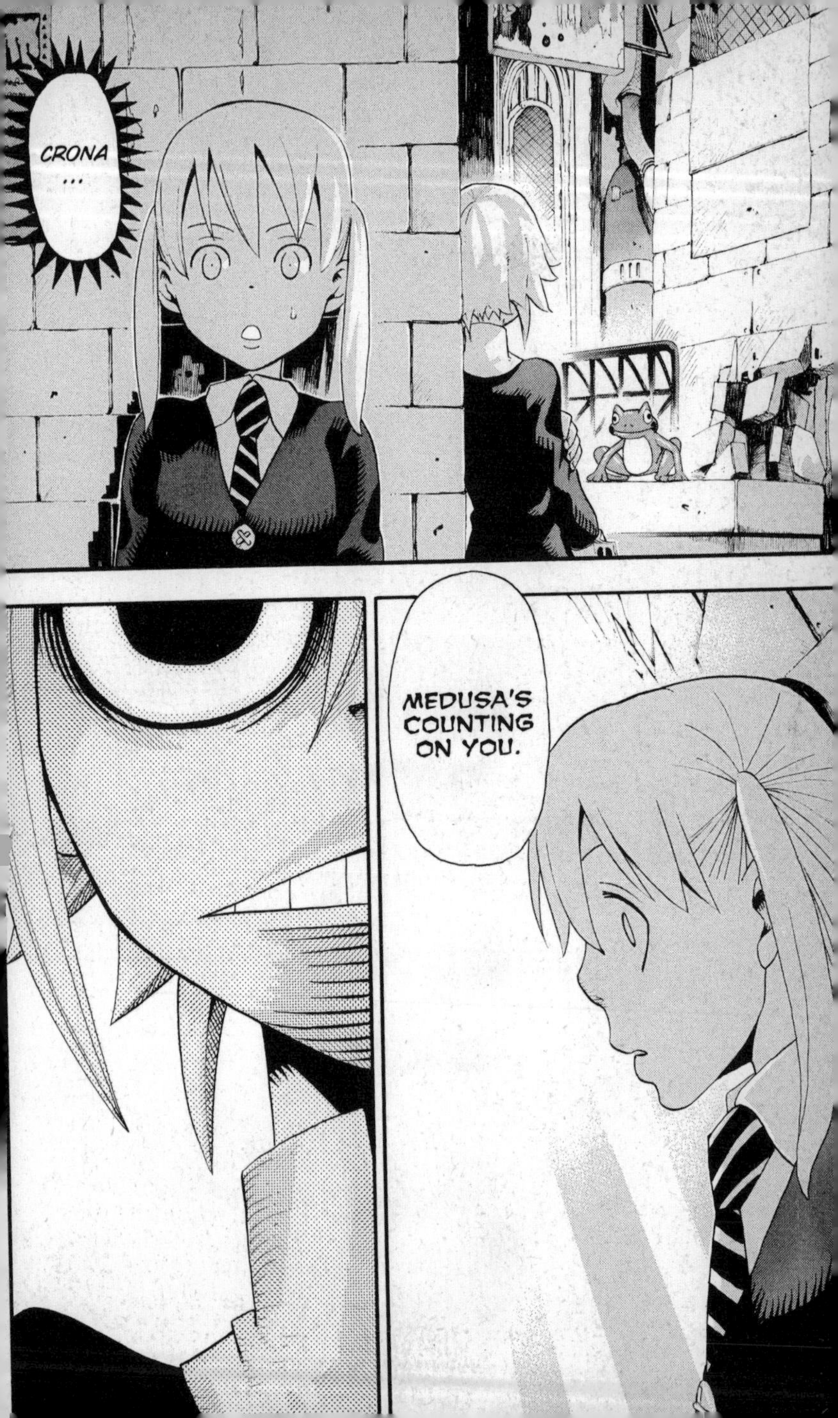
CRONA ...
MEDUSA'S COUNTING ON YOU.

SOUL EATER

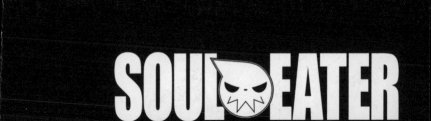

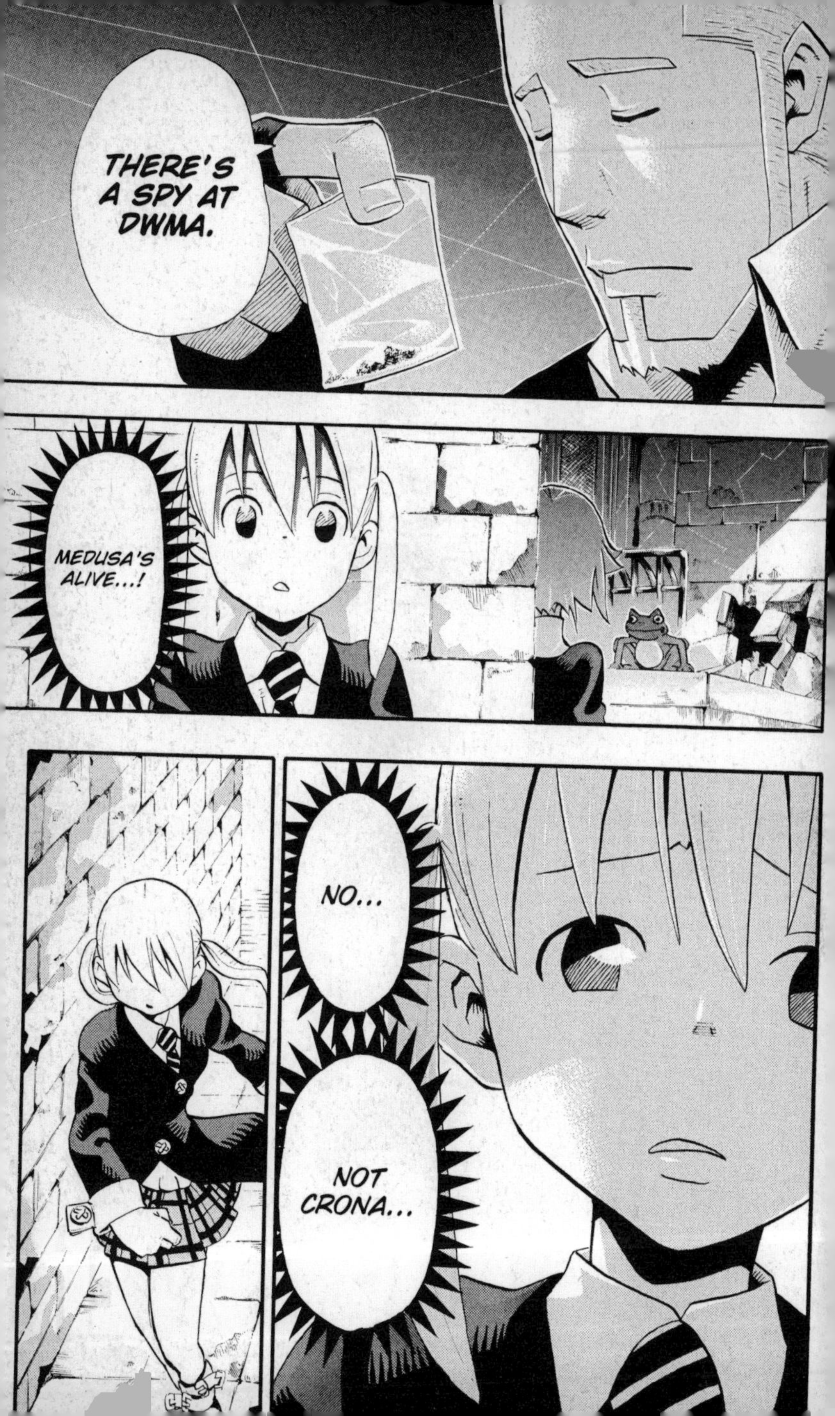
THERE'S A SPY AT DWMA.
MEDUSA'S ALIVE...!
NO...
NOT CRONA...

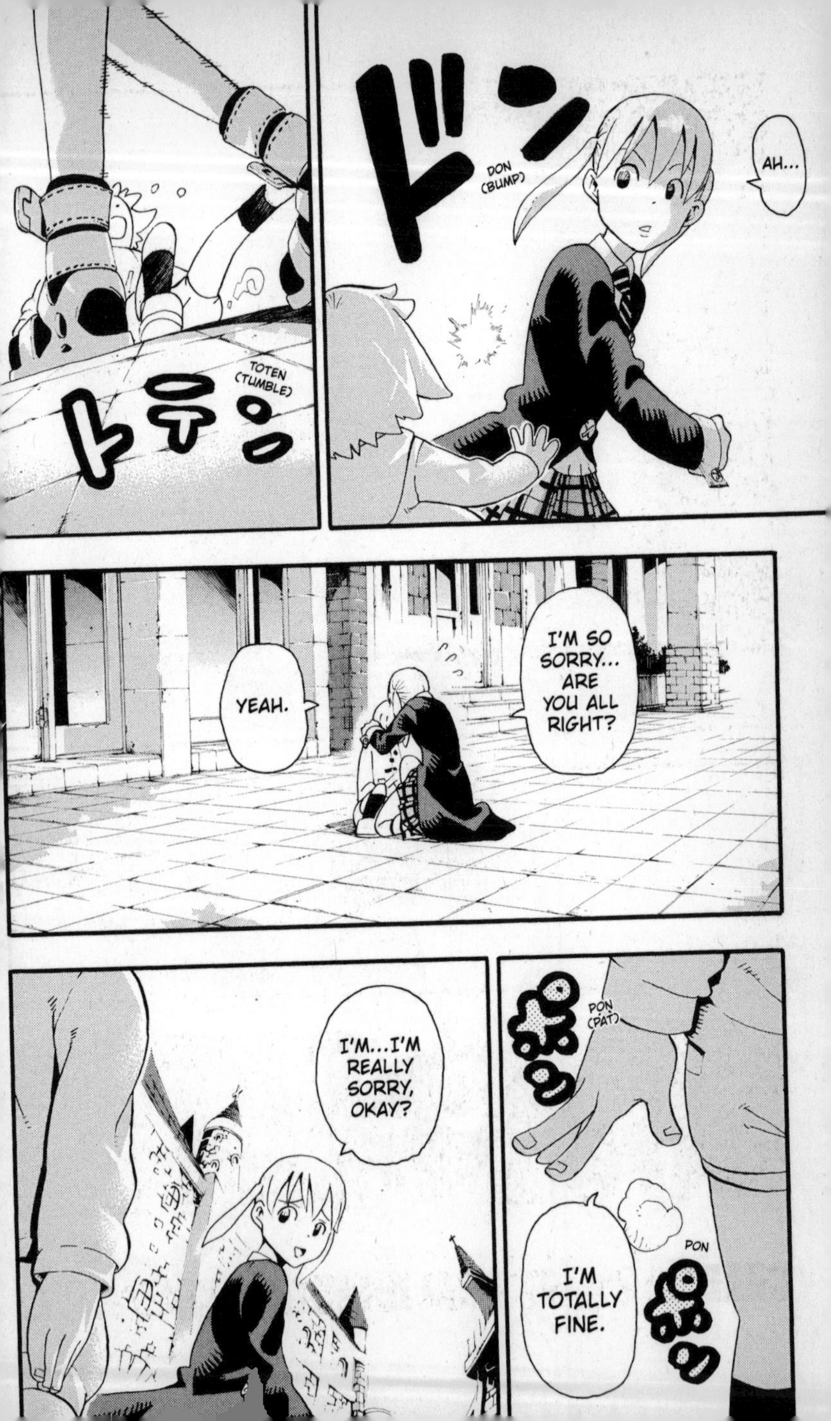
AH...
DON (BUMP)
TOTEN (TUMBLE)
I'M SO SORRY... ARE YOU ALL RIGHT?
YEAH.
PON (PAT)
I'M TOTALLY FINE.
PON
I'M...I'M REALLY SORRY, OKAY?

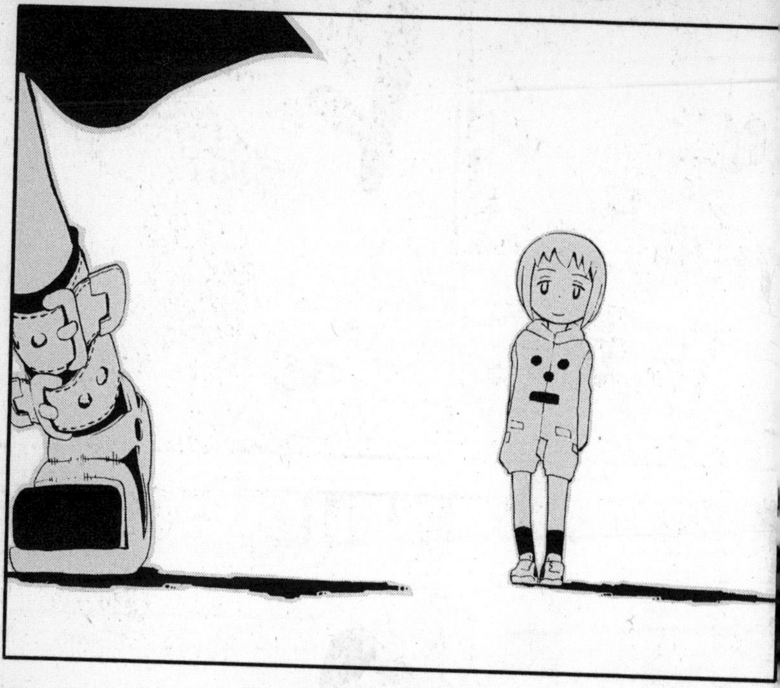

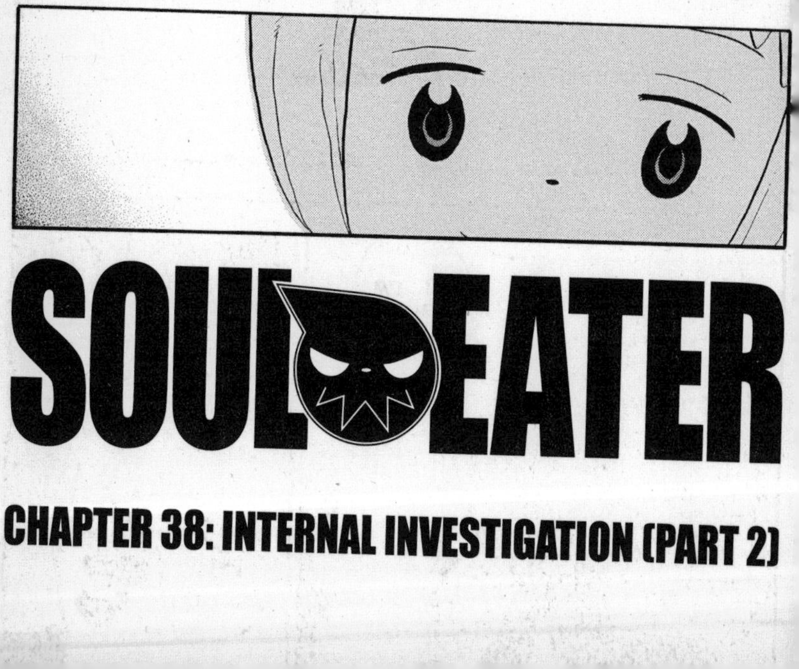

SOUL EATER

CHAPTER 38: INTERNAL INVESTIGATION (PART 2)

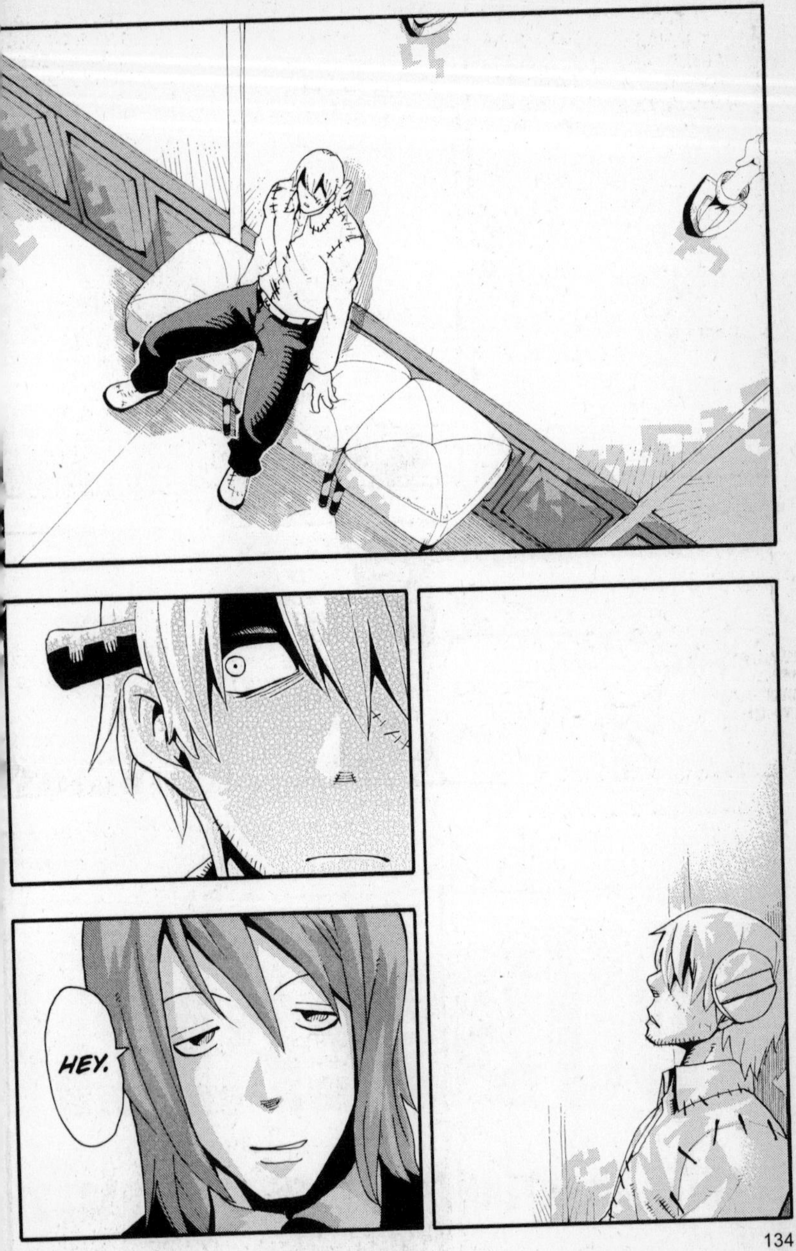
HEY.

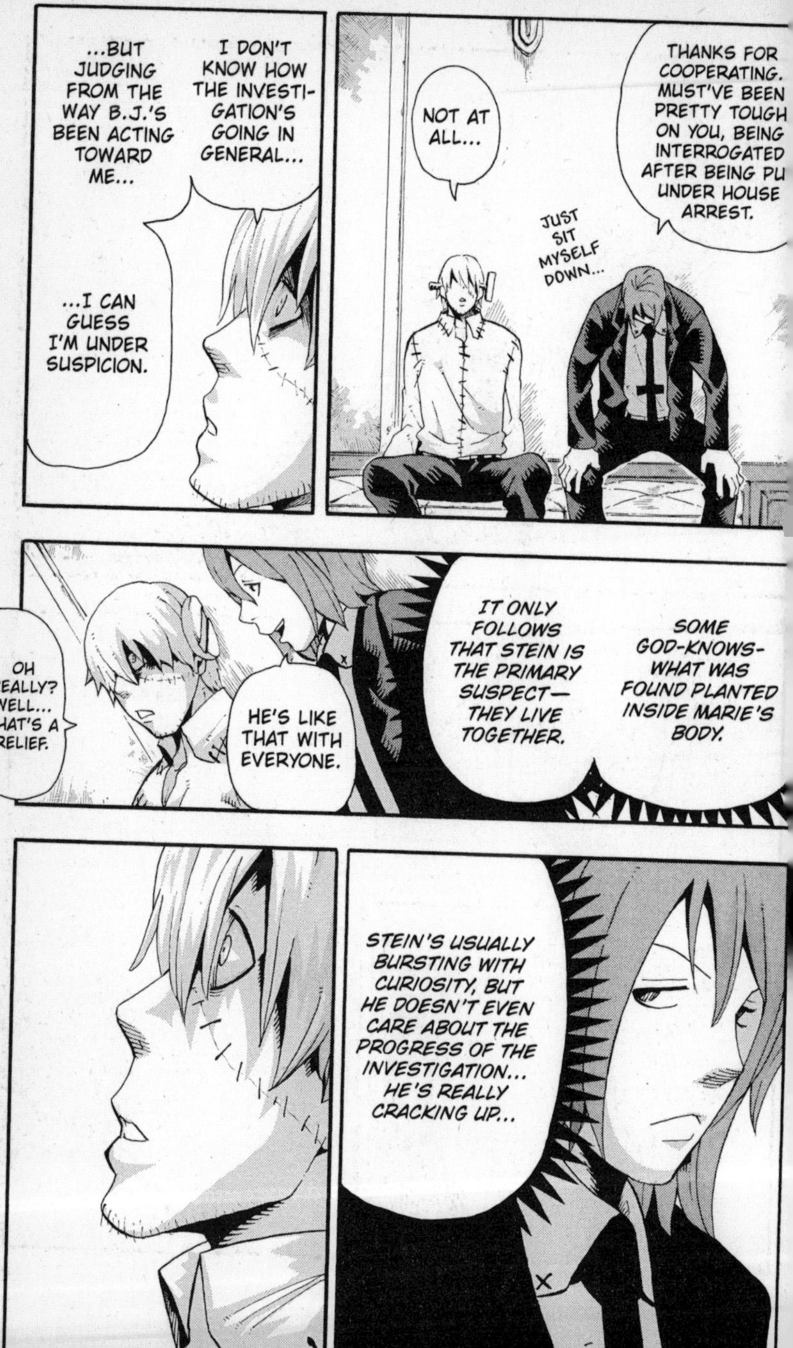
THANKS FOR COOPERATING. MUST'VE BEEN PRETTY TOUGH ON YOU, BEING INTERROGATED AFTER BEING PU UNDER HOUSE ARREST.
NOT AT ALL...
JUST SIT MYSELF DOWN...
I DON'T KNOW HOW THE INVESTI-GATION'S GOING IN GENERAL...
...BUT JUDGING FROM THE WAY B.J.'S BEEN ACTING TOWARD ME...
...I CAN GUESS I'M UNDER SUSPICION.
SOME GOD-KNOWS-WHAT WAS FOUND PLANTED INSIDE MARIE'S BODY.
IT ONLY FOLLOWS THAT STEIN IS THE PRIMARY SUSPECT— THEY LIVE TOGETHER.
HE'S LIKE THAT WITH EVERYONE.
OH REALLY? WELL... THAT'S A RELIEF.
STEIN'S USUALLY BURSTING WITH CURIOSITY, BUT HE DOESN'T EVEN CARE ABOUT THE PROGRESS OF THE INVESTIGATION... HE'S REALLY CRACKING UP...

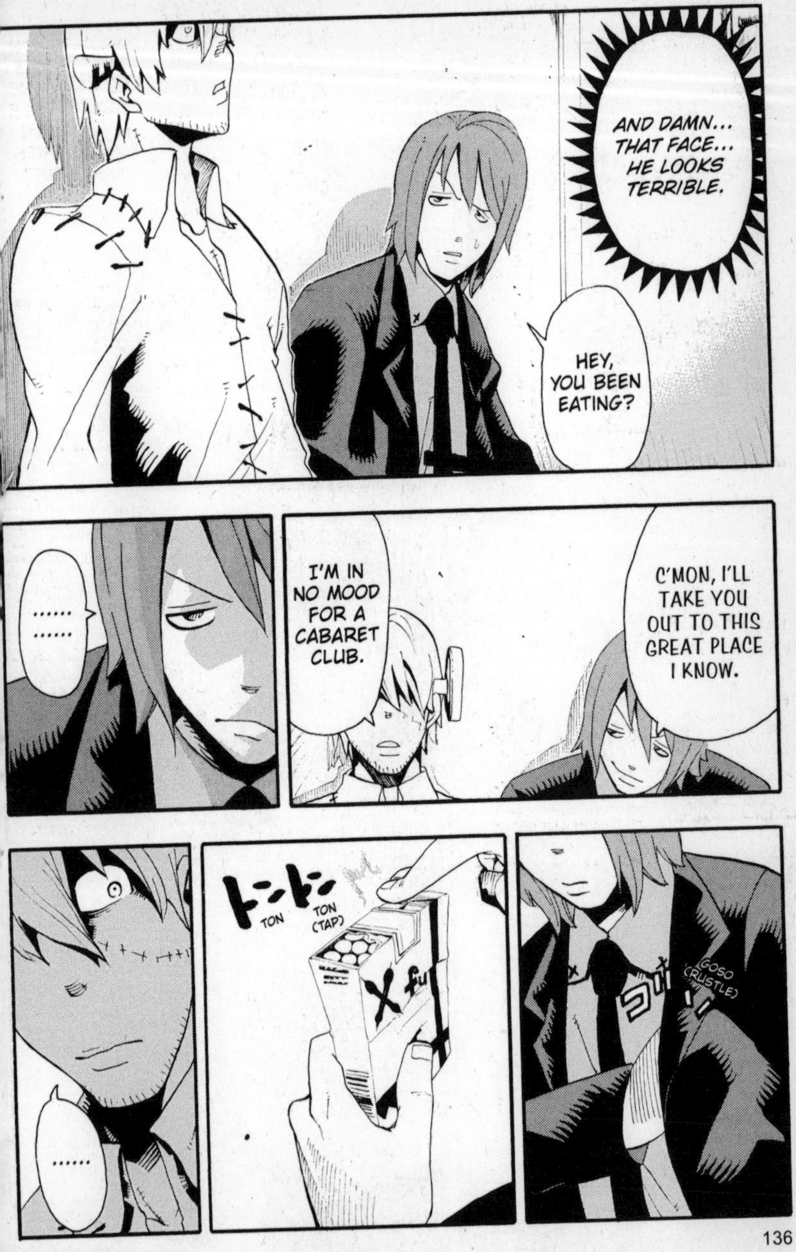
AND DAMN... THAT FACE... HE LOOKS TERRIBLE.
HEY, YOU BEEN EATING?
C'MON, I'LL TAKE YOU OUT TO THIS GREAT PLACE I KNOW.
I'M IN NO MOOD FOR A CABARET CLUB.
......
......
GOSO (RUSTLE)
トントン
TON
TON (TAP)
......

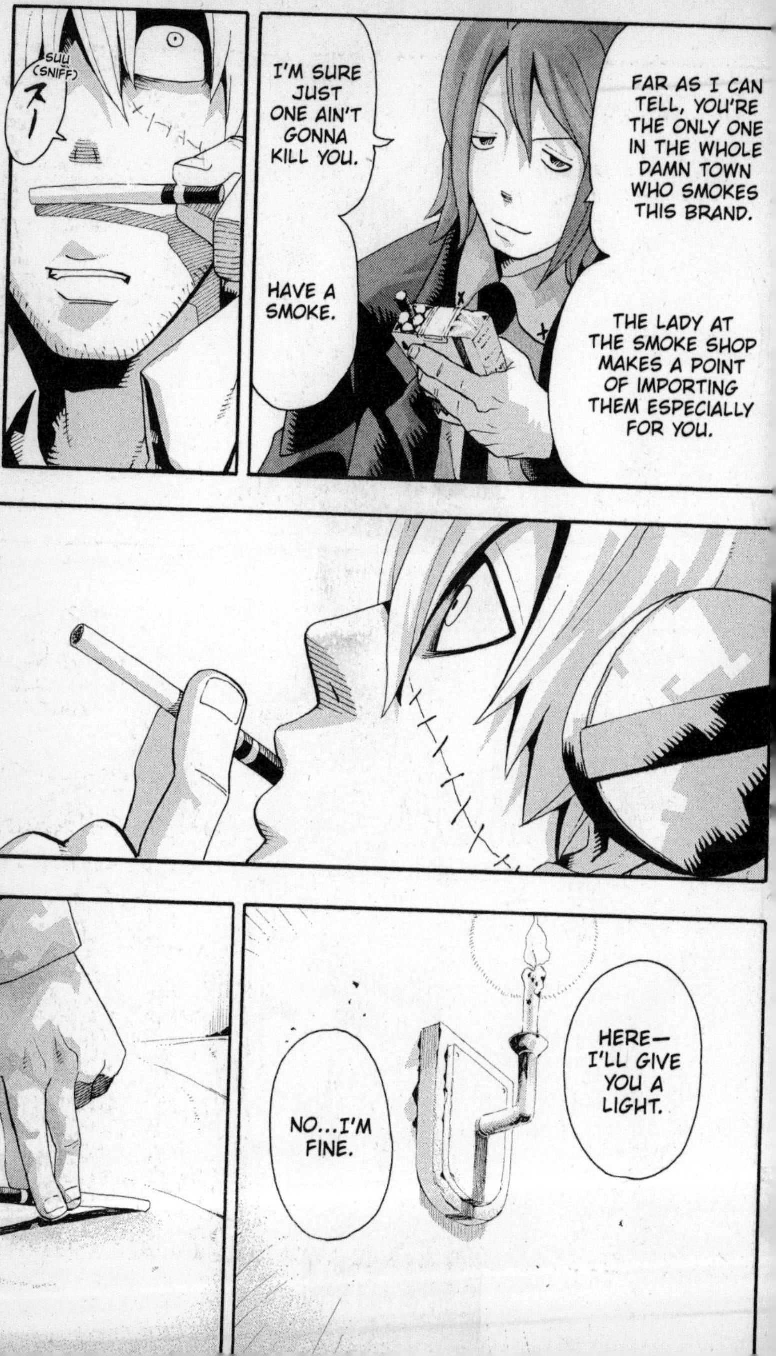
FAR AS I CAN TELL, YOU'RE THE ONLY ONE IN THE WHOLE DAMN TOWN WHO SMOKES THIS BRAND.
THE LADY AT THE SMOKE SHOP MAKES A POINT OF IMPORTING THEM ESPECIALLY FOR YOU.
I'M SURE JUST ONE AIN'T GONNA KILL YOU.
HAVE A SMOKE.
SUU (SNIFF)
スー
HERE— I'LL GIVE YOU A LIGHT.
NO...I'M FINE.

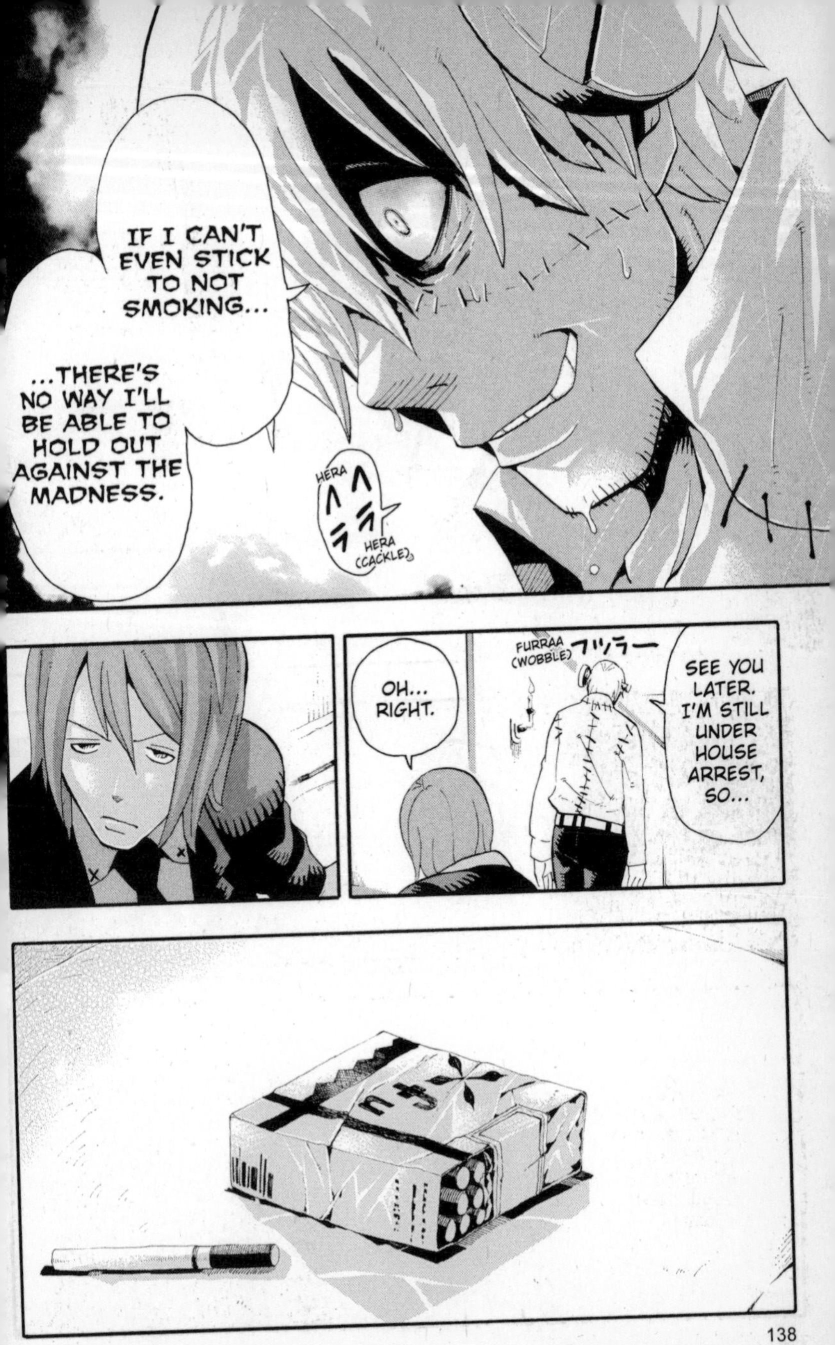
IF I CAN'T EVEN STICK TO NOT SMOKING...
...THERE'S NO WAY I'LL BE ABLE TO HOLD OUT AGAINST THE MADNESS.
HERA ヘラ ヘラ HERA (CACKLE)
SEE YOU LATER. I'M STILL UNDER HOUSE ARREST, SO...
FURRAA (WOBBLE) フツラー
OH... RIGHT.

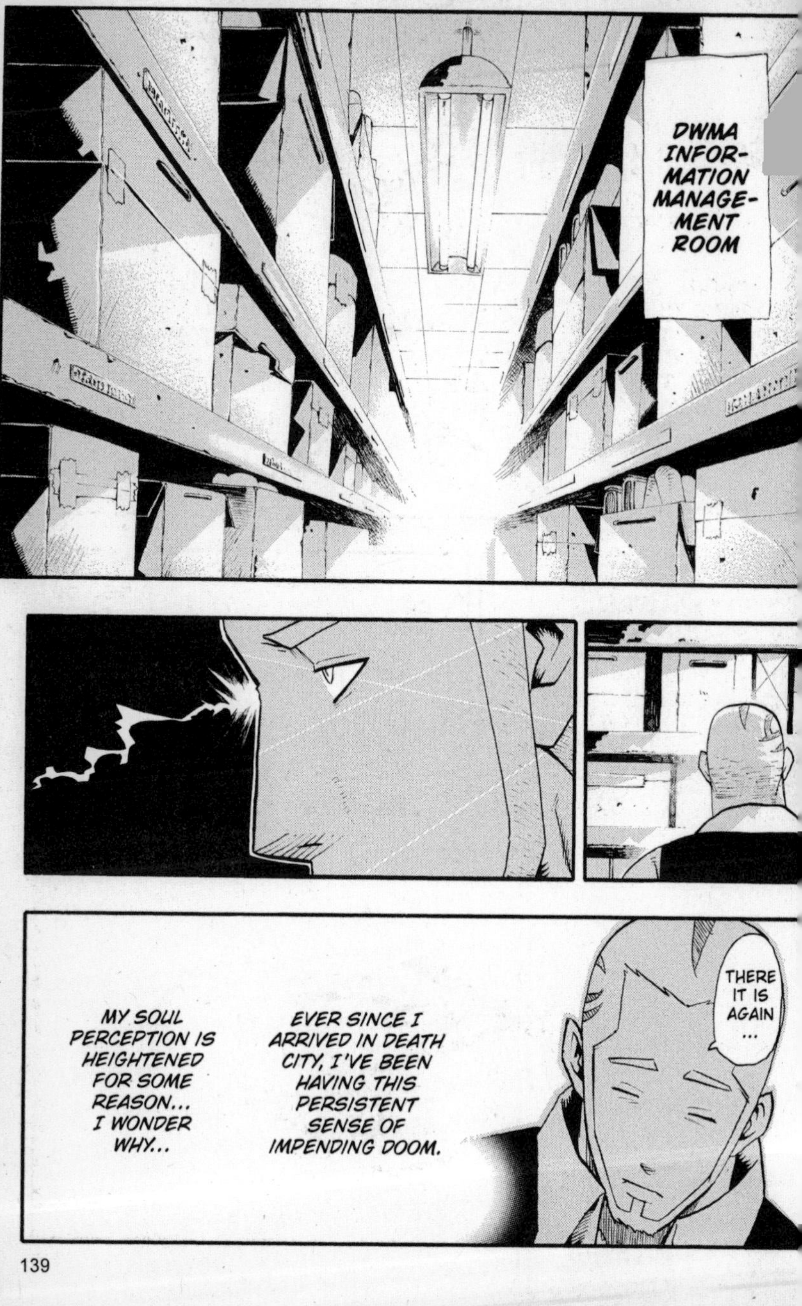
DWMA INFORMATION MANAGEMENT ROOM
THERE IT IS AGAIN...
EVER SINCE I ARRIVED IN DEATH CITY, I'VE BEEN HAVING THIS PERSISTENT SENSE OF IMPENDING DOOM.
MY SOUL PERCEPTION IS HEIGHTENED FOR SOME REASON... I WONDER WHY...

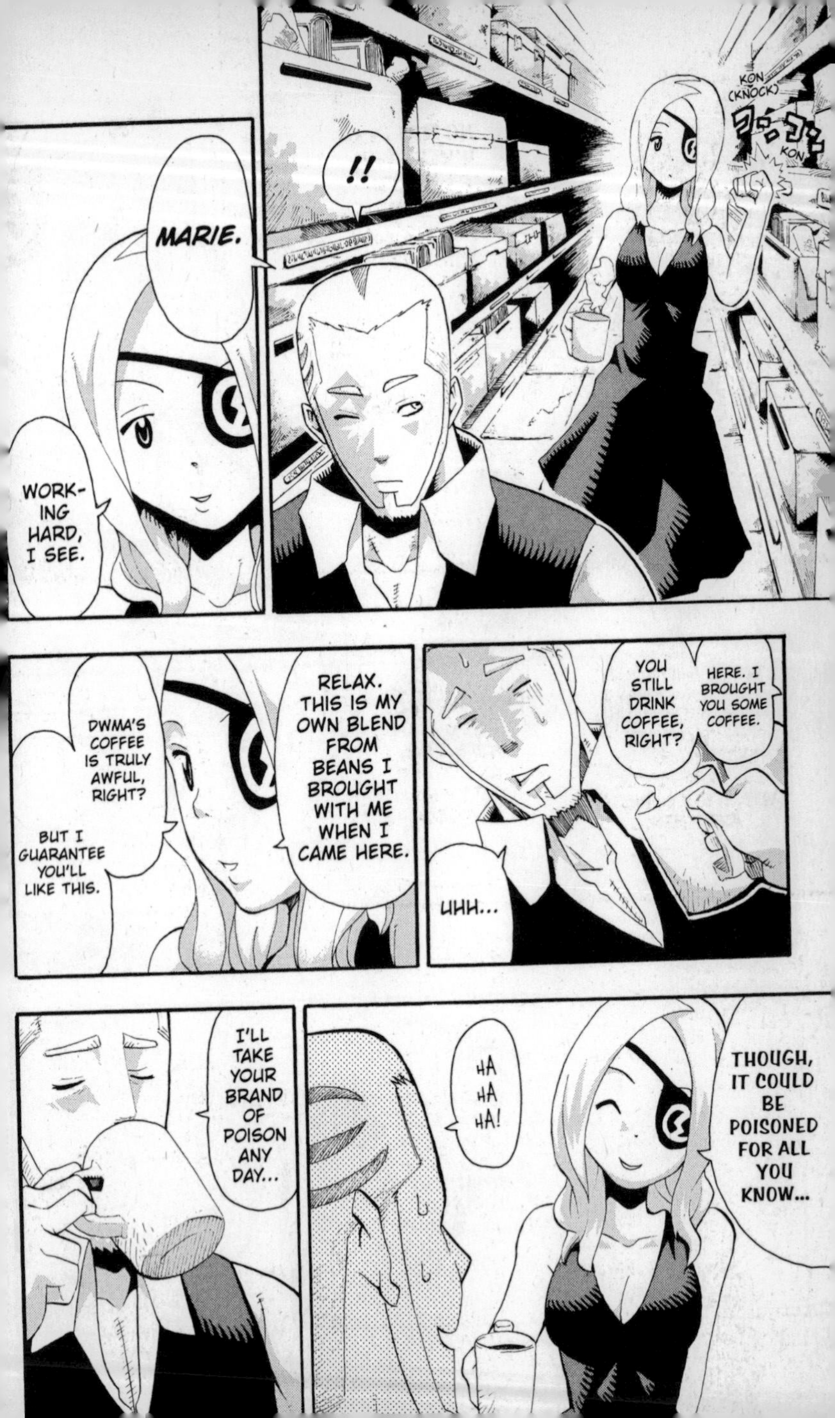
KON (KNOCK) KON
!!
MARIE.
WORKING-ING HARD, I SEE.
HERE. I BROUGHT YOU SOME COFFEE.
YOU STILL DRINK COFFEE, RIGHT?
UHH...
RELAX. THIS IS MY OWN BLEND FROM BEANS I BROUGHT WITH ME WHEN I CAME HERE.
DWMA'S COFFEE IS TRULY AWFUL, RIGHT?
BUT I GUARANTEE YOU'LL LIKE THIS.
THOUGH, IT COULD BE POISONED FOR ALL YOU KNOW...
HA HA HA!
I'LL TAKE YOUR BRAND OF POISON ANY DAY...

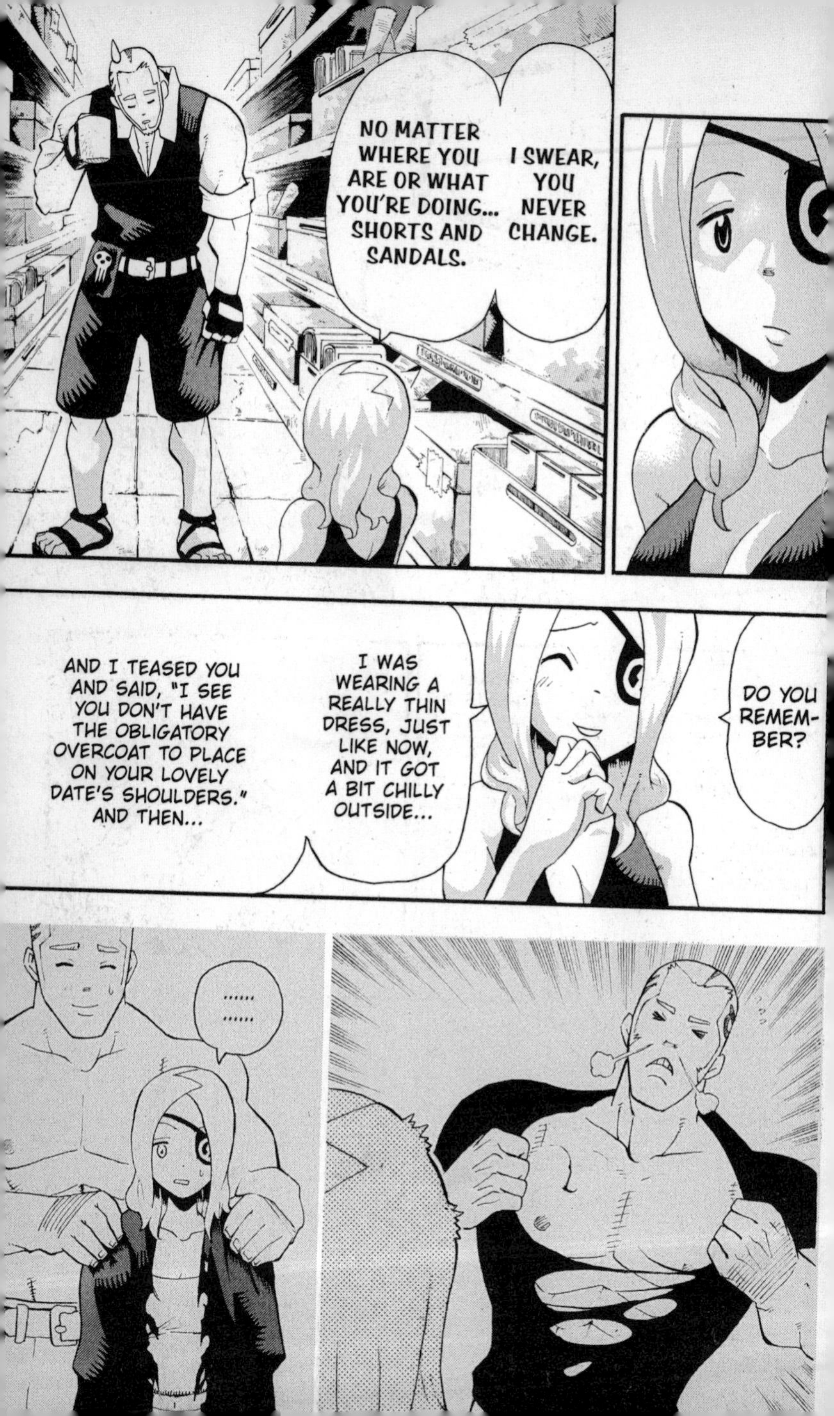
I SWEAR, YOU NEVER CHANGE.
NO MATTER WHERE YOU ARE OR WHAT YOU'RE DOING... SHORTS AND SANDALS.
DO YOU REMEM-BER?
I WAS WEARING A REALLY THIN DRESS, JUST LIKE NOW, AND IT GOT A BIT CHILLY OUTSIDE...
AND I TEASED YOU AND SAID, "I SEE YOU DON'T HAVE THE OBLIGATORY OVERCOAT TO PLACE ON YOUR LOVELY DATE'S SHOULDERS." AND THEN...
......
......

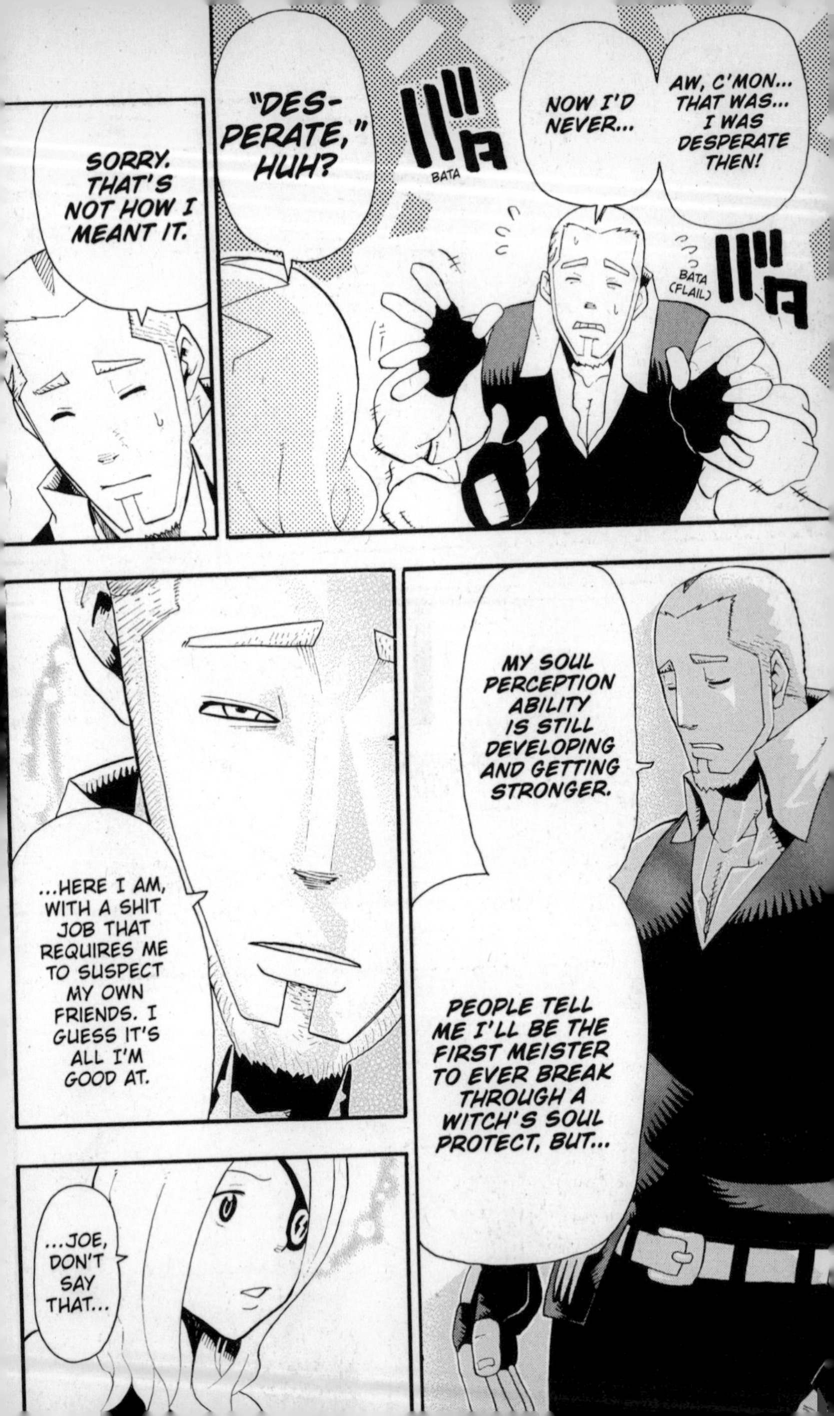
AW, C'MON... THAT WAS... I WAS DESPERATE THEN!
NOW I'D NEVER...
BATA (FLAIL)
BATA
"DES-PERATE," HUH?
SORRY. THAT'S NOT HOW I MEANT IT.
MY SOUL PERCEPTION ABILITY IS STILL DEVELOPING AND GETTING STRONGER.
PEOPLE TELL ME I'LL BE THE FIRST MEISTER TO EVER BREAK THROUGH A WITCH'S SOUL PROTECT, BUT...
...HERE I AM, WITH A SHIT JOB THAT REQUIRES ME TO SUSPECT MY OWN FRIENDS. I GUESS IT'S ALL I'M GOOD AT.
...JOE, DON'T SAY THAT...

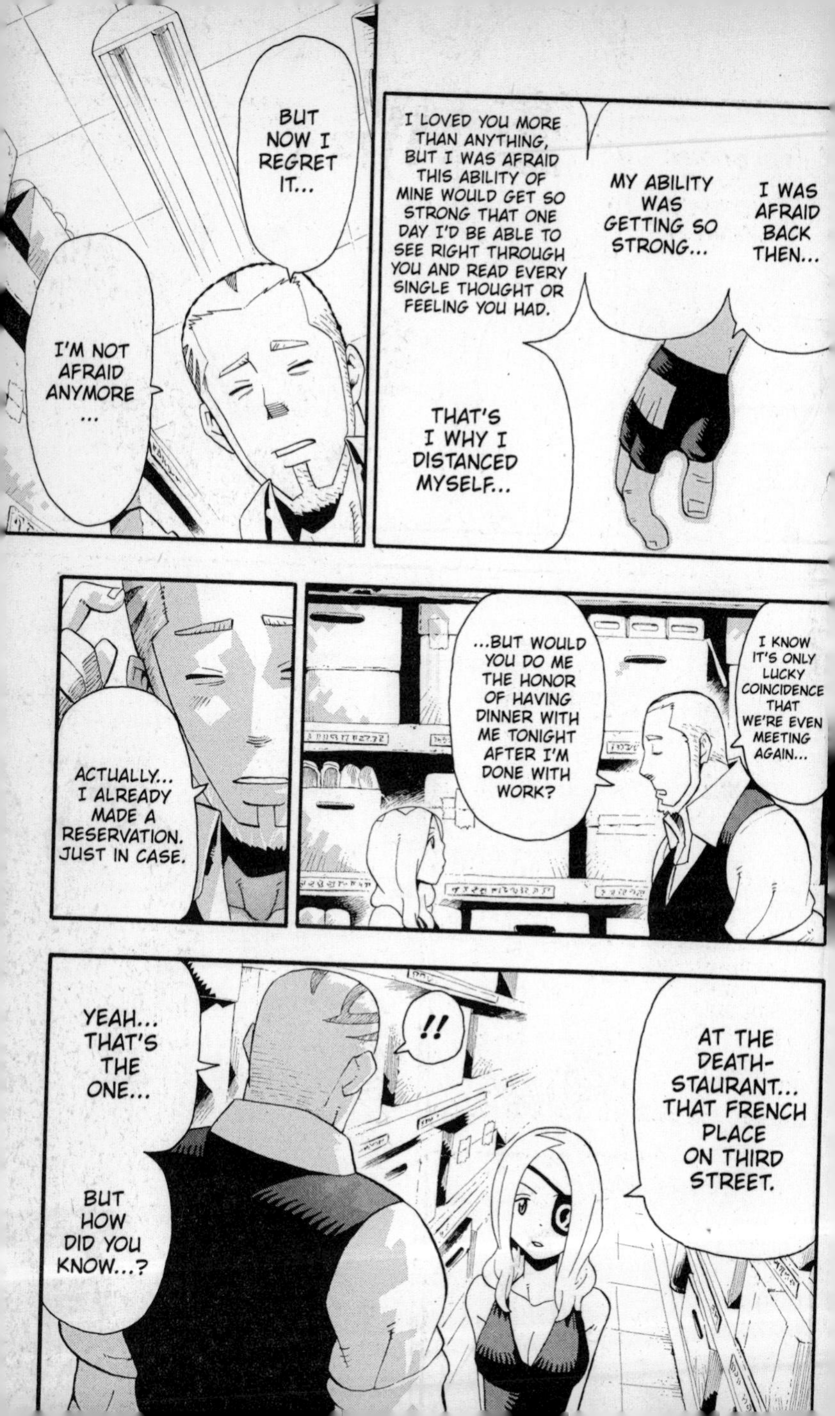
I WAS AFRAID BACK THEN...
MY ABILITY WAS GETTING SO STRONG...
I LOVED YOU MORE THAN ANYTHING, BUT I WAS AFRAID THIS ABILITY OF MINE WOULD GET SO STRONG THAT ONE DAY I'D BE ABLE TO SEE RIGHT THROUGH YOU AND READ EVERY SINGLE THOUGHT OR FEELING YOU HAD.
THAT'S I WHY I DISTANCED MYSELF...
BUT NOW I REGRET IT...
I'M NOT AFRAID ANYMORE...
I KNOW IT'S ONLY LUCKY COINCIDENCE THAT WE'RE EVEN MEETING AGAIN...
...BUT WOULD YOU DO ME THE HONOR OF HAVING DINNER WITH ME TONIGHT AFTER I'M DONE WITH WORK?
ACTUALLY... I ALREADY MADE A RESERVATION. JUST IN CASE.
AT THE DEATH-STAURANT... THAT FRENCH PLACE ON THIRD STREET.
!!
YEAH... THAT'S THE ONE...
BUT HOW DID YOU KNOW...?

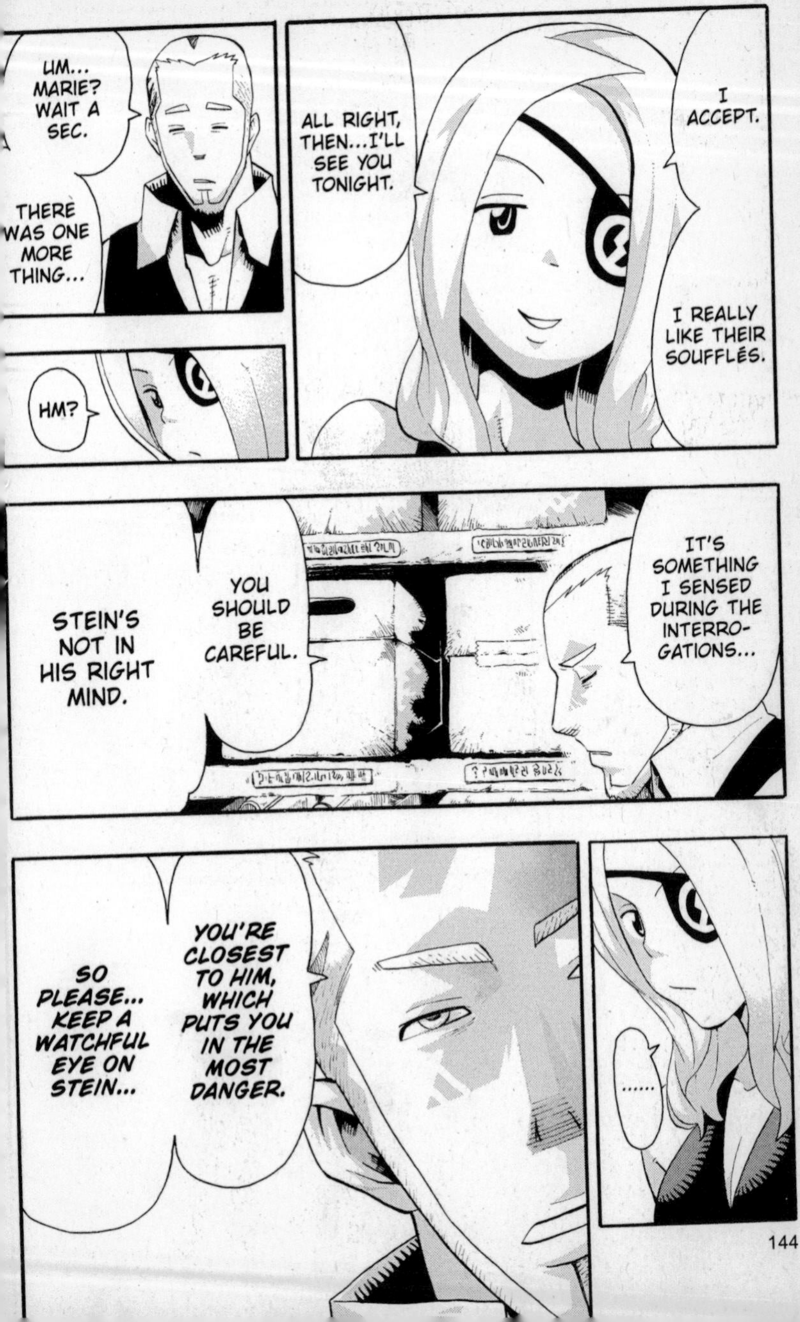
I ACCEPT.
I REALLY LIKE THEIR SOUFFLÉS.
ALL RIGHT, THEN...I'LL SEE YOU TONIGHT.
UM... MARIE? WAIT A SEC.
THERE WAS ONE MORE THING...
HM?
IT'S SOMETHING I SENSED DURING THE INTERROGATIONS...
YOU SHOULD BE CAREFUL.
STEIN'S NOT IN HIS RIGHT MIND.
......
YOU'RE CLOSEST TO HIM, WHICH PUTS YOU IN THE MOST DANGER.
SO PLEASE... KEEP A WATCHFUL EYE ON STEIN...

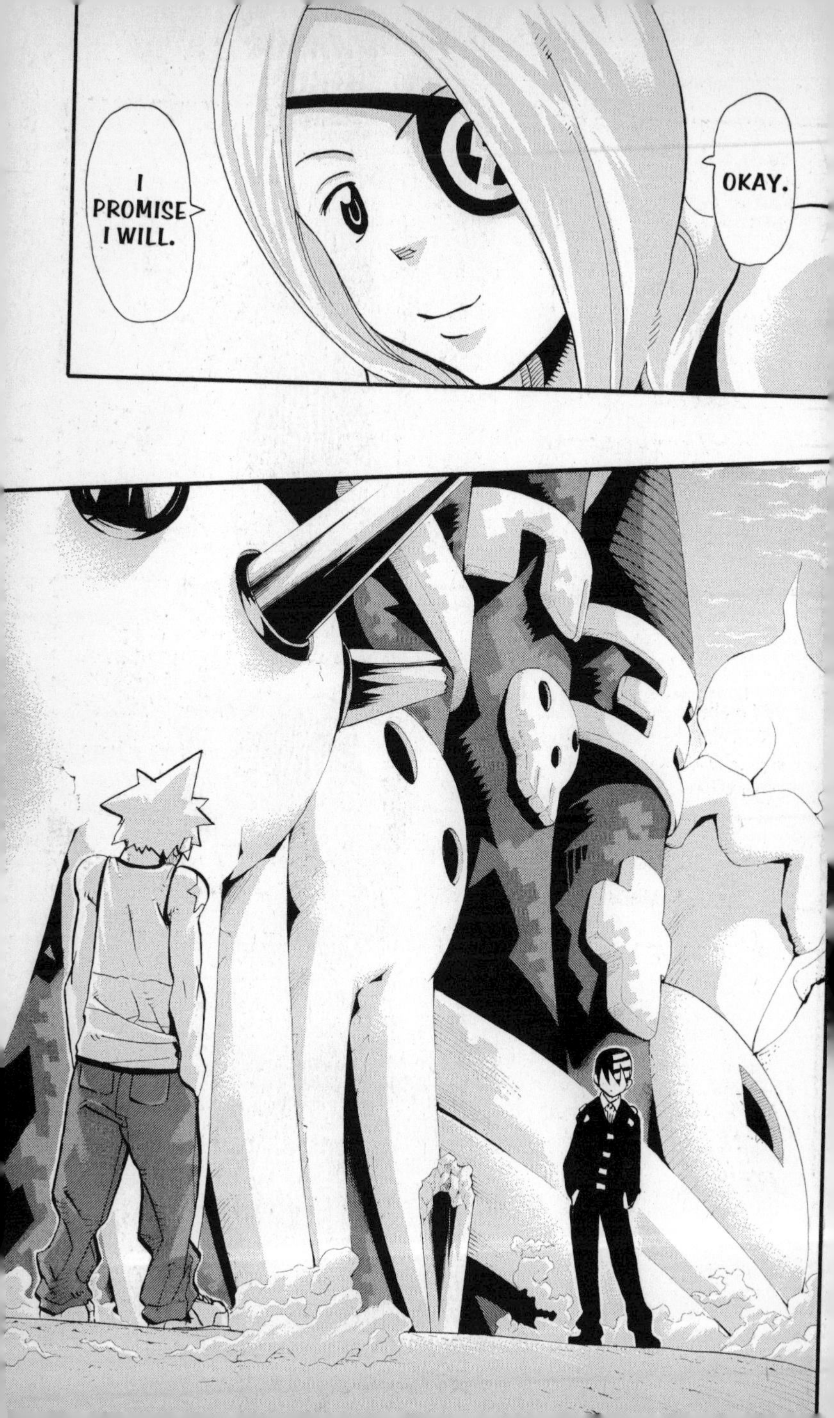
OKAY.
I PROMISE I WILL.

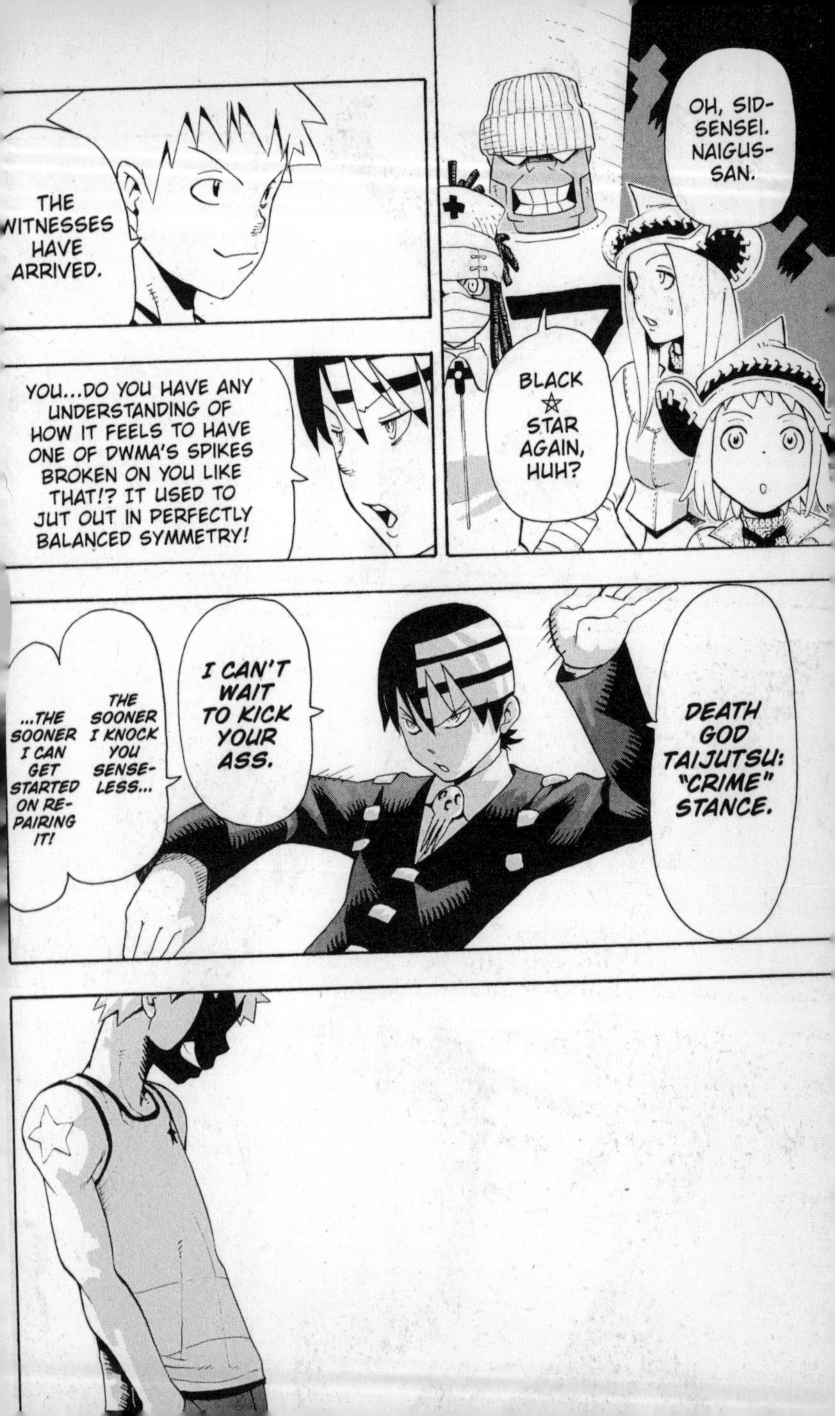
OH, SID-SENSEI. NAIGUS-SAN.
BLACK ☆ STAR AGAIN, HUH?
THE WITNESSES HAVE ARRIVED.
YOU...DO YOU HAVE ANY UNDERSTANDING OF HOW IT FEELS TO HAVE ONE OF DWMA'S SPIKES BROKEN ON YOU LIKE THAT!? IT USED TO JUT OUT IN PERFECTLY BALANCED SYMMETRY!
DEATH GOD TAIJUTSU: "CRIME" STANCE.
I CAN'T WAIT TO KICK YOUR ASS.
THE SOONER I KNOCK YOU SENSE-LESS...
...THE SOONER I CAN GET STARTED ON RE-PAIRING IT!

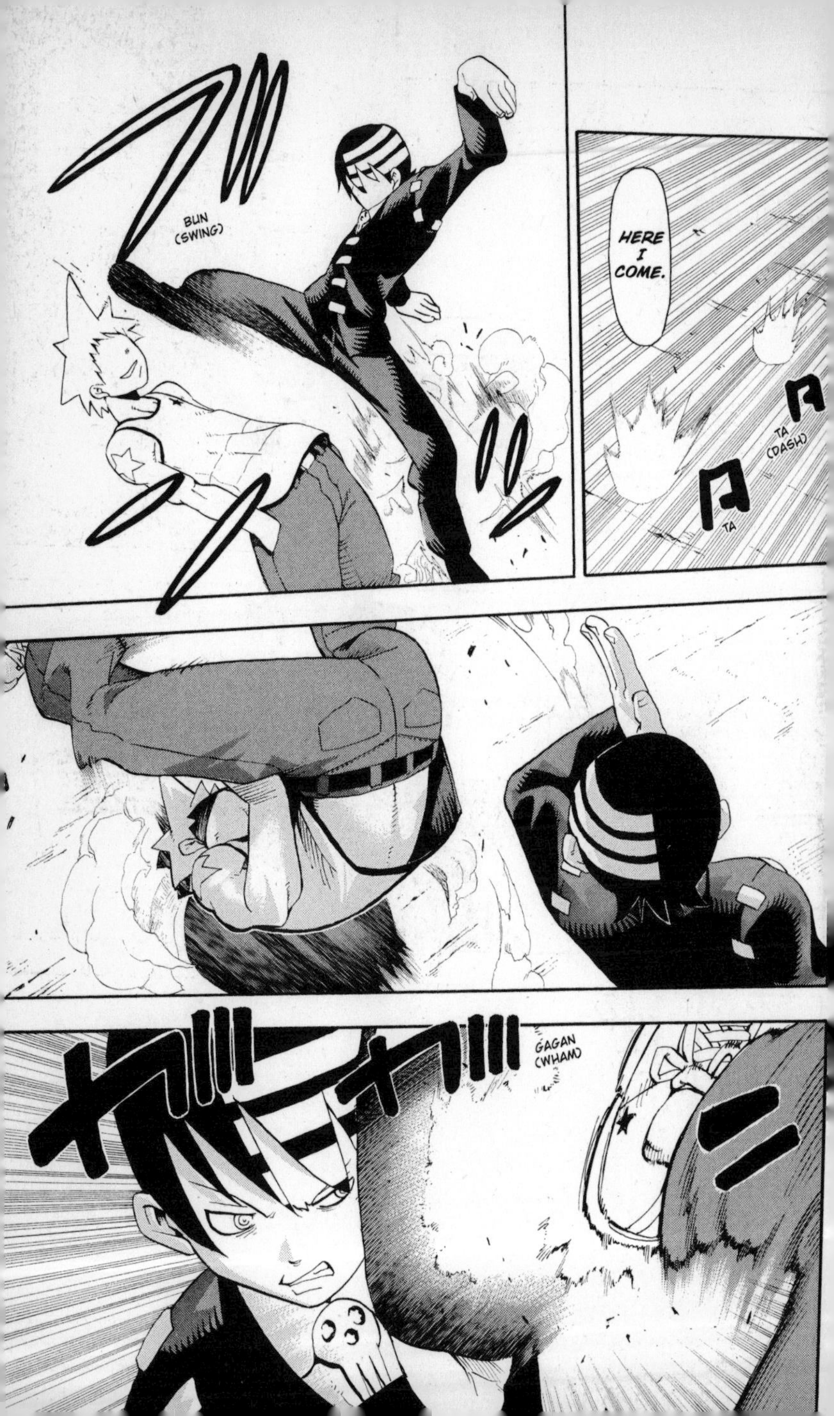
HERE I COME.
TA (DASH)
TA
BUN (SWING)
GAGAN (WHAM)

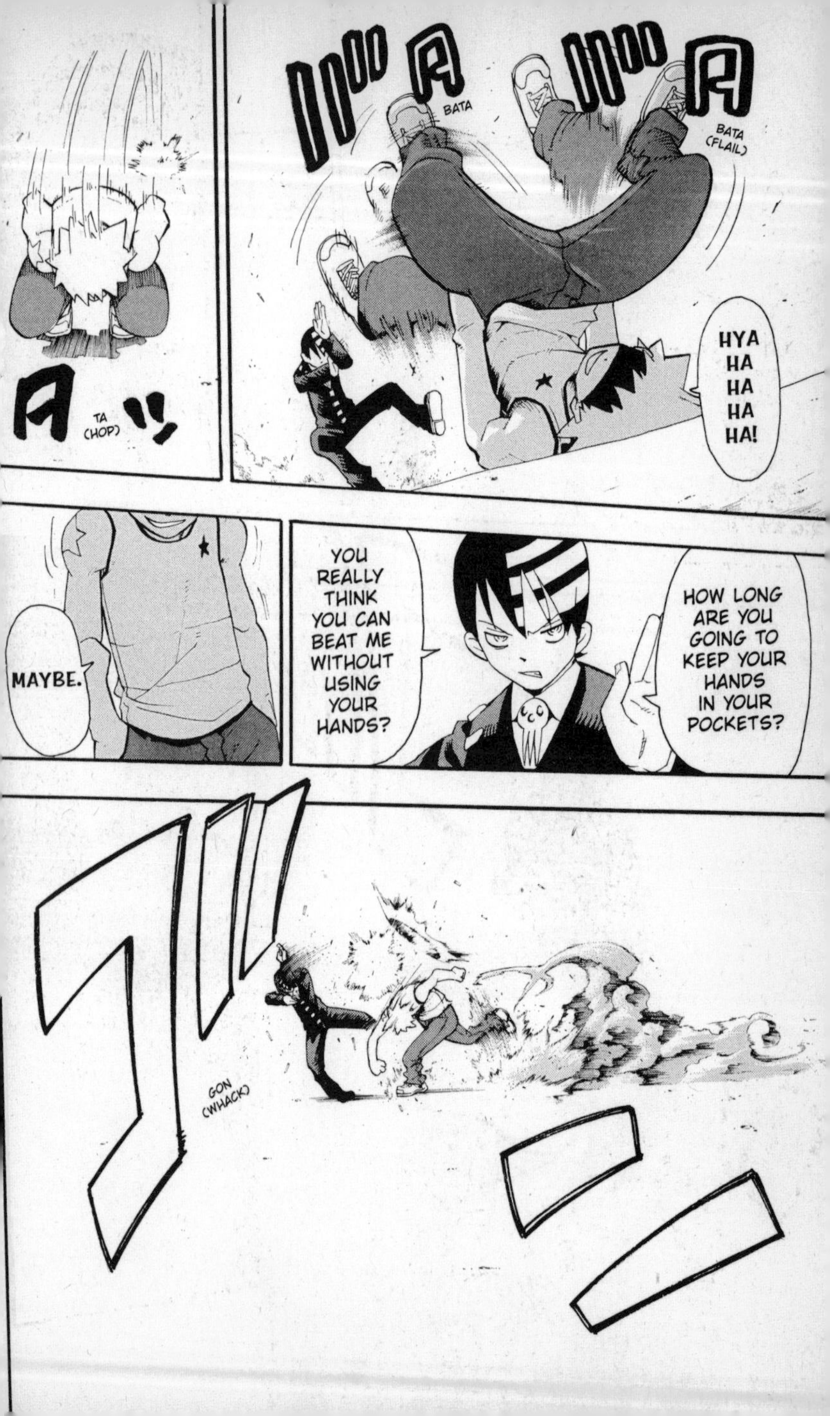
BATA
BATA (FLAIL)
HYA HA HA HA HA!
TA (HOP)
HOW LONG ARE YOU GOING TO KEEP YOUR HANDS IN YOUR POCKETS?
YOU REALLY THINK YOU CAN BEAT ME WITHOUT USING YOUR HANDS?
MAYBE.
GON (WHACK)

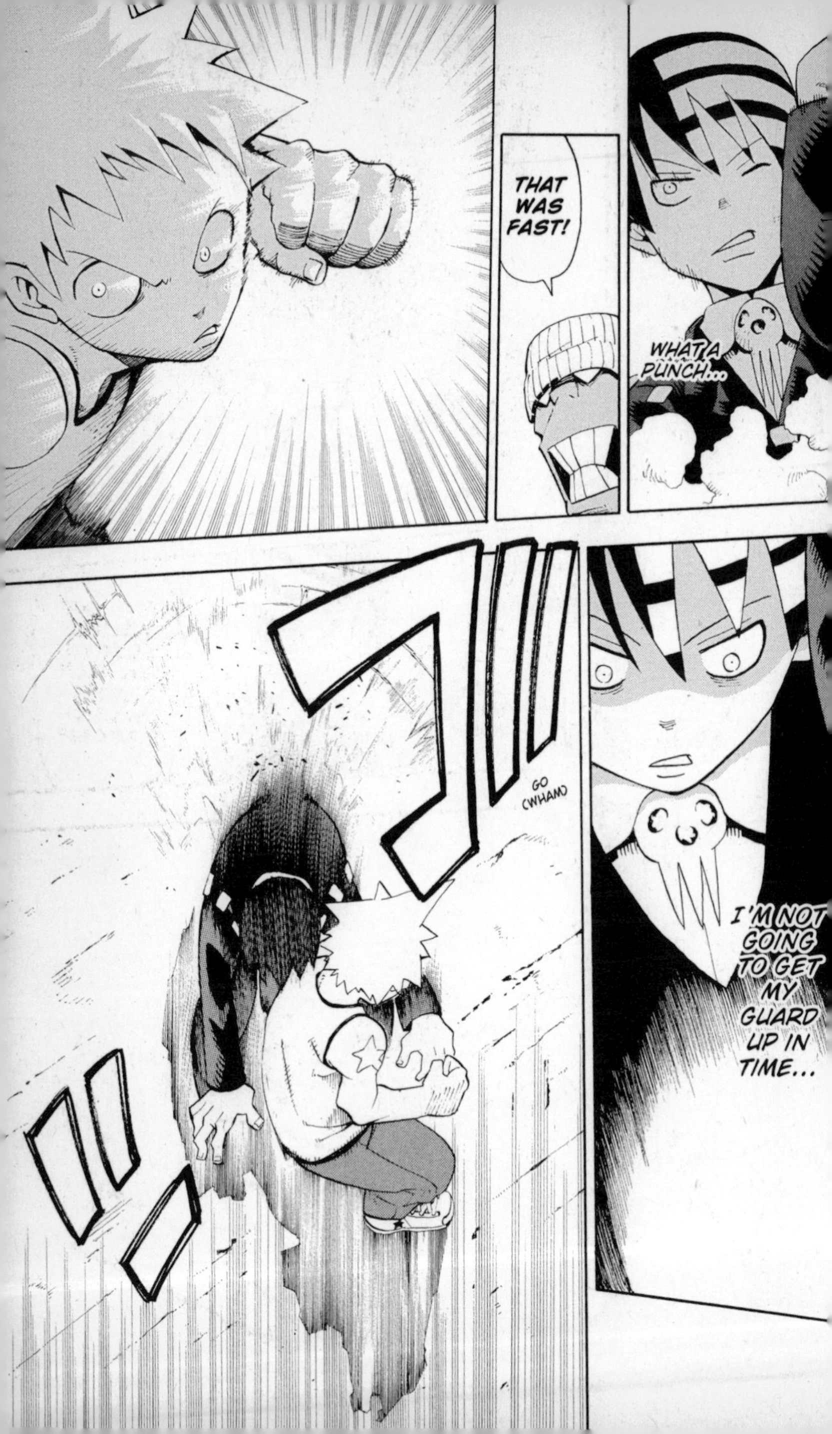
WHAT A PUNCH...
THAT WAS FAST!
I'M NOT GOING TO GET MY GUARD UP IN TIME...
GO (WHAM)

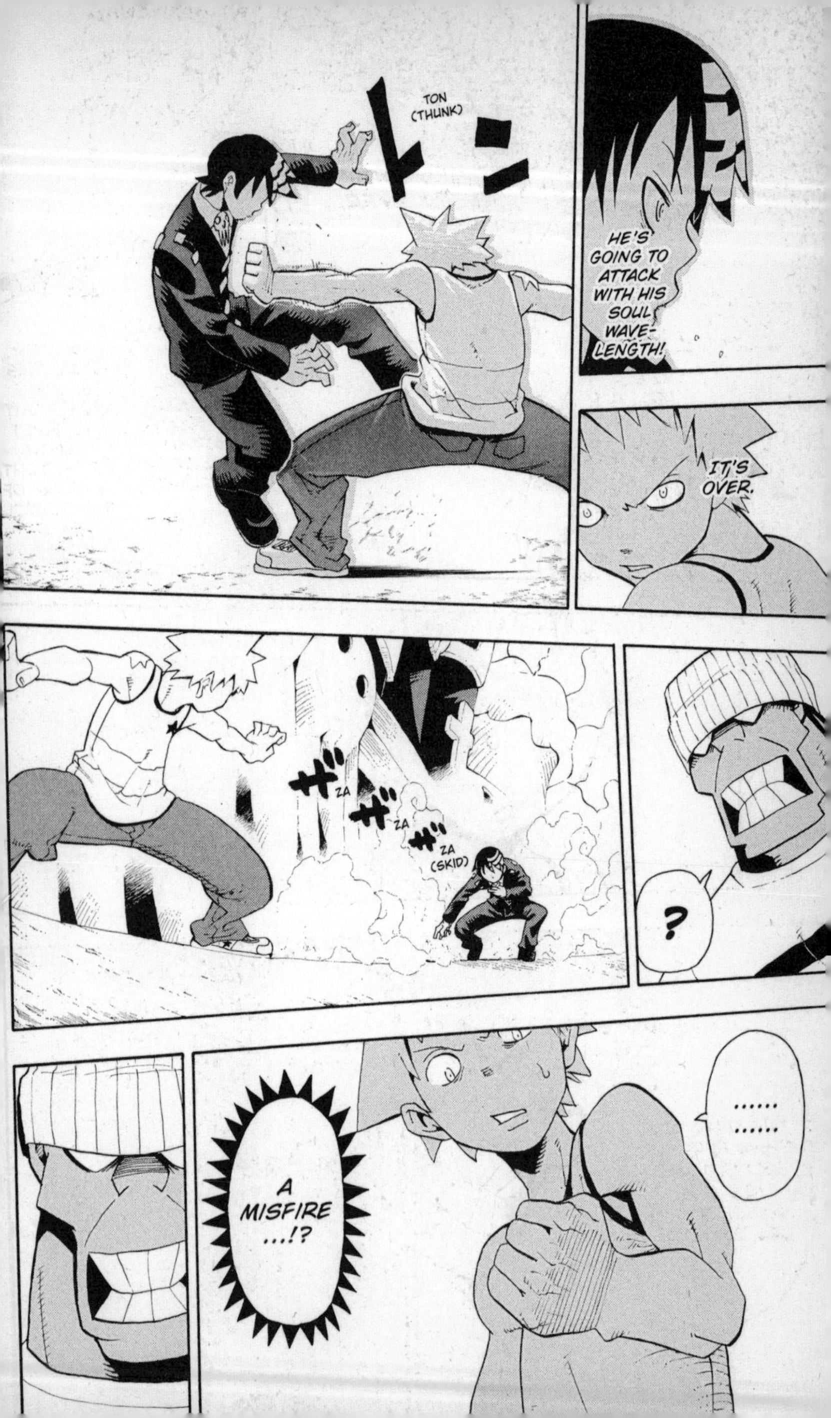
HE'S GOING TO ATTACK WITH HIS SOUL WAVE-LENGTH!
IT'S OVER.
TON (THUNK)
?
ZA
ZA
ZA (SKID)
......
......
A MISFIRE ...!?

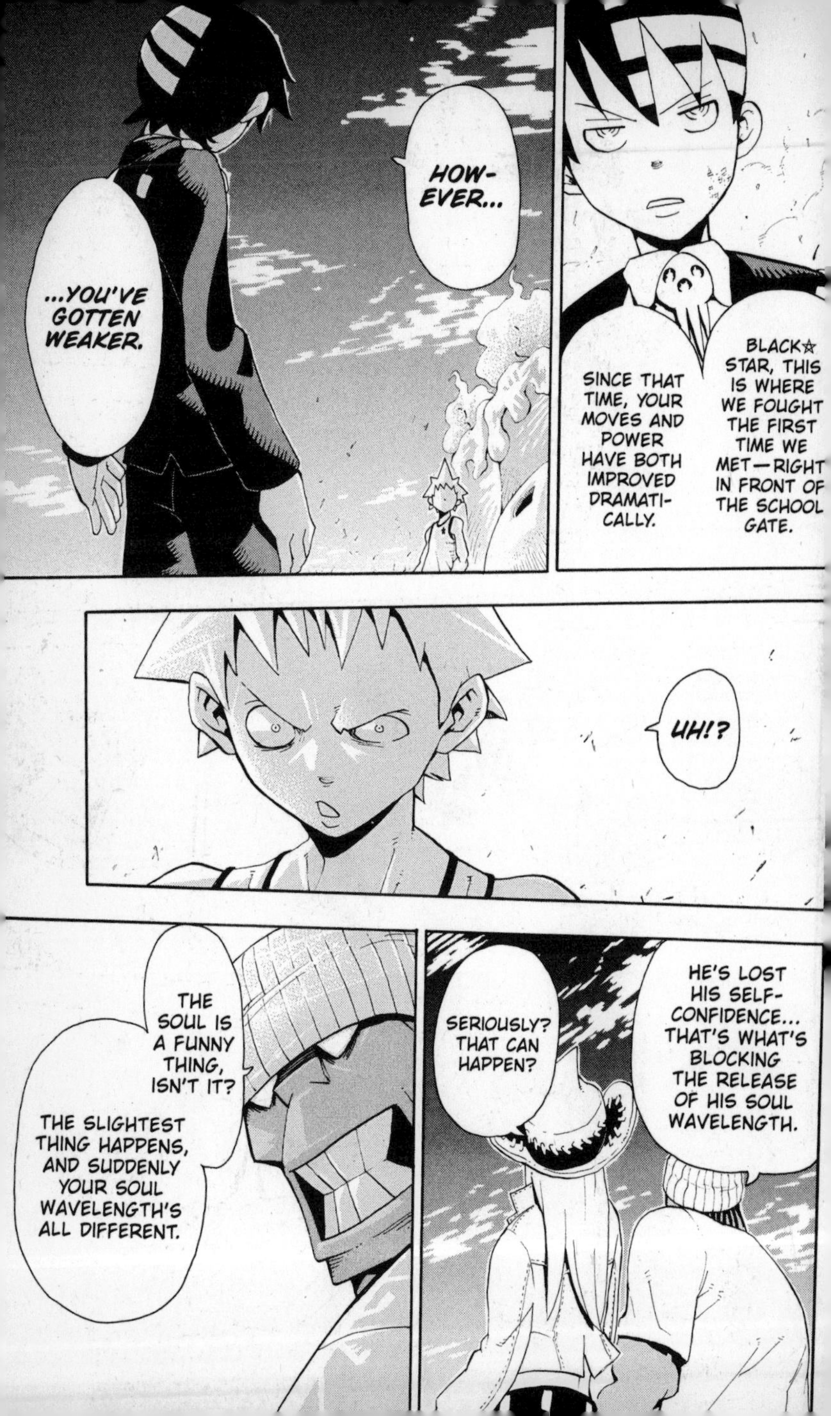
BLACK☆ STAR, THIS IS WHERE WE FOUGHT THE FIRST TIME WE MET—RIGHT IN FRONT OF THE SCHOOL GATE.
SINCE THAT TIME, YOUR MOVES AND POWER HAVE BOTH IMPROVED DRAMATICALLY.
HOWEVER...
...YOU'VE GOTTEN WEAKER.
UH!?
HE'S LOST HIS SELF-CONFIDENCE... THAT'S WHAT'S BLOCKING THE RELEASE OF HIS SOUL WAVELENGTH.
SERIOUSLY? THAT CAN HAPPEN?
THE SOUL IS A FUNNY THING, ISN'T IT?
THE SLIGHTEST THING HAPPENS, AND SUDDENLY YOUR SOUL WAVELENGTH'S ALL DIFFERENT.

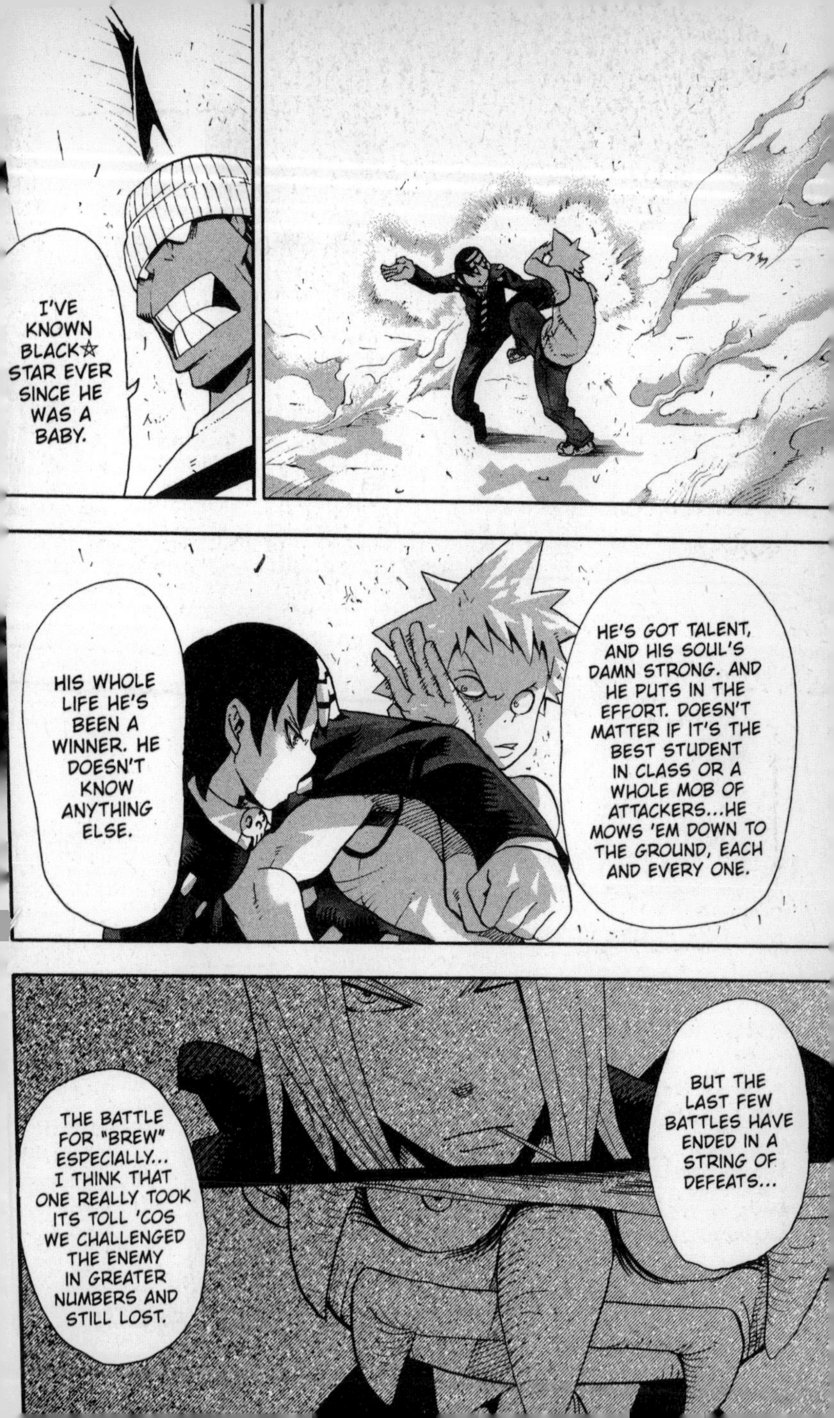
I'VE KNOWN BLACK☆STAR EVER SINCE HE WAS A BABY.
HE'S GOT TALENT, AND HIS SOUL'S DAMN STRONG. AND HE PUTS IN THE EFFORT. DOESN'T MATTER IF IT'S THE BEST STUDENT IN CLASS OR A WHOLE MOB OF ATTACKERS...HE MOWS 'EM DOWN TO THE GROUND, EACH AND EVERY ONE.
HIS WHOLE LIFE HE'S BEEN A WINNER. HE DOESN'T KNOW ANYTHING ELSE.
BUT THE LAST FEW BATTLES HAVE ENDED IN A STRING OF DEFEATS...
THE BATTLE FOR "BREW" ESPECIALLY... I THINK THAT ONE REALLY TOOK ITS TOLL 'COS WE CHALLENGED THE ENEMY IN GREATER NUMBERS AND STILL LOST.

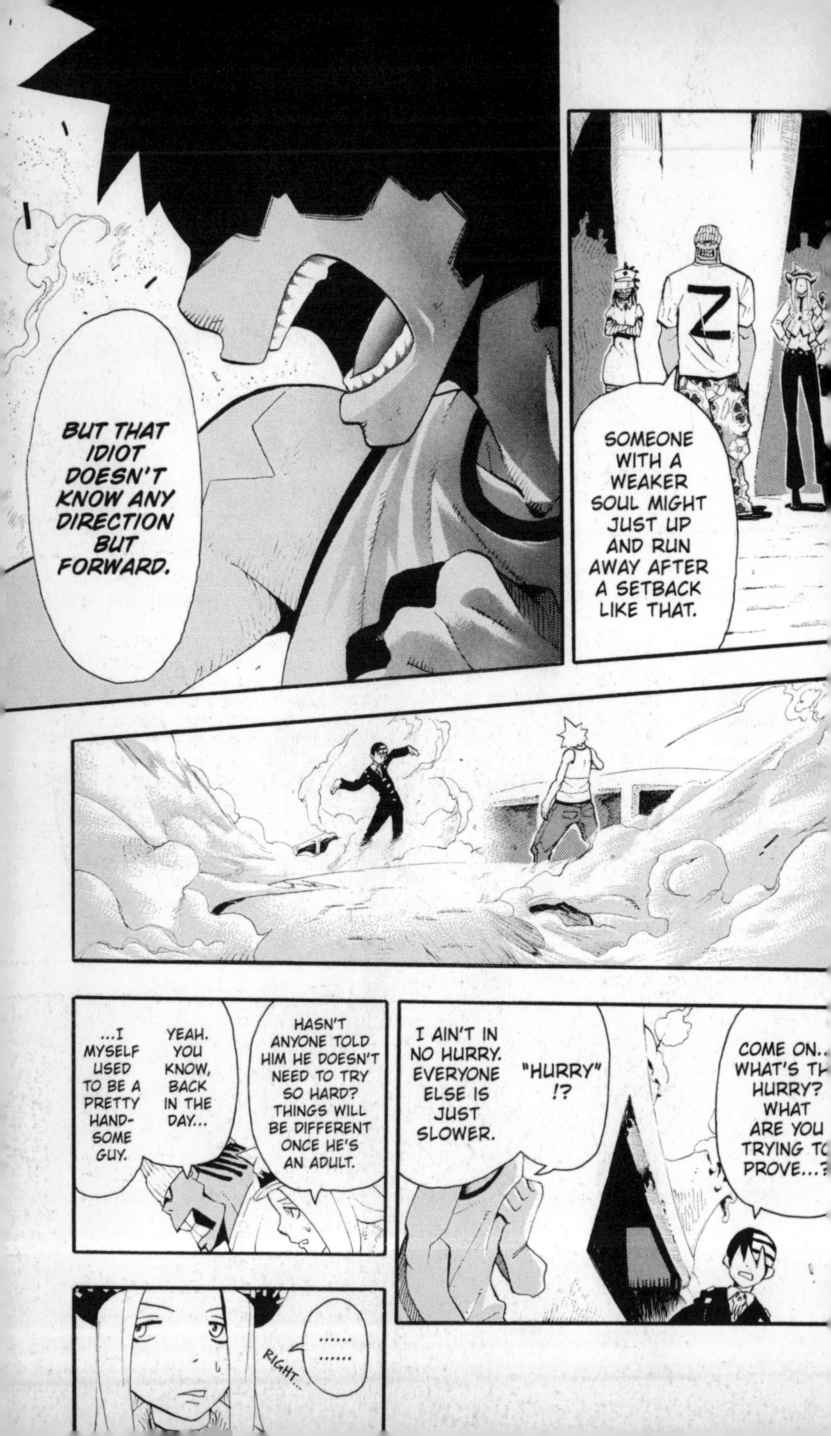
SOMEONE WITH A WEAKER SOUL MIGHT JUST UP AND RUN AWAY AFTER A SETBACK LIKE THAT.
BUT THAT IDIOT DOESN'T KNOW ANY DIRECTION BUT FORWARD.
COME ON... WHAT'S TH HURRY? WHAT ARE YOU TRYING T PROVE...?
"HURRY" !?
I AIN'T IN NO HURRY. EVERYONE ELSE IS JUST SLOWER.
HASN'T ANYONE TOLD HIM HE DOESN'T NEED TO TRY SO HARD? THINGS WILL BE DIFFERENT ONCE HE'S AN ADULT.
YEAH. YOU KNOW, BACK IN THE DAY...
...I MYSELF USED TO BE A PRETTY HANDSOME GUY.
......
......
RIGHT...

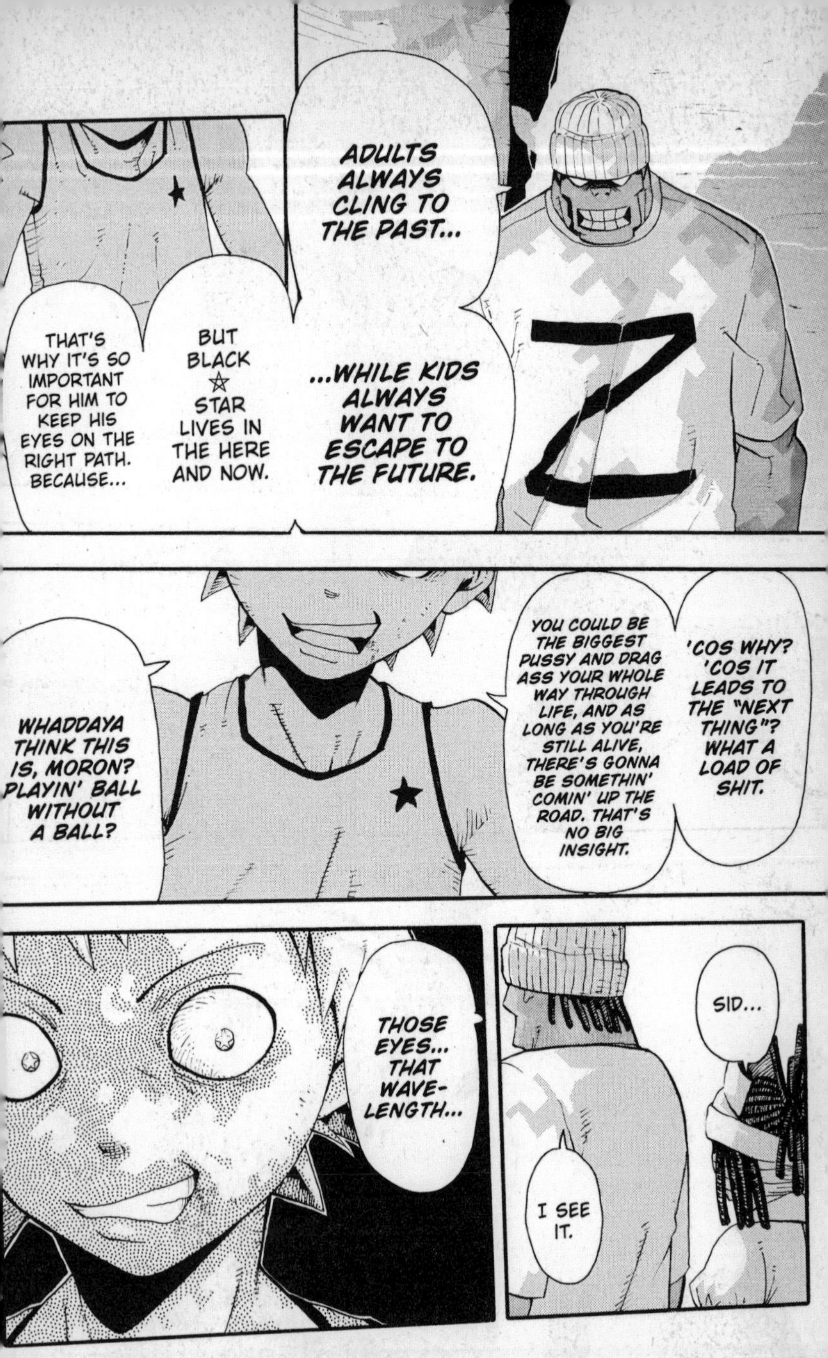
ADULTS ALWAYS CLING TO THE PAST...
...WHILE KIDS ALWAYS WANT TO ESCAPE TO THE FUTURE.
BUT BLACK☆STAR LIVES IN THE HERE AND NOW.
THAT'S WHY IT'S SO IMPORTANT FOR HIM TO KEEP HIS EYES ON THE RIGHT PATH. BECAUSE...
'COS WHY? 'COS IT LEADS TO THE "NEXT THING"? WHAT A LOAD OF SHIT.
YOU COULD BE THE BIGGEST PUSSY AND DRAG ASS YOUR WHOLE WAY THROUGH LIFE, AND AS LONG AS YOU'RE STILL ALIVE, THERE'S GONNA BE SOMETHIN' COMIN' UP THE ROAD. THAT'S NO BIG INSIGHT.
WHADDAYA THINK THIS IS, MORON? PLAYIN' BALL WITHOUT A BALL?
SID...
I SEE IT.
THOSE EYES... THAT WAVE-LENGTH...

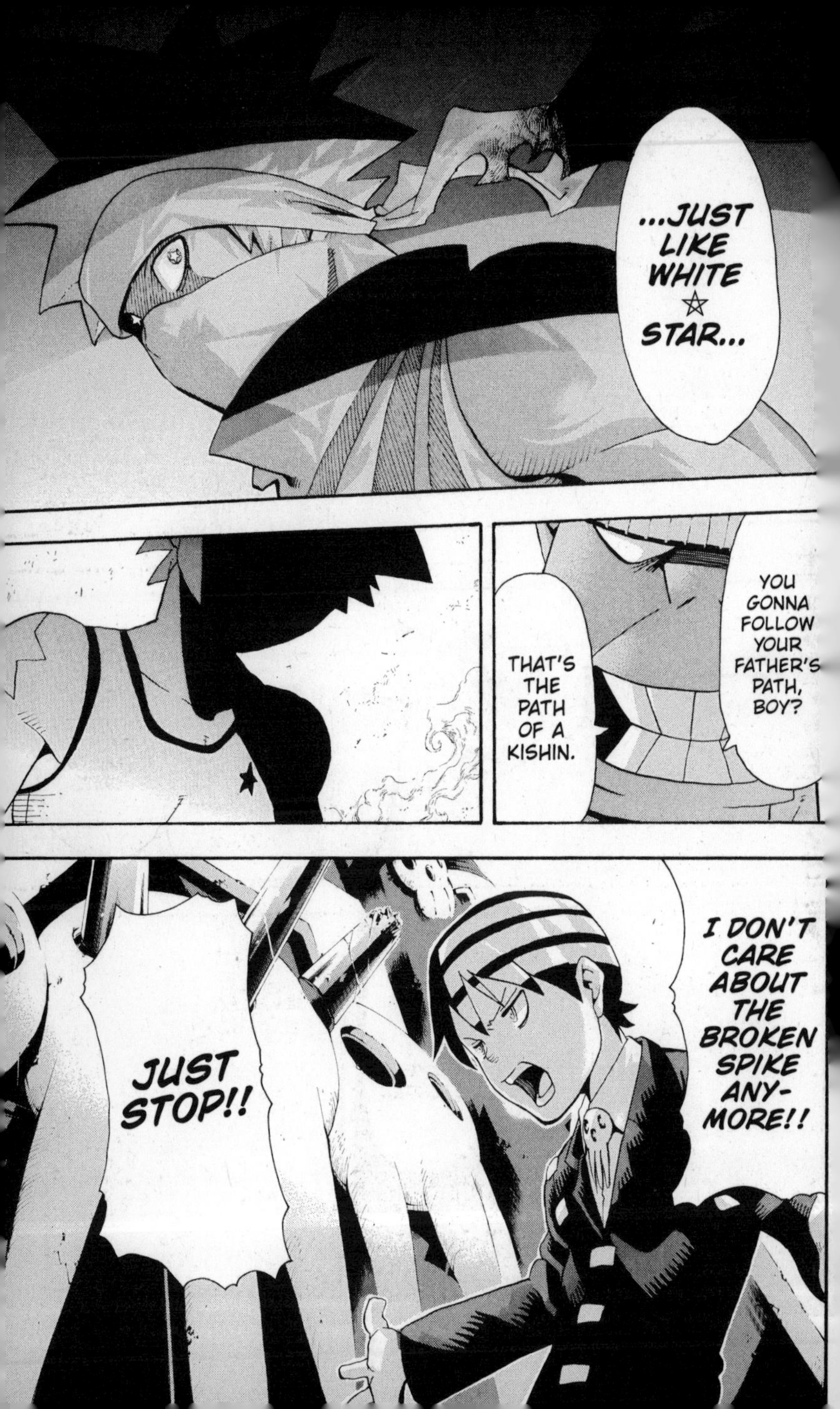
...JUST LIKE WHITE ☆ STAR...
YOU GONNA FOLLOW YOUR FATHER'S PATH, BOY?
THAT'S THE PATH OF A KISHIN.
I DON'T CARE ABOUT THE BROKEN SPIKE ANY-MORE!!
JUST STOP!!

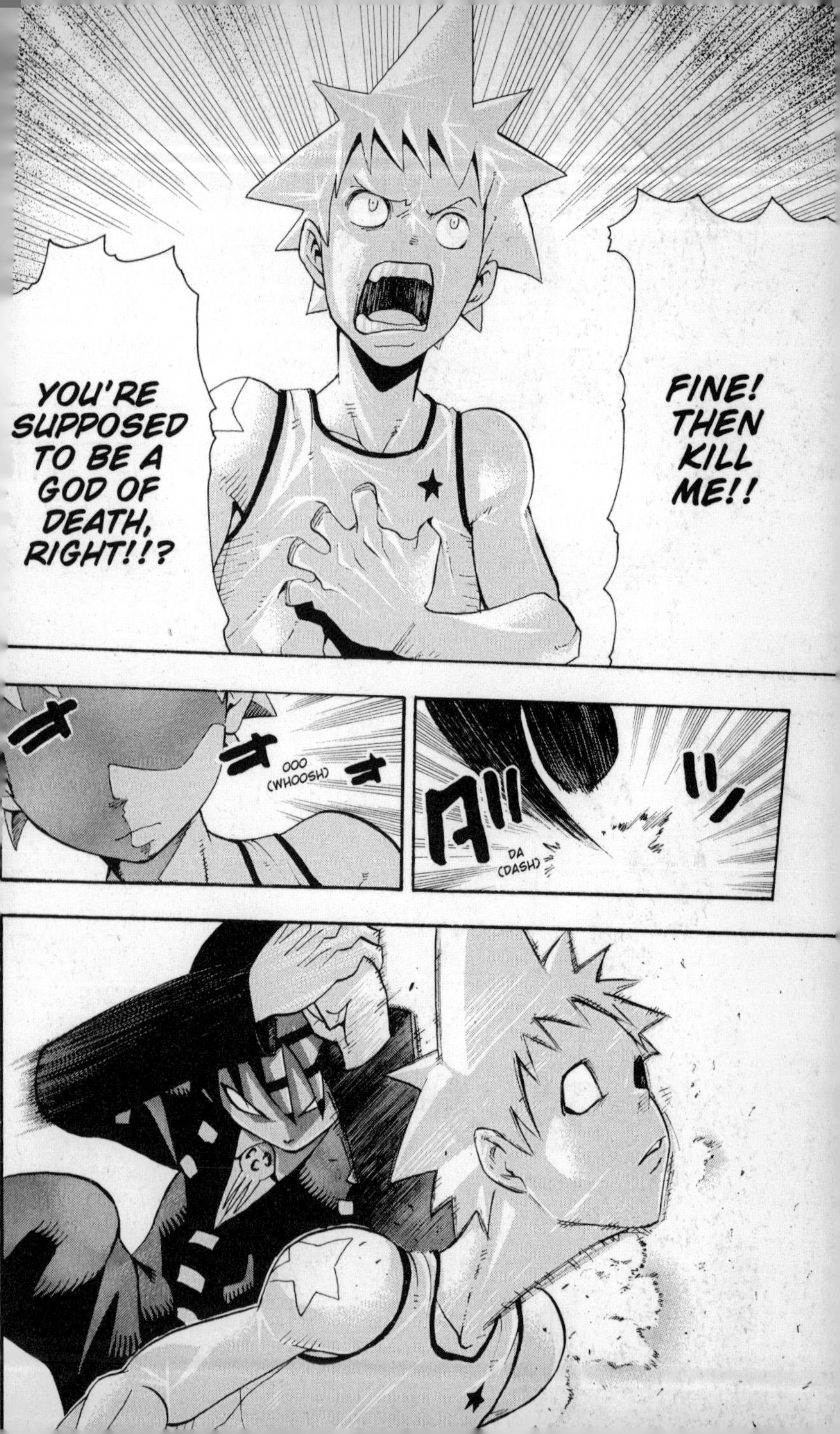
FINE! THEN KILL ME!!
YOU'RE SUPPOSED TO BE A GOD OF DEATH, RIGHT!!?
DA (DASH)
OOO (WHOOSH)

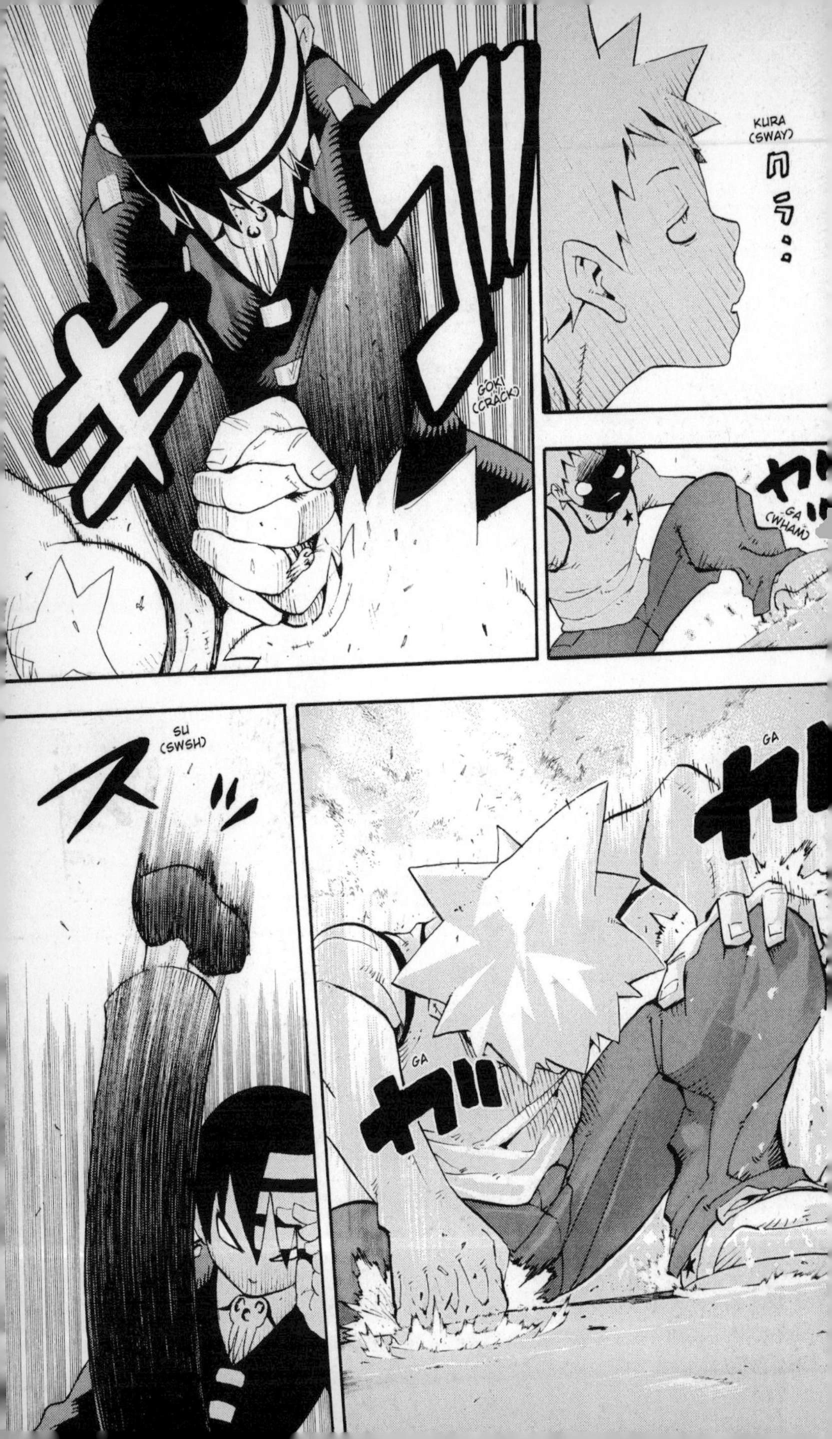
KURA (SWAY)
GA (WHAM)
GOKI (CRACK)
GA
GA
SU (SWSH)

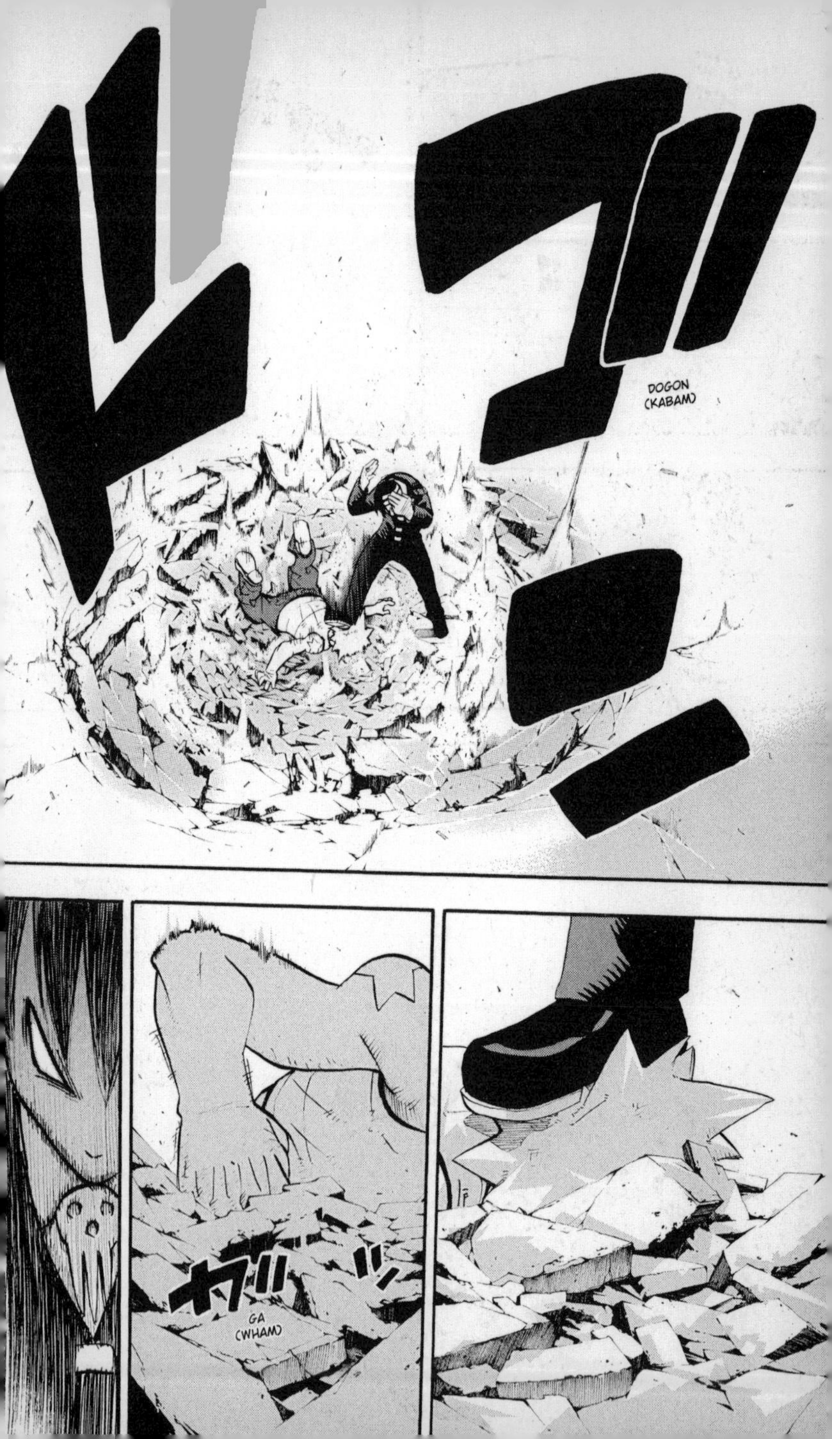
DOGON
(KABAM)
GA
(WHAM)

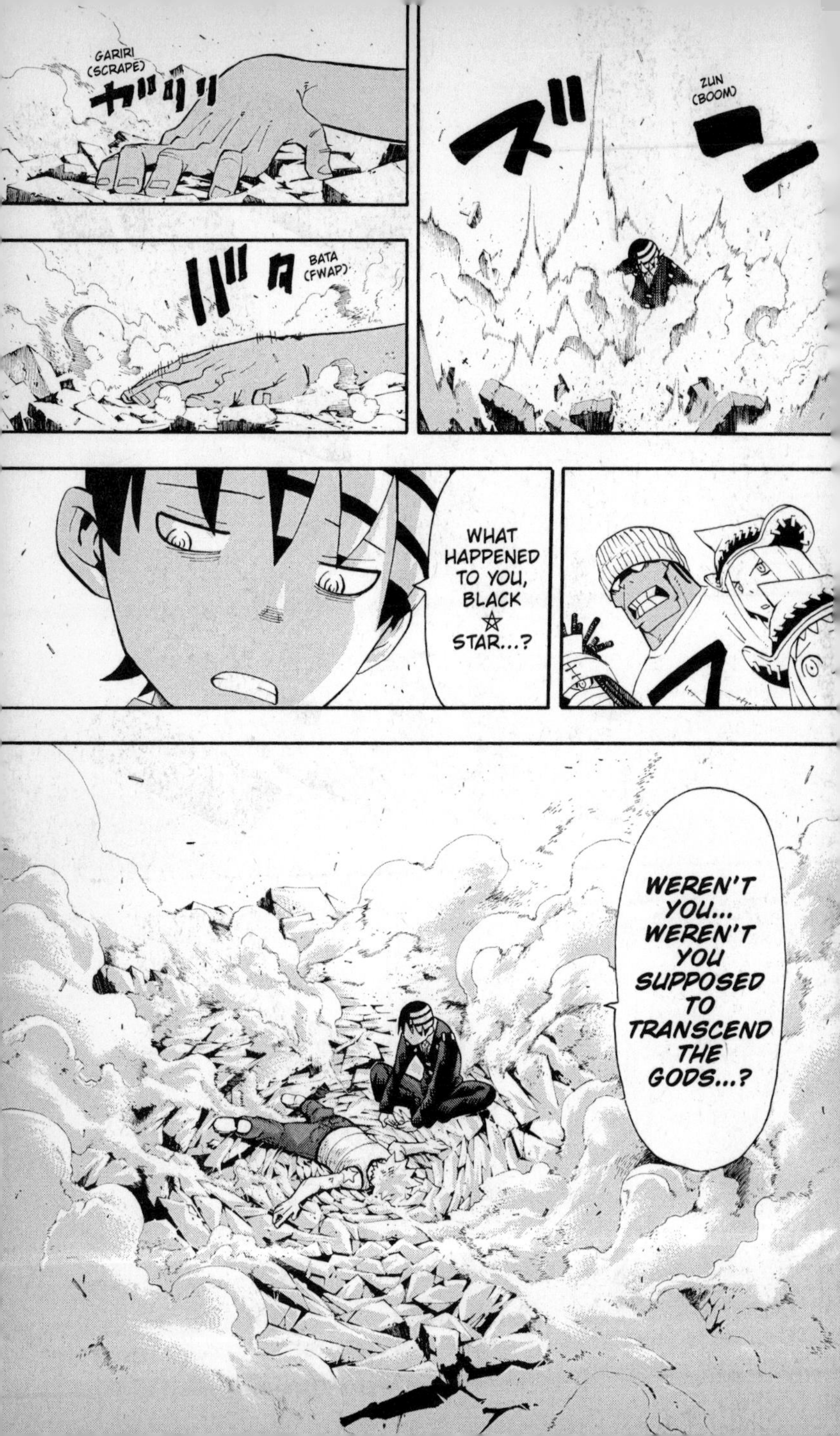
ZUN (BOOM)
GARIRI (SCRAPE)
BATA (FWAP)
WHAT HAPPENED TO YOU, BLACK☆STAR...?
WEREN'T YOU... WEREN'T YOU SUPPOSED TO TRANSCEND THE GODS...?

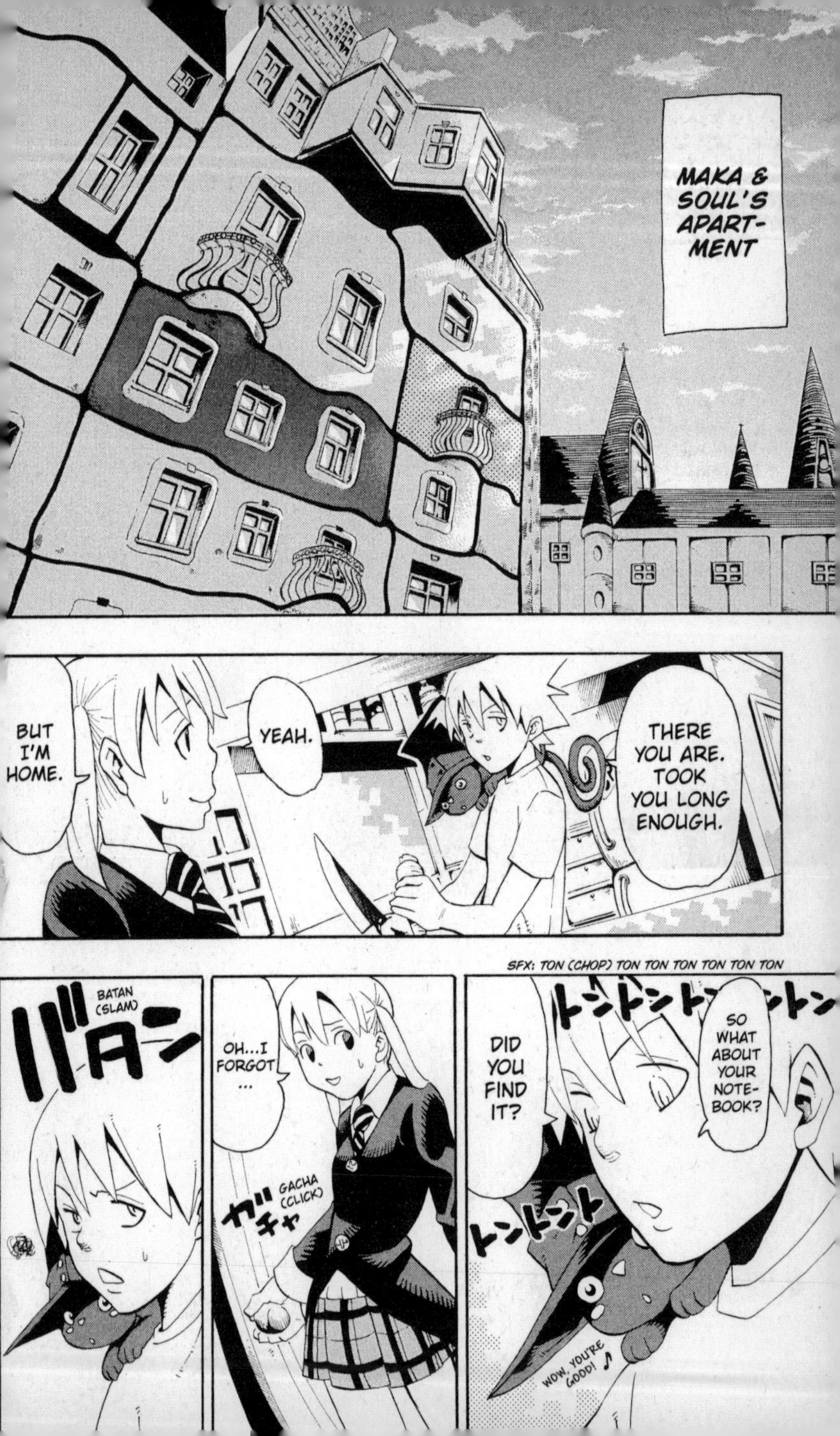
MAKA & SOUL'S APARTMENT
THERE YOU ARE. TOOK YOU LONG ENOUGH.
YEAH.
BUT I'M HOME.
SFX: TON (CHOP) TON TON TON TON TON TON
SO WHAT ABOUT YOUR NOTE-BOOK?
DID YOU FIND IT?
WOW, YOU'RE GOOD! ♪
OH...I FORGOT ...
GACHA (CLICK)
BATAN (SLAM)

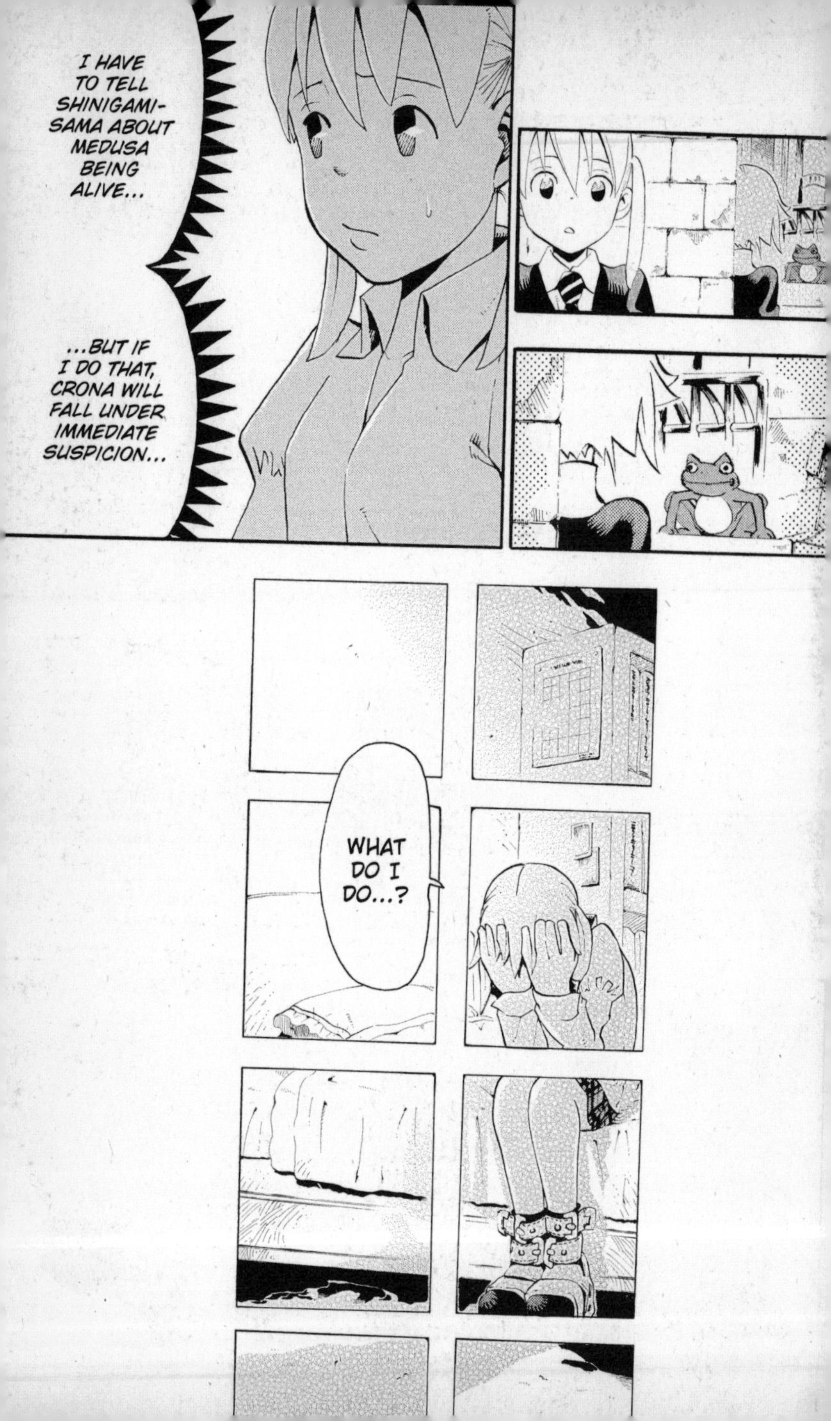
I HAVE TO TELL SHINIGAMI-SAMA ABOUT MEDUSA BEING ALIVE...
...BUT IF I DO THAT, CRONA WILL FALL UNDER IMMEDIATE SUSPICION...
WHAT DO I DO...?

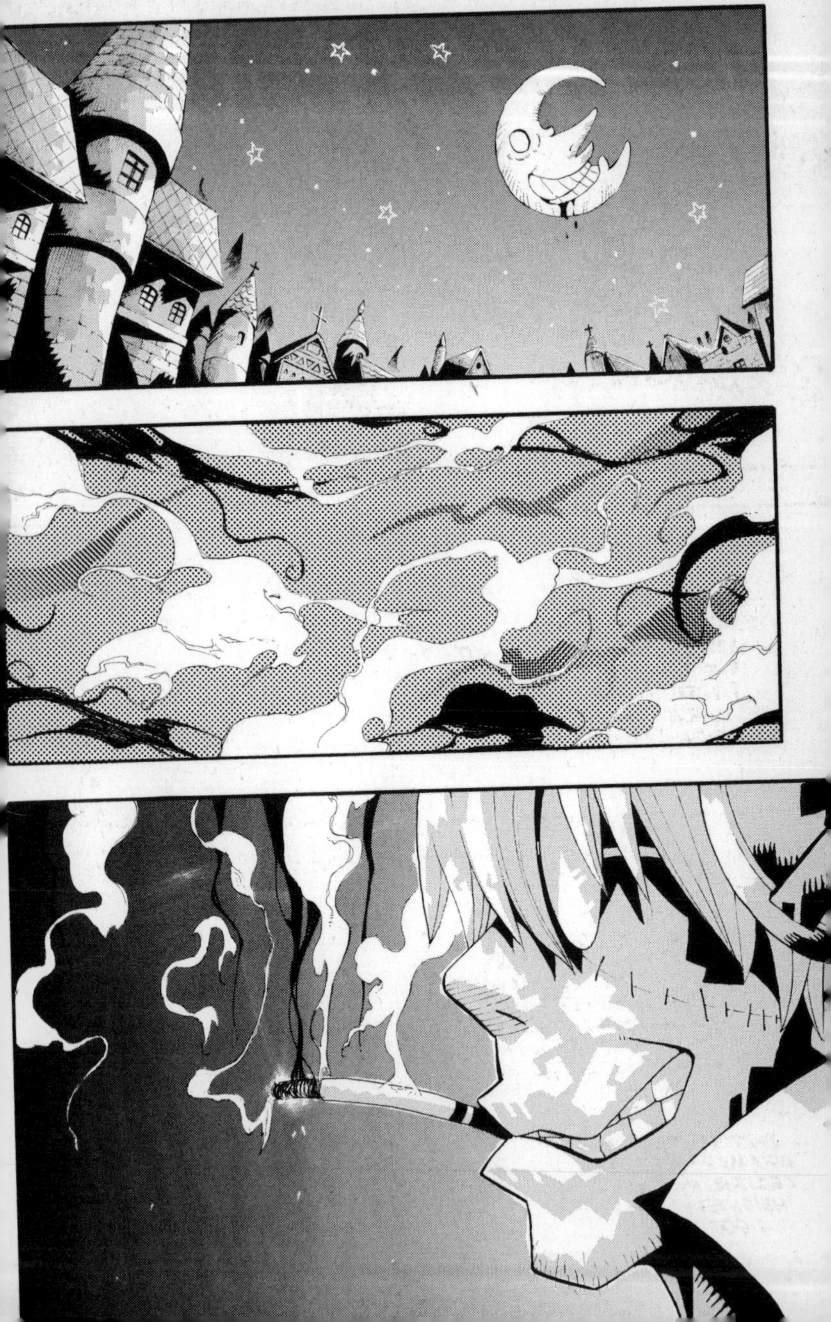

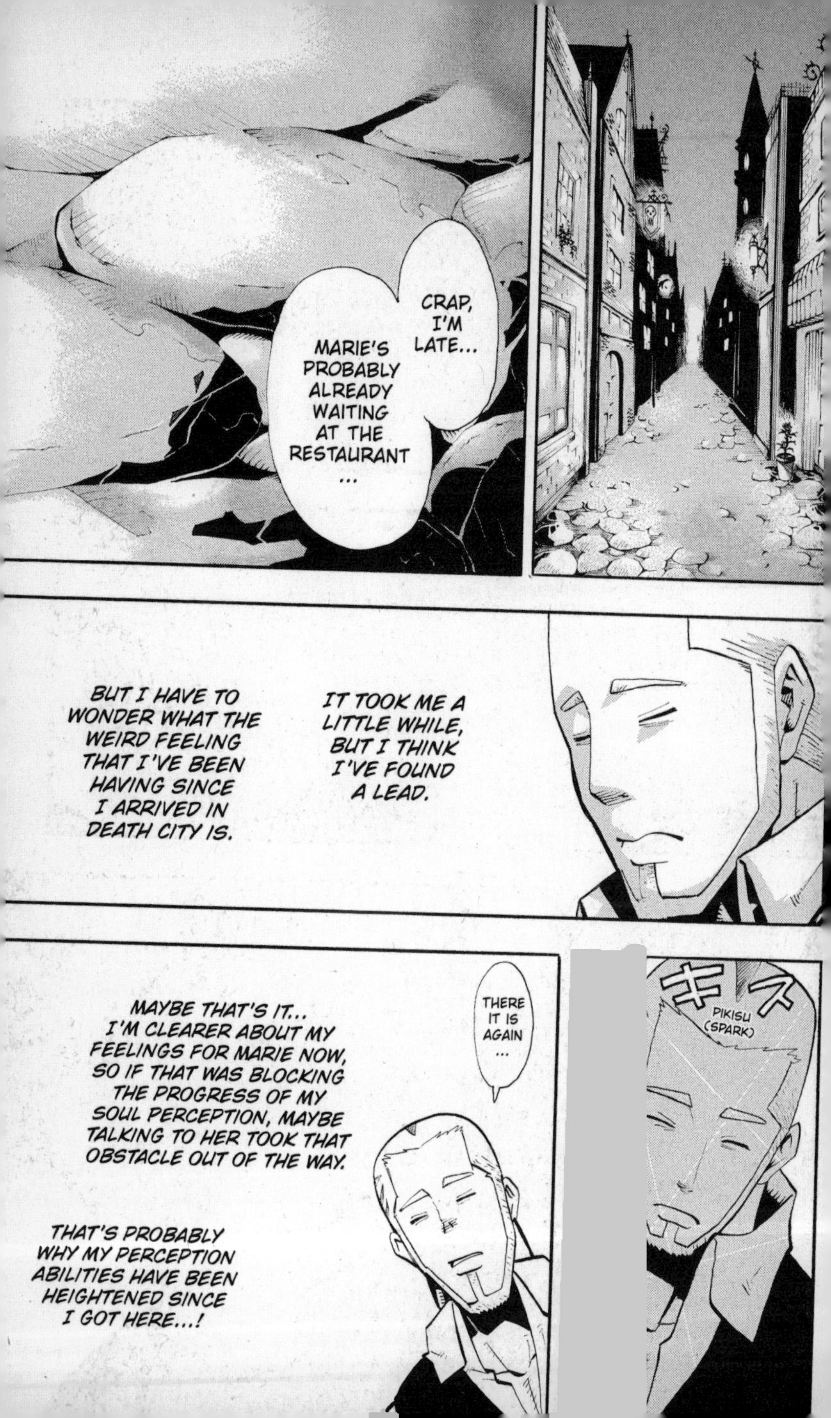
CRAP, I'M LATE...
MARIE'S PROBABLY ALREADY WAITING AT THE RESTAURANT...
IT TOOK ME A LITTLE WHILE, BUT I THINK I'VE FOUND A LEAD.
BUT I HAVE TO WONDER WHAT THE WEIRD FEELING THAT I'VE BEEN HAVING SINCE I ARRIVED IN DEATH CITY IS.
PIKISU (SPARK)
THERE IT IS AGAIN...
MAYBE THAT'S IT... I'M CLEARER ABOUT MY FEELINGS FOR MARIE NOW, SO IF THAT WAS BLOCKING THE PROGRESS OF MY SOUL PERCEPTION, MAYBE TALKING TO HER TOOK THAT OBSTACLE OUT OF THE WAY.
THAT'S PROBABLY WHY MY PERCEPTION ABILITIES HAVE BEEN HEIGHTENED SINCE I GOT HERE...!

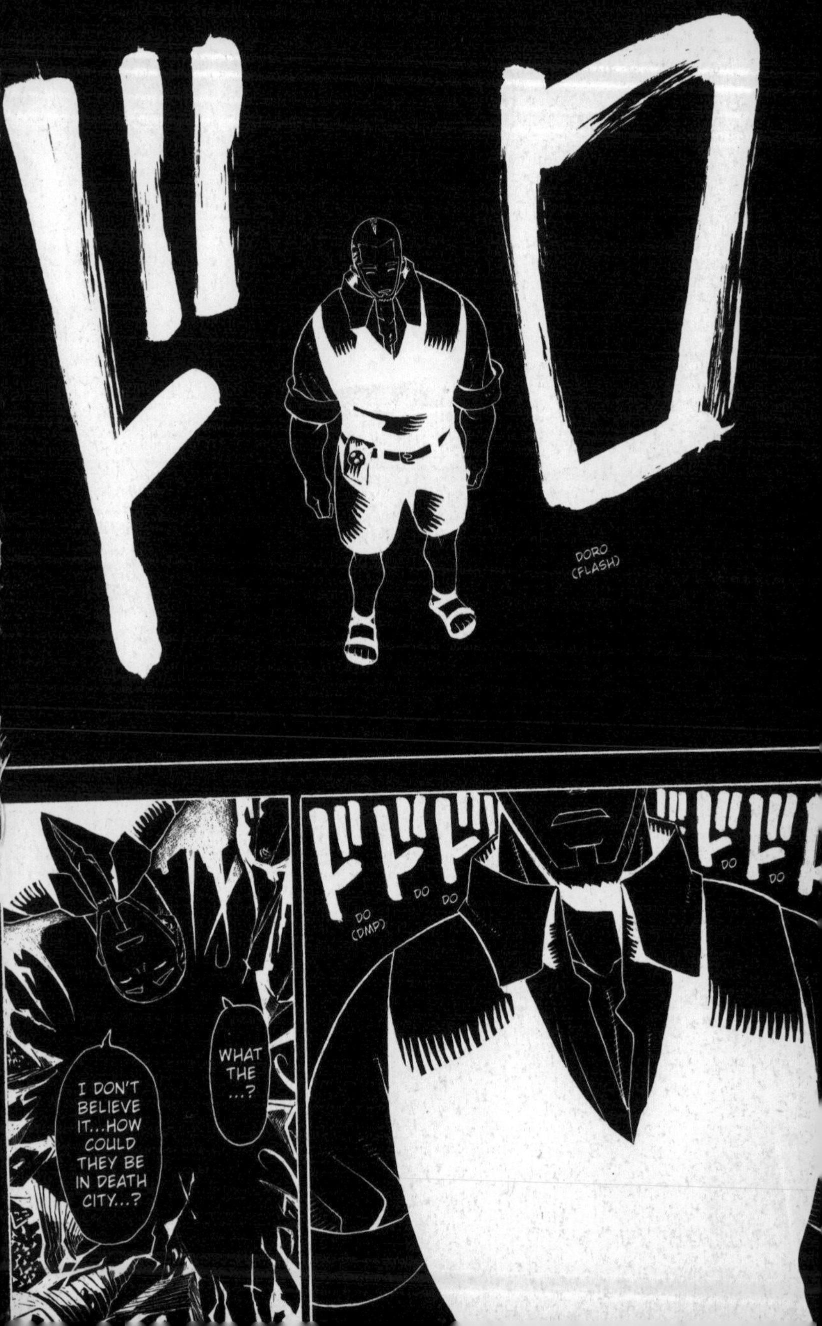
DORO (FLASH)
DO
DO
DO
DO
DO (DMP)
WHAT THE ...?
I DON'T BELIEVE IT...HOW COULD THEY BE IN DEATH CITY...?

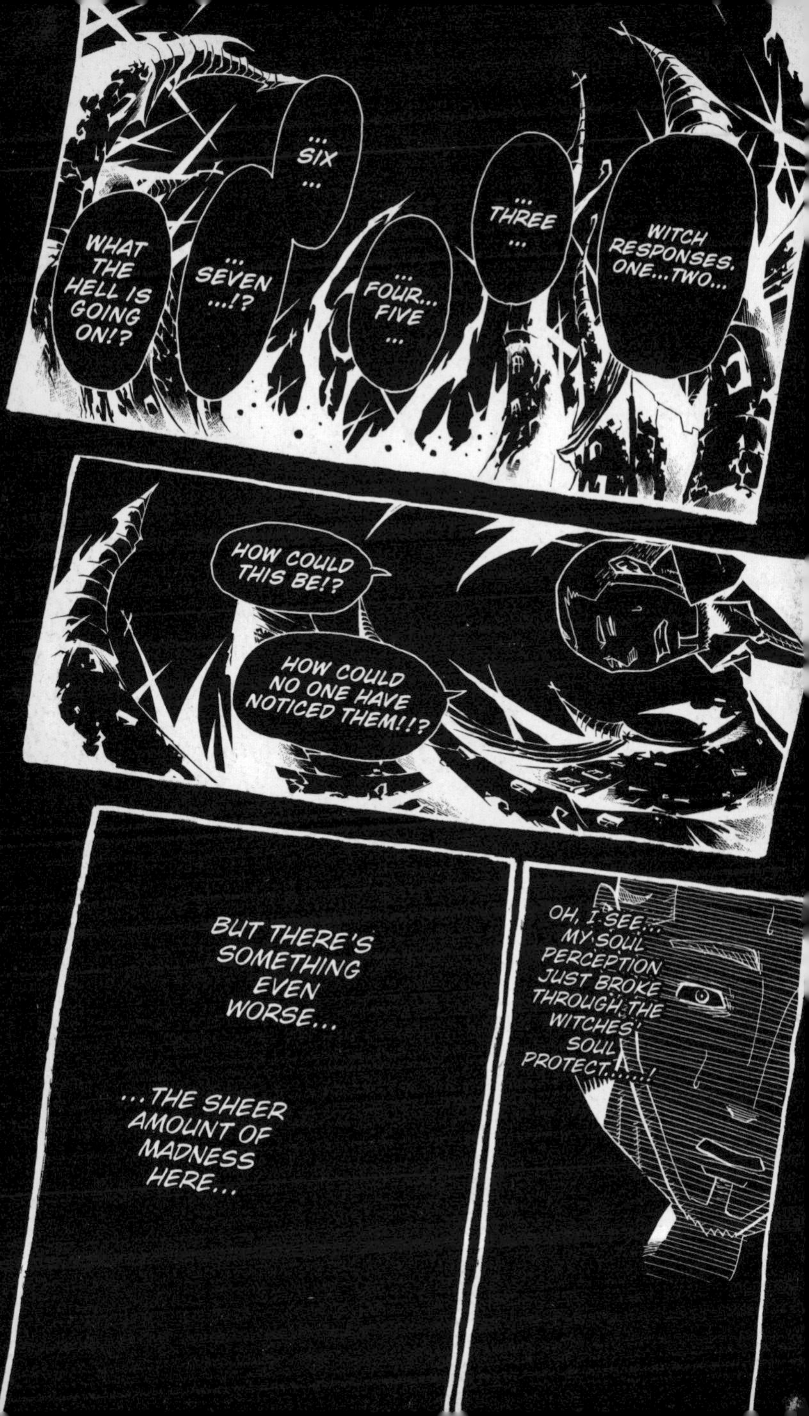
WITCH RESPONSES. ONE...TWO...
...THREE...
...FOUR...FIVE...
...SIX...
...SEVEN...!?
WHAT THE HELL IS GOING ON!?
HOW COULD THIS BE!?
HOW COULD NO ONE HAVE NOTICED THEM!!?
OH, I SEE... MY SOUL PERCEPTION JUST BROKE THROUGH THE WITCHES' SOUL PROTECT......!
BUT THERE'S SOMETHING EVEN WORSE...
...THE SHEER AMOUNT OF MADNESS HERE...

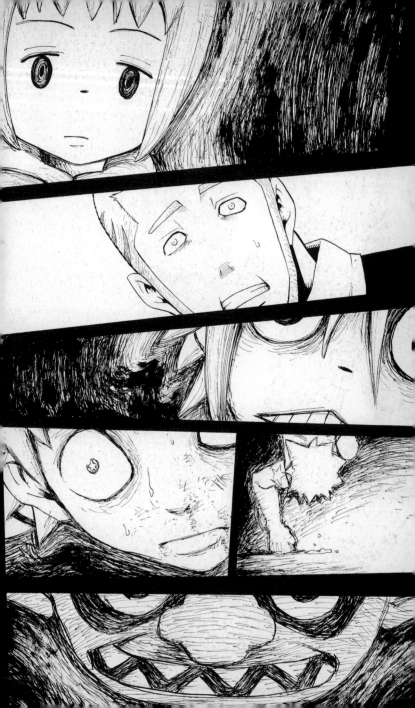

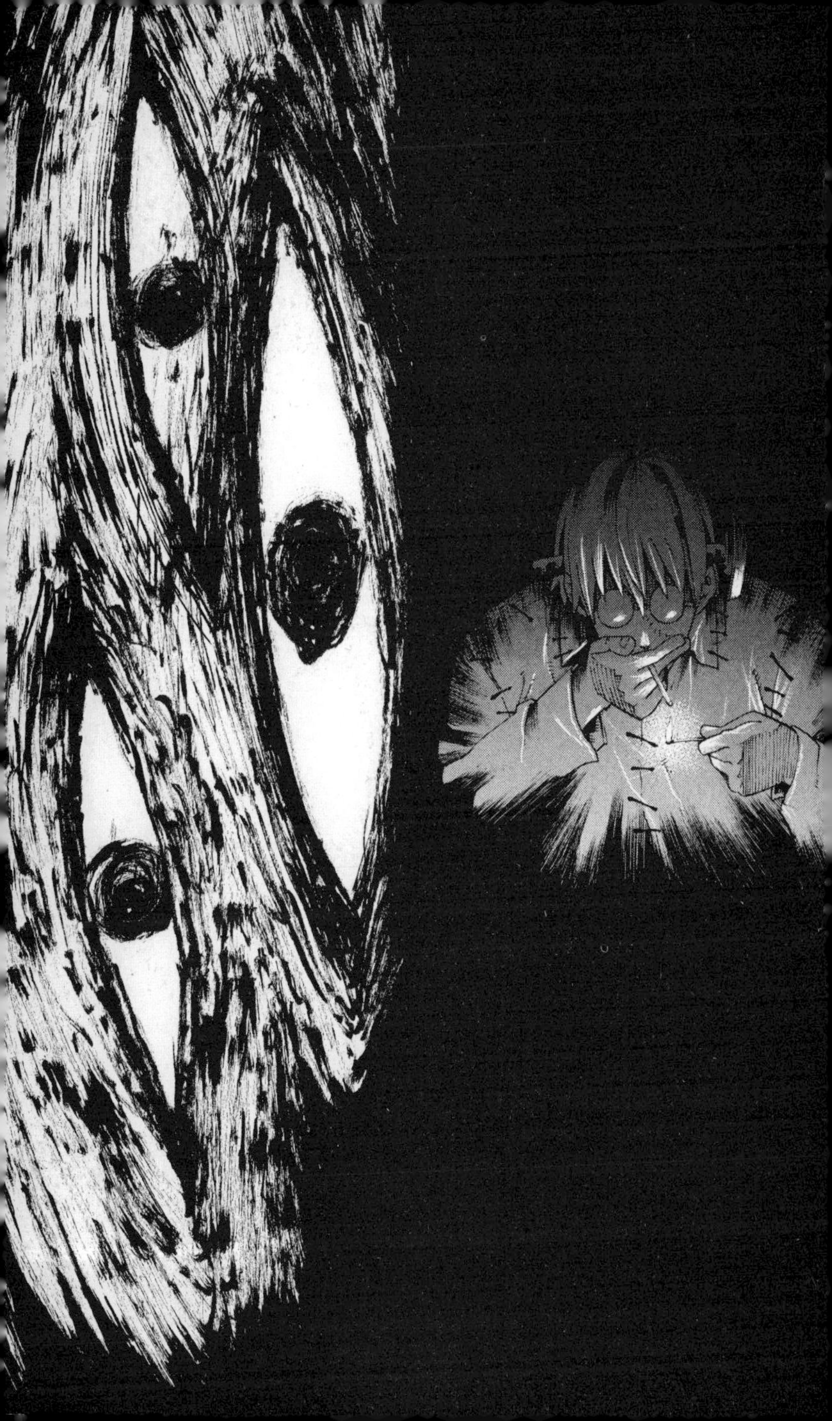

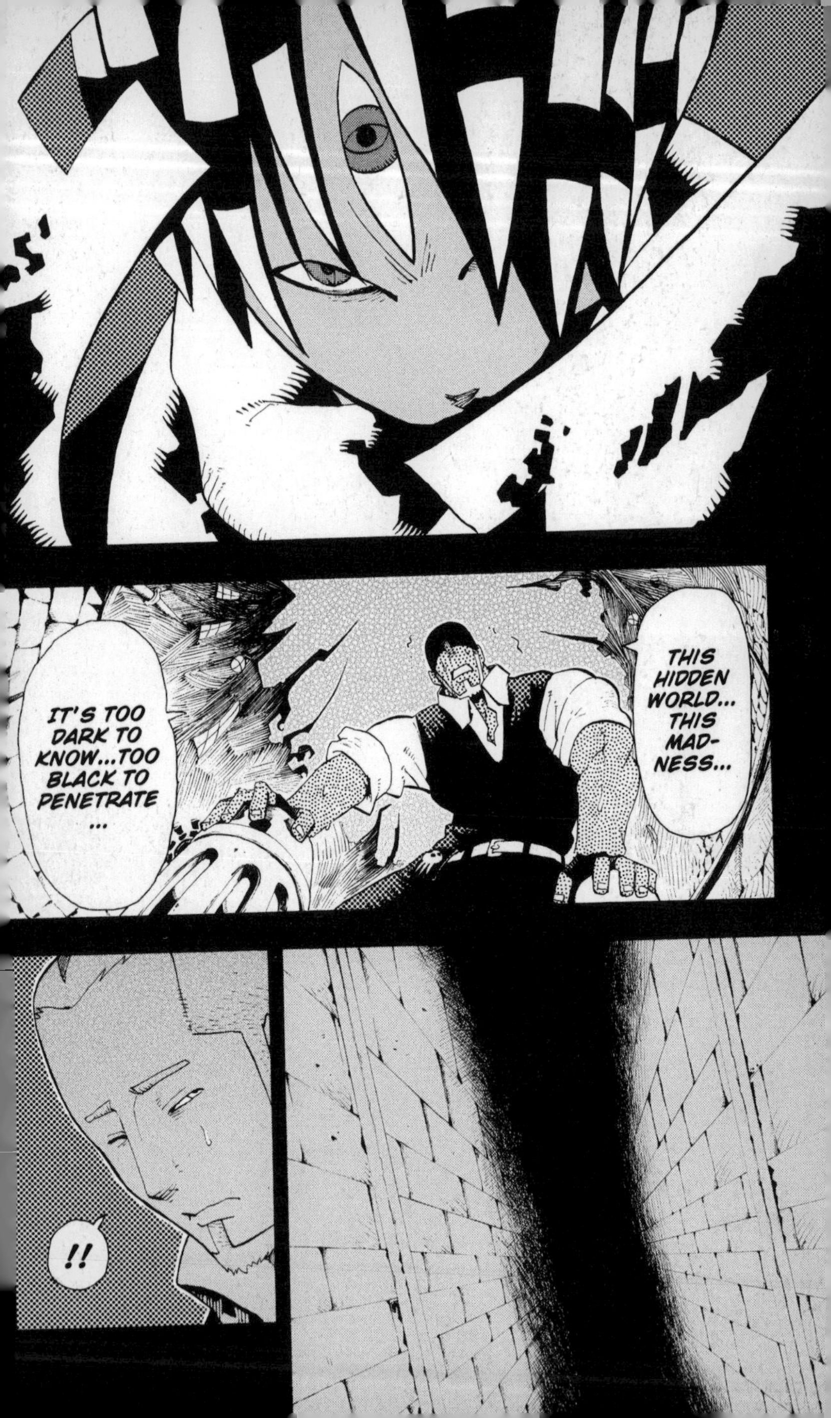
THIS HIDDEN WORLD... THIS MAD-NESS...
IT'S TOO DARK TO KNOW...TOO BLACK TO PENETRATE ...
!!

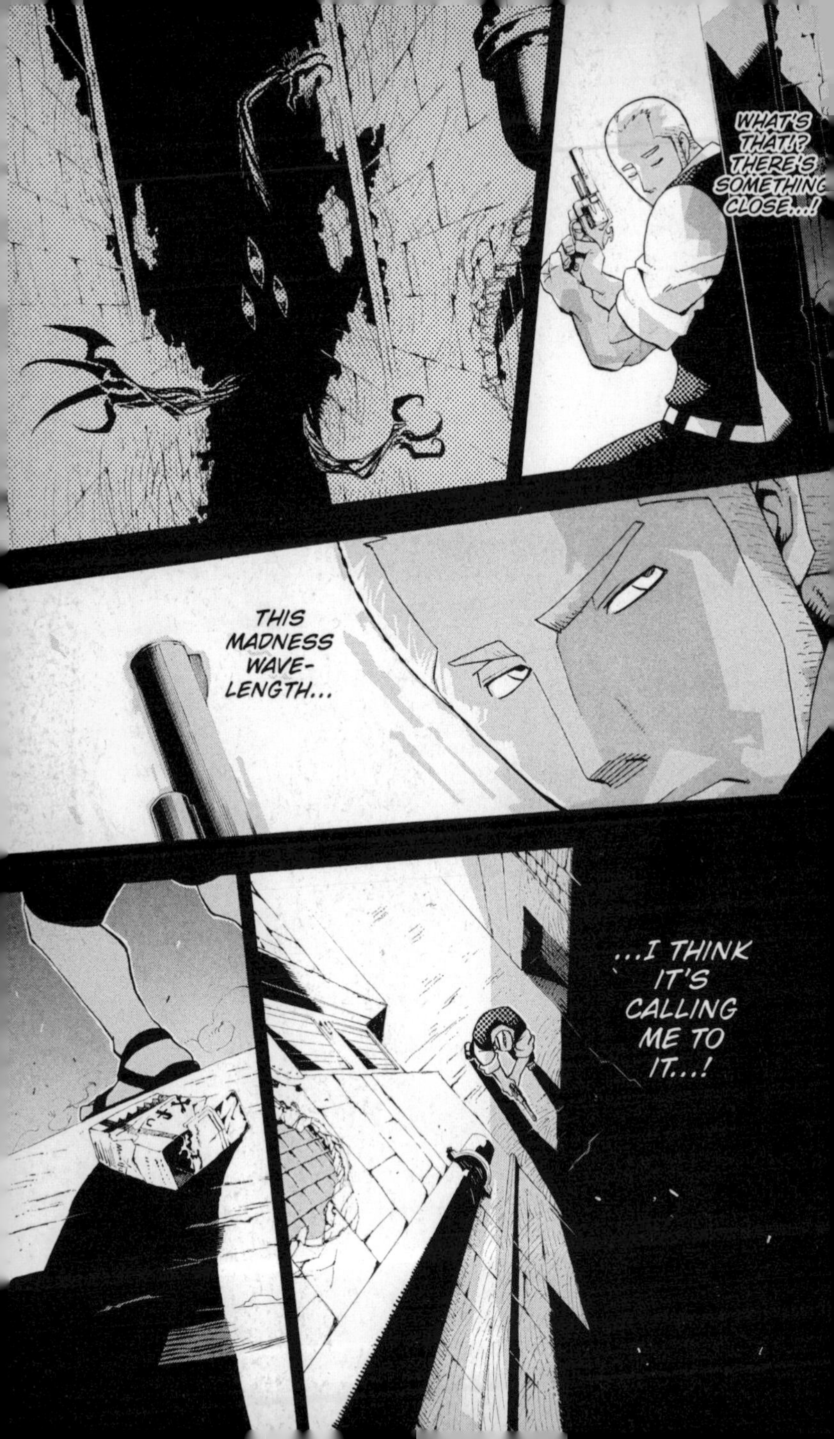
WHAT'S THAT!? THERE'S SOMETHING CLOSE...!
THIS MADNESS WAVE-LENGTH...
...I THINK IT'S CALLING ME TO IT...!

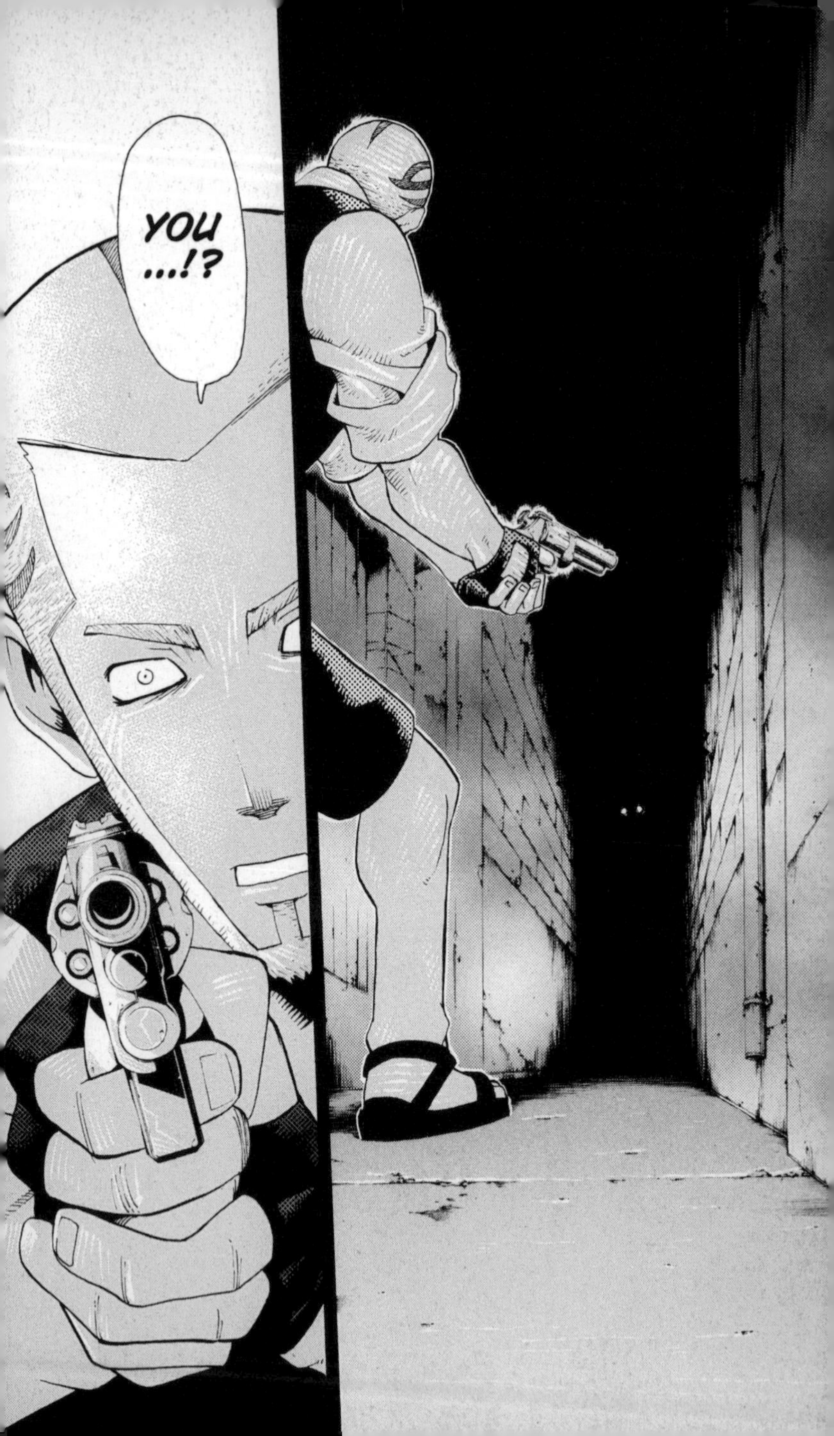
YOU ...!?

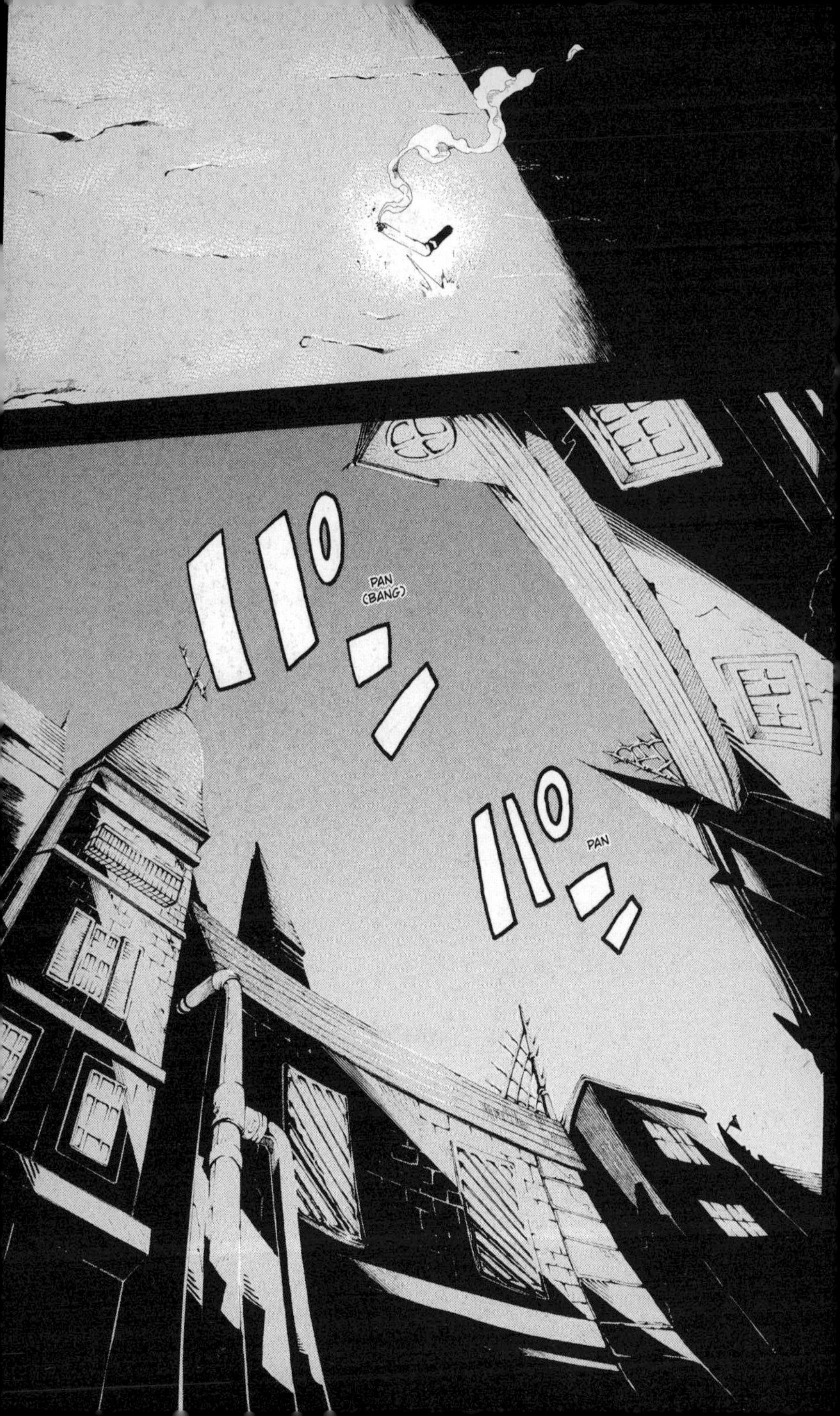
PAN
(BANG)
PAN

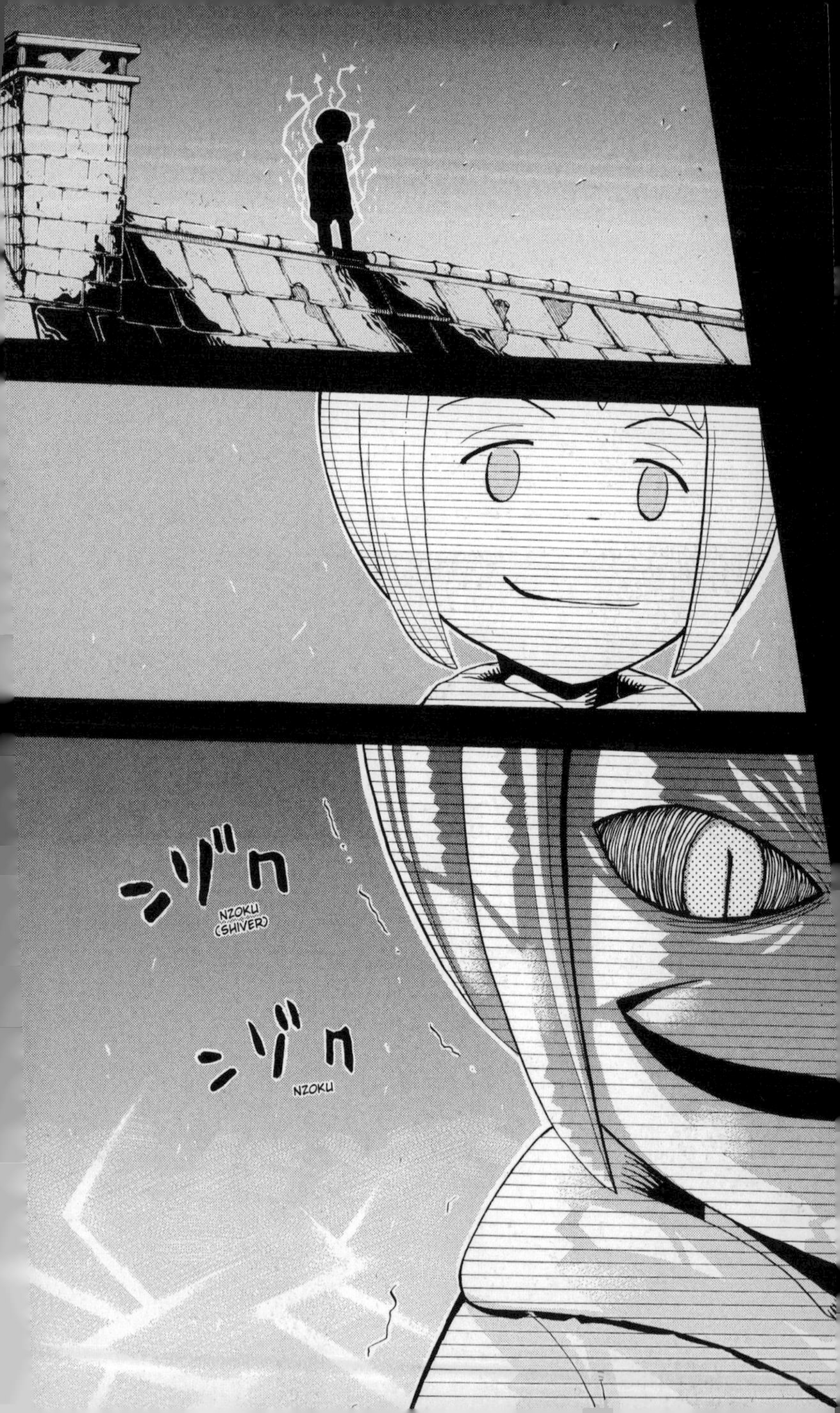
ゾク
NZOKU (SHIVER)
ゾク
NZOKU

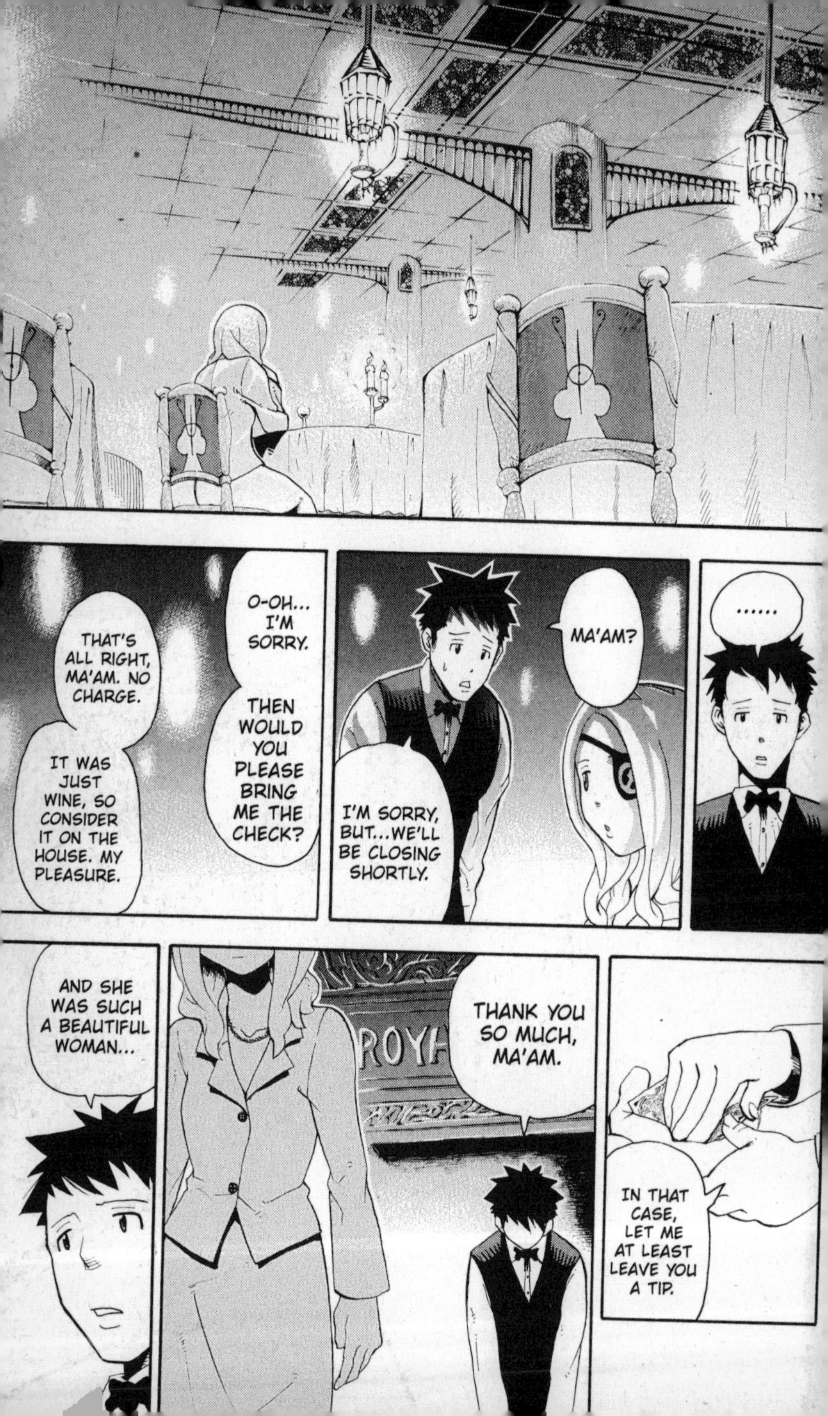
......
MA'AM?
I'M SORRY, BUT...WE'LL BE CLOSING SHORTLY.
O-OH... I'M SORRY.
THEN WOULD YOU PLEASE BRING ME THE CHECK?
THAT'S ALL RIGHT, MA'AM. NO CHARGE.
IT WAS JUST WINE, SO CONSIDER IT ON THE HOUSE. MY PLEASURE.
IN THAT CASE, LET ME AT LEAST LEAVE YOU A TIP.
THANK YOU SO MUCH, MA'AM.
AND SHE WAS SUCH A BEAUTIFUL WOMAN...

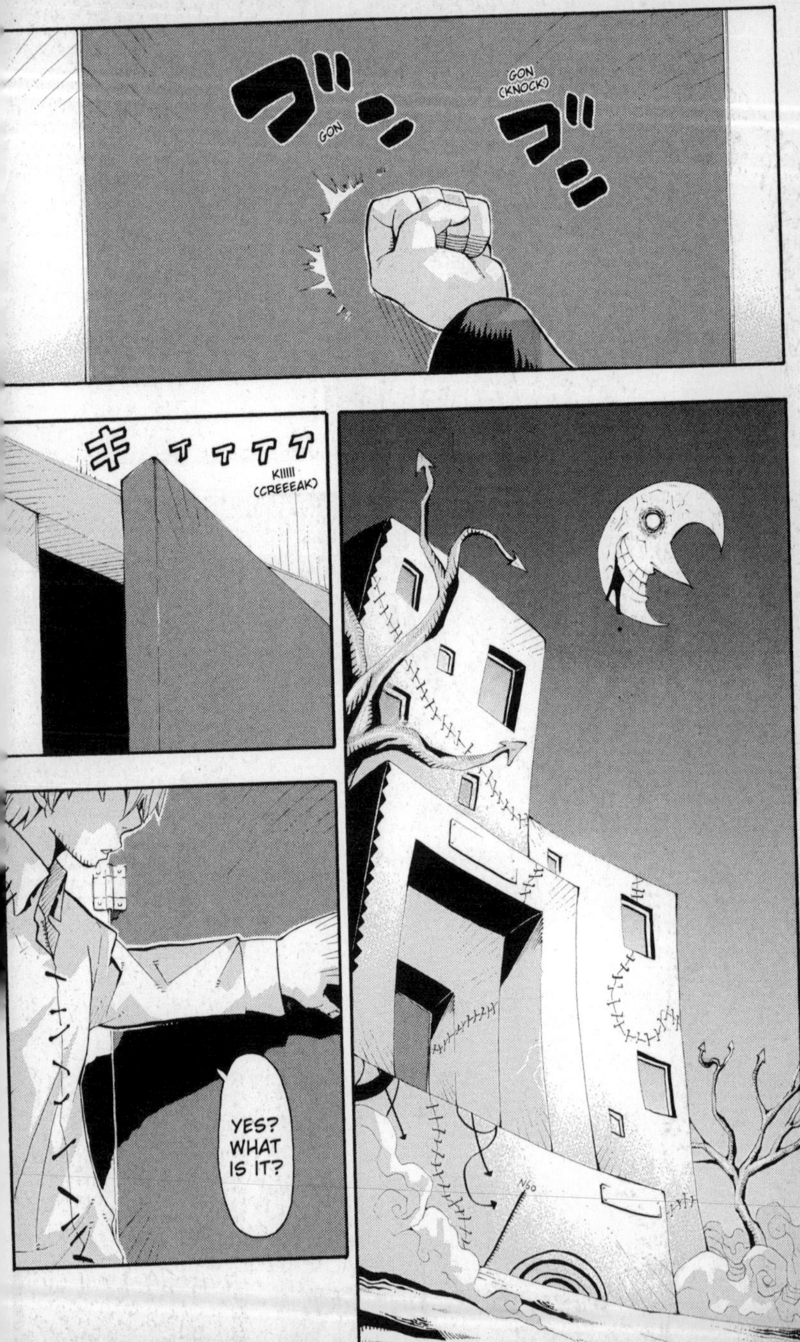

ゴッ
GON (KNOCK)
ゴッ
GON
キィィィィ
KIIIII (CREEEAK)
YES? WHAT IS IT?

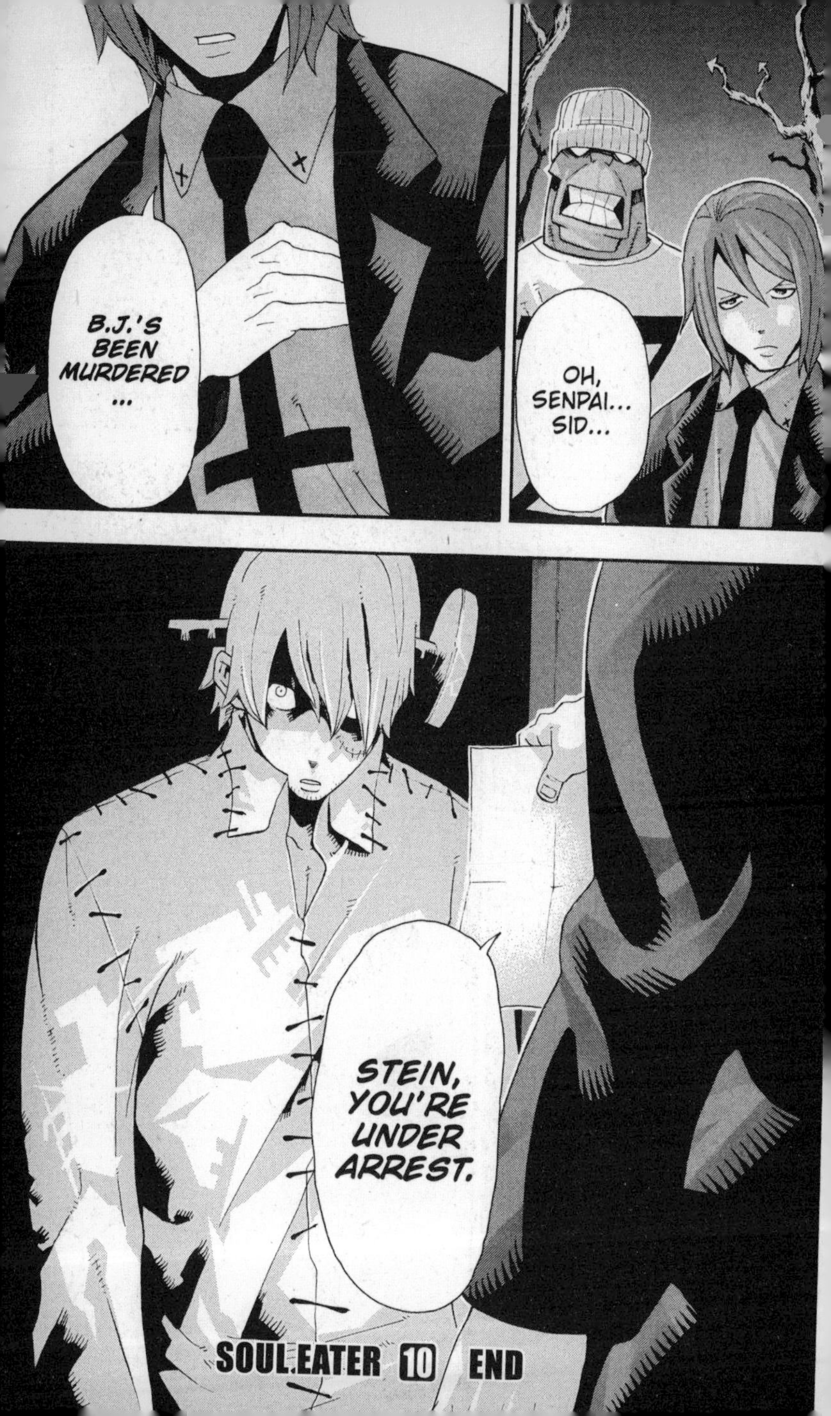
OH, SENPAI... SID...
B.J.'S BEEN MURDERED ...
STEIN, YOU'RE UNDER ARREST.
SOUL EATER 10 END

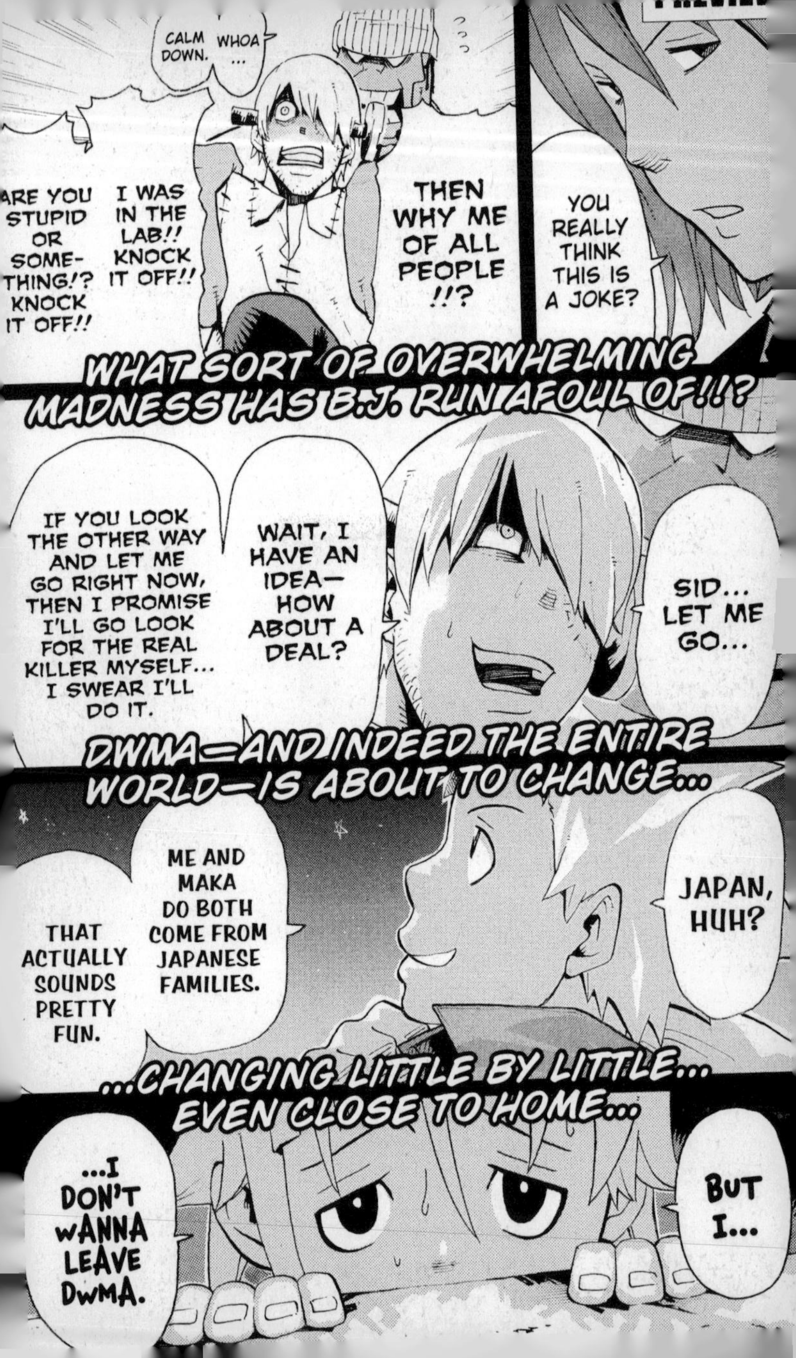

YOU REALLY THINK THIS IS A JOKE?
WHOA...
CALM DOWN.
THEN WHY ME OF ALL PEOPLE!!?
I WAS IN THE LAB!! KNOCK IT OFF!!
ARE YOU STUPID OR SOMETHING!? KNOCK IT OFF!!
WHAT SORT OF OVERWHELMING MADNESS HAS B.J. RUN AFOUL OF!!?
SID... LET ME GO...
WAIT, I HAVE AN IDEA—HOW ABOUT A DEAL?
IF YOU LOOK THE OTHER WAY AND LET ME GO RIGHT NOW, THEN I PROMISE I'LL GO LOOK FOR THE REAL KILLER MYSELF... I SWEAR I'LL DO IT.
DWMA—AND INDEED THE ENTIRE WORLD—IS ABOUT TO CHANGE...
JAPAN, HUH?
ME AND MAKA DO BOTH COME FROM JAPANESE FAMILIES.
THAT ACTUALLY SOUNDS PRETTY FUN.
...CHANGING LITTLE BY LITTLE... EVEN CLOSE TO HOME...
BUT I...
...I DON'T wANNA LEAVE DwMA.

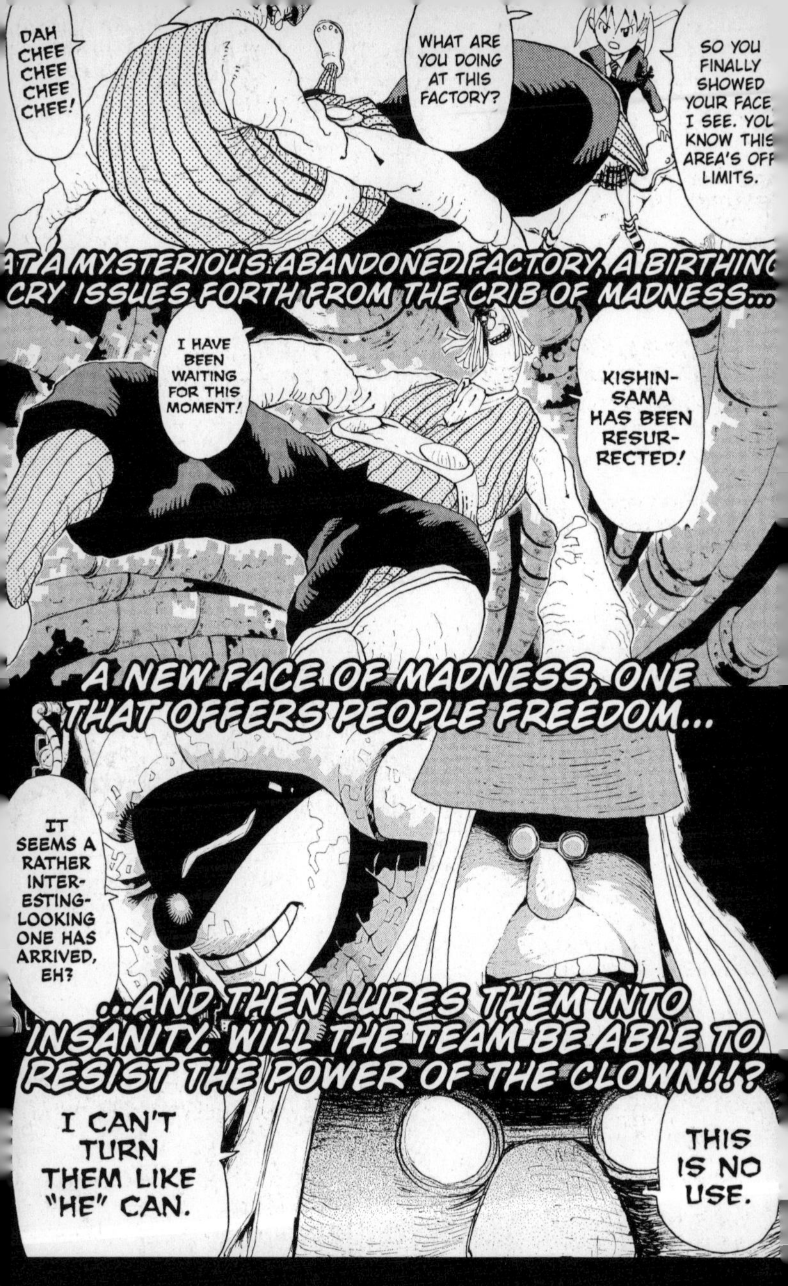
SO YOU FINALLY SHOWED YOUR FACE I SEE. YOU KNOW THIS AREA'S OFF LIMITS.
WHAT ARE YOU DOING AT THIS FACTORY?
DAH CHEE CHEE CHEE CHEE!
AT A MYSTERIOUS ABANDONED FACTORY, A BIRTHING CRY ISSUES FORTH FROM THE CRIB OF MADNESS...
KISHIN-SAMA HAS BEEN RESURRECTED!
I HAVE BEEN WAITING FOR THIS MOMENT!
A NEW FACE OF MADNESS, ONE THAT OFFERS PEOPLE FREEDOM...
IT SEEMS A RATHER INTERESTING-LOOKING ONE HAS ARRIVED, EH?
...AND THEN LURES THEM INTO INSANITY. WILL THE TEAM BE ABLE TO RESIST THE POWER OF THE CLOWN!!?
THIS IS NO USE.
I CAN'T TURN THEM LIKE "HE" CAN.

Continued in Soul Eater Volume 11!!

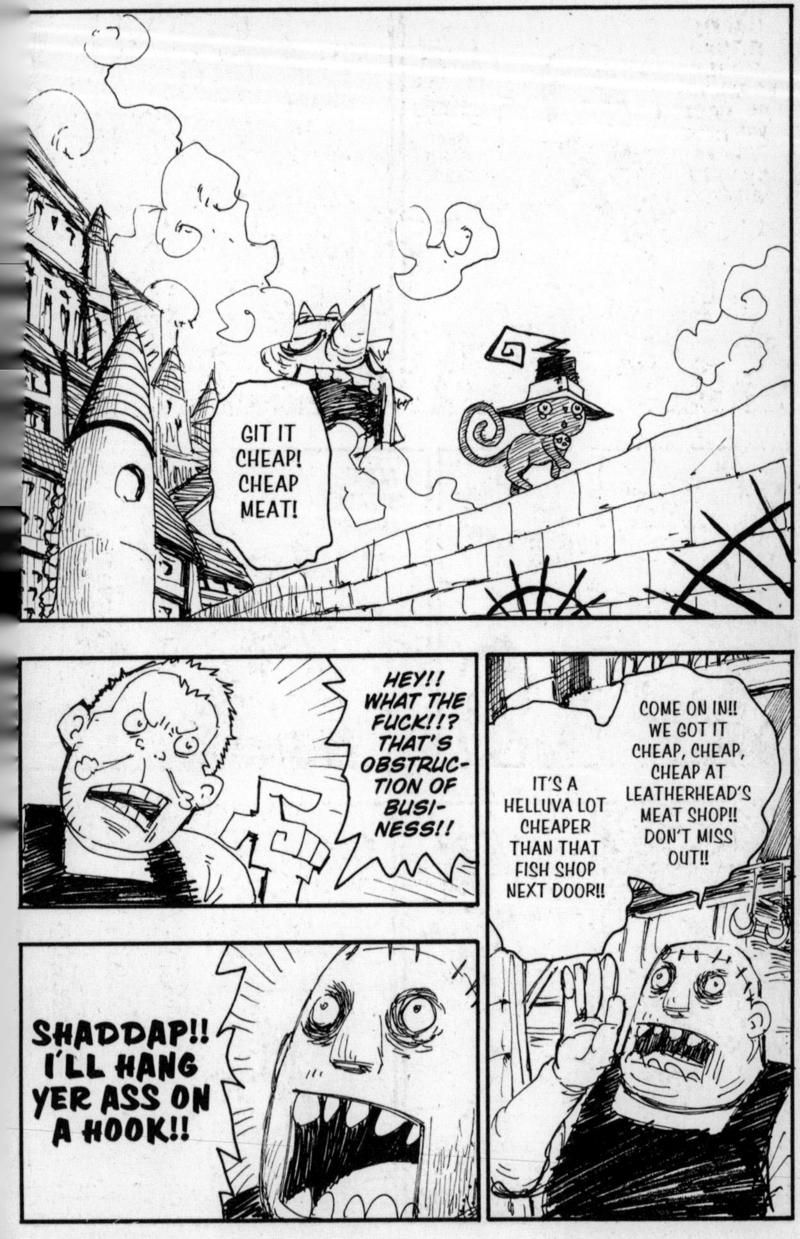
GIT IT CHEAP! CHEAP MEAT!
COME ON IN!! WE GOT IT CHEAP, CHEAP, CHEAP AT LEATHERHEAD'S MEAT SHOP!! DON'T MISS OUT!!
IT'S A HELLUVA LOT CHEAPER THAN THAT FISH SHOP NEXT DOOR!!
HEY!! WHAT THE FUCK!!? THAT'S OBSTRUCTION OF BUSINESS!!
SHADDAP!! I'LL HANG YER ASS ON A HOOK!!

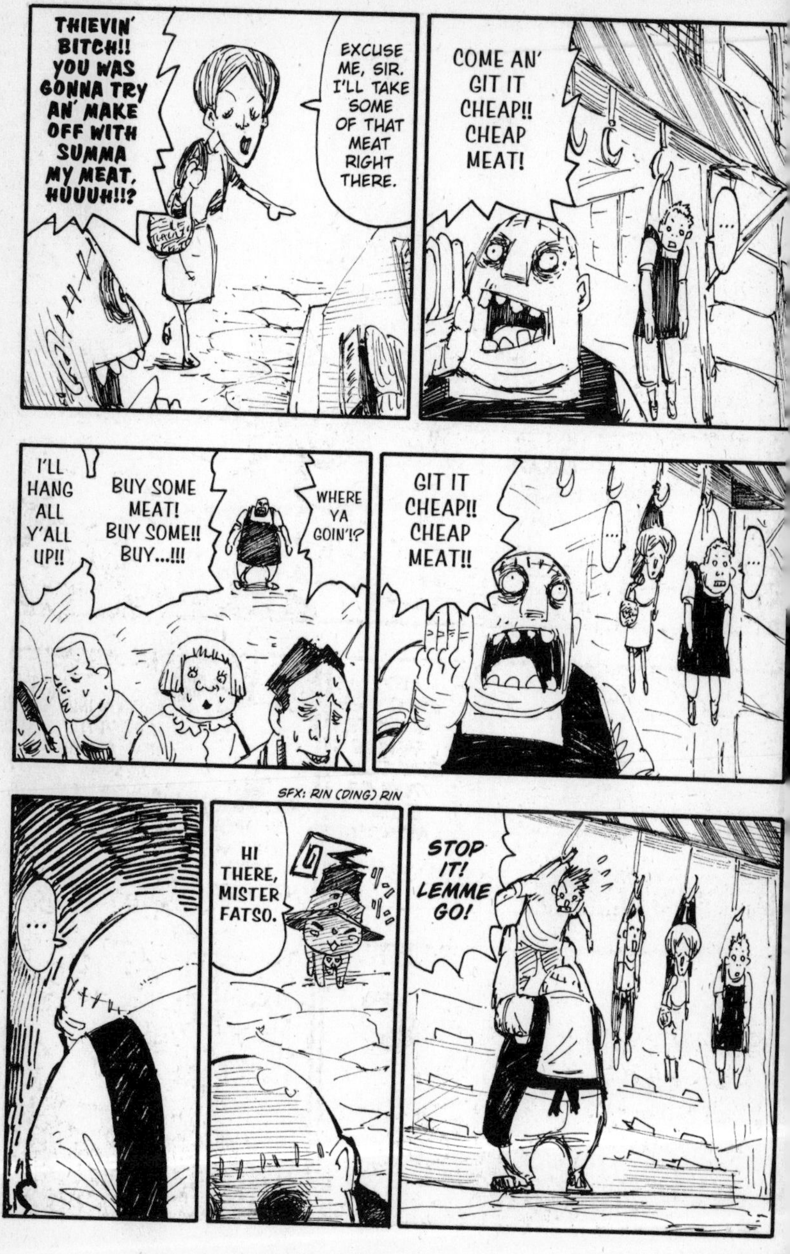
COME AN' GIT IT CHEAP!! CHEAP MEAT!
...
EXCUSE ME, SIR. I'LL TAKE SOME OF THAT MEAT RIGHT THERE.
THIEVIN' BITCH!! YOU WAS GONNA TRY AN' MAKE OFF WITH SUMMA MY MEAT, HUUUH!!?
GIT IT CHEAP!! CHEAP MEAT!!
...
...
WHERE YA GOIN'!?
BUY SOME MEAT! BUY SOME!! BUY...!!!
I'LL HANG ALL Y'ALL UP!!
STOP IT! LEMME GO!
SFX: RIN (DING) RIN
HI THERE, MISTER FATSO.
...

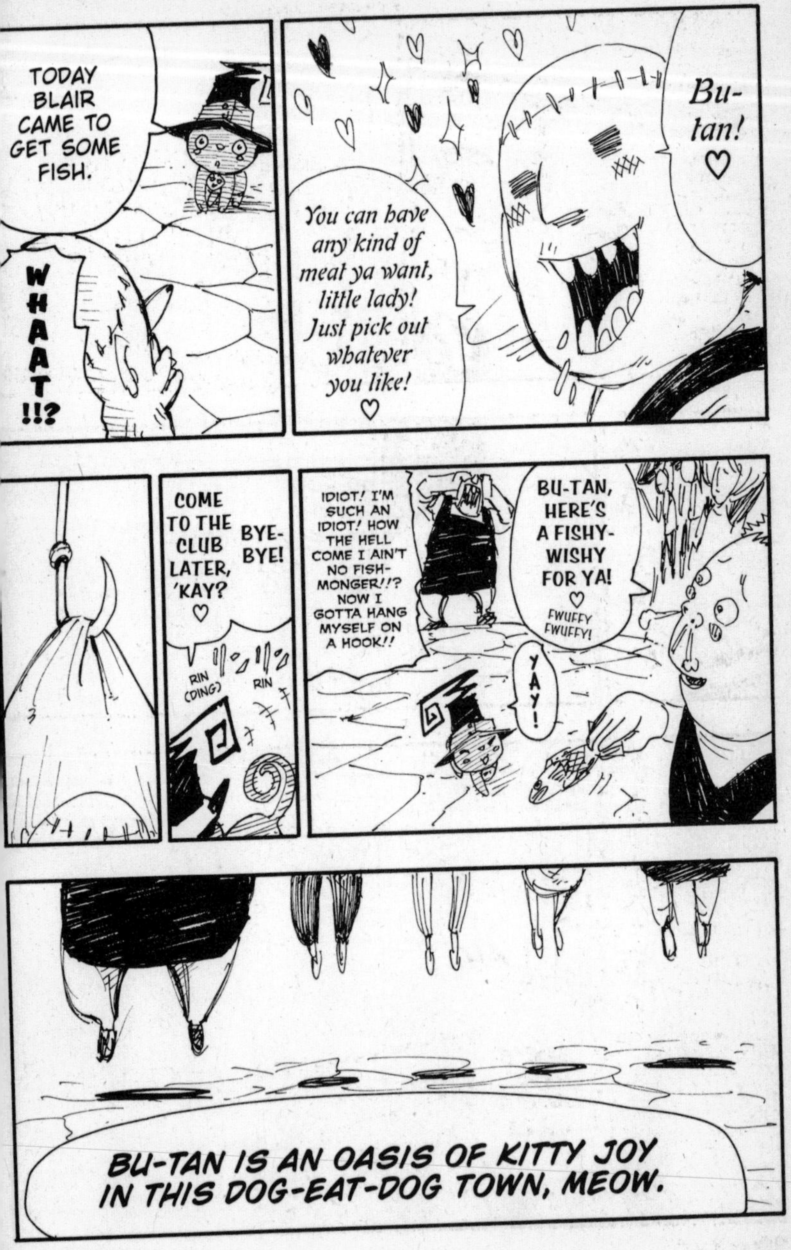
Bu-tan! ♡
You can have any kind of meat ya want, little lady! Just pick out whatever you like! ♡
TODAY BLAIR CAME TO GET SOME FISH.
WHAAAT!!?
BU-TAN, HERE'S A FISHY-WISHY FOR YA! ♡
FWUFFY FWUFFY!
YAY!
IDIOT! I'M SUCH AN IDIOT! HOW THE HELL COME I AIN'T NO FISH-MONGER!!? NOW I GOTTA HANG MYSELF ON A HOOK!!
BYE-BYE!
COME TO THE CLUB LATER, 'KAY? ♡
RIN
RIN (DING)
BU-TAN IS AN OASIS OF KITTY JOY IN THIS DOG-EAT-DOG TOWN, MEOW.

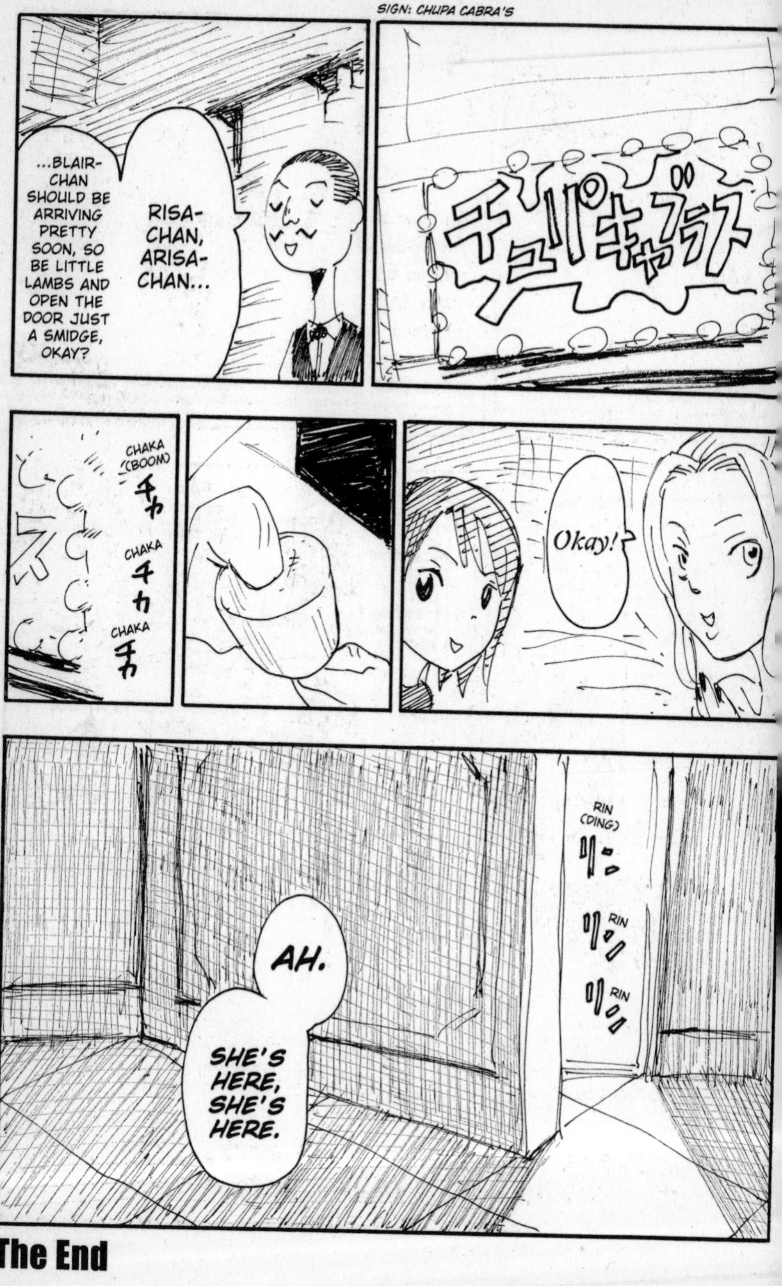
SIGN: CHUPA CABRA'S
チュパキャブラス
RISA-CHAN, ARISA-CHAN...
...BLAIR-CHAN SHOULD BE ARRIVING PRETTY SOON, SO BE LITTLE LAMBS AND OPEN THE DOOR JUST A SMIDGE, OKAY?
Okay!
CHAKA (BOOM)
チカ
CHAKA
チカ
CHAKA
チカ
RIN (DING)
リン
RIN
リン
RIN
リン
AH.
SHE'S HERE, SHE'S HERE.

The End

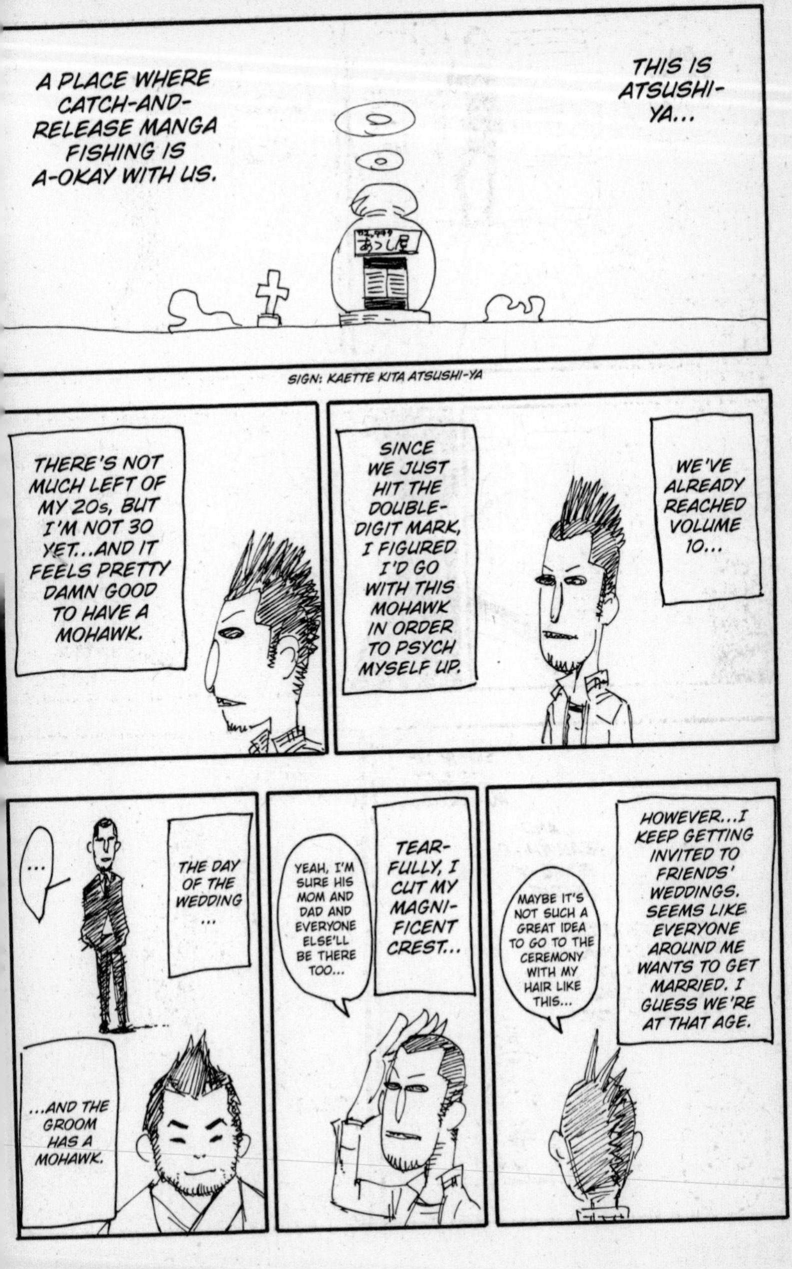
THIS IS ATSUSHI-YA...
A PLACE WHERE CATCH-AND-RELEASE MANGA FISHING IS A-OKAY WITH US.
SIGN: KAETTE KITA ATSUSHI-YA
WE'VE ALREADY REACHED VOLUME 10...
SINCE WE JUST HIT THE DOUBLE-DIGIT MARK, I FIGURED I'D GO WITH THIS MOHAWK IN ORDER TO PSYCH MYSELF UP.
THERE'S NOT MUCH LEFT OF MY 20s, BUT I'M NOT 30 YET...AND IT FEELS PRETTY DAMN GOOD TO HAVE A MOHAWK.
HOWEVER...I KEEP GETTING INVITED TO FRIENDS' WEDDINGS. SEEMS LIKE EVERYONE AROUND ME WANTS TO GET MARRIED. I GUESS WE'RE AT THAT AGE.
MAYBE IT'S NOT SUCH A GREAT IDEA TO GO TO THE CEREMONY WITH MY HAIR LIKE THIS...
TEARFULLY, I CUT MY MAGNIFICENT CREST...
YEAH, I'M SURE HIS MOM AND DAD AND EVERYONE ELSE'LL BE THERE TOO...
THE DAY OF THE WEDDING...
...
...AND THE GROOM HAS A MOHAWK.

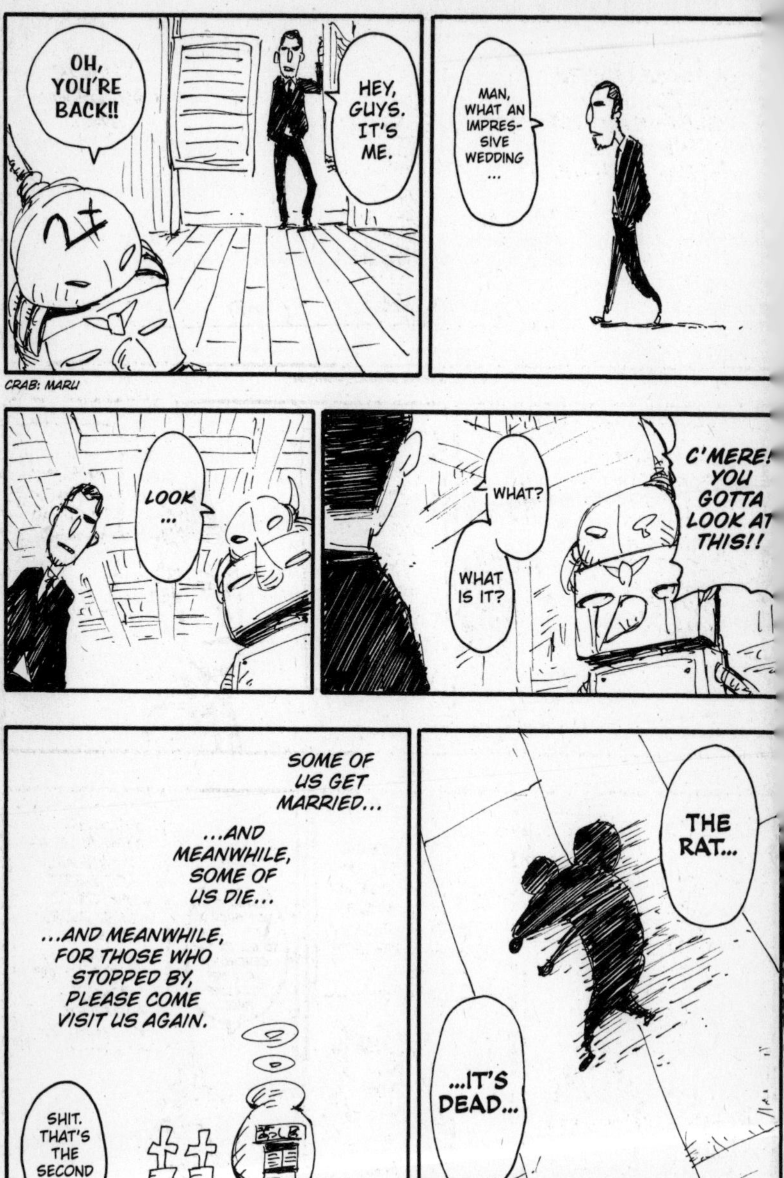
MAN, WHAT AN IMPRES-SIVE WEDDING ...
HEY, GUYS. IT'S ME.
OH, YOU'RE BACK!!
C'MERE! YOU GOTTA LOOK AT THIS!!
WHAT?
WHAT IS IT?
LOOK ...
THE RAT...
...IT'S DEAD...
SOME OF US GET MARRIED...
...AND MEANWHILE, SOME OF US DIE...
...AND MEANWHILE, FOR THOSE WHO STOPPED BY, PLEASE COME VISIT US AGAIN.
SHIT. THAT'S THE SECOND ONE...

CRAB: MARU

ranslation Notes

ommon Honorifics

o honorific: Indicates familiarity or closeness; if used without permission or reason, ddressing someone in this manner would constitute an insult.

san: The Japanese equivalent of Mr./Mrs./Miss. If a situation calls for politeness, this is the ail-safe honorific.

sama: Conveys great respect; may also indicate that the social status of the speaker is ower than that of the addressee.

kun: Used most often when referring to boys, this indicates affection or familiarity. Occasionally used by older men among their peers, but it may also be used by anyone eferring to a person of lower standing.

chan: An affectionate honorific indicating familiarity used mostly in reference to girls; also used in reference to cute persons or animals of either gender.

senpai: A suffix used to address upperclassmen or more experienced coworkers.

sensei: A respectful term for teachers, artists, or high-level professionals.

Page 87
"B.J." is for "Buttataki Joe" (his name in Japanese order), and **"Whack-a-Mole"** (mogura-ataki, literally "mole-hitting" in Japanese) is sort of a title/nickname taken from his sur-name. Joe's last name, **Buttataki**, literally means "beating the crap out of (things/people/etc.)"—the name says it all. In other words, he's a heavy-hitting type of investigator, sent in to bust heads and take names where others might fail.

Page 180
The suffix –tan is a cutesy form of –chan, and the name "Blair" can be shortened to "Bu" in Japanese, so **Bu-tan** is just a cutesy form of Blair-chan.

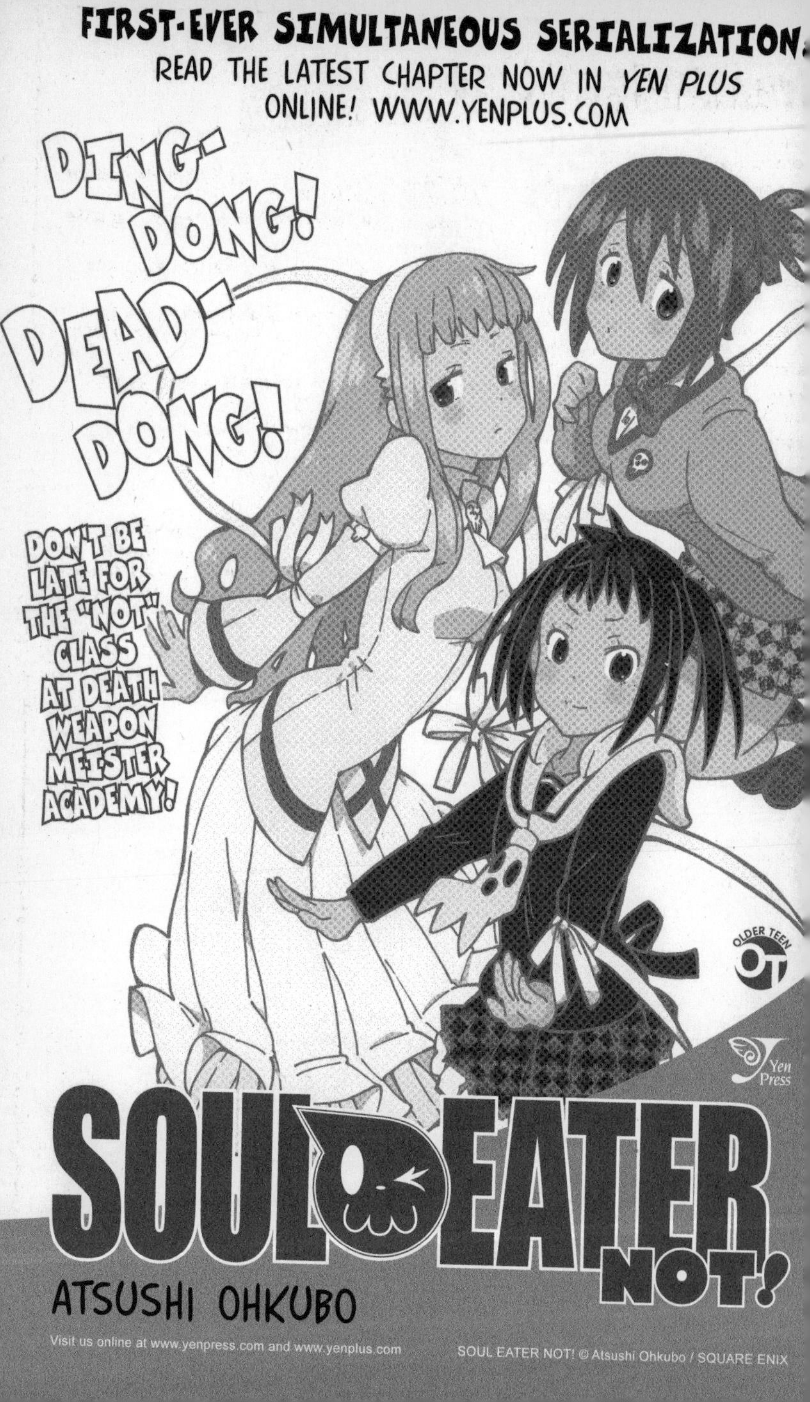

FIRST-EVER SIMULTANEOUS SERIALIZATION.
READ THE LATEST CHAPTER NOW IN YEN PLUS ONLINE! WWW.YENPLUS.COM
DING-DONG!
DEAD-DONG!
DON'T BE LATE FOR THE "NOT" CLASS AT DEATH WEAPON MEISTER ACADEMY!
OLDER TEEN OT
Yen Press
SOUL EATER NOT!
ATSUSHI OHKUBO
Visit us online at www.yenpress.com and www.yenplus.com
SOUL EATER NOT! © Atsushi Ohkubo / SQUARE ENIX

Can't wait for the next volume? You don't have to!

Keep up with the latest chapters of some of your favorite manga every month online in the pages of YEN PLUS!

READ IT THE SAME DAY AS JAPAN!

SOUL EATER NOT?

MAXIMUM RIDE

SOULLESS

WITCH & WIZARD

THE INFERNAL DEVICES CLOCKWORK ANGEL

Visit us at ww.yenplus.com for details!

SOUL EATER NOT! © Atsushi Ohkubo / SQUARE-ENIX • Maximum Ride © James Patterson, Illustrations © Hachette Book Group • Soulless © Tofa Borregaard, Illustrations © Hachette Book Group • Witch & Wizard © James Patterson, Illustrations © Hachette Book Group • The Infernal Devices: Clockwork Angel © Cassandra Clare, Illustrations © Hachette Book Group

WANT TO READ
MANGA ON YOUR IPAD?

Now for iPhone too!

Download the *YEN PRESS* app for full volumes of some of our bestselling titles!

Nightschool © Svetlana Chmakova

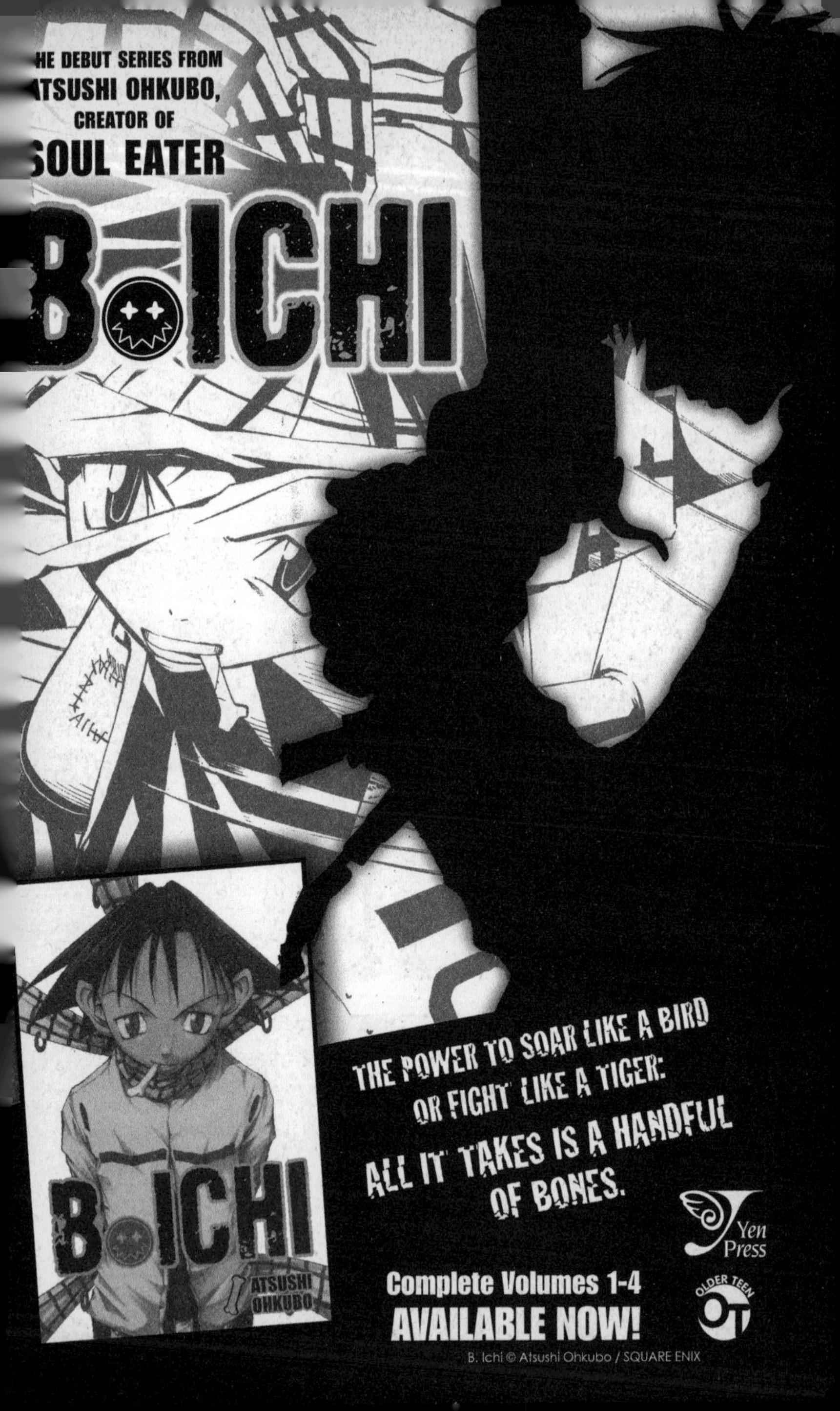

HE DEBUT SERIES FROM
ATSUSHI OHKUBO,
CREATOR OF
SOUL EATER
B. ICHI
B. ICHI
ATSUSHI OHKUBO
THE POWER TO SOAR LIKE A BIRD
OR FIGHT LIKE A TIGER:
ALL IT TAKES IS A HANDFUL
OF BONES.
Yen Press
Complete Volumes 1-4
AVAILABLE NOW!
OLDER TEEN OT
B. Ichi © Atsushi Ohkubo / SQUARE ENIX

COME TO IKEBUKURO,
WHERE TOKYO'S WILDEST
CHARACTERS GATHER!!

DURARARA!!

DRRR!! ×1

AYDRE
EXTRAC

DOCTOR W
REDENTIA

POWE
EBUKU
A HEDONIS
INFORMA

RIDER" A
MOTORC

CREATOR
RYOHGO
NARITA

CHARACTER
DESIGN
SUZUHITO
YASUDA

ART
AKIYO
SATORIGI

THEIR PATHS CROSS, THIS ECCENTRIC CAST
LIVES A TWISTED, CRACKED LOVE STORY...

AVAILABLE NOW!!

DEALING WITH THE DEAD IS EVEN WORSE THAN DEALING WITH THE DEVIL!

ZOMBIE-LOAN

BY PEACH-PIT

AVAILABLE NOW.

www.yenpress.com

Yen Press

ZOMBIE-LOAN © PEACH-PIT/SQUARE ENIX
Yen Press is an imprint of Hachette Book Group USA.

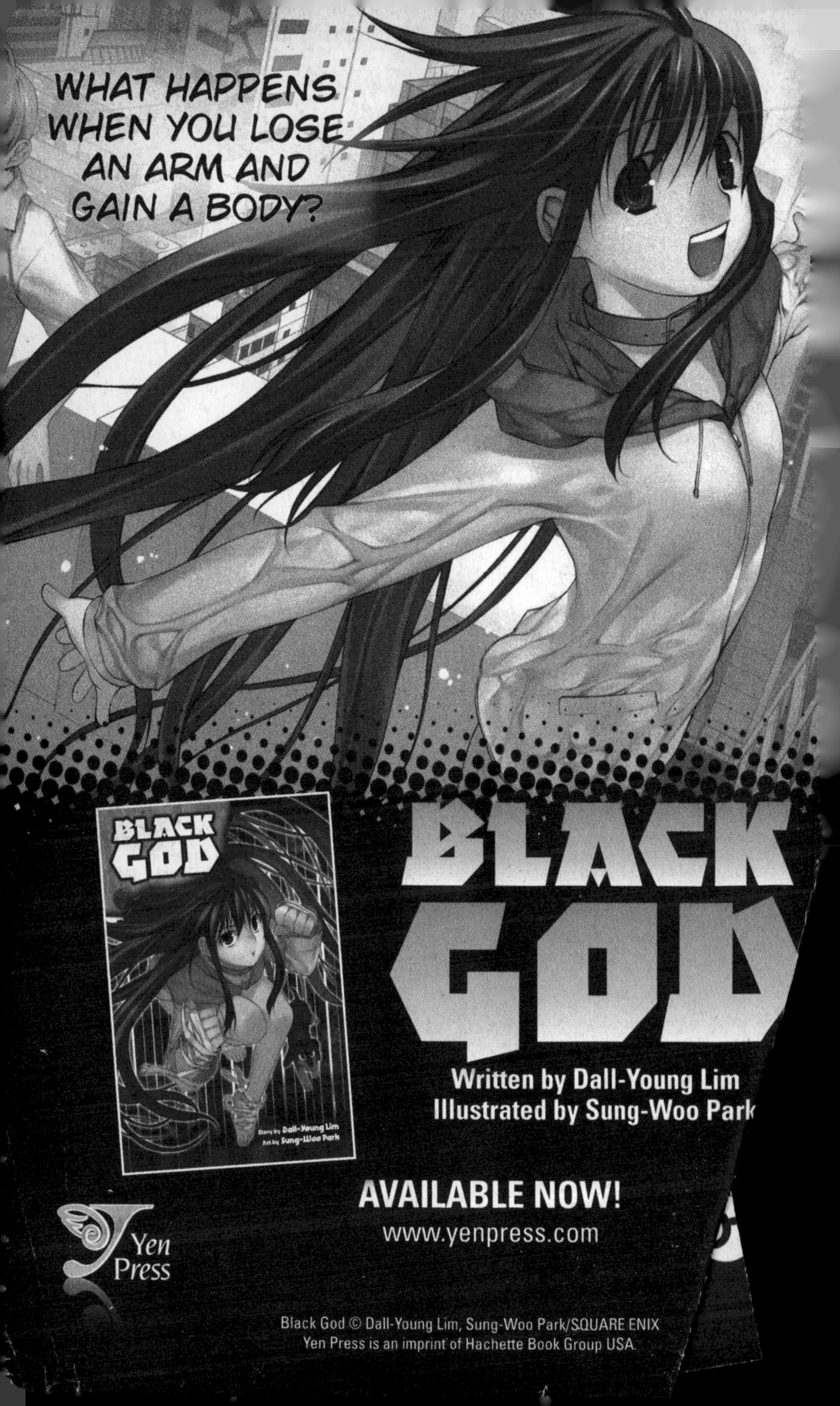
WHAT HAPPENS WHEN YOU LOSE AN ARM AND GAIN A BODY?
BLACK GOD
Story by Dall-Young Lim
Art by Sung-Woo Park
BLACK GOD
Written by Dall-Young Lim
Illustrated by Sung-Woo Park
AVAILABLE NOW!
www.yenpress.com
Yen Press
Black God © Dall-Young Lim, Sung-Woo Park/SQUARE ENIX
Yen Press is an imprint of Hachette Book Group USA.

SOUL EATER ⑩

ATSUSHI OHKUBO

Translation: Jack Wiedrick

Lettering: Alexis Eckerman

This book is a work of fiction. Names, characters, places, and incidents are the product of the author's imagination or are used fictitiously. Any resemblance to actual events, locales, or persons, living or dead, is coincidental.

SOUL EATER Vol. 10 © 2007 Atsushi Ohkubo / SQUARE ENIX. All rights reserved. First published in Japan in 2007 by SQUARE ENIX CO., LTD. English translation rights arranged with SQUARE ENIX CO., LTD. and Hachette Book Group through Tuttle-Mori Agency, Inc.

Translation © 2012 by SQUARE ENIX CO., LTD.

All rights reserved. In accordance with the U.S. Copyright Act of 1976, the scanning, uploading, and electronic sharing of any part of this book without the permission of the publisher is unlawful piracy and theft of the author's intellectual property. If you would like to use material from the book (other than for review purposes), prior written permission must be obtained by contacting the publisher at permissions@hbgusa.com. Thank you for your support of the author's rights.

Yen Press
Hachette Book Group
237 Park Avenue, New York, NY 10017

www.HachetteBookGroup.com
www.YenPress.com

Yen Press is an imprint of Hachette Book Group, Inc. The Yen Press name and logo are trademarks of Hachette Book Group, Inc.

First Yen Press Edition: August 2012

ISBN: 978-0-316-07114-7

10 9 8 7 6 5 4 3 2 1

Printed in the United States of America